D1737201

M

WITHDRAWN
UTSA LIBRARIES

HITLER'S
LUFTWAFFE
IN THE
SPANISH CIVIL WAR

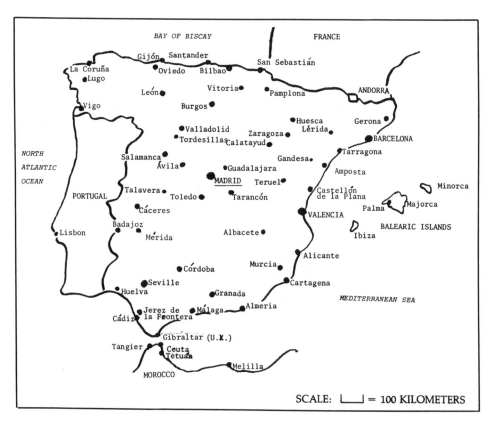

SPAIN. This map presents an overall view of Spain that locates many of the cities mentioned in this book and provides a reference point for each of the area battle maps that accompany the text. All the maps have been prepared by the author.

HITLER'S LUFTWAFFE IN THE SPANISH CIVIL WAR

RAYMOND L. PROCTOR

Contributions in Military History, Number 35

Greenwood Press
Westport, Connecticut • London, England

Library of Congress Cataloging in Publication Data

Proctor, Raymond L.
  Hitler's Luftwaffe in the Spanish Civil War.

  (Contributions in military history, ISSN 0084-9251 ;
no. 35)
  Bibliography: p.
  Includes index.
  1. Spain—History—Civil War, 1936-1939—Participation,
German. 2. Spain—History—Civil War, 1936-1939—
Aerial operations. 3. Spain. Ejército Nacional.
Legión Cóndor. 4. Spain—History—Civil War, 1936-1939—
Regimental histories. I. Title. II. Series.
DP269.47.G3P76 1983   946.081   83-5526
ISBN 0-313-22246-0 (lib. bdg.)

Library of Congress Catalog Card Number: 83-5526
ISBN: 0-313-22246-0
ISSN: 0084-9251

First published in 1983

Greenwood Press
A division of Congressional Information Service, Inc.
88 Post Road West
Westport, Connecticut 06881

Printed in the United States of America

10 9 8 7 6 5 4 3 2 1

Contents

Maps   vii

Acknowledgments   ix

1   Phase One: Unwilling Involvement   3

2   Phase Two: "Magic Fire"   11

3   Phase Three: The Airlift from Africa   25

4   Phase Four: Warlimont and Mission "Guido"   39

5   Phase Five: Creation of the Legion   53

6   Phase Six: Warlimont versus Faupel   71

7   Combat, Problems, and Reorganizations   79

8   Málaga, Jarama, and Guadalajara   101

9   Battle in the North   117

10 Fall of Bilbao   133

11 Battle of Brunete   145

12 Termination in the North   157

13 New Commander and Teruel   171

14 The Aragón Offensive   187

15 The Levante Offensive   205

Contents

16   Battle of the Ebro   221
17   Catalonia to Döberitz   237
     Consequences   251

     Select Bibliography   267
     Index   275

Maps

	Overall View of Spain	*frontispiece*
1	Airlift from Africa, July-October 1936	27
2	German View of Spain, August 1936	32
3	Nationalist Advance on Madrid, October 1936	50
4	Battle of La Coruña Road, January 1937	88
5	Battle of the Jarama, 6-25 February 1937	106
6	Battle of Guadalajara, 7-18 March 1937	111
7	Battle in the North, 30 March-30 April 1937	120
8	Fall of Bilbao, June 1937	140
9	Battle of Brunete, 7-26 July 1937	148
10	Final Operation in the North, August-October 1937	160
11	Battle of Teruel and Alfambra, January and February 1938	179
12	Aragón Offensive, 9 March 1938	189
13	From Belchite to the Sea, 11 March-15 April 1938	196
14	Mediterranean Offensive, April-July 1938	208
15	Battle of the Ebro, 25 July-6 August 1938	222
16	The Ebro Bulge, 7 August-16 November 1938	228
17	Catalonian Campaign, 23 December 1938-10 February 1939	241

Acknowledgments

The writer would like to acknowledge some of the organizations and people who made this work possible. In Spain, my thanks go to the Spanish War Ministry for granting unlimited availability of the records of the Servicio Histórico Militar, and the Spanish Air Ministry for access to its Historical Division. The officers and men of these organizations were most kind with their assistance. Conde Morphy Colonel (retired) Antonio Galbis Loriga, former military adjutant to Generalissimo Franco and King Juan Carlos, gave valuable assistance. Brigade General Barsen García-Lopez of the Spanish Air Force granted much of his time and hospitality, as did Colonel Francisco Lízarraga Gil. My thanks to Lt. General (retired) Lacalle, former Spanish Air Minister, for his valuable comments. The help of Lt. General José L. Aramburu Topete (Spanish Combat Engineers) was most valuable. The guidance in the early stage of research by the late Colonel (Spanish Air Force) Manuel Alonso y Alonso is most memorable. Dr. Angel Viñas Martin gave considerable information on the first phase of the German involvement. Many other officers of the Spanish Armed Forces lent assistance, as did the officers of the American Military Attaché in Madrid. The late Generalissimo Franco's personal encouragement and best wishes were very much appreciated.

In Germany, help was given by the United States Liaison Office in Munich. The assistance of Dr. Horst Boog and Colonel (West German Air Force) Dr. Klaus A. Maier of the Military Research Center, saved much time in Freiburg. The officials of the German Military Archives of

Freiburg were very helpful in locating documentary material and pro-
viding microfilm copies. The account of the second phase of German involvement would have been impossible without the gracious cooperation,
candid comments, and pertinent papers of the late General a.D. (*ausser
Dienst*-retired from active service) Walter Warlimont. The enthusiastic
assistance in locating former officers of the Condor Legion by the late
General a.D. Hasso von Manteuffel was most rewarding, as well as the
counsel granted by General a.D. Burckhardt Müller-Hillebrand, the former first officer of General Halder. Valuable insight into the Condor
Legion's structure and operations was contributed by the late General
a.D. Hermann Plocher, the second chief of staff of the Legion. He also
gave many details of the battles of Teruel, Aragón, and the Río Ebro.
The reflections and analyses of the dynamic General a.D. Martin Harling-
hausen, commander of the Legion Seaplane Squadron, was a great contribution. Colonel a.D. Douglas Pitcairn, of the "Mickey Mouse" Fighter
Squadron, related details of the assembly, sea journey, and organization
of the Legion in Spain, as well as the first difficult months of operations.
The outstanding German fighter ace and commander, General a.D. Adolf
Galland, granted valuable assistance for the period he was in Spain.
Colonel a.D. Herbert Wittmann graciously recounted information on the
Legion's bomber operation. Colonel a.D. Franz Brey provided much data
and papers relative to the Legion General Staff. To all of these gentlemen,
and others, this writer is deeply grateful for their help and warm
hospitality.

Greatly appreciated was the financial assistance from the Idaho Research Foundation and the University of Idaho History Department. In
addition, the clerical assistance of the History Department was most
valuable, particularly that of Mrs. Dayle Williams. Mrs. Elke Eroschenko,
formerly of Germany, spent much of her time working on the German
translations. And I am greatly indebted to my wife for her hours of typing
and verification of source material.

Any errors existing in this work are the responsibility of the writer,
with apologies extended to the many people who gave their time and
assistance.

HITLER'S
LUFTWAFFE
IN THE
SPANISH CIVIL WAR

1

Phase One: Unwilling Involvement

The infant *Luftwaffe* of the Third Reich initially, and unwillingly, became involved in the Spanish Civil War (1936-1939) because of a strange set of circumstances unknown to either the *Luftwaffe* command or the Berlin government. These began in the early hours of 18 July 1936, the day that the Spanish radio station at Las Palmas, Grand Canaries, announced to the world that elements of the Spanish military had risen in revolt against the Popular Front government of Spain. During the next few days and weeks the German involvement, although modest and very restricted, escalated as the Spanish struggle became an arena of not only international concern but political ideologies, and soldiers from many different lands were to be fighting on the ground in Spain and in the skies above the battlefields. Finally Berlin reversed its prohibition and permitted a few German airmen and planes in Spain to engage directly in combat. The aircraft, however, carried the markings of the Spanish Nationalists.

Then in late October 1936, unknown to the few Germans actively serving in Spain and the Nationalist leadership, the German government made the decision to increase the German involvement in the form of a composite air organization of about 5,000 men with their equipment. This organization was composed of a Bomber Group, Fighter Group, Reconnaissance Squadron, Seaplane Squadron, Antiaircraft (flak) Group, and the required ground support squadrons. The Germans already committed to Spain would be incorporated into its ranks. The organization was to be known as the "Condor Legion" and was committed as a combat force to the Nationalists' cause until their final victory in the spring of 1939.

All of this began 18 July 1936 with the flight of a single German transport plane (Ju-52) of the German national commercial airline. The aircraft identification was D-APOK, but was nicknamed "Max von Müller." It was on its regular scheduled flight from Bathurst (Gambia) to Villa Cisneros in the then Spanish Sahara, and from there on to Las Palmas in the Grand Canaries. It was flown by Flight Captain Alfred Henke, a thirty-four-year-old professional pilot who had flown for several years in Latin America. He had been flying this remote route for some time and had never encountered any trouble. He made his landing at Villa Cisneros and cleared the continuation of his flight with the Spanish authorities. Again airborne and out over the Atlantic, he was handed a message by his radio operator. Henke was surprised to note that the message was in Spanish but carried the proper *Lufthansa* designation:

D-APOK must land Villa Cisneros and remain for new orders—
Bezltgsa[1]

According to the German records, Henke decided to follow the instructions and returned to Villa Cisneros to find out what this was all about. He made his landing at 3:00 p.m. and was taken directly to the military governor. The Spaniard explained that, as far as he knew, an uprising had taken place in Morocco, the Canaries were under martial law, and the revolt was extending all over Spain; but even to himself the situation was not at all clear.

Henke was unaware that a few days earlier there had been a very unusual meeting between his *Lufthansa* representative Otto Bertram and some very important Spaniards in Las Palmas which was to have a profound impact on his aircraft and crew. It began on 13 July when Bertram received a call from a Doctor Guerrero, who was the physician of General Amadeo Balmes Alonso (Las Palmas military governor), who, like General Francisco Franco in Tenerife, was living in semi-exile on orders of the new government in Madrid. The doctor made an appointment to meet with the *Lufthansa* representative, and at that time he advised Bertram that General Luis Orgaz y Yoldi, also living in exile, would like to meet with him midmorning of 15 July in the doctor's office. The German had no idea what was taking place, and as he sat with the Spaniards, he did not know that General Orgaz was understandably distraught and that he, along with other Spanish officers, was deeply involved in a grave conspiracy against the new government in Madrid. The designated leader of the circle was General José Sanjurjo Sacanell, who was living in exile in Portugal. Most of the organizational planning was in the hands of General Emilio Mola Vidal, who plotted in his office as military governor of Pamplona. In all, some seven major generals were involved. Included was the former supporter of the Republic, General Gonzalo Queipo de Llano y Serra, who had been appointed commander of the *Carabineros* (Customs Guards).[2]

Due to the structure of the Spanish military establishment, the Spanish forces in Africa, which were composed of the Spanish Foreign Legion, the Moorish *Regulares*, and select units of the Spanish Army, constituted the most valuable components of what could be called a Spanish standing military force. If there should be fighting in the course of a military uprising, the active support for such an attempted coup by the Army of Africa was indispensable. The backing by General Franco, who carried so much influence with the African forces, although possibly not absolutely critical, was most assuredly desirable. Franco, although holding utterly no sympathy for the Popular Front government, initially had rejected solicitations to join in the circle of conspirators headed by Mola and Sanjurjo. There has been much speculation as to exactly when he did decide to commit himself to the cause of revolt, but it seems as though he came to these conclusions sometime after the middle of June 1936.[3]

The uprising would be carried out in Africa late on 17 July and was to be followed early the next morning by the forces in Spain. It was imperative that a suitable aircraft be available to fly General Franco to Spanish Morocco to assume direct command of these professional forces. From the existing evidence, it appears that General Orgaz did not know that his fellow conspirators had made arrangements for such an aircraft to be chartered in England. In any event, in that his meeting with Otto Bertram was in the morning, it was impossible for the general to know that this aircraft was en route from Casablanca, French Morocco, to the Canaries; but with a vital refueling stop at Cape Juby, a remote Spanish military base on the fringe of the Spanish Sahara. The plane, which was a twin-engine de Havilland, *Dragon Rapide*, had been chartered by Luis Bolín, a Monarchist journalist in England.[4] It was flown by a young Englishman, Captain Bebb. Besides the crew and Bolín, the *Dragon Rapide* carried a retired British Major Pollard along with his daughter and her girl friend. The passengers and crew had no idea of the purpose of their flight other than for an exciting adventure along the coast of Africa. They had been invited, however, hopefully to distract attention from Bolín, who was well known.

After their arrival at Casablanca, Bolín learned of the murder of Calvo Sotelo, a conservative member of the Cortes, in Madrid.[5] Suspecting things might take a quick turn, Bolín decided to send the *Dragon Rapide* on to the Canaries but he should remain in Casablanca. This meant that he had to entrust a coded message to the British major for delivery in the Canaries. Pollard accepted without asking questions.

With no knowledge of this, General Orgaz was deeply concerned. The uprising was to take place Saturday morning, 18 July; it was now Wednes-

day, 15 July. He absolutely had to have an airplane to fly General Franco
to the major military forces in Africa which would be in open revolt. As
far as the general knew, the only plane which would be in the islands
that day would be the German commercial transport, which was scheduled
to arrive that morning. He hoped to be able to procure the aircraft temporarily for their cause and at the same time not reveal the purpose to
which it would be used. His request of Bertram was basic—to be loaned
an aircraft to fly to the peninsula.

However, in formulating his appeal, he must have intimated that the
flight might be involved in some sort of political action. The result was,
quite correctly, that the *Lufthansa* manager, as a foreigner in Spain,
would not involve himself or his company in the internal affairs of the
Spaniards. He pointed out that he was merely a district chief with very
limited capabilities; as such he could not allocate any aircraft for a flight
other than those established in his well-defined directives.[6] To one familiar
with the circumstances it is easy to envision that General Orgaz was in
a state of near panic. However, he need not have been too greatly dis-
arranged because his needed plane, the twin-engine de Havilland *Dragon
Rapide*, landed at the airfield of Gando, near Las Palmas, that same
afternoon.

In a very strange accident for a professional soldier, General Amadeo
Balmes had killed himself with a pistol during target practice. This gave
General Franco an excuse to leave Tenerife by boat for Las Palmas to
attend his former companion's funeral. Importantly, he was to seize the
Canaries and meet his plane to fly to Tetuán, Morocco. He was advised
by a message from Melilla that the Legion had been forced to act prematurely and Franco was forced to step up his plans in the islands. There
was some fighting with the Assault Guards, but finally at 5:15 a.m. on
the morning of 18 July, he announced on the radio the uprising and its
purpose. Flight Captain Bebb had been advised to have his aircraft ready
for departure with new passengers who arrived in the early afternoon.
A little after 2:00 p.m. General Franco was on his way to Casablanca to
join Luis Bolín. After a short and very restless sleep they took off at
5:00 a.m. the following morning and landed at Tetuán two hours later.

Hardly had the Spaniards landed at Tetuán than General Franco wanted
to sent the *Dragon Rapide* back to the Canaries for General Luis Orgaz.
"I need him here!" he told Bolín.[7] The latter pointed out that it would
take him some sixteen hours flying time, and that they were not contracted for such a flight. Bolín also noted that for their cause they were
greatly in need of aircraft. Franco wanted to know where they could be
obtained. Bolín ruled out France and the Soviet Union for obvious reasons. He suggested he might be able to accomplish something in England,
but there Juan de la Cierva could do it better, if it was at all possible.
Bolín did not think that he could be of any help in Germany because he
could not speak the language; however, he could manage in Italian.

It was immediately decided that Bolín should leave for Rome, but via Lisbon; here he could advise General Sanjurjo as to the progress of the uprising in Africa and their dire need of aircraft. General Franco now gave Bolín a hurriedly written memorandum which authorized him, in Franco's name, to negotiate in England, Germany, and Italy for twelve bombers and three fighters—along with an unspecified amount of bombs.[8] Thus, only after about two hours on the ground at Tetuán, Bolín, Bebb, and the *Dragon Rapide* were on their way to Portugal. In Lisbon, General Sanjurjo was delighted to learn that Franco had been able to join the Army of Africa, and at the same time (as leader of the revolt) he hurriedly endorsed Franco's authorization for Bolín to negotiate for aircraft in the name of the rising.[9]

There was some discussion about the possibility of using the *Dragon Rapide* to fly Sanjurjo into Spain; however, because it was not known for certain which fields that could accommodate the aircraft were in the hands of the rebel forces, it was decided to use another, smaller airplane, which was now available. For the Spanish general this was an unfortunate decision because he was to die in the crash of this plane a few hours after this meeting.[10] But the *Dragon Rapide* and Bolín continued on to Marseille where Bolín took another aircraft to Rome.

The same day, 19 July, the decision was made in the Canary Islands to reopen the airways to *Lufthansa* flights. This word was finally passed to Flight Captain Henke in Villa Cisneros. Thus, once again the Ju-52 "Max von Müller" was soon airborne for its interrupted flight to Las Palmas, where it landed at 11:37 a.m. on 20 July.[11]

It can be assumed that General Orgaz had by now received word from Franco that he was needed in Morocco, because Orgaz again approached the *Lufthansa* representative, Otto Bertram. This time the local German consul was included in the discussion. General Orgaz now took a firmer line with the Germans. He informed them that he was forced to requisition one of their aircraft for a short flight to serve the requirements of the Spanish military authorities. Bertram stood his ground as firmly as he had when the general had approached him several days earlier. He again noted, most strongly, that he was absolutely forbidden to become involved in any way with the internal affairs of a foreign country. Despite his objections, Captain Henke was now given written instructions (in Spanish) directing him to make his aircraft and crew available for a mission under Spanish military orders. But still Orgaz had not yet physically taken possession of the airplane. This then was the first direct German involvement in the Spanish Civil War, an involvement which was assumed under violent protest.

The next day the relations between the Spanish military and the Germans became even more strained. After several urgent calls from the Spaniards, Bertram finally agreed to put in an appearance. It probably came as no surprise when he was now handed a note which advised that

Henke's Ju-52 had been seized; along with its crew it was to be placed at the disposal of the Spanish military.

The following day, 22 July, General Orgaz assumed an even more definite stand. He bluntly informed the Germans that he would need the aircraft that same evening to fly to Spanish Morocco. However, it is obvious that Orgaz was concerned about the legal ramifications of his demands, because he now softened his insistence with the fact that he would assume personal responsibility for his actions; along with this he would deposit a bill of credit for 90,000 pesetas in the name of *Lufthansa* in the Bank of Spain. This bill of credit would be insurance for the aircraft and crew. Orgaz then gave the German consul a note which advised that the aircraft along with its crew were now commandeered by the Spanish military; however, both would be released very soon.[12] That same night, the Ju-52 with its German crew took off for Tetuán with Orgaz and several other Spanish officers as passengers. They reached their destination at 5:30 a.m. the morning of 23 July.

Even though General Orgaz had promised that the aircraft and crew would be released once they reached Tetuán, this proved not to be the case. The later German study of the events curtly notes: "General Orgaz went back on his word."[13]

Notes

1. An accurate account of the Ju-52, D-APOK can be found in the very fine and detailed work by Angel Viñas, *La Alemania nazi y el 18 de julio* (Madrid, 1977), pp. 317-385. Most of the German documents pertaining to the German military forces in the Spanish conflict have been lost or destroyed. The material that has been found is located in the West German Archives in Freiburg. These files have been used extensively in this writing and will be cited as "Freiburg" plus the individual file and page number, and/or occasionally other identifying information. In 1940, a special study of the German involvement in Spain was compiled, based on the then existing documentation by the German Air Ministry. It was highly classified and carried the code name of "Magic Fire." Due to the lack of documentation today, such as valuable Unit War Diaries, this compilation is invaluable to a study of the German involvement in Spain. However, in the initial period there is a confusion as to dates of events. It must be remembered that this study does reflect the "official" German position at the time. This does not detract from its value, however. Where the "Magic Fire" compilation is used, it will be cited as "Freiburg, MF," along with the appropriate file number and other necessary identification. For the "Magic Fire" account of the Ju-52, D-APOK see Freiburg, MF, RL 2/v. 3187.

2. George Hills, *Franco. The Man and His Nation* (New York, 1967), pp. 234-235.

3. Ibid. Hills summed up Franco's position rather well. "Franco's attitude was as incomprehensible to the Right as to the Left. The Left could not believe that he was not a conspirator; the Right could not understand why he was not." p. 204.

4. Luis Bolín gives his account of the saga of the *Dragon Rapide* in his *Spain: The Vital Years* (New York, 1967), pp. 11-54. The flight log of Captain Bebb is also reproduced.

5. Calvo Sotelo earlier had been finance minister during the dictatorship of Primo de Rivera. Many observers believe that it was his murder by government uniformed officers which finally made the different factions opposing the Popular Front settle their differences, at least temporarily, and join in revolt.

6. Viñas, *La Alemania nazi*, p. 316.

7. Bolín, *Vital Years*, p. 52.

8. Ibid., pp. 52-53.

9. Ibid., pp. 161-162.

10. A small plane had been sent by General Mola. The pilot was Juan Ansaldo. He had to take off from a small field and, losing power, crashed into a stone wall. Ansaldo managed to escape the burning plane but could not free the general. Later he described these events in his book *¿Para qué. . .?* (Buenos Aires, 1951).

11. Freiburg, MF, RL 2/v. 3187. The proper sequence of events is in Viñas, *La Alemania nazi*, pp. 357-360.

12. Freiburg, MF, RL 2/v. 3187.

13. Ibid.

2

Phase Two: "Magic Fire"

When Captain Henke and the crew were forbidden to reenter the aircraft's cabin, Henke angrily demanded a meeting with the senior Spanish officer. Later in the day the German was able to have a brief talk with Franco and was told by the general that very important moves were under consideration, and that the German pilot and his plane would probably be involved. However, at this moment the Spanish general did not reveal his intentions.[1]

By this time the insurrection was six days old, and to some extent (considering the deplorable communications) its scattered leadership was able to evaluate their successes and failures. To the evaluator, the failures must have seemed by far to outweigh the successes. In brief, the rebels precariously held about one-third of Spain. They had been successful in Navarre, where General Mola, with the support of the Carlists, had secured Pamplona. The rebels tentatively occupied a wide belt from the French border through Castile to Portugal, excluding the northern Basque provinces as well as the rich mining district of Asturias. The flamboyant General Queipo de Llano, in a ridiculous storybook *coup de main*, had managed to seize Seville with far more bluff and bravado than strength. However, Seville along with Granada and Cádiz were mere rebel enclaves in a vast stretch of southern Spain still held by the Popular Front.

Loyal government forces, augmented by armed union militias and anarchist groups, were able to hold the very important districts of Madrid, Barcelona, Valencia, and the entire Mediterranean coast along with half of the border with France. Scattered through these zones were many isolated rebel-held towns, villages, or fortifications (such as Albacete, Oviedo, Gijón, Alcázar of Toledo, and the monastery of Santa María de la Cabeza). Many of these were eventually to be overrun by government forces, but others were able to hold out until they were relieved by friendly forces.

For the cause of the insurrection, a cursory survey of the military forces reveals a trying situation. On the seas the cause was fundamentally hopeless because most of the fleet remained in the hands of the Popular Front. Cells of the navy crews had seized the ships and killed most of the officers, whose bodies were thrown overboard. On 19 July, the destroyer *Churruca* did manage to ferry a unit of Moorish troops to the mainland; but following this effort for the rebels the crew seized the ship, and its officers met the same fate as the rest of the officers of the fleet.

Most of the Spanish Air Force was also in the hands of the government. The later German study placed the strength of the air force at approximately 300 aircraft (generally antiquated) of all types. Of this number, at least 230 remained under government control. Luis Bolín gives the rebel strength in Morocco as three old Breguets and a Dornier flying boat.[2]

Because of the carnage of the first few days of fighting it is most difficult to define the ground forces of the opposing sides. The paper strength of the Spanish army at the time has been put at 121,000, but at the moment of the insurrection it is figured (from the ration records) that at least 60,000 men were on leave. Of the remainder, the Nationalists on the mainland controlled about 23,000 and the government some 33,000. Spain also had paramilitary forces which must be considered. They were in the form of the Civil Guard, Assault Guards, and *Carabineros*. The rebels were supported by 14,200 Civil Guards, 500 Assault Guards, and 6,000 *Carabineros*. Remaining with the government were 10,000 Civil Guards, 3,500 Assault Guards, and 8,750 *Carabineros*.[3] The government thus controlled over half of the army and paramilitary forces. It should be noted that many of the men were trapped on a given side by the circumstances of the moment, when in fact their sympathies lay with the other, and when given the opportunity, they deserted to the other forces. This was done singly, in small groups, and at times even in complete units.

To the above forces one must add the strength of the so-called militia units. George Hills, using reliable Nationalist and Popular Front sources, puts the Nationalists' combined Carlist and Falange militia strength at initially 12,400 and the Popular Front militia (including Socialists, Communists, Trotskyites, and Anarchists) at 27,000.[4] The militia strength on both sides was to increase very quickly. Since Spain had compulsory military service, it can be assumed that most of the so-called militiamen were able to handle small arms to some extent. For manpower reserves, the government had the great advantage because it controlled all the major population centers—upon which it could enforce a draft. Again, in general, those drafted would have had at least limited prior military training.

In the matter of resupply, the government again held the great advantage because it dominated all of Spain's industrial regions. In addition, with its control of the entire Mediterranean coast, most of the Bay of Biscay, and a large stretch of the French border, resupply from abroad was no problem. In the important area of finances it controlled the gold reserves of the Bank of Spain.

The Socialist leader Prieto y Tuero was largely justified when he noted that the rebels had ". . .gone off their heads. How can they hope to be saved?"[5] And Karl Schwendemann (counselor in the German Embassy) on 25 July wrote a summary of events up to that time. His views were: ". . .it is hardly to be expected in view of all this that the military revolt can succeed, but the fighting will probably continue for some time."[6]

The major hope for the rebels lay in the well-trained professional Army of Africa. Including the Spanish Foreign Legion, Moorish *Regulares*, and the Spanish units, this force totaled 24,000. To this were quickly added some 6,000 Moroccan Guards. But other than for the very few men who had been carried to the mainland on 19 July, the entire force was bottled up in North Africa. When asked what he proposed to do, General Franco understandably replied: "Everything that might be feasible and necessary. Everything, except surrender."[7] Not only did they have to move the Army of Africa to Spain, but at the same time augment their limited supplies. Also, it should be noted here that the death of General Sanjurjo left the rebels lacking in any recognized centralized leadership. Each commander had been, and still was, acting on his own initiative and limited resources. This extended from General Mola in the north (who had cast his force in revolt desperately short of a basic supply of ammunition) to Queipo de Llano in Seville and Franco in Africa.

It has been noted that as early as 19 July, Franco had sent Luis Bolín to Italy to try and obtain a few aircraft. If he should be successful, these few bombers could strike at the government airdromes from which its aircraft had bombed North Africa. At the same time they could be used to scatter the government fleet—as well as protect troop convoys across the straits. But it was not known if Bolín would succeed. Under these gloomy circumstances it was but natural that Franco and his staff would consider all other alternatives. Support from the Popular Front government of France was out of the question; besides, the Madrid government had already placed frantic orders for aircraft with Paris.[8] Any assistance from England was hardly likely, but still the Monarchist flyer Colonel (later General) Alfredo Kindelán attempted to obtain aircraft through close British friends.

By the time that Captain Henke landed his plane at Tetuán the leaders in Africa had decided to approach Germany for possible assistance. At the moment this was viewed as the only possible recourse. But how would this be accomplished?

There was no diplomatic contact between the insurgents and the German Reich. Nor was there any established liaison with individual highly placed German political or military officials. It has frequently been speculated that there was a deep connection between the insurgents and the agents of Admiral Canaris of German Military Intelligence. This, however, has no base in historical fact. It is true that there was to develop a very close relationship between the German admiral and General Franco, and that Canaris was to play a very enigmatic role in German-Spanish relations during the Second World War. And, following the war his widow was to live in Spain on a Spanish government pension. Still, all of this should not lead one to assume that Canaris was one of the moving forces behind the Civil War.

Through the nature of their positions some of the Spaniards did know personally some of their German counterparts. It was recognized that if the Spaniards should approach any German officer, he would have to pass their request on to the responsible ministries of the Reich. The deciding office would be the Ministry of Foreign Affairs, which would have to determine if German assistance could be viewed as being in the national interest of the Reich. Undoubtedly that ministry would take a very cautious view of the international risks that would be brought about by even the most modest involvement in what assuredly could be viewed, at the time, as a strictly Spanish affair, and one that appeared to have little chance of success.

Still, General Franco and his staff made the decision to move in this direction. There was a communications channel through the German Consulate in Tetuán to a German officer assigned to the Attaché Service. Posted to the attaché offices in Paris and Lisbon was General Kühlenthal, known both to Franco and the capable Arabist Lt. Colonel Juan Beigbeder (himself a former attaché to Germany). It was decided that the colonel should send a short personal "very urgent" message to Kühlenthal, but "on the word of Franco of Spain." This message was dispatched late in the evening of 22 July, and was forwarded the afternoon of the following day to the Reich foreign minister in Berlin. The message simply stated that a new Nationalist government had been founded in Spain and requested that he send ten transport aircraft to Morocco. The "contract will be signed afterwards."[9]

Any feeling of doubt about the results of this overture was to be justified by the very rapid negative response of the Reich Foreign Ministry upon receipt of the message.[10] Even before the dispatch of the message to Kühlenthal the Spaniards were considering approaching Germany through a channel which might be able to bypass the professional government ministries of the Reich. This was through the communications channel of the National Socialist party.

In Morocco there was a small German colony which was in the main connected with German business firms and well known by both Spanish civil and military authorities. Included in the German colony was an even smaller group associated with the "Foreign Organization" (*Auslandsorganisation,* or simply A.O.) of the Nazi party. This party group had communications channels to its party headquarters office in Berlin, which lay outside the official civil and military structure of the German government. In Berlin, the head (*Gauleiter*) of A.O. was Ernst Wilhelm Bohle, who had direct contact with the Nazi party leadership such as Rudolf Hess and ultimately the *Führer* himself. The Chief *(Ortsgruppenleiter)* of the small A.O. group in Spanish Morocco was one Adolph Langenheim, and another member was Johannes Bernhardt. As events evolved, the latter was to prove to be the most important.[11]

In April 1933, Bernhardt, along with Langenheim and six others of the colony, had joined the Nazi party. Bernhardt's party number was 1,572,819 and Langenheim's was 1,572,863.[12] Langenheim and Bernhardt as German businessmen had occasion to confer with the German consul in Tetuán, the German Embassy in Madrid, the Foreign Office, and Langenheim as the local head of the party (small as it was) would have had contact with the office of the A.O. and its chief, Ernst Bohle, in Berlin. As near as can be determined, Langenheim's last visit to Berlin prior to 18 July 1936 was in May of that year. It can be assumed that he discussed with the Berlin office conditions in Spain as he saw them. If so, it is difficult to determine if this had any impact upon Bohle, or indeed if Langenheim had been able to see him personally.

During the prior six years, Bernhardt's company had had many business negotiations with the Spanish civil and military authorities in the protectorate. These dealings included materials from communications equipment, stoves, and cameras, to the manufacture of artillery targets for the Army of Africa. He was understandably well known to the Spaniards not only through his business contacts but socially as well. It was a colonial environment, and it was not uncommon for Europeans living in such an environment to group themselves together socially. And among the Spanish military he was respected because of his former experience as an artillery officer in the Great War (World War I). He was known to many Spaniards by the nickname "Tónie." General Franco, however, up until this time was not one of his acquaintances.

Hardly being an admirer of the political Left, Bernhardt understandably would identify himself with the cause of the Spanish insurrection. On 21 July, he called briefly on some of the officers of the Spanish staff and in a gesture of sympathy stated that he was at their service. Preoccupied with their problems, and they had many, the Spaniards were appreciative but seemingly not overly concerned at this moment. Later he was able to meet briefly with General Franco and offered to go to Berlin and act in their behalf. Now Bernhardt and Langenheim were soon to become directly involved in the Spanish scheme of things.

The desperate and determined officers in Morocco resolved that they should make a petition directly to the German chancellor. If their emissary should be able to reach Hitler personally, they would be able to bypass all the Reich ministries and their objections to any German support for their cause. They could approach Hitler on the grounds that their insurrection was indeed a move against the strong possibility of a communist state arising on the western end of the Mediterranean. To prevent this, the limited material support requested of Germany would be in fact assisting in a blow against the enemy of the Reich.

Where such an ideological appeal to Germany might give rise to sympathy, it would not necessarily result in the much-needed aircraft. Here German interests and risks would have to be measured. These could partly be answered by the possibility of increased German commerce with a Nationalist Spain, along with opening Spanish mineral resources to Germany, which up until now were so greatly dominated by British financial interests. Also, it could be noted that the Spaniards' request was modest, and furthermore payment would be forthcoming. In addition, their expressed need would be for transport aircraft, which could be dispatched to Spain through commercial means rather than military channels. This maneuver could be used to lessen any international criticism of the Reich.

Importantly for the officers in Morocco, the channel existed by which they could attempt a direct approach to the German leader. Bernhardt had expressed his willingness to cooperate. Equally important was that the means to transport him to Germany lay in Captain Henke and his Ju-52.

When Henke finally learned what was being proposed, he was adamantly opposed to becoming involved in any way. Part of his concern was the possibility of jeopardizing his company, *Lufthansa*, and at the same time his own position with the company, for what he viewed as a hopeless cause of the *general de bandidos*.[13] The chief of A.O. in Tetuán, Langenheim, an elderly man, was not enthusiastic either about becoming involved in Spanish affairs. Still, after much persuasion on the part of Bernhardt and his wife, as well as a bank deposit of a sizeable amount of French francs to cover the cost of the operation, Langenheim and Henke reluctantly agreed to carry out the mission.

The Spaniards selected aeronautical engineer Captain Francisco Arranz Monasterio, who had just been appointed chief of staff of the Rebels' diminutive air force in Morocco, to accompany the Germans. Finally in the afternoon of 23 July, the very hastily drawn plans were put into effect, and at 5:00 p.m. the Ju-52 with its passengers of Bernhardt, Langenheim, and Captain Arranz departed Tetuán. Their first stop was at the airfield of Tablada, which is near Seville. Here the Germans and Arranz contacted General Queipo de Llano to advise him of their mission. The German account of events notes that Queipo de Llano expressed pleasure over the remote possibility of material assistance coming from Germany.[14]

Their intentions were to depart Seville about 1:00 a.m. of 24 July and fly on to Marseille; however, because of engine and radio problems their takeoff was delayed until 9:00 a.m.[15] Without additional mishaps, after landing in Marseille and Stuttgart, they landed later that same day at the airfield Gatow near Berlin—not at Tempelhof as has often been reported. Berlin had been advised by radio of their intended arrival, and the delegation was deliberately diverted to Gatow to ensure thay they maintained a low profile. They were to be guests of *Lufthansa* rather than any official department of the Reich government.[16]

The following day, 25 July, Hans Heinrich Dieckhoff of the German Foreign Office noted in a memorandum that his office had been advised the previous day by the War Ministry of the arrival of the Spanish mission. He agreed with the War Ministry that the delegation "should not be received by any official military authorities." Furthermore, he urged the head of the A.O. that the Nazi party organization should not permit the Spanish delegation to come into contact with German political officials. Dieckhoff was specific that *Gauleiter* Bohle should be "against promoting their [the Spaniards'] plans here in any way." Also, he advised that no arms shipments to the Spanish rebels be considered.[17] Foreign Minister Neurath emphatically agreed to his memorandum. Dieckhoff then reinforced his memorandum with a personal telephone conversation with *Gauleiter* Bohle of the A.O.

Bohle, in contrast to the position taken by the German Foreign and War offices, must have been influenced by the reports of his A.O. organizations as to the nature of the political-ideological events south of the Pyrenees. In any event, he immediately made the decision to ignore the instructions and advice of the professionals of the War and Foreign offices. *Gauleiter* Bohle now placed a direct phone call to the "second man" in the National Socialist party, Rudolf Hess, who was at the moment in Thuringia, and informed him of the objectives of the delegation from Morocco. Hess, on his part, seems to have made a hasty decision to consider the question further;[18] he now ordered the delegates to be flown to meet with him in Thuringia. Bernhardt and Langenheim departed at once, but oddly the Spanish captain was left behind in Berlin.

When Hess met with the Germans from Morocco, he must have been moved with sympathy in face of their description of events. He concluded that he would immediately contact Hitler, who was in Bayreuth attending the opera festival. By phone, Hess successfully prevailed upon Hitler to receive the Germans speaking for the Spaniards. Hess then notified Bohle, in Berlin, of Hitler's decision and ordered him immediately to Bayreuth accompanied by the head of the legal office of A.O. and several high-ranking Nazi officials.

It was late at night, 25 July, when Bernhardt, Langenheim, and another representative of the A.O. were ushered into the *Führer*'s presence. The former presented Hitler with a letter from General Franco and then translated it into German with comments. The letter itself has never been found in the stores of German archival materials, but years later Bernhardt was to relate to Dr. Viñas its contents, in general, as well as the events that transpired at this meeting.[19] Franco's letter noted that the rebels' struggle was against anarchy and communism and contained a description, written by Franco, of the situation in Spain as of 23 July. Attached to it was a request for infantry weapons, antiaircraft guns, and aircraft (including ten transport aircraft).

Hitler had already been provided with the latest information on events in Spain as gathered by his ministries, and thus neither Franco's letter nor Bernhardt's comments came as a great surprise. Hitler took the position that the cause of the insurrection had deteriorated even further. Also, he showed misgivings about German support if the struggle should be a lengthy one. He then plied Bernhardt with many questions, some of which the latter could not answer. Hitler then went into a lengthy monologue reciting all that he knew, or thought he knew, about Spain. His visitors maintained a discreet silence for nearly two hours and watched Hitler, forgetting supper, go from a position of reserve and lack of confidence in the revolt to a position of curiosity. When advised by Bernhardt of Franco's dire financial status, Hitler responded: "You cannot begin a war like that."[20] At Hitler's probing, Bernhardt admitted that the conflict could last for months, and if Franco did not receive help immediately, his chance for success would be greatly reduced. Hitler commented, "He is lost."[21]

But then surprisingly he ordered that they be joined by the war and air ministers, Generals von Blomberg and Goering respectively. In a few words, Hitler informed them of his intention of helping General Franco and his insurrection. The war minister knew that his department, as well as the Foreign Office, had already informed Hitler of their objections and apparently accepted the *Führer*'s position now as being irrevocable. On the other hand, Hermann Goering objected strongly, noting that Germany itself lacked military equipment and that at the same time any assistance from the Reich might precipitate difficult international problems. Hitler's position was that it would be wise to run the risk of international complications; Franco did not need men, but he must have equipment and aircraft to move the troops from Africa to the mainland. Hitler, surprisingly, took the view that where Germany's help could not be extended as a gift, it could be granted on credit.[22]

Air Minister Goering immediately shifted his position of objections to one of enthusiasm for the idea. Whether this was because of his desire to please his *Führer* or indeed to test his new *Luftwaffe* as he was to proclaim after the war is open to debate.[23] The conference was then joined by a German admiral who to this date has not been identified, but according to Bernhardt—there is no reason to doubt him—was not Admiral Canaris, chief of *Abwehr*, as has been suggested.[24]

The navy would be responsible for the surface shipment of men and materials, but the ultimate responsibility would be vested in the hands of General Goering and his Air Ministry. Possibly fearing that the movement of aircraft and personnel would dilute his very small air force, as well as still being concerned about precipitating an international incident, Goering suggested that the planes and crews should come from *Lufthansa*. Hitler followed this with the order that they should be camouflaged so as not to be recognizable as property belonging to the German government. And importantly, absolute secrecy was to be maintained. To remove the German government further from involvement, a private company would be established through which the materiel would be moved. It would be charged with the responsibility, and it would, at the same time, be dealing with a single individual; the individual would be General Franco.

The meeting finally came to an end between 1:30 a.m. and 2:00 a.m., 26 July. The decision was made! Germany, on the sole decision of the *Führer*, was to be involved in mischief south of the Pyrenees.

Even though it was Sunday, events moved with amazing speed. Naval Commander Lindau, in Hamburg, was called out of bed and by 7:00 a.m. was being flown south in Hitler's personal aircraft. Goering's sub-secretary of air, General Erhard Milch, flew to Bayreuth and arrived a little after 1:30 p.m. to meet with Lindau and Hitler. In only about two hours, in the greatest of secrecy, the plans for German action were formulated. Then both Milch and Lindau flew north the same afternoon with the general piloting the plane.[25]

By 5:30 p.m. General Milch met with a group of specialists who had already been ordered by phone to assemble. At 7:30 p.m. General Helmuth Wilberg arrived at the Air Ministry and was charged with forming a "Special Staff" to be responsible for all phases of the German involvement. This staff was to become known as "Special Staff W."[26] Absolute secrecy was to be maintained. Not even other military personnel who would contribute to the operations of the staff were to know what it was all about. The operation was to go by the code name "Magic Fire."[27]

Meanwhile, the two Germans from Morocco and the Spanish Captain Arranz were preparing to return to Tetuán in, of all things, the same aircraft D-APOK with the same flight captain Alfred Henke at the controls. That same day, 27 July, the crew off-loaded everything possible so as to accommodate the maximum fuel load, some of which was stored in gas cans in the cabin to be used for in-flight refueling. Henke and his passengers took off and flew over Switzerland, then along the French/Italian coast and the Spanish coast to Morocco. After more than ten hours in the air they landed at Tetuán about 1:00 p.m., 28 July, to be greeted by a crowd of very anxious Spanish officers. Captain Arranz was able to report that Germany would be shipping twenty Ju-52 aircraft, six He-51 fighters, twenty pieces of antiaircraft artillery, and munitions, as well as the personnel to support them.[28]

Hardly had Flight Captain Henke landed his aircraft when he and his crew were making it ready to air lift the first contingent of Spanish troops across the Straits of Gibraltar. But still, he had to remove the German identification. It is rather ironic that Henke, who had so adamantly opposed his aircraft and crew becoming involved in Spanish affairs, would be the first pilot to make the one-hour airlift to Seville and thereby initiate the first military airlift of an army in history.

To handle the transfer of equipment, a private Spanish/German company was established, and at General Franco's suggestion, it was named *Hispano-Marroquí de Transportes, S.L.*, but better known by the abbreviation *HISMA*.[29] The following morning a second *Lufthansa* Ju-52 landed at Tetuán. If the Spaniards had any doubts of the honesty of the German offer for assistance, they were now quickly dispelled.[30]

In Germany, preparations for assistance were moving at a hectic pace and involved many people, organizations of the government, and commercial companies. The materials had to be drawn from military stores, packed, and shipped to the port of Hamburg; ships had to be provided to carry the materiel; and trained military personnel and technicians had to be drawn from the ranks of the still small *Luftwaffe*. The security was the responsibility of the *Gestapo*, and the Hamburg Customs Office was advised to remain out of the picture. To move the materiel and personnel, the German Navy worked through the firm of Mathis & Rhode Company freight office. The steamship *Usaramo* was contracted from the Woermann Line.[31]

The Junker firm at Dessau, south of Hamburg on the Elbe River, was instructed to remove the German national markings and dismantle the aircraft, including ten Ju-52s and six He-51 fighters, which were to be shipped by sea. They were packed in camouflaged crates and shipped to the port the following day. The antiaircraft batteries were shipped in vans labeled "Moving Materials." In order to acquire the proper personnel, specifically flight and ground crews, the Air Ministry directed the commanders of the Fighter wings at Dortmund and Döberitz and the Bomber squadrons at Merseburg, Gotha, and Ansbach to pull capable personnel from their units. In all, the personnel complement included twenty-five officers and sixty-six noncommissioned officers, soldiers, and civilian technicians. Besides the flight crews for the Ju-52s they included pilots for the six He-51s, one medical officer, radiomen, and mechanics. To call these men "volunteers," however, is not accurate. According to Lieutenant Hans Trautloft in his *Memoirs*, he was called in by his commander and told to pack his bag because he had volunteered for a very secret mission. Within two hours he was on his way from his base near Cologne to Dortmund and then on to the fighter squadron "Freiherr von Richthofen" at Döberitz where he reported 29 July, to join several other officers who had already arrived. Only single men had been selected, and in an attempt to divorce the *Luftwaffe* from the venture, the officers resigned their commissions and were placed on the reserve list.[32] They turned in their uniforms and were issued civilian clothing and cheap identical suitcases.

Even though they were on the military reserve list, they were under military orders and military law. They were placed under the command of Major Alexander von Scheele, a very pleasant man who had served in World War I and had lived for years in Latin America but had been recalled to active duty. He and his personnel were given specific orders that forbade them to fly any combat missions for General Franco, including bomber, fighter, or reconnaissance missions. The He-51s could, however, protect the lumbering transports.[33] The manner in which his men and equipment were to be used was left up to his judgment.

It would be impossible to pull this number of men from Germany and simply have them drop out of sight from their families for an unknown period of time. They were sworn to strict secrecy, but a mailbox was opened for them in Berlin under the name of Max Winkler, to which they and their families could write. This procedure was much the same as that used for those men who received their training in the secret operation in Russia, which had come to an end only a couple of years earlier.

The assembled men were inspected the morning of 31 July by Generals Milch and Wilberg and learned what was expected of them, and they were again warned not to become involved in combat of any kind. Then in mufti and with their identical cheap suitcases they boarded buses which took them to the small rail station of *Lehrter* in Berlin at 11:00 a.m. They were traveling under the name "*Reisegesellschaft Union*" (Tourist Group Union). After dark they boarded the *Usaramo*, which was now loaded with 773 crates. Either shortly after or before midnight, 31 July, the *Usaramo* weighed anchor for its destination Cádiz, Spain. It arrived in Spanish waters on 6 August.

While the *Luftwaffe* fighter and bomber unit commanders were selecting their volunteers, nine Ju-52s and crews were being withdrawn from the commercial airline *Lufthansa*. As noted, on 28 July, before Major von Scheele's command gathered in Döberitz, Flight Captain Henke had already flown to Morocco and immediately started the air bridge from Africa to Spain. The existing German documents do not indicate when the other aircraft flown to Morocco arrived, but they do note that their route was from Dessau-Stuttgart or Friedrichshafen (the old German zeppelin base) and then on to San Remo, and finally Morocco or Seville in southern Spain. After departing Stuttgart or Friedrichshafen, the flight was about eleven hours (nonstop) at an altitude of 5,000 meters.[34]

One of the last *Lufthansa* aircraft had a problem. The crew of Ju-52 D-AMYM took off from Germany 8 August and by mistake landed at the Madrid airport at 10:00 a.m. They thought they were landing in Seville because both Madrid and Seville operated on the same radio frequency. Upon landing, a German civilian advised them of their error and they took off immediately. But still confused, the crew then landed at an airfield near Badajoz in Madrid-controlled Spain. The government in Madrid, now alerted, had the crew arrested and the aircraft impounded. Later, a Spanish pilot flew the plane back to Madrid, where the German ambassador in Madrid had entered a violent objection to the seizure and impoundment of a German commercial aircraft and its crew. After questioning the crew at some length they were turned over to the German Embassy. But there was at the same time quick reaction in Berlin. There a Spanish officer, Lt. Colonel Luis Riaño, was put under guard and not permitted to leave Germany. However, by 15 August Berlin learned that the Ju-52 crew was in the German Embassy. Concerned about the safety of Germans in Madrid, Berlin now ordered six *Lufthansa* planes to fly Germans from that city to Marseille, where they were to be picked up by other German aircraft.[35]

Still, in the first eight days after Captain Henke landed his Ju-52 at Tetuán, by stripping the interior of the arriving planes and jamming about 35 soldiers and their basic equipment into the cabins, the German aircraft and crews had flown 1,207 men to southern Spain. By the end of the second week an additional 1,282 had been moved.[36] Air sickness of some of the soldiers made even worse what was already a difficult situation. Additional troops were to be moved by the limited number of Spanish planes. The first major military airlift was well under way.

Notes

1. Freiburg, MF, RL 2/v. 3187.
2. Freiburg, MF, RL 2/v. 3191, pp. 7-8, and Luis Bolín, *Spain: The Vital Years*, p. 174.
3. George Hills, *Franco. The Man and His Nation*, pp. 240-241.
4. Ibid., p. 241.
5. Ibid., p. 242.

6. *Documents on German Foreign Policy 1918-1945* (Washington, D.C., 1950) (hereafter cited as *GD*), Series D, Vol. III, Doc. No. 11.

7. Brian Crozier, *Franco* (Boston, 1967), p. 192.

8. Luis Bolín, *Spain: The Vital Years*, p. 174, and Freiburg, MF, RL 2/v. 3191, pp. 8-9, and *GD*, Series D, Vol. III, Doc. No. 3, dtd. 23 July 1936.

9. *GD*, Series D, Vol. III, Doc. No. 2.

10. *GD*, Series D, Vol. III, Doc. No. 5. Dieckhoff, of the Foreign Ministry, was specific: "In the view of the Foreign Ministry, compliance with the Spanish request is out of the question at this time."

11. For the complete story of Bernhardt, see Angel Viñas, *La Alemania nazi y el 18 de julio*, pp. 276-284, upon which the following is drawn.

12. Ibid., p. 283.

13. Ibid., p. 326.

14. Freiburg, MF, RL 2/v. 3187.

15. Ibid.

16. Viñas, *La Alemania nazi*, p. 319.

17. *GD*, Series D, Vol. III, Doc. No. 10.

18. Viñas, *La Alemania nazi*, pp. 335-337.

19. Ibid., p. 339.

20. Ibid., p. 341.

21. Ibid.

22. Ibid., p. 342.

23. *GD*, Series D, Vol. III, p. 2, n. 2.

24. Viñas, *La Alemania nazi*, p. 342.

25. Ibid., p. 344.

26. Freiburg, MF, RL 2/v. 3187.

27. Ibid.

28. Freiburg, MF, RL 2/v. 3187, and Viñas, *La Alemania nazi*, p. 384.

29. Viñas, *La Alemania nazi*, p. 386.

30. Ibid., p. 385.

31. Freiburg, MF, RL 2/v. 3187.

32. Hans Trautloft, *Als Jagdflieger in Spanien: Aus dem Tagebuch eines deutschen Legionäres* (Berlin, 1940), pp. 7-12.

33. Freiburg, MF, RL 2/v. 3187, p. 20.

34. Ibid., pp. 22-23.

35. Ibid.

36. Ibid., p. 21.

3

Phase Three: The Airlift from Africa

The airlift from Africa was not without its problems. At first dawn the planes would leave for Seville and Jerez de la Frontera. Within the first five days a temporary airstrip at Jerez became the main destination because it was closer than the over-one-hour flight to Seville. The reduction of the flights to forty minutes was extremely important for fuel economy. Care had to be exercised to prevent the infantry soldiers from overloading the aircraft. At times it was necessary to break up small infantry units temporarily, and this was not too popular with the troops. The seats and everything else that could be dispensed with were removed, and the soldiers sat on the floor with their knees drawn up to their chins with their rifles propped between their feet. The Germans quickly learned that the best time to operate was in the morning and evening. Through the noon hours there usually were strong winds which not only raised the fuel consumption but induced air sickness among the troops. One man getting sick in the hot, crowded aircraft often prompted others to follow suit in a very messy manner. Flights were usually made at altitudes between 2,500 and 3,500 meters to avoid antiaircraft fire from the government ships.[1]

At the end of the first week in August as the *Usaramo* entered the harbor of Cádiz, the Nationalist forces of the South had made the link with General Mola's troops of Army North. The *Usaramo* immediately began to unload its passengers and crates of war materiel. The officers and men were shipped to Seville by special train where prior billeting had been arranged.

The officers, civilians, and some of the mechanics, were quartered in the Cristina Hotel, a very charming hotel on the *Jardines de Cristina*. Ground personnel were quartered in German pensions in the city and the balance of the mechanics was housed at the airfield of Tablada.

Major von Scheele organized this small force into five different groups. Of course, at the same time he was to assume control over the aircraft and crews already involved in the airlift from Africa (see map 1). The first group was the transport force which was placed under Lieutenant Baron von Moreau and stationed at the airport in Tetuán.[2] The second group was the bomber force which was equipped with the Ju-52s, but with Spanish crews, placed under the command of Flight Captain Henke. Lieutenant Kraft Eberhard was to command two forces; one unit was the small squadron of six He-51 fighters based at Tablada near Seville. It would come directly under Captain Houwald and was to train Spanish pilots to operate the fighters. Lieutenant Eberhard's other responsibility was the ground support forces at the airfield and the small communications section. A temporary maintenance depot and communications center was established in Salamanca. The fifth group was the flak training force under Lieutenant Hermann.

Initially the maintenance of aircraft in Seville was made the responsibility of *Lufthansa* which was augmented by military and civilian specialists. Later this was turned over to representatives of H & O Wilmer.

As the "Tourist Group Union," which now called themselves "volunteers," established their operation, the airlift from Africa continued as rapidly as the limited number of aircraft would permit. But problems quickly began to arise. To make as many trips as possible, the crews would eat while their aircraft were being refueled and loaded with troops. Hundreds of Spanish and Moorish troops and Legionaries were camped near the airfield at Tetuán awaiting their turn, and in company strength hundreds more were arriving daily. The cook fires could be seen burning day and night. It would not be until after dark that the flight crews would repair to their billets for much-needed rest. The mechanics would now take over the planes for reservicing. The conditions were most primitive, and the work was carried out by lanterns and headlights of service vehicles.

The conditions at Tablada were hardly better. The airfield and its service equipment had deteriorated badly over the past five years. The Germans complained that even the most primitive equipment, had it been available, would have been a great help. Thus the flight and maintenance crews were cast on their own initiative. Still, in the week of 10 to 16 August 1936, 2,853 armed men and 7,985 kilos of materiel were flown from Africa to Spain. The climate was most difficult for the northern Europeans; in an aircraft out in the broiling sun, it can be absolutely intolerable. It was not unusual that from time to time the Germans would drop from heatstroke. The Spaniards, well aware, through the centuries

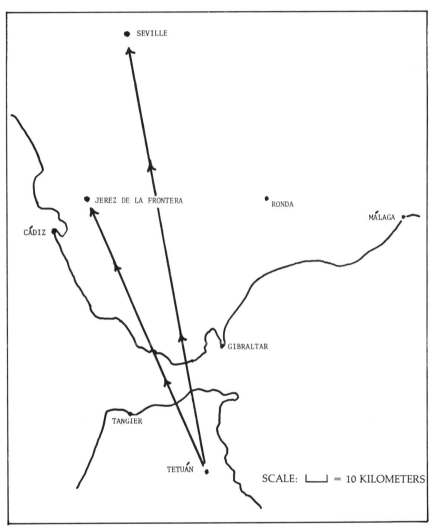

Map 1. Airlift from Africa, July-October 1936.

had adapted the problem into their living habits—work in the cooler hours of the forenoon and after the fierce sun dips into the Atlantic to the west.

Even though the Germans were supposed to maintain a low profile, all Seville knew who they were and why they were there. For one thing there were their distinctive white suits on which they wore the HISMA pin. The purpose of the pin was to show that the individual was connected with the HISMA Company, which at the time was charged with taking care of the many administrative problems such as quartering, provisioning, and clothing of personnel.

The German transport crews were disturbed by antiaircraft fire from the Madrid warships *Churruca* and *Jaime I*. They felt that they could and should put an end to the problem but they were still denied an active combat role. For one of the Ju-52s with Spanish markings, with a Spanish crew to have attacked one of the warships would not have been a violation of German orders because the aircraft had technically been sold to the Spanish Nationalists. But for a German to be involved in any air strike would be in direct violation of orders given them by Generals Milch and Wilberg. These orders were reinforced when Major von Scheele asked for such permission. The German "Magic Fire" documents note that this forced von Scheele to act "on his own initiative and determine that an aircraft should attack. . . ." Two Ju-52s were pulled from the transport mission, and for two days and nights the crews struggled to conform the transports to carry bombs. It was most difficult because they did not have the proper tools or trained personnel. By radio they had learned that the battleship *Jaime I* was in the Bay of Málaga. At 4:00 a.m., 13 August, the two aircraft were airborne with bombs slung in crude bomb racks. (There were two bomb racks that were included in the equipment that had arrived on the *Usaramo*, but they were either forgotten or not located by this time.)

In the first aircraft, the commander was Lieutenant Baron von Moreau. The second was commanded by Flight Captain Henke and carried Lieutenant Count Hoyos and a Spanish naval officer as observer. Lieutenant von Moreau's aircraft became lost in the clouds and did not reach Málaga.[3] Flight Captain Henke, however, did reach Málaga, but the battleship *Jaime I* was not tied to the pier; still, in the grey hours of the dawn they located it far out in the bay. The Ju-52 attacked from an altitude of 400 meters and dropped three bombs. The second bomb struck the bridge, and the Ju-52 returned to base. From the Madrid radio it was learned that the *Jaime I* was out of commission and had to be towed to the naval base at Cartagena. Some works state that the Ju-52 which struck the *Jaime I* was flown by Lieutenant Baron von Moreau, and several Germans interviewed by the writer have stated the same, but still the German study was specific in naming Flight Captain Henke. What is important about the event, besides for a time removing the annoying battleship from action, was that it did signal an event, although not fully recognized at the time, that the purely support and noncombative role of the Germans was drawing to a close. The news of the event was received with delight by the other crews, and some began to pressure Major von Scheele to permit them to enter combat as members of the Spanish Foreign Legion, a position which at the time was being held by Italian crews who were supporting the Nationalists with Italian aircraft. Still, Berlin would not consent.

Only two days following the strike against the warship the Germans lost their first blood when noncommissioned officers (NCOs) Helmut Schulze and Herbert Zech died in the crash of their Ju-52 at Jerez de la Frontera.[4]

On 23 August 1936, Flight Captain Henke and Lieutenant Baron von Moreau once again manned the controls of German aircraft with Nationalist markings.[5] With the inception of the revolt Spanish Colonel Moscardó with a force of nearly 1,300 young soldiers, *Guardia Civil*, cadets, and civilian volunteers (along with about 500 women and children) had been besieged in the old fortress of the Alcázar of Toledo. All of these days they had been under direct artillery fire, at point-blank range from across the river, aerial bombardment, mine explosions, and infantry assaults. It appeared a heroic effort for a lost cause, but they repeatedly withstood all efforts of the attackers. The attention of the entire world was focused on the valor of the defenders, as well as those who were equally determined to storm their defenses. In the early morning hours of this day, Flight Captain Henke's aircraft flew low over the shattered towers and crumbling walls of the old fortress and dropped food, medical supplies, and letters to the defenders. A few hours later Baron von Moreau repeated the feat and dropped his supplies into the courtyard of the fortress. It was a message that those inside had not been forgotten.

In the rush to gather the materials to ship on the *Usaramo*, the proper tools were not included to reassemble the He-51 fighters. As a result this took much longer to accomplish than had been anticipated. The first aircraft were not assembled until 10 August and then were test flown to the satisfaction of Lieutenant Eberhard.[6] As noted, the German fighter pilots were supposed to act as instructors for the Spanish, who insisted on taking the aircraft over immediately. The German record curtly states: "Since the Spaniards did not have any experience in flying the German planes, one aircraft crashed and another was blown to pieces over the front the first day. Therefore great importance was put on assembling the other three aircraft."[7]

The German report notes that it was with reluctance that Franco directed the first Nationalist air attack against Madrid on 3 August. The planes struck at the War Ministry with minimal effect. Knowing of the buildup of aircraft in the Madrid sector, on 24 August the Nationalists struck the airfields of Getafe and Cuatro Vientos with twenty-one aircraft with 200 bombs. Many grounded aircraft were destroyed, but the number is not given. The limited number of Nationalist aircraft were now diverted against enemy ground forces in the Guadarramas where the fighting had intensified. In face of increased fighter opposition the Germans also diverted four of their He-51 fighters to a Spanish squadron at Escalona. On the very first mission two of the aircraft crashed. This was most distressing to the German flyers. The Spanish pilots had proven they were brave and determined but that they lacked the skill to handle the German craft. With the concurrence of Major von Scheele the German pilots took the remaining fighters back and still against orders from Berlin, flew into battle. On 25 August, the German flyers Lieutenant Eberhard and Lieutenant Trautloft had their first, but not last, victories of the Spanish war with one each. The next day Lieutenant Knüppel was to claim the third German victory.

Throughout this period the Nationalist troops were under enemy aerial attacks directed against Córdoba, Puertollano, and Valdepeñas. At the same time the Nationalists with their limited force were striking at the government fleet harbors but without any measurable success.

Meanwhile the airlift from Morocco continued. Of the original twenty aircraft (Ju-52s) sent to Spain, ten had been turned over to the Spaniards. One had made the error of landing at Madrid and was still in the hands of the Popular Front, and the other nine were still committed to the airlift by the Germans. The shortage of fuel and required overhaul of engines of these planes slowed but did not stop the airlift. This was particularly noted between 17 and 23 August with the decrease to 698 men in troops transported, but at the same time the tonnage of materials moved rose to 11,646 kilos. Although aircraft maintenance was a problem, the greatest issue was lack of fuel. Between the two, maintenance and fuel, there were some days when only four aircraft were available for the mission. On two successive days, flights had to be cancelled simply because fuel was not available. Every possible way was used to find each liter from private sources, firms, factories, and even from the French airport at Tangier. At the same time, what fuel could be located was of very poor quality. Then there was the problem of loading the fuel by hand from cans. They desperately needed fuel pumps from Germany, but they were partly able to meet this problem in a very unusual way. Jerez de la Frontera is the center of the great sherry wine region of Spain. In the wineries pumps are used to move the fine aging wine from one great cask to another. These were soon put to refueling aircraft. However, the wine pumps' capacity was but three liters a minute.

Adding benzol and gasoline together was done "by eye," and the mixing was accomplished by rolling the full drums over the ground. This problem was partly alleviated on 13 August by the arrival of the ship *Kamerun* with fuel. According to the air crews, their planes would have been grounded the following day had not this ship arrived. The Italians were having the same problem, but by 16 August fuel arrived from Italy, and some 1,500 barrels of fuel and 170 barrels of oil were made available for the Germans. In the last week of August, 1,247 men and 3,511 kilos of materiel were moved. And von Scheele was still trying to induce Berlin to permit him to deploy German personnel and aircraft directly into combat. Possibly because of concern for the resulting international repercussions, Hitler still demurred.

In the first week of September, 1,204 men and 36,847 kilos of materiel were flown. In the second week of the month the numbers were increased to 1,398 troops and 46,780 kilos of equipment. But in the last week of the month the figures were raised to 1,552 men and 68,450 kilos of materiel. This was followed in the period 30 September to 11 October with the movement of 1,610 troops and 25,550 kilos of equipment. In the German count by the latter date, 11 October, 13,000 troops and 270,199 kilos of war impedimenta of all kinds had been transported across the narrow waters to Seville or Jerez de la Frontera. These figures do not reflect the personnel that were transported (with their equipment) to Spain by the nine Italian bomber/transport aircraft or those moved by the Spaniards both by air and sea.[8] As near as this writer has been able to determine, this was accomplished without the loss of an aircraft and its load, other than for the crash of the Ju-52 on 16 August at Jerez de la Frontera resulting in the deaths of the first two Germans. The first military airlift of an army and its supplies was drawing to a surprisingly successful conclusion. And one must concede that it reflected highly on the professionalism of the flight and maintenance crews who operated under most primitive and trying conditions. Later, Hitler was to maintain that General Franco should thank the Ju-52s for what was to be his ultimate victory. This comment of the German *Führer*, of course, can be seen as an overstatement. One can speculate that in all probability without the Ju-52s and their crews, both air and ground, the troop movement from Africa ultimately could have been made, but it would certainly have taken longer. But the fact remains that the German airlift was made at a time when the Army of Africa was so terribly needed to form and reinforce the battle-columns fanning out in Andalusia driving to join with Mola's Army North, and struggling to seize Mérida, Badajoz, Cáceres, and Talavera (see map 2). The original battle-columns were very small and their ranks were continually being thinned. Their replacements in the main were coming from Africa. Eventually Spanish Legionaries and Moorish *Regulares* as well as Spaniards were able to raise the spectacular siege of the Alcázar of Toledo and drive on to the outskirts of southern Madrid. And importantly, General Mola and his Army North had received their gravely needed ammunition.

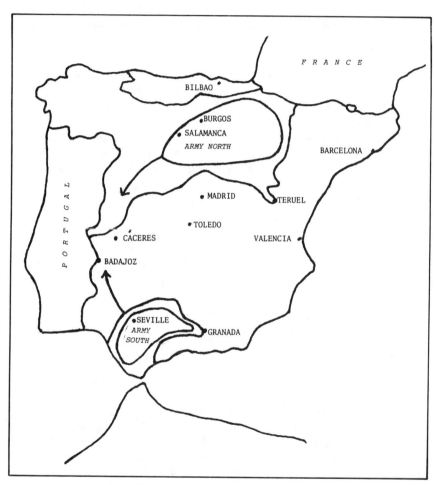

Map 2. German View of Spain, August 1936.

By the middle of October 1936, the airlift was practically completed. But even before that, more and more aircraft were being diverted from the transport mission to one of direct support of the advancing battle-columns. In addition, more equipment was headed for Spain almost before the *Usaramo* made its first docking at Cádiz.

During the first days of August 1936, General Franco had asked increased support from "Special Staff W" in order to offset the increasing number of fighters being supplied the Popular Front from France. In view of this, it was decided to ship six additional He-51s to Spain from existing German squadrons. The planes were to have standard and interchangeable equipment and with low operational hours on the engines. The materiel was gathered in the next few days and by 11 August was ready for delivery. Besides the six He-51 fighters the materiel included:

2 Ju (type Guinea) Reconnaissance planes
15 bomb racks for the Ju-52
960 bombs of 50 kilos
10,000 bombs of 10 kilos
10,000 bombs of 1 kilo (B.L.II)
150,000 rounds of machine gun ammunition

The same agencies in Hamburg that handled the materiel for the first shipment of the *Usaramo* were alerted to handle this materiel. This time the ship *Wigbert*, also of the Woermann Line, was selected.

This time the land transport of the materiel was through the Pankower Transport Company (Pankower is a suburb of Berlin). The security procedures, as earlier, were to be followed. However, the German record of the movement denounced the manner in which the materiel was packed, which completely compromised the security. Even bomb identifications were visible. As in the case of the *Usaramo*, the ship's crew had to sign papers which sealed them to secrecy. The ship was provided with radio, code machine, and communications personnel. The radio call letters were the call signs of German ships which were, at the moment, in far-off waters and could not be raised by calls from Germany. The *Wigbert* sailed for Cádiz at 4:00 p.m., 14 August.

Before the *Wigbert* approached the west coast of Spain, the final preparations were being made for yet another shipment to the Spanish Nationalists. But this time the materiel was destined for General Mola and his Army of the North. General Mola was very hard-pressed even for ammunition and rifles and through his emissaries had directly approached the Germans for help. The leading Spanish generals in revolt (Franco in Africa, Queipo de Llano in Seville, and Mola in the North) were still acting very much as independent war lords who were attempting to acquire materials from all available sources. Mola's plea was for 8,000 rifles and 10 million rounds of ammunition.[9] This was followed by a request for fighter planes, bombs, hand grenades, and small arms. The Spanish port to receive the supplies Mola hoped to be La Coruña. The War Ministry in Berlin made the decision to honor the request for army materials, not aircraft, which would have to come through the *Luftwaffe*. The company of VELTJENS was ordered to supply 3,500 rifles and 3.5 million rounds of ammunition, the balance to be drawn from German army stores. Included was the request for 10,000 hand grenades, which was rejected by the army. They were, however, delivered to VELTJENS by the German arms industry. To keep the army records clear, VELTJENS paid 90,000 pounds sterling to the army depot for the munitions drawn from its stock. The balance of the payment was to come from copper which would be shipped to Germany from Spain. The munitions were loaded on the ship *Girgenti*, which cleared Hamburg for La Coruña on 22 August.

General Wilberg of "Special Staff W" was deeply concerned about this entire affair. The fact that these materials were put together by the VELTJENS Company and at the request of General Mola certainly was in contradiction to what General Wilberg and his "Special Staff" understood were the procedures to be followed. The "Special Staff" was to handle all requests for aid from Spain, and these must come through no one other than General Franco. Furthermore, the destination of all shipments would also be determined by the little general in Africa.

Still the ship *Girgenti* cleared into Spanish waters and put into the port of La Coruña on 26 August. After it unloaded its materials for General Mola, the ship proceeded to Huelva, Spain, where it was loaded with Spanish ore for Germany. In addition, the ship took on board cases containing the bodies of the first two Germans to die in the cause of the Spanish Civil War, the noncommissioned officers Helmut Schulze and Herbert Zech.

A week before the *Girgenti* arrived in Spanish waters, the ship *Wigbert*, which had sailed from Hamburg on 14 August with the six additional He-51 fighters and bombs, arrived in the harbor of Lisbon. The unloading was conducted through Bernhardt and the firm of Marcus & Harting of Lisbon. This was arranged through the minister president of Portugal, Antonio de Oliveira Salazar, who ordered the ship unloaded and its cargo moved to the Spanish border as soon as possible. To ensure that this would be accomplished, Salazar made the required personnel available. The unloading and transport were accomplished in twelve hours. The munitions were then shipped to Seville, Cáceres, and León.

General Wilberg went to Spain during the middle of August to assess personally the situation and at the same time to confer with General Franco. The Spaniard took the opportunity to ask that he be provided with more light or medium aircraft. Wilberg was receptive, and Berlin, on 18 August, decided to fulfill Franco's request with twenty He-46 tactical aircraft. It was decided to have the aircraft dismantled and crated, along with munitions, and that the navy would have the ship *Usaramo* ready for transport the moment Hitler's Supreme Command (*OKW*) gave its permission. This permission came quickly. Because the crates for the aircraft were too large to be moved by train, the shipment to Hamburg was made by forty vans. Besides the He-46s, the *Usaramo* was loaded with thirty-seven crates of ammunition, aircraft parts, grease, tools, plywood, chemicals, and radios. Then once again the port authority complained that the method of packing had compromised security.

As the *Usaramo* was being loaded, it was obvious that the German assistance to the Nationalist cause in Spain had escalated far beyond the modest commitment that Hitler had made that night thirty days before in Bayreuth. On 25 August (the day the German fighter pilots claimed their first aerial victories) the war minister, General von Blomberg, called into his office Lt. Colonel Walter Warlimont of the Army General Staff. An artillery officer and brilliant staff officer, Warlimont was noted as well for his knowledge of economic matters. Blomberg had come to the conclusion that he had to have an officer in Spain who would establish a command section with General Franco's headquarters. It was viewed that events had outpaced Major von Scheele, as head of the transport mission, and the HISMA Company. Neither could function as a centralized military command, nor could they act as direct military advisors to General Franco. At the same time it was felt that Germany should discuss with Italy their mutual involvement. Blomberg advised Colonel Warlimont that he was being sent to Spain to be placed in charge of all German involvement, both military and economic, and at the same time would be the German military advisor to General Franco. First, however, he would accompany Admiral Canaris to meet with General Roatta to work out German/Italian cooperation.

Colonel Warlimont was surprised at this development. Even as a General Staff officer he had no knowledge of the development of German involvement in the Spanish affair. Because of the secrecy surrounding the operation, the only knowledge he had of events in Spain was what he had heard as rumors or read in the German press.

Thirty-seven years later, when this writer discussed these affairs with the late retired General Warlimont (formerly of the Operations Staff of *OKW*), he still had in his possession a copy of General von Blomberg's orders to him, which were dated 31 August 1936. General Warlimont then translated the document. It was Order WA/L No. 44/36 Chief: dated 31 August 1936.

1. Order German Minister of War, General von Blomberg to Army, and Air Force. Last day of August 1936. Corresponding to the Orders of the *Führer*, I designate Lt. Colonel Warlimont of the General Staff as my representative at the High Command Nation-

alist Armed Forces in Nationalist Spain. He probably will take up his duties on 3 September 1936. The appendix to this Order contains his tasks and submission of reports to the Home Office.

/s/ General von Blomberg
Minister of War

1. Appendix: Directive Army, Navy and Air Force and Lt. Colonel Warlimont.
1st Task: To examine all possibilities and proposals for supporting the Nationalists of Spain by the German Armed Forces.
2nd Task: Advise the Spanish Nationalist High Command.
3rd Task: Keep in mind German interests in the fields of military-political and economic matters.
4th Task: Cooperate with the representatives of the Italian forces in Spain.

2. Directives for carrying out these tasks:
    1. All German forces on Spanish soil in whatever capacity are hereby being subordinated to the representative of the German Minister of War.
    2. The military commanders of those specific units are responsible for their own specific operations. The military reports of the Spanish soil, in contrast to the Navy, will be forwarded exclusively to the Minister of War by his representative.
    3. Parts of the German Navy staying in Spanish waters have to correspond in case of need to the demands of my representative as far as this will be possible within the general task.

The directive is clear. Colonel Warlimont was being sent to Spain charged with all the responsibility for the war minister of matters pertaining to all military, political, and economic matters in Spain, as well as to be the German advisor to General Franco.

On 27 August, the day after the *Usaramo* left port for its second voyage to Spain, Admiral Canaris, along with Lt. Colonel Warlimont, met with General Roatta of Italy in Rome. It was decided that in spite of the so-called arms embargo General Franco's requests should be honored and that Italy and Germany should share the requests equally. Once again it was specifically noted that materials should go only to Franco, but now their use should be supervised by the Italian and German military.

Both Roatta and Canaris noted that open involvement in the Spanish conflict was prohibited. It should be noted here, however, that this was agreed to just the day before Hitler made the decision, 28 August, for German personnel to become actively engaged in combat.

At their meeting, General Roatta had not decided who the Italian counterpart to Colonel Warlimont would be. But the two officers would report to Italian Military Intelligence (*SIM*) in Rome on the evening of 3 September and would depart immediately for Spain. Their transportation would be handled by the Italians. The Italian and German officers would operate under Spanish command during offensive actions. Both officers were ordered to refrain from any political discussion relative to Spanish affairs, but besides their military roles, the officers were charged with handling the monetary payments for materials shipped; this would be either in cash or goods.

The following day, 28 July, Warlimont flew back to Berlin to put his affairs in order and to meet with General Wilberg and the "Special Staff W." Admiral Canaris, on the other hand, remained in Rome to meet with the Italian foreign minister, and the *Duce*'s son-in-law, Count Ciano, who had played an important role in convincing Mussolini to respond to Franco's original appeal. Ciano's view was that it was the duty of both Germany and Italy to support the Spanish Nationalists not only in materiel, but also in personnel. He emphasized that it was imperative that the two nations should have a common plan and understanding, so that their efforts would be successful. Ciano noted that the Italian support of the Nationalists was charged to him by the orders of the *Duce*.

Ciano also noted that he knew German personnel had been denied an active combat role, while, on the other hand, Italian flyers had absolute freedom of action. In that Admiral Canaris did not know that Berlin that very day was rescinding its prohibition, all he could do was to advise the minister that this decision was in the hands of the War Ministry.

Notes

1. Freiburg, MF, RL 2/v. 3187.
2. Ibid., pp. 30-31.
3. Freiburg, MF, RL 2/v. 3187, p. 38.
4. R. Hidalgo Salazar, *La ayuda alemana a España 1936-39* (Madrid, 1975), Appendix I.
5. Freiburg, MF, RL 2/v. 3187, Part II, p. 16.
6. Hans Trautloft, *Als Jagdflieger in Spanien: Aus dem Tagebuch eines deutschen Legionäres*, p. 25.
7. Freiburg, MF, RL 2/v. 3187, p. 34.
8. Salazar, *La ayuda alemana*, p. 53. Captain Salazar, using Spanish records, reveals a slightly different count of the totals. He places the troops moved at 13,962 with 500 tons of materiel which included 36 pieces of artillery and 127 machine guns. By surface ships the Spanish moved to Algeciras by convoy 3,000 combatants, six batteries of artillery, automobiles, and ambulances, as well as other very bulky materiel.
9. Also see *GD*, Series D, Vol. III, Docs. No. 33 and 41.

4

Phase Four:
Warlimont and
Mission "Guido"

Because of the urgency of the situation Colonel Warlimont's departure date was moved up to the first of the month. He flew to Rome where he met with his Italian counterpart and was surprised to learn that he was no less than General Roatta. The two immediately left Rome for the port Gaeta where they boarded an Italian cruiser and sailed to Tangier. Once aboard the cruiser he changed from mufti into an Italian naval officer's uniform and continued wearing it until he was in the Nationalist-controlled Protectorate of Morocco. They arrived in Tangier without problems and were met by the Italian attaché. Remaining with him through the day, they were brought up to date on events relative to Spain as far as he knew. The following morning they drove to Tetuán, where they boarded one of the German Ju-52s of the transport mission and were flown to Seville. There they met with General Queipo de Llano, where, according to Warlimont, they gained very little. On the morning of 5 September, they flew from Seville to the picturesque medieval city of Cáceres, Estremadura, where General Franco's headquarters was temporarily located in the old section of the city. Roatta gave a very short speech of introduction to Franco, and Warlimont presented his orders from General Blomberg. Then, and even years later, Warlimont was convinced that Franco did not know of their mission. But under the trying conditions with which the little Spanish general was faced, he was in no position to reject, out of hand, any assistance. In that all German and Italian officers were using pseudonyms, in a futile effort to maintain security, Warlimont was henceforth known as either *Guido* or *Wolters-dorff*.

The appointment of Colonel Warlimont to "Magic Fire" as supreme commander over German forces to be engaged in military operations, as well as military advisor to General Franco, with its possible international political repercussions, was a decided turning point from the Reich's previous position. The German study of the events takes the view that the Reich was responding to actions that had been taken by France, which had immediately supplied war materials, including aircraft, along with advisors to Madrid. Furthermore, on 17 August, French trains had arrived at Irún and Puigcerda with war materials destined for the Popular Front. Also, the Popular Front was moving combat forces from Catalonia to Irún and subsequently San Sebastián through southern France on the other side of the Pyrenees. Meanwhile, the delivery of French warplanes continued. Included were bombers from the French Air Force flown by French crews from the French air base at Villa Coublay. By the middle of August, the Germans placed thirty French aircraft as having been flown to Barcelona. Included in this number were twelve twin-engine bombers and eighteen Dewoitine fighters. By 22 August, twenty-five additional French planes and crews had arrived in Madrid.

At the end of August, in the Madrid area, the government had at its disposal sixty foreign aircraft. Among these were thirty-five French and six English. Six French "mail pilots" had also arrived.[1] At the airfield of Getafe, south of Madrid, were thirteen aircraft of French, Dutch, and American origin. At the Spanish air base of Cuatro Vientos, southwest of Madrid, on the highway to Navalcarnero, there were twenty French single-engine fighters, some with French pilots, and twelve Dewoitine fighters. In Barcelona there were six French planes and nineteen French pilots, which were quartered at the airport outside of the city.

However, based on information provided by retired Colonel General Jaenecke (formerly chief of staff of the "Special Staff W"), General Karl Drum (also formerly of the *Luftwaffe*) in his special unpublished study of the Condor Legion took a different view:

> At this point the scope of Italian military aid to Spain, which had achieved impressive proportions, played a much larger role in Hitler's deliberations than proved to be justified in view of the fact, soon clear, that Italy's contribution had been grossly overrated.[2]

With the decision to commit German forces under Warlimont, Berlin increased the tempo of its shipments of war materials. The machinery that had been established in the first days of "Magic Fire" was still used and perfected. Mistakes learned were eliminated. But still the security was strictly adhered to. For example, the movement of flak, which at first was made by van, was changed to removing the gun barrels which were packed in crates. The bases of the guns and vehicles were covered with tarpaulins and moved to the harbors separately. There the unit commanders personally observed the loading. As a safety precaution, in the event it appeared as though the guns might fall into enemy hands, they were mined to be destroyed at a moment's notice.

Problems arose, however, because of the poor packing procedures. The dock workers were well aware that they were handling munitions and in accordance with the normal labor agreements for such work the laborers demanded a 100 percent pay increase. Because of the delicate nature of the affair the authorities refused to grant the raise. Thereupon, the dock workers threatened to let some crates of ammunition drop. Of this affair the German record notes: ". . .this was stopped by threatening to have the *Gestapo* take care of the matter."[3] The dismantled Heinkel aircraft shipped in crates in the past had presented a problem in that they had been packed in crates 4 meters high and transported to Hamburg by truck. The truck loading was to the height of 5.25 meters and thus it was necessary to remove power lines across the roads and cut down many trees. Telephone lines were frequently torn down by the high loads. To prevent these problems and hopefully to control security, "Special Staff W" ordered that moving the aircraft henceforth would be accomplished by train.

When Colonel Warlimont reported on 5 September to General Franco's headquarters, he immediately attempted to learn as much as possible about a situation of which he had only limited knowledge. He was surprised that they had practically no tanks, antitank guns, or heavy artillery. In a later meeting with Franco (he could not recall the exact date) he, not Franco as it is so frequently written, suggested that he might attempt to obtain a tank battalion, several antitank guns, and a flak battery from Germany. He could not request heavy artillery because the German army, at that time, had very few in its inventory. In addition, he would request the required German personnel to train the Spanish troops in their operation and maintenance. He did not, however, suggest that these Germans be used directly in combat. Franco quickly agreed.

Warlimont then submitted his request to Berlin according to the procedures given to him by General von Blomberg. Warlimont later commented:

> To my astonishment, all of my proposals were accepted by Berlin! Some of the batteries arrived late in October. I did not know of the arrival of the tank unit until General Franco called me into his office, now in Salamanca, and advised me that it was in Estremadura. At that time he asked me to accompany him to welcome and inspect the unit.[4]

"Special Staff W" responded to Warlimont's request in a manner which far exceeded his guarded expectations. From the German Army it drew:

8—20mm Cannon—with one cannoneer for each cannon.

20—PAK (antitank cannon)—with five platoons of troops and four trucks, plus two instructors for each platoon.

41—Tanks and armored cars (the tanks were Mark I). The personnel comprised a command staff, two companies of troops, and a field maintenance unit. Together there were 10 officers and 225 men (under Major von Thoma).

10—*Kübelwagen* (a Jeep-like vehicle)—with one driver for each unit.

The army personnel were formally transferred to the *Luftwaffe*. Warlimont commented: "There was much rivalry between the Army and the *Luftwaffe*! I was transferred from the Army to the *Luftwaffe* to get along with them. Most of this was because of Goering himself. The move did improve relations."[5]

The tanks were the very light Mark I panzers armed only with a single machine gun. And, "When we arrived at the tank unit the commander, the then Major von Thoma, had it lined up for inspection."[6]

The noted British historian B. H. Liddell Hart in his *The German Generals Talk* relates that following World War II, when he interviewed the then General von Thoma, the panzer commander stated he was sent to Spain when the Civil War broke out, "for it was seen that Spain would serve as the 'European Aldershot.' "[7] Furthermore, he actually started on the night that the revolt began and met with Franco at Mérida where he arranged with Franco how Germany could help his cause, and then stated the first Krupp Mark I panzers arrived in September. Unfortunately these comments of von Thoma have appeared in many writings and have been accepted as the whole of the matter, thereby linking Germany with Franco from the very beginning of the uprising.

When General Warlimont was questioned by this writer about this, the general was most adamant. "This was absolutely impossible! There were absolutely no German tanks in Spain until in October when von Thoma arrived with the companies that I had requested from Berlin." General Warlimont followed this up in a letter from Tegernsee, dated 10 July 1974, which reads in part:

. . . it remains for me to assure you that General von Thoma's story of this first appearance in Spain, of which I already know from Liddell Hart's account, does in no way correspond with the facts. It is hard to believe that an officer of his standing went as far as that and apparently only *"ad majorem gloriam suam."* I recollect every step of this development, which led to his mission, as follows:

1. During my first conversations with General Franco at Cáceres early in September 1936, in which various possibilities of future German military aid were being discussed, I, in conformity with my general task, suggested to him to have a battalion of light tanks sent to Spain. General Franco did not hesitate to consent.
2. A few weeks later the battalion arrived by sea in Seville and on Spanish orders was sent to a Spanish military training camp in western Spain.
3. After General Franco had been informed of the arrival, he invited me to fly there with him in order to welcome the battalion.
4. On this occasion I presented him to the then Major von Thoma, its commanding officer.

I should not like to conclude this account without mentioning that von Thoma, later on, rendered precious services to the cause of General Franco.[8]

The tank force was to become known as *Drohne*, and even though the personnel were to train Spanish combat and maintenance crews and were not to become engaged in battle, at times the latter was the case. The day Warlimont and Franco welcomed the tank force they flew back to the headquarters at Salamanca. They had hardly landed when Franco called Warlimont into his office.

Franco was very upset. He had just been advised that very heavy Russian tanks had arrived at Cartagena. They carried a crew of four and were armed not only with machine guns but cannon of 37 and 50mm. This was very grave news; the Nationalists had nothing like them and neither did Germany.[9]

Franco did at that time express to Warlimont the hope that he could obtain some comparable equipment, but Warlimont had to discourage him:

I could only advise Franco that not even Germany had any heavy tanks. I could only propose to him that we might be able to send additional antitank guns. But this would have to be decided by Berlin.[10]

According to Warlimont, Franco never again voiced to him any requests for deliveries of materiel or personnel from Germany.

When Warlimont arrived in Spain, he found the aerial capability of the Nationalists as augmented by Germany and Italy very limited and the enemy decidedly superior both numerically and technically. The Nationalists had a strike force of twelve German Ju-52 bombers and seven Italian

Savoia-81 bombers. In the fighter arm the Nationalists had six Italian Fiat CR-32 fighters, but they were not then operational. Being assembled and in transit were twelve of the short-range German He-46 reconnaissance craft. The manning of the latter was to be shared equally by German and Spanish crews. Also being assembled at the time were twelve additional He-51 fighters. This was hardly a formidable aerial armada.

The Spanish pilots still had not acquired the necessary skill to handle the He-51s, and as a result German pilots were repeatedly committed to an air defense role. Even though facing a superior numerical and technical enemy force, by 11 September the German pilots had destroyed eleven enemy aircraft. With the few available fighters and trained pilots committed to air defense, the small strike force of bombers was frequently thrown against the enemy without fighter cover. The tactical missions of the Nationalist aircraft were under the orders of the chief of the Nationalist Air Force, General Alfredo Kindelán. Kindelán was one of the founders of the old Spanish Air Force. As a captain in the Riff Wars, he commanded a squadron of aircraft which was one of the very earliest applications of aviation in military history. With the Nationalist uprising, he was on the retired list but placed his services to their cause. He was to become one of the key figures in the Nationalist Supreme Command and was to work closely with the German airmen from the moment of their commitment to Nationalist Spain.

At this time the newly created small German Fighter Squadron was stationed at Cáceres, but refueling of the aircraft had to be accomplished at the airstrip of Talavera. In the latter part of the month some of the fighters were moved to Talavera as an alert defense force because of increased enemy air strikes against the Nationalist battle-columns. Also at this time a three-aircraft German bomber flight came into existence at Cáceres. Of the twenty German Ju-52s sent to Spain back in July, ten had originally been turned over to the Spaniards. Of the ten transport versions drawn from *Lufthansa* one had landed in Madrid by mistake and was still in the hands of the enemy. One had crashed and killed a crew at Jerez de la Frontera on 15 August. Of the remaining eight planes, four were still committed to the transport mission from Africa and three had been withdrawn to be reconfigured as bombers to form the bomber flight stationed now at Cáceres. Commanded by Captain von Moreau, this flight was to be known as "Flight Pablo." In time it would grow to be a full bomber squadron, but this was still many weeks in the future. The tenth of the original *Lufthansa* planes was now being used as a courier plane.

The bomber "Flight Pablo" flew its first strike on 14 September, the same day it arrived at Cáceres. It was an armed reconnaissance mission against enemy troop concentrations between Santa Olalla and Talavera. The "Pablo" flight was now committed daily, sometimes flying two or more missions on the same day. The mission of 15 September was very effective with the destruction of a 5 million-liter fuel depot at Alcázar de San Juan, and then a second mission against the enemy forces attempting to storm the Alcázar of Toledo. The strikes were tactical rather than strategic and were usually flown at altitudes of 500 to 800 meters.

At this same time, the few German-flown fighters were being operated in the same area on alternate days with the Italian fighters, which were now operational. Each tried to divide their efforts between bomber protection and aerial defense of the advancing battle-columns. On 17 September, a German He-51 flight learned of the great disadvantages of their planes when they encountered an enemy bomber flight striking a friendly battle-column protected by a single Dewoitine and one Hawker-Fury fighter. The single Dewoitine fighter charged into the He-51 formation and forced the entire German flight onto the defensive. The Dewoitine did not break off its attack until a second He-51 flight arrived. There was no doubt in the minds of the German crews that their biwing, open cockpit He-51 fighters were completely outclassed. The He-51 plane was not only obsolescent, but was now obsolete as a fighter aircraft. This engagement alone had much to do with the subsequent evaluation of air superiority.

During the last week of September the "Pablo" flight moved to León and repeatedly struck in the area of the Cantabria in direct support of friendly battle-columns and against Oviedo. There was one attempt to drop supplies to the beleaguered garrison of the Alcázar of Toledo, but it was driven off by heavy antiaircraft fire. This brought the flight back to attack the besieging forces with high explosives and fire bombs. It also temporarily disrupted enemy resupply by setting a train afire. The fact that the "Pablo" flight was striking targets in such a wide area and so many times a day gave observers the impression that the strike forces were much larger than the three aircraft actually involved.

That same week, the small German fighter squadron moved to Vitoria and assisted the bombers in their repeated strikes against the enemy headquarters in Bilbao. The fighters did manage to shoot down two enemy aircraft, which temporarily caused the opposition to withhold its planes from direct contact.

On 28 September the He-51s returned to the operating facility that had been established on the airstrip at Ávila. It was this day that the Germans lost their first fighter pilot, Lieutenant Eberhardt Heftner. Lieutenant Heftner took off from the airfield at Vitoria but quickly developed engine trouble. He was unable to return to the field, and his plane crashed into the plaza of Vitoria. It exploded on impact and burst into flames.

Colonel Warlimont was concerned about the repeated demands that were being imposed on the limited German crews and aircraft by the Spanish command. He insisted that this be changed and as the supreme German commander assumed direct command over the German forces and full control over their mission assignment. Warlimont then ordered the "Pablo" flight to stand down from all missions from 28 September to 11 October for repair and engine overhaul, as well as crew rest.

The general mission of "Magic Fire" was now changed to the mission of Warlimont, known as "Guido." This included both German air and ground elements. But the air function was still known as "Magic Fire" even though it was within the "Guido" structure.

Between 28 August and 30 September, "Special Staff W" greatly increased its shipments to Spain. This was largely on the suggestion of Warlimont, but according to him a great share of the materials was shipped on the initiative of the "Special Staff." Warlimont's initial request for the tank companies and antitank guns along with flak have already been noted and are not reflected below. In addition only the major items will be noted.

> 24—additional He-51 fighters for the Nationalist Air Force
> 12—additional He-51 fighters to reinforce the German squadron
> 3—Bf-109 (still in the experimental stage which had been denied earlier)
> 6,000—rounds of 37mm ammunition
> 6,000—rounds of 88mm ammunition (flak)
> 40 million—rounds of 7mm rifle ammunition
> 40 million—rounds of machine gun ammunition
> 20,000—rounds of 2cm grenades
> 86,200—kilos of bombs from 10-kilo to 500-kilo
> Communications equipment—including radios, telephone switchboards, field phones, and 500 kilometers of field wire
> 25—light all-purpose trucks
> 20—5-ton trucks

Additional aircraft were shipped for experimentation. These were a single He-50 and two Hs-123 planes with flight and maintenance crews. The Hs-123 was an early version of a plane tested for dive-bombing, built by Henschel, the locomotive manufacturer of Germany, which was to be known to the Spaniards as "Angelito." The He-50 was a combination reconnaissance dive-bomber built by Heinkel. Both were single-engine biplanes. The He-50 had a crew of two, but the Hs-123 was a single-place aircraft. As it proved, neither aircraft was suitable for dive-bombing, but they were both adapted to low-altitude support of ground forces and performed well on the Eastern Front during World War II. The aircraft and crews were loaded on the *Wigbert* on 8 September. Once in Spain, they were assigned to an Experimental Squadron (*Versuchskommando*) that was just being organized.

In this same time period, three additional Ju-52 bombers and crews were sent to Spain to reinforce the Ju-52s, which were being formed into the German bomber squadron being organized from the transport mission aircraft. The "Special Staff" also drew from the navy two float planes and crews, which would have the mission of protecting the German cargo ships arriving in Spanish waters. These were an He-59 twin-engine bi- plane, which was a reconnaissance bomber with a crew of four and could accommodate the 500-kilo bomb, and an He-60 single-engine biplane mainly used for reconnaissance. The navy also provided the flight crews and maintenance personnel, who, as in the case of the army, were transferred to the *Luftwaffe*. In Spain they were originally stationed at Cádiz. Later these two aircraft were to be expanded into a full seaplane squadron.

There was a problem in obtaining the 40 million rounds of 7mm am- munition. By the date of delivery only 5 million rounds were available in the German Arms & Munitions factory at Borsigwalde and an additional 17 million rounds were found at other locations throughout Germany. The plants at Borsigwalde and Karlsruhe were ordered to increase their monthly production to the point where, by 25 November 1936, these two plants were producing 25 million rounds.

These shipments were quickly followed by twelve additional flight per- sonnel for the He-51 Fighter Squadron taking form in Spain; six crews for the He-46 light reconnaissance planes; pilots for the Bf-109 fighters; and as well three staff officers who would be assigned to Major von Scheele's small staff, Captain Moreau who was organizing the Bomber Squadron (known as "Group Moreau"), and Lieutenant Eberhard in the Fighter Squadron (to be known as "Group Eberhard").

Between 26 August, when the *Usaramo* once again sailed from Ham- burg, and 5 October 1936, eleven German merchant ships departed for Spain. Five of these, chartered through Hautz & Schmidt Company, sailed from Stettin with 389 officers and men and with 22,268 tons of war materiel. All of these ships, except the *Nyassa*, sailed directly to Seville and arrived between 4 October and 18 October. The *Nyassa* stopped for two days at El Ferrol to unload naval supplies and then continued to Seville with its remaining cargo, which included the 88mm flak battery.

Three days after the *Nyassa* departed Stettin, the Moscow radio gave a full and accurate report as to its cargo and destination. This fully in- dicates that the Soviets, through their intelligence agents and Communist sympathizers in the ports of Germany, had a firm grasp of the matter despite all of the security measures taken by the "Special Staff W."

On the other hand, German and Nationalist Intelligence reported that on 25 August twenty-five rail cars had arrived in Popular Front Spain through Marseille with war materials marked "farm equipment." Also, the Mexican ship *Janisco* delivered 30,000 rifles and 10 million rounds of ammunition of Belgian manufacture through Marseille. These were followed on 18 September by the ship *Maggalhanes*, which delivered four aircraft and thirty machine guns, along with an unspecified amount of ammunition, to a Spanish government port. Soviet deliveries were now arriving in large quantities. General Queipo de Llano, in Seville, reported that on 29 September forty-seven Soviet aircraft had arrived, with thirty stationed in Valencia, three in Barcelona, and seven in Cartagena.

The German shipments noted above were added to in October by tons of rifles, machine guns, and ammunition, as well as the raw materials to produce finished ammunition. In addition, there were twenty antitank guns, but the caliber was not specified. Importantly, eighteen additional He-51 fighters were destined for the Nationalist Air Force along with six more Ju-52 bombers. At this time the first two He-70 medium reconnaissance bombers and five courier-type aircraft were delivered. The materials were initially in the hands of German personnel but were to be turned over to the Spanish as their crews were properly trained.

By the end of October 1936, the Germans were directly supporting in Spain a bomber force with twenty-four Ju-52 bombers and two He-70 medium reconnaissance bombers; a fighter force with thirty He-51 fighters; and the newly formed Experimental Squadron with three aircraft, an He-50 and two Hs-123s. All of the materiel and personnel were the responsibility of Colonel Warlimont.

Colonel Warlimont believed that the course of events was moving too fast for one man to handle the mission properly as ordered by the German War Ministry. The rapid influx of German personnel and equipment, the demands being levied upon them, the additional materiel being delivered directly to the Spanish, as well as the economic control, were such that he felt things were starting to slip through his fingers. Economic matters from the beginning had been handled largely by Johannes Bernhardt, and Warlimont found him competent. Warlimont now suggested to General Wilberg that a clear division be made between military and economic matters, with Bernhardt and HISMA to assume the responsibility for the latter. At the end of September, Warlimont and Bernhardt flew to Berlin in one of the now regularly scheduled courier flights and closed the matter with Hermann Goering.

Colonel Warlimont had come to some strong conclusions of his own relative to the fighting in Spain. He had made many trips to the front and had gained the impression that, regardless of anything Germany would be able to do, the fighting would go on for a long, long time. Germany could send materials that, along with the materiel from Italy, might possibly help fill the gap between what the Nationalists had and what the Popular Front had, which was being so greatly added to from foreign sources. He was also of the opinion that this foreign assistance would continue to grow. Still, he was of the opinion that regardless of what Germany and Italy could provide, the successful conclusion of the war for the Nationalists would in the end have to come from support within Spain. He viewed the war not as a traditional conflict in which he had been trained as a professional soldier, but as a guerrilla conflict with all of its terrible implications. It was not the kind of a war which the Germans knew or could fully understand. "It was a terrible conflict on all sides."[11]

Warlimont was opposed to sending German troops to fight in the war as combat forces. This he "strongly recommended to Berlin" both in communications and during his short trips back to Germany. Berlin, however, and one would assume Hitler, made a different evaluation which caused Warlimont to later comment: "It was a most disagreeable surprise to me that my recommendations were not followed in Berlin. I had no idea what was taking place in the headquarters of the *Führer*."[12]

On 30 September, the Nationalist commanders were no longer operating as private war lords but had pooled their efforts when the Burgos *Junta* named General Franco as the Nationalist supreme commander (generalissimo) and chief of state of Nationalist Spain. Still, the Nationalist forces could hardly be called a modern army. They remained small battle-columns which, at high costs, were converging upon Madrid from the south (see map 3), or had fanned out from General Mola's command into Aragón, attempting to seize the strategic passes of the Sierra de Guadarrama and to close the border with France at Irún. The battle-columns made up of *banderas* of the Foreign Legion and companies of Moorish *Regulares*, as well as companies of Spaniards from the Army of Africa which had battled north from Seville were tough, trained professionals, but their numbers were limited. The civilian volunteers joining the companies of the spirited Carlists and Falange were increasing the battle-columns but the numerical superiority still lay with the Popular Front forces being swollen by the ranks of the unions and anarchist militiamen. Also, foreign troops were arriving to fight in the ranks of the Madrid forces. The Communist-sponsored and recruited International Brigades were being formed in Albacete under the devoted French Communist André Marty.

Not only was the amount of military equipment being delivered to the Madrid government a matter of concern, but also the superior quality of armor and aircraft along with the trained military personnel to operate them. Also, the Popular Front forces were far superior to the Nationalists in artillery. Although many of the batteries of Spanish guns had fallen to the battle-columns of the Army of Africa, there was still no comparison in relative strength. The increased number of higher performance foreign aircraft and crews gave the Popular Front decided air superiority, par-

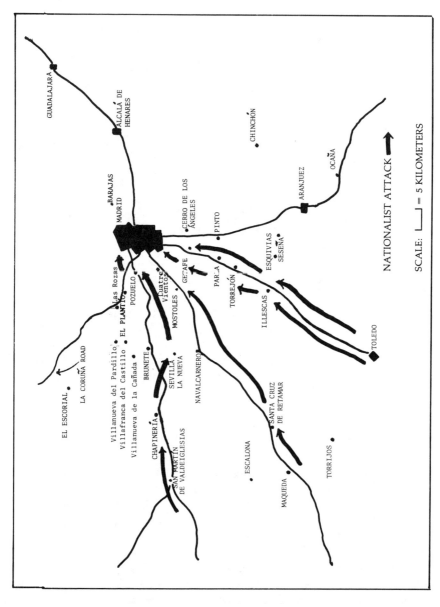

Map 3. Nationalist Advance on Madrid, October 1936.

Source: The author drew the disposition of forces on all of the battle maps from the description in the "Special Staff W" summaries and, where they exist, from the General Staff operational reports and battle maps.

ticularly in fighter aircraft. The French Squadron headed by the French "poet" André Malraux was included in this force. Furthermore, it was believed that this aerial superiority would continue to grow as more men and materials arrived, particularly from France and the Soviet Union. The general military balance was such that the Germans did not feel that Franco had the strength to take Madrid and that he himself recognized this.[13]

Where some observers might feel that the Nationalists were of the opinion that the struggle would be a short and easy one, the Nationalists themselves certainly felt otherwise. Several weeks before the creation of the Supreme Command, the Nationalists had set in motion the machinery to bring more troops under arms by calling up different classes of reserves as well as encouraging volunteers. In addition, schools were being established early in September 1936 to train troops, as well as schools for the *Alférezes Provisionales* (Provisional Second Lieutenants). Many of the instructors of these schools were to come from the ranks of German active duty and reserve officers. Where the German tank companies were known as *Drohne*, these instructors were known as *Imker* (Beekeeper). Importantly, the Nationalists had not, as was the case on the other side, destroyed the organic divisions of the old Spanish Army that had come under their control. The Nationalists used the headquarters of these divisions as a base upon which to build eventually a Spanish Nationalist Army. This was, of course, many months in the future. It was the status of forces at the moment that was the great concern in Berlin. By the end of October, the Nationalists had realized some 14,000 casualties, and it is estimated, from the best sources available at this writing, that the entire Nationalist force attempting to converge upon Madrid numbered some 20,000 men, but only 4,500 of these could be committed for the first assault which it was hoped would be in mid-October. In Berlin, the view was being formulated, without discussing it with either Colonel Warlimont or General Franco, that for the military situation to be changed in favor of the Nationalists, an increased commitment of the German armed forces would be necessary.

According to the German documents, it was decided that the increased Soviet and international Communist organizations' involvement was most alarming and something would have to be done. Where this thinking might have an ideological appeal, General Jaenecke, who at the time was chief of staff of "Special Staff W," later expressed a different view. He saw Hitler's decision as being at least partly based on the increased Italian commitment. "For Hitler, despite his firmly emphasized friendship for Mussolini and his sympathies for Fascist Italy, was not really interested in permitting Italy to become too strong in the Mediterranean."[14] Whatever the case the German study summed this up with the brief comment:

The Germans thus viewed the entire Russian commitment as a threat on the part of Russia to European peace, and thereby it was necessary to bring about, on the part of Germany, a victory by Franco in the German interest. This was the basis of the creation of the Condor Legion.[15]

This was the third phase of German involvement in Spain. Operation "Magic Fire" and Mission "Guido" were now replaced by Exercise "Rügen."

Notes

1. Freiburg, MF, RL 2/v. 3187, No. 11, p. 19.
2. General Karl Drum, "The German Luftwaffe in the Spanish Civil War (Condor Legion)," (special unpublished study for the USAF), p. 18.
3. Freiburg, MF, RL 2/v. 3187, Part II, p. 20.
4. Warlimont statement to the writer.
5. Ibid.
6. Warlimont's comments to the writer.
7. B. H. Liddell Hart, *The German Generals Talk* (New York, 1948), pp. 92-93.
8. The letter was written in English as here reproduced.
9. Warlimont's comment to the writer.
10. Ibid.
11. Comment to the writer.
12. Ibid.
13. Freiburg, MF, RL 2/v. 3187, Part IV, p. 8.
14. Drum, "The German Luftwaffe," p. 18.
15. Freiburg, MF, RL 2/v. 3187, Part II, p. 43.

5

Phase Five:
Creation of the Legion

The thinking for creating the Condor Legion began in Berlin after the arrival of massive materiel from the Soviet Union for the Popular Front, when it appeared that the Nationalists would not be able to capture Madrid in October.

The month of October was most trying to the exhausted Nationalist battle-columns as well as imposing a seemingly impossible strain on the limited Nationalist Air Force in which the newly organized German small combat flights were repeatedly called upon. On 5 October, after dropping leaflets asking the civilians to leave the area, for two hours the German flyers struck at the railroad lines and military barracks near Madrid.

It was not only the Madrid sector that was of major concern to General Franco. Since the very first day of the uprising, 2,000 troops and 1,000 civilian volunteers, under the leadership of Colonel Antonio Aranda Mata, had been surrounded in the strategic city of Oviedo. Their reduced ranks had held out all these weeks against seemingly impossible odds. In this sector, on 5 October, the Nationalists encountered enemy tanks, and it was quickly proven that the enemy had air superiority. To meet this threat, five German-flown He-51s from the walled city of Ávila were sent to the airfield of León to support Nationalist bombers trying to open relief routes to Oviedo.

The following day two German-flown Ju-52s and six fighters were moved from Salamanca and Ávila to Barahona to support the Nationalist storming of the enemy fortified in the ancient cathedral city of Sigüenza, north of the Saragossa-Madrid highway. After intensive bombing by the German flyers of enemy troop concentrations, the ground assault was made on 8 October. Several aircraft were hit by ground fire but none were lost. The Nationalist infantry stormed into the city that same afternoon, and the enemy was quickly fleeing toward Madrid. As a result, German flyers now struck at the rail line in an attempt to cut off this retreat. The Germans viewed this operation as a fine example of what could be accomplished with close cooperation between ground troops and air power.

While the Ju-52s were supporting the infantry at Sigüenza, the six light tactical He-46s were committed to cover friendly forces that were in danger at Navalperal. The German records then make the interesting comment: "Between 11 and 14 October the Spanish Nationalist offensive for Madrid was interrupted so that the Nationalists could celebrate the fiesta of the Virgin of Pilar."[1] But the Nationalists still did not relent in their efforts to relieve the beleaguered garrison in Oviedo. On 12 October, the German "Pablo" flight was again moved from Salamanca to León from where it flew to drop supplies to the battered garrison.

The Nationalists and Germans estimated that in this sector alone they were faced with a force of about 60,000 men. Because of this, General Franco shifted his reserves, five battalions of Moroccans (about 8,000 men) from the Madrid sector to the northeast. Through difficult terrain and weather, as well as determined enemy resistance, the relief battle-columns realized sizeable losses. The enemy at the same time was being supported by warships off the coast and additional war supplies were arriving by sea. The few German flyers were now committed. With this small air support, Legionaries and Moors, on 17 October, battled their way into the city and joined with the remaining defenders. Still the enemy maintained pressure on the Nationalists, and Franco had to shift even more forces from the Madrid front for their support.

The Germans again had to divide their limited air flights on 14 and 15 October. Serious ground fighting erupted in the Sierra de Gredos and German He-46s, with Italian fighters for cover, were committed as direct ground support for friendly infantry. The Italians shot down three enemy aircraft, near Navalcarnero on 21 October, the same day that the He-46s struck hard at enemy troops at Navalperal de Pinares.

Colonel Warlimont knew of the arrival of Soviet ships carrying heavy tanks and aircraft at Cartagena and a large concentration of new enemy aircraft at Málaga. On 15 October, he ordered all available aircraft to strike at this force. The fact that this raid could be carried out by only two Ju-52s, two Stukas, and two seaplanes (protected by three Italian fighters) shows that the Nationalist air strength was stretched very thin. The raid was considered only a moderate success. The following day the single He-60 seaplane again bombed and strafed the air facility at Málaga where three enemy planes on the ground were hit and two burst into flames. The seaplane then shot down a Breguet biplane that crashed into the sea just off Málaga. The He-60 itself had problems; on its return flight it ran out of fuel and let down at sea, but was taken in tow by a Nationalist ship.

Because of the easy access of Soviet and other ships to the ports of Popular Front Spain, Warlimont believed that it was necessary for the Nationalists to have additional long-range armed reconnaissance craft in the area. By radio, he requested that Berlin send twelve additional He-59s to Spain as quickly as possible.

Because of the vast flow of Soviet equipment and personnel through Cartagena, five bombers of the "Pablo" and "Pedro" flights (the "Pedro" flight was the second flight of three aircraft to be created out of the reconformed Ju-52 transports of the transport mission) were ordered flown from Salamanca to Seville and then Granada for strikes against Cartagena. Supported by three Italian Savoia bombers, the Ju-52s made their first attack against Cartagena the night of 26-27 October, with questionable results.

The following day the entire picture of the aerial war changed. Enemy bombers, without fighter escort, bombed the Nationalist airfields at Seville, Mérida, Cáceres, and Salamanca. These bombers had never been seen before and were correctly suspected to be new Soviet high-speed planes. In the record there is the terse comment: "With their [enemy] new type of aircraft, a new phase of the air situation started."[2]

As "Pablo" and "Pedro" flights were attempting to disrupt the enemy source of supply from Cartagena, General Franco moved his headquarters from Cáceres to Salamanca to be closer to the fighting approaching Madrid. Franco now directed all aerial support to cover attacking battle-columns.[3] At the moment there were thirty-three German-flown planes involved in the Spanish war. At Ávila were six reconnaissance/tactical He-46s and the fighter squadron of fourteen fighters, which included the flights of Lieutenants Eberhard, Houwald, and Trautloft. There were the six former transports based at Salamanca consisting of the flights "Pablo" of Captain Baron von Moreau and "Pedro" of Captain Joester. Not committed to the Madrid front were two Ju-52 transports, which were flying a courier route Salamanca-Seville-Tetuán, and the two seaplanes (He-59 and He-60) based at Cádiz. The seaplane flight was supported by the Experimental Flight ("Michelis") of Stukas operating from Jerez de la Frontera.

By 28 October, the five battle-columns of the colorful General José Varela Iglesias were poised for their next attack, which they hoped would carry them to about five kilometers from the entrance to Madrid. His combined force now numbered probably some 7,000 effectives, but they were spread over a front more than fifty kilometers wide and facing far superior forces.[4]

Their problems were added to early the next morning when the Nationalist airfields came under heavy aerial bombardment by the Soviet two-engined high-speed Katiuska SB-2 bombers. These bombers could carry a bomb load of 1,700 pounds and had a range of 900 miles. Because of their basic design they were known to the Nationalists as the "Martin" bomber. They could outrun the antiquated German He-51s as well as the Italian Fiat CR-32 fighters. Almost at the same time, Major Heli Tella Cantos, with his battle-column, attempting to advance up the Toledo—Madrid road, came under heavy artillery fire from two armored trains and heavy field guns. His column was also badly bombed and strafed by the Soviet Polikarpov I-15 fighters. With their chub nose these fighters were known as "Chato"; however, Nationalist flyers came to call them "Curtiss" because of their basic lines. Because these aircraft are repeatedly referred to in writings and the existing documents as "Curtiss," this designation will be used in this narrative. The Curtiss was very vicious with its four machine guns at high speed.

To the right of Major Tella's column, Colonel Monasterio's horse cavalry column also came under heavy attack from Soviet aircraft. But equally important, the horsemen were faced with something they had never seen before. They were confronted by fifteen of the 10-ton Soviet T-26 tanks. These tanks were armed with two machine guns and a 45mm cannon firing from a revolving turret. A vicious, but unequal, battle developed between the cavalrymen and the steel monsters in the area of Seseña, south of Madrid. The T-26 tanks were followed by a counterattack from the able Communist commander Lister with his force equipped with new Soviet 105mm Howitzers and 45mm antitank guns. Monasterio's cavalrymen managed to blunt the enemy attack and destroy two of the Soviet tanks, but the Nationalists now knew full well what was in store for them on the battlefield.[5]

The Soviet aircraft were flown by Russian pilots under General Yacob Schmouskievich who (like the Germans and Italians) had assumed an alias, "Douglas." The Soviet tank crews were commanded by Major Paul Arman, or "Greisser," and the Soviet artillery batteries were under General Nikita Voronov. The Nationalists responded immediately by striking, with six to nine bombers, the airfields of Getafe and Cuatro Vientos. At Getafe, one bomb tragically fell out of the target area and hit a school, killing dozens of children.[6]

While the bitter battle raged around Seseña, Admiral Canaris appeared in General Franco's headquarters. It was then, 30 October, that both Franco and Colonel Warlimont learned for the first time that Berlin had made the decision to commit additional German military forces to Franco in the form of a unique, and in many respects revolutionary, air organization which eventually would be known as the Condor Legion. This came as a surprise, and at the same time a disappointment, to Warlimont.

It also came as a surprise to General Franco because "General Franco had not asked for it and indeed did not want it."[7]

There were four stipulations attached by Berlin: (a) The leadership of all German air units in Spain would be under the German commander who would be the sole advisor to Franco in matters pertaining to these air units. Outwardly, however, Spanish leadership would be maintained. (b) All existing German pilots, aircraft, antiaircraft, and air communications units, along with their rear echelons, currently in Spain would be integrated into this air unit. (c) Protection of the German air bases [by the Spaniards] would be required if necessary, and (d) "More systematic and active conduct of the war with regard to ground and aerial operations and with regard to cooperation between the two for the purpose of quick occupation of the harbors important for Russian supplies."[8] Franco had to recognize these "demands without reservations."

Even though he had not asked for this sort of assistance, it is not difficult to determine why Franco would have agreed to the demands of Berlin. He was now faced with massive Soviet aid to his enemy on the battlefield, and this Soviet armor and air power certainly had placed his forces in a very delicate position.

Colonel Warlimont, on his part, could see that his role in Spanish-German affairs would soon be radically changed. Indeed, as early as 17 October, General von Blomberg had suggested to the Foreign Office that a "quasi" chargé d'affaires of sufficient rank be sent to the Burgos government to relieve Warlimont of his duties.[9] This was agreed to by the Foreign Ministry, but Warlimont, at this time, was not aware of this.[10]

Meanwhile, events in Germany had been moving at a hectic pace. Because the forces to be sent to Spain were from the new *Luftwaffe*, the ultimate responsibility rested with General Goering, but the entire effort would be handled by General Wilberg and his "Special Staff W." But this staff had to be expanded to meet these new demands. One of the additional officers posted to the "Special Staff" was Major Hermann Plocher. Plocher was a tall, broad-shouldered, powerful Swabian from the Black Forest. Even though a member of the General Staff, the major (because of the secrecy surrounding "Magic Fire") had no idea of the extent of the German involvement in Spain. Unfortunately, there is hardly any existing German documentary material that covers this important period. Most of the information presented here resulted from lengthy interviews with the late Major General a.D. (*ausser Dienst*-retired from active service) Hermann Plocher, who died 7 December 1980, and other German officers involved with events of this time. The only *War Diary* of any of the units involved that exists is the *War Diary* of the Communications Group, and it ends 26 March 1937.

When Plocher joined the "Special Staff W" in mid-October, he was surprised to learn of his mission, which was to assist in drawing the plans for the creation of the Condor Legion; this had been given the code name "Exercise Rügen." This was supposed to be a winter operation in the Baltic Sea. Personnel, aircraft, flak batteries, communications equipment, and all support materiel would have to be drawn from existing *Luftwaffe* units, many of which themselves were in the organizing stage. Tactical and support unit commanders were ordered to screen their personnel and select the best trained single men available. The personnel selected were moved under orders for "Exercise Rügen," but they had no idea where they were destined to go or what they would soon become involved in. "They definitely were not volunteers!"[11] Each case was different; for example, a pilot would be called in by his commander and asked if he would like to volunteer for a special assignment, which would be interesting and exciting, and where he would be able to do much flying, but he could not be told any more about it at this time. Others were simply assigned.

Some of the fighter pilots and maintenance crews were drawn from squadrons of the "Richthofen Wing." In this squadron was Lieutenant Douglas Pitcairn who was one of the last fifteen pilots to graduate from the *Reichswehr* secret training base deep in Russia. When he returned from Russia he was, like the other pilots, sworn to secrecy as to his training and assigned to a motorcycle Reconnaissance Battalion in East Prussia. Much to his disgust, the only flying he was able to do was from time to time with a "sport" flying club. It was not until 1935, when Germany announced the birth of the new *Luftwaffe*, that these carefully covered pilots were able to pin on their wings and join the fighter squadrons which were being formed and equipped with whatever aircraft they could obtain. When Hitler ordered remilitarization of the Rhineland, Pitcairn was in the first flight of German fighters to put on a fake show of strength over Cologne.[12]

Pitcairn and others proceeded to Stettin where they boarded the steamship *Berlin* and the *Osorio* of the Hamburg South American Line. Others were processed through Swinemunde.

In Berlin, on orders from General Goering, General Hugo von Sperrle, a veteran observer of the Great War, was named commander. Most writings on the Condor Legion list as the first chief of staff Lt. Colonel Baron von Richthofen. However, General Drum in his special study for the United States Air Force (USAF) maintains that from the beginning until January 1937 the chief of staff was Lt. Colonel Holle. Baron von Richthofen took over at that time.[13]

General Sperrle was a huge man with a mammoth girth (somewhat like Goering) that was a result of his overfondness for fine foods and wines. He considered himself a great gourmet; the food must be perfect and served in a perfect manner. He was not considered a brilliant man, but he was smart to the point of being clever, sly, and crafty. He was very impatient, not only in military matters but in his personal nature as well. This was revealed at the slowness of his companions when playing cards. He was considered tough and very demanding, but he had a robust sense of humor. He had very strong personal convictions as to how things should be done and could be extremely blunt. He was so abrupt that in no way could he be considered a diplomat. Still, he was considered a good officer and competent commander.[14] In Spain he was known by the pseudonym of "Sander."

Baron von Richthofen was a graduate engineer and very intelligent. He came to conclusions quickly, so much so that it would startle one. Like Sperrle, he was a very impatient man, which became evident when playing cards, which he also enjoyed. Even in time of crises he made snap decisions, but usually these decisions were correct. He could make people accept his conclusions and convictions, not because he was the commander, but by going to great extents to convince others that he was right. He frequently gave way to his frustrations in Spain when confronted with what he considered Spanish slowness and overly great concern for planning each operation in minute detail. That once they committed themselves to a line of actions, they would not deviate he found most annoying. He was very demanding of himself and he expected the same devotion to duty in others. He was far more of a diplomat than Sperrle, but some of his men viewed him, at times, as being more than a little inflexible in his own opinions. Still, he was considered a dedicated, exceptional, and even brilliant commander.[15]

The first name given to the air formation of "Exercise Rügen" was "Iron Rations," but this was shortly changed to "Iron Legion." According to General Plocher, Goering wanted only names of birds used. He carried this to the point of wanting all the individual units of the Legion also to be given the names of birds, and the Legion as a group should be known as the "Condor Legion." Plocher found trying to use the bird designation for all the units far too complex and too confusing and therefore changed the names of the specific units to the "88" designations; still, the unit as a whole was to remain known as the "Condor Legion." Some of the unit designations were: the Legion General Staff became S/88; the Bomber Group (*Kampf*) K/88; the Fighter Group (*Jagd*) J/88; Reconnaissance Group (*Aufklärung*) A/88; Antiaircraft (Flak) F/88; Seaplane Squadron AS/88, and the Communications Group Ln/88.

The original Legion order of battle drawn by Major Plocher seems simple on paper, but it was to go through many modifications before the Legion returned to Germany. The Legion consistently shifted its structure to meet with new operational problems and organizational matters. Originally there was the Bomber Group (K/88) which comprised three squadrons. Each squadron had twelve Ju-52 bombers. The Ju-52s currently being flown in Spain at that time by German crews were to be assigned as a fourth squadron when the Bomber Group became operational. The "Experimental Flight" was also attached to the Bomber Group, but as it evolved, this flight was usually directly controlled by the Legion staff.

The Fighter Group (J/88) originally was also designated as a three-squadron group with nine fighters (He-51) for each squadron. Once in Spain the fighter squadron already formed there was attached to the group as the fourth squadron. The Reconnaissance Squadron (A/88) was divided into two flights with a total of twelve aircraft. The short-range flight had the He-45s and He-46s. The long-range flight was equipped with the He-70 and Do-17. The Seaplane Flight already in Spain was increased to a Reconnaissance/Bomber Squadron (AS/88) with twelve long-range He-59s on floats, one short-range He-60 and a Ju-52, also on floats, for support.

The Flak Group (F/88) when incorporated with the batteries existing in Spain constituted eight batteries. There were to be five batteries of heavy 88mm guns with four mobile guns per battery. One of these batteries was converted from the heavy searchlight section, and the other was made up from the battery "Aldinger," which had been sent to Spain as a training battery for the Spanish. Also, there were two light batteries comprised of twelve 20mm guns and three 37mm guns per battery. The light batteries were supported by searchlight sections. There was an eighth battery with all caliber guns, to train the Spaniards, and a flak ammunition column. The light guns were moved by two-wheeled trailers and had to be dismounted for firing.[16]

The Communications Group (or Signal Battalion) constituted five companies of telephone, radio, flight security, and aircraft warning. There was also an aircraft maintenance group, vehicle maintenance section, ordnance, guards, photographic section to support the reconnaissance, quartermaster, intelligence, military police, medical, band corps, and a legal officer. Throughout its commitment the manning of the Legion was always fluctuating, but it usually maintained its strength at about 5,000 men.[17] The final report of the Legion, dated 20 May 1939, showed a personnel strength of 5,136 men, civilians, and officers.

In its original form the Legion was authorized, including what it gained from the flights already in Spain, approximately 119 combat and support aircraft. The total number of vehicles was about 1,500, but they started with 100 different types, and this was to be increased to 125 different types.

It is generally believed that the German tank companies and antitank platoons of *Drohne*, under Major von Thoma, operated as an integral part of the Legion. This was not the case. These troops remained under the orders of the German and Spanish armies. The only direct involvement of the Legion General Staff with the men of *Drohne* was to provide personnel services. In no way did the Legion commander exercise operational control over the men of the panzers or the instructor (*Imker*) group.[18] But the Legion communications sections did always have a communications link between the Legion staff and the *Drohne* group.[19]

General Sperrle departed for Seville via Rome on 31 October. In Germany, some of the men selected for "Exercise Rügen" boarded their ships at Stettin and put to sea. The troops were in uniform because they were supposed to be going on a winter exercise. They were puzzled when their ships turned west, and before they reached the English Channel, they were ordered to turn in their uniforms and wear civilian clothing. It was not until they passed through the channel and entered the Bay of Biscay that they learned where they were going and what was in store for them.[20] Most of the officers and men became caught up in what they could see as a great adventure.

General Sperrle arrived in Spain before the first ships from Stettin put into Cádiz or Seville. On 5 November, he issued orders restoring to duty the men who had been separated from the German services when they were originally sent to Spain. They were then reorganized to be incorporated into the new organization which would begin to arrive.[21]

The aircraft and crews that were to make up the Bomber Group (K/88) were assembled at Lechfeld not far from Augsburg. From here they flew to the Italian airfield Champino Nord near Rome and then over Ostia and the Italian naval base of Cagliari on the southern tip of Sardinia. Then they flew to the Balearic Islands and on to an area west of Málaga, from there over the Serranía de Ronda. From Seville they were dispersed to different Nationalist airfields, including Salamanca and León. They were aided in this operation by ships of the Italian Navy which were at holding stations along the route to act as direction finders. In reality, the German military pilots had very little if any experience in long-range flights. Not to overtax the Italian facilities, the ships were limited to a maximum of ten per day. There were thirty-three aircraft involved.

Lieutenant Pitcairn and his colleagues shortly docked at Cádiz.[22] They did not immediately go to Seville but remained in Cádiz for about two weeks. It was an exciting time for all. They had left Germany coming into the grips of winter and were now in mild southern Spain. They were surprised to be greeted by signs in Spanish on lampposts which read: "Otto is here!" In Seville they were finally issued a uniform. At first it was a Spanish uniform but very quickly replaced by what General Plocher described as "basically a uniform for German labor forces" but using Spanish-type insignia.[23]

After the troops had been billeted, they began the laborious task of assembling their equipment. Things progressed well under the circumstances because there were experienced personnel available who had gone through all of this before and had learned how to overcome what initially might appear as insurmountable problems. Still, it would take days to reassemble the aircraft, test-fly them, and fire their machine guns to the satisfaction of engineers and pilots. It was now close to the end of November 1936.

What is surprising is that the companies that were to form the Communications Group (Ln/88) were not included with the first shipment. It was not until 5 November that the communications staff and the 1st and 5th Companies were assembled in Münster. In their *War Diary* was written: "We went to an unknown future."[24] They arrived at Stettin the following day, and some sections boarded the ship *Fulda* before nightfall.

Like the ships that had sailed before them, they sailed north through the Kattegat. Both officers and men were issued civilian clothing on 8 November, and the troops were assembled to listen to orders and a message from General Sperrle and to learn where they were going and why. All officers, civilian technicians, and men were then given a series of inoculations by grinning medical corpsmen with their big needles. On the morning of 9 November, they sailed through the waters of the Skagerrak, the naval battle area of the Great War in which some of the men had lost members of their families. By now at least a third of the complement was violently seasick, partly because of the inoculations but mainly from very heavy seas that night. The next morning the seas calmed somewhat as they sailed through the North Sea. They approached the English Channel in the dark and sailed between Calais and Dover without lights. "The lights on shore looked beautiful." But on 11 November, while still in the channel, they encountered a very bad storm with extraordinarily heavy seas. Many of the men again became sick and could picture the problems encountered by the Spanish Armada. The heavy seas continued out into the Atlantic. To enliven matters, the communications men printed a newspaper. There were two separate editions, the *North Sea Edition* and the *Channel Edition*.[25]

As they entered the Bay of Biscay on 13 November, they were still encountering disagreeable seas which lasted until they passed Cape Finisterre. From there the weather turned mild and then warm and sunny as they sailed south off Portugal. On 15 November, they entered the Gulf of Cádiz and about noon arrived off the mouth of the Río Guadalquivir. They sailed upstream and dropped anchor about eight kilometers south of Seville. "Here we were greeted enthusiastically by people along the banks of the river."[26]

It was not until the next day that they arrived in Seville and started immediately to disembark. The same day the entire group was quartered in the Cuba Hotel. The hotel must not have been in very good condition because the *War Diary* notes that they immediately started cleaning it up. They did not expect the heavy vehicles and personnel of the telephone and radio companies for at least another eight days and ". . .we hoped to fill these empty days by learning the language and the culture of Spain."[27] This, however, was not to be the case. The next day a small detachment was sent to Melilla, North Africa, to establish a finder station. Also, they had to contact the Spanish Postal System so they could patch telephone and teletype connections to Franco's headquarters in Salamanca. It was not until 2 December that all of the personnel, equipment, and vehicles of the Communications Group were to arrive in Spain.

Hardly had the first ship with the Condor Legion left its port on the Baltic when it was obvious to the most confirmed optimist that the Nationalist assault against Madrid would be a failure. The Nationalists simply did not have the strength to carry the city now that it was reinforced by Soviet heavy tanks, armored cars, and high-performance aircraft.

On 2 November, the Madrid command committed a force of 14,000 men, reinforced by forty-eight Soviet tanks and nine armored cars in a large counterattack against the battle-columns advancing up the Toledo and Aranjuez roads. Their objective was to double-envelop and destroy Major Tella's column. With their mass and uncontested armor, one would assume they would realize great success. They advanced south from the *Cerro de los Angeles*, "Hill of the Angels," now renamed "Hill of the Reds" by Madrid.[28]

As earlier, there was not the proper concentration of armor and coordination with infantry, and the counterattack was shattered even though some elements did advance as far as Torrejón de Velasco. The proper use of tanks was a factor which seemed repeatedly to escape the leaders of the Popular Front forces and their Soviet allies. Using an early version of the "Molotov cocktail" the determined cavalrymen of Colonel Monasterio, on Major Tella's right flank, destroyed two of the T-26 tanks and although badly bloodied, the Nationalist battle-columns were in pursuit.

By 7 November, the Nationalist battle-columns were in position, some as near as seven kilometers from Madrid's *Puerta del Sol*. General Varela's columns were now reinforced to a total strength of 12,000 but only 5,000 constituted the assault force, supported by twenty-four field guns and thirty light Italian and German tanks. They were faced by a defense force of 33,700, which was quickly reinforced by the arrival of the first of the International Brigades and 4,000 men in Buenaventura Durruti's anarchist brigade from Aragón. These forces were supported by forty-four additional heavy and medium caliber Soviet cannon, as well as the Soviet aircraft operating from the hard-surfaced runways near Madrid. All fell under the able Spanish General Miaja, but the real command was in the hands of the Communists and the Russians. For the Nationalists this was hardly a desirable ratio with their offensive force being outnumbered by more than three to one. Major Barroso of Franco's battle staff was not only gloomy about the possibilities of success but considered it hopeless. They ". . .[we] were merely a finger of an army." He advised

General Franco that they did not possess the strength and it was a "hopeless task."[29] Franco's position was: "Let Varela try it. He's always been lucky."[30] Additionally, unknown to Varela was the fact that his enemy was able to realign its defense forces to meet his main point of attack. One of his officers had been killed in the destruction of one of the light Italian tanks and on his body the enemy found Varela's complete battle plan. What is amazing is that Varela's troops were able to do as well as they did. But take Madrid they could not, although some momentarily managed to fight their way to the *Plaza de España*.

As the Nationalists battled their way through the *Casa de Campo*, across the Río Manzanares, and then from room to room in the University City (in a terribly bloody hand-to-hand struggle), the defenders had control of the air. At the onset the Nationalist air strength constituted twelve Ju-52s (including the five of the German "Pablo" and "Pedro" flights), six SM-81 bombers flown by mixed Spanish and Italian crews, eighteen Fiat CR-32 fighters, also flown by Spanish and Italian pilots, and ten newly acquired Italian RO-37 close ground support planes.[31] Included were none of the Condor Legion units which were in transit from Germany. This was hardly a formidable air armada. As early as 3 November, a Soviet squadron of I-16 (Rata) fighters had shot down five Nationalist aircraft without a single loss.[32] This was but the beginning of growing success by the government pilots.

General Varela repeatedly called for direct aerial support of his attack columns, but the lumbering bombers, even though both the He-51 and Fiat fighters tried to protect them, were not able to penetrate the Soviet aerial screen. Then on 11 November, Soviet bombers struck the German-flown He-51 squadron of Lieutenant Eberhard at Ávila. Notable damage was inflicted on the squadron, which was caught on the ground. This did not halt Varela's repeated requests for aerial support for his bloodied infantry, but there were few planes available and they were all highly vulnerable. As the hand-to-hand fighting raged in the University City, hot aerial combat raged and the rattle of machine gun fire could be heard in the skies over Madrid. On 13 November, there was a spectacular dogfight between thirteen Soviet Curtisses and fourteen Fiats directly over the heart of the city. Planes were lost by both sides. At the same time, in response to a plea for support, Lieutenant Eberhard led a flight of his remaining He-51s into the bloody battle for the *Casa de Campo*. Two planes were to be seen going down in flames, but only one parachute floated down into Madrid. Eberhard crashed with a machine gun bullet in his heart. The oscillating parachute held his adversary—a Russian pilot. The Russian was mistaken as a German by a Madrid mob and stomped to death. This naturally infuriated the Soviet leadership, who demanded that henceforth any downed flyer would immediately be taken to the nearest military facility. This Soviet order turned out to be favorable to the Germans in that some of the later downed German flyers were saved in this manner, and when there was a lull in the fighting, at times there would be an exchange of prisoners.

The same day that Eberhard died, one of his fellow pilots, Lieutenant Oskar Herici, landed his badly damaged fighter at Alcorcón. After the plane rolled to a stop, Herici stood up in the cockpit and fell over dead. He too had a bullet in his heart. His companions could never understand how he had managed to land the plane.[33] Not only had planes been damaged two days earlier by the Soviet squadron, but now the German squadron had lost two of its highly respected pilots. Eberhard had claimed his first victory back on 25 August, three days before Hitler committed the German pilots to battle. The squadron he had organized out of the remaining six original He-51 fighters sent to Spain was now badly battered and desperate. The German pilots fully knew that regardless of their skill as pilots and aerial gunners, they were hopelessly outclassed by the superior Soviet craft flown by skillful Russian pilots, some of whom they might have flown with in the skies over the Don Basin not too many years before.

While most of the Legion was still in its formative stage, the three bomber squadrons of K/88, under the command of Major Fuchs, put their aircraft in commission at Salamanca on 15 November, for the first direct participation of any of the units of the German Legion, as such, in the Spanish conflict. Their commitment at this time was not, however, in support of the desperate struggle for Madrid. There was great apprehension over the vast flow of heavy Soviet equipment through the Mediterranean ports of Cartagena and Alicante. In hopes of disrupting this flow, the Bomber Group was ordered to Seville. The operation had been in the planning for some time. It was known that there was a major problem of flying the bombers over the Sierra Nevada between Seville and Cartagena because of extreme icing conditions. Thus, by surface transport tons of fuel had been deposited at Melilla in North Africa. The Communications Group had by now also established there a finder station and a weather section to coordinate the flight operations. The bombers took off from Seville and landed at Melilla, fully loaded with bombs, shortly after noon. The refueled planes left Melilla in elements of two aircraft, with ten minutes between flights. Without fighter cover, they flew across the narrow waters of the Mediterranean and up the coastline of Spain to Cartagena. The first element was over the target at 5:30 p.m. and started a bombardment which lasted into the night. Two merchant ships were destroyed and others damaged. Most of the other ships fled the harbor for the open sea.[34] There was heavy antiaircraft fire and some of the bombers were hit, but there was no serious damage to the flights. All planes recovered in North Africa. This was the first combat experience of almost every one of the crewmen, and it was with a feeling of relief known only to airmen that it was successfully concluded without any losses. They had not shut off the flow of materials, but for a time they did slow the operation through Cartagena.

Shortly after the Legion bombers returned to Salamanca, on 18 November, a mixed flight of German and Spanish bombers struck hard at the enemy field at Alcalá de Henares hoping to catch the Soviet fighter aircraft on the ground. They managed to penetrate the enemy fighter screen but encountered heavy antiaircraft fire. The results of the mission were questionable, and one German craft was hit by ground fire. Bombardier Wilhelm Harjes was badly wounded and died before his bomber returned to base.[35] As near as this writer can determine, Airman Harjes was the first member of the Condor Legion to die in combat.

Also on 18 November the largest aerial bombardment of Madrid to date began, and it lasted until 22 November.[36] It appears that this series of raids came about through the insistence of the Germans. But it is difficult to determine if this was because of General Sperrle himself or upon orders that he might have received from Berlin. Prior to this particular moment, General Franco had established a bomb safety zone in Madrid to avoid civilian casualties. The area was determined by *Calle Zurbano* in the west, *Paseo de Ronda* in the north, *Calle Velázquez* in the east, and *Calle Goya* in the south.

The new air raids against Madrid were carried out by from thirty to as many as fifty bombers. There were Ju-52s of the Legion, the Nationalist Air Force, and the Italian SM-81 bombers. Unfortunately the German records of this period do not exist, and it is difficult to determine exactly what transpired between Berlin and the Legion commander. All fighters possible were ordered to protect the bombers, but the German He-51 squadrons were still in the process of being reassembled in southern Spain. Because of the great vulnerability of the bombers, as well as the inadequacy of all the fighters when faced with Soviet aircraft, the bombing of Madrid was quickly switched to a night operation.

Much to the distress of the Germans, their bomb-sighting mechanisms were very primitive and under the most ideal circumstances left much to be desired in a daytime strike. Never during World War II did the Germans ever develop the pinpoint bombing capability realized by the United States Air Force with its famous bombsight. Neither did the Royal Air Force which relied on massive pattern bombings and darkness for protection. The switching from daylight to night bombing against Madrid resulted in the same sort of indiscriminate bombing that was to be the rule of the Allies later. But with the small number of aircraft involved and with their limited bomb loads the amount of damage done must be considered minimal. In the case of Madrid, in all the raids between 14 and 23 November 1936, there were 244 civilian casualties, 875 wounded, and 303 buildings damaged.[37] Undoubtedly among the dead and wounded were some who were strong supporters of the Nationalist cause. But regardless, the loss of civilian lives in any conflict is a great tragedy. The raids were, in fact, a great benefit to the Popular Front with its capitalization on the sympathetic propaganda which resulted.

At the moment the air strikes were being made against Madrid, a German panzer section was committed by the Nationalist command to the Húmera-Pozuelo sector east of the *Casa de Campo*. They were immediately contained by the Soviet T-26s and quickly withdrew, knowing they were completely outclassed. The German command now issued orders that the panzers should avoid any contact with the superior enemy armor. Any effort to do battle would be a useless waste of tanks and lives, and Berlin was immediately informed of this decision.

The Nationalist Command Post assembled on 23 November. General Franco recognized that any further effort to carry Madrid by frontal assault would be futile and a continuous waste of his elite units. Some of the Legion *banderas* and Moroccan *tabores* were so badly shattered that they were dissolved and the survivors assigned to other units as replacements. Volunteer units had suffered equally with one battalion of 500 reduced to only 40 men. The superiority of the Soviet fighter planes forced the air operation into hours of darkness and thus greatly reduced its effectiveness. Bad weather, which would continue for some time, was beginning to limit this operation. General Franco now ordered General Varela to break off any further attempted ground assaults and secure his own positions and straighten his lines west of Madrid from Húmera to Pozuelo in order to contain any attempted rupture of the Nationalist front by the Madrid brigades, which were undoubtedly soon to come. Franco's aim was to attempt a double envelopment which would encircle Madrid and bring the entire city under siege, but this would require a far larger force than what he had at his disposal.

The Bomb Group (K/88) of the Condor Legion took advantage of the remainder of November 1936 to evaluate the lessons learned in these few weeks, and the Legion staff attempted to gather the various scattered units of the Legion into an operational organization well tied together with land and radio communications. These efforts were interrupted on 27 November 1936 when the Legion responded to a request from General Queipo de Llano in Seville.

Since the first days of the Nationalist uprising, there was a sizeable force of the Civil Guards, volunteers, women and children, and refugees from anarchist-held Andújar (twenty miles south) who were under siege by government forces in the sanctuary of Santa María de la Cabeza and nearby Lugar Nuevo.

The ragtag battle-columns of Queipo de Llano had not been able to fight their way through to relieve the surrounded garrison and he called for help. On 27 November 1936, Captain Baron von Moreau, who had

demonstrated his skill at such operations during the famous siege of the
Alcázar in Toledo, took off with a flight of Ju-52s from Salamanca, led by
a Spanish Ju-52, piloted by the Spanish Captain Pardo. They landed at
San Pablo (near Seville) where they were joined by a flight of the armed
reconnaissance He-70s from the Reconnaissance Squadron (A/88) of the
Condor Legion. It was not until 29 November that the five Legion planes,
guided by the Spanish Ju-52s, were able to make their first supply drop
on the embattled sanctuary. The Ju-52s and the He-70s then strafed
enemy artillery and machine gun positions firing on the defenders. The
German planes repeated this operation through the remainder of 1936 to
the end of April 1937. During this period tons of supplies were dropped
to the defenders, as well as tons of bombs on the attack forces gathering
about the sanctuary. On 25 January 1937, Lieutenant Kaufmann flew his
Ju-52 in a flight from Santander against Andújar. Over the target his
plane was hit by ground fire and crashed, killing all the crew. On 1 May
1937, a single Ju-52 on a resupply mission to the now ruined sanctuary
sensed something was wrong, and the German crew returned to base
without making their supply drop. The sanctuary had been overrun by
a force of two full Mixed Brigades with tanks and six batteries of 75mm,
105mm, and 124mm guns.[38]

The Condor Legion effort to assist the beleaguered defenders of the
sanctuary at Santa María de la Cabeza was only one of many factors in
the story of the Legion the last weeks of 1936 and early months of
1937. Besides being called upon to support friendly ground forces directly, it went through an organizational change, as well as a change in
equipment. Also in December, proposals were made in Berlin which, had
they been fulfilled, could have had a decided impact upon the whole
conduct of the Spanish Civil War.

Notes

1. Freiburg, MF, RL 2/v. 3187, Part V, p. 11.
2. Ibid., p. 21.
3. Warlimont commented to this writer that he was always disturbed that
the Spanish would insist on deploying all available aircraft in direct infantry
support rather than striking at the source of supply.
4. George Hills, *The Battle for Madrid* (London, 1976), p. 83.
5. Ibid., p. 84. Franco knew the tanks were in the area but assumed, wrongly,
that they would be held back by the Río Tajo.
6. Ibid., pp. 84-85.
7. Comment of Warlimont to the writer.
8. *GD*, Series D, Vol. III, Doc. No. 113, and Enclosure.
9. *GD*, Series D, Vol. III, Doc. No. 103.
10. Warlimont's comment to the writer.
11. Plocher's comment to the writer.
12. Interview of the writer with Colonel a.D. Douglas Pitcairn. At the time

of this writing, Colonel Pitcairn is about seventy years old. He was a lieutenant colonel when the war ended. In 1954, Pitcairn was called back to duty with the new West German Air Force but was considered too old for a combat pilot and was assigned to G-2 of the General Staff. He retired in 1972 with the rank of colonel. If the reader is confused by the name Pitcairn, as indeed was this writer, it can be explained by the colonel's comments. He is a descendant of the Pitcairn clan of Scotland which emigrated to Germany in the seventeenth century because of religious persecutions. Some other interesting members of the Pitcairn family are Major Pitcairn, who was the first British officer to be killed in the American Revolution, and Midshipman Pitcairn, who served on a British frigate and after whom Pitcairn Island in the South Seas is named.

13. General Karl Drum, "The German Luftwaffe in the Spanish Civil War (Condor Legion)," (special unpublished study for the USAF), p. 45.

14. Comments by General Plocher which were reinforced by Colonel Pitcairn.

15. Comments to the writer by General Plocher, who later served as von Richthofen's chief of staff. Colonel Pitcairn held much the same view. Von Richthofen's impatience is revealed in the few parts of his personal diary that have been made public.

16. Drum, "The German Luftwaffe," pp. 38-40.

17. General Plocher could not recall the exact number of men sent to Spain at this time, but suggested it probably was around 5,000.

18. General Plocher's comment to the writer.

19. Even with the enthusiastic assistance of the noted panzer commander, the late General Hasso von Manteuffel, the writer was unable to locate any officers who served with this unit. General Plocher commented to the writer: "I did have contact with Major von Thoma when I arrived in Spain as the second Chief of Staff of the Legion, but it was not from the Legion that von Thoma received his orders. His orders came directly from Berlin. I was repeatedly advised that the German Army units in Spain were only to instruct the Spaniards, they were not to fight. Only in the gravest battles did the instructors themselves engage in combat. I do know that by the end of the war some Germans were actually operating as leaders of tank units manned by Spaniards."

20. Comment of Colonel Pitcairn.

21. Hans Trautloft, *Als Jagflieger in Spanien: Aus dem Tagebuch eines deutschen Legionäres*, p. 123.

22. Pitcairn could not recall the exact date.

23. Comments of General Plocher.

24. Freiburg, *War Diary* of the Communications Group Ln/88, hereafter cited as Freiburg, Ln/88 *War Diary*.

25. Ibid. This document states that copies of these papers were attached to the diary. However, they have not been found.

26. Ibid.

27. Ibid.

28. Hills, *The Battle for Madrid*, p. 88.

29. Ibid., pp. 91-92.

30. Ibid.

31. The Italian Romero-37 was a two-place biplane made on a sport plane design used for close ground support and reconnaissance. It had a top speed of 335 knots

and was armed with two machine guns and could carry twelve light bombs.

32. Hugh Thomas, *The Spanish Civil War*, 2d ed. (New York, 1977), p. 482. The author quotes Jesús Salas Larrazábal, *La guerra de España desde el aire* (Barcelona, 1969), p. 133. In fn. 1, Thomas states that Lieutenant Eberhard was the first German officer to die in Spain. This is not correct. The first was Lieutenant Eberhardt Heftner, who died in the crash of his aircraft in the Plaza of Vitoria.

33. Comment of Pitcairn to the writer.

34. Drum, "The German Luftwaffe," p. 74, and R. Hidalgo Salazar, *La ayuda alemana a España 1936-39*, p. 128.

35. Salazar, *La ayuda alemana*, p. 129. There is a bit of confusion here because in the Appendix 1, Salazar lists Harjes as being killed 8 December over Alcalá de Henares.

36. Many writers state that these large strikes against Madrid began on 15 November. This would have been impossible with the entire Legion bomber fleet deployed against Cartagena at that time.

37. Hills, *The Battle for Madrid*, p. 106, refers to Ramón Salas Larrazábal, *Historia del ejército popular de la República*, 4 vols. (Madrid, 1974), p. 2522, who gathered the data from Madrid municipal records.

38. Salazar, *La ayuda alemana*, pp. 129-132, and Thomas, *The Spanish Civil War*, 2d ed., pp. 630-631. There has been little written in English of this most spectacular siege which had lasted these many months. The most complete work in Spanish is Julio de Urrutia, *El cerro de los héroes* (Madrid, 1965).

6

Phase Six:
Warlimont versus
Faupel

When Admiral Canaris (on 30 October) informed General Franco and Colonel Warlimont of the creation of the Condor Legion, the latter envisioned a drastic change in his personal position in Spain. As early as 17 October, General von Blomberg of the War Ministry had recommended that Warlimont be replaced by a chargé d'affaires from the Foreign Ministry, who would be posted to the Nationalist government.[1] The position fell to retired infantry Lt. General Wilhelm von Faupel.

General Faupel had a long and varied career as an imperial officer and following the Great War was associated with different Free Corps units during the revolutionary upheavals of 1918-1919.[2] In the 1920s he served as a military advisor to different South American countries, where he became proficient in the Spanish language and knowledgeable of Latin customs. Although he was not, at the time, a member of the Nazi party, he was closely connected with *Gauleiter* Ernst Bohle, the head of *Auslandsorganisation* (A.O.), who had been so instrumental in obtaining Hitler's initial assistance for Nationalist Spain. There is little doubt that Bohle, through the assistance of Rudolf Hess, prevailed upon Hitler himself to assign Faupel to Salamanca even though he was posted through the Foreign Ministry of Baron von Neurath.[3] Initially, Faupel was given the long title "German Diplomatic Representative to the Spanish Nationalist Government," but he always considered himself a full ambassador and the dispatches in the German documents usually referred to his office as the "Embassy."[4]

Warlimont was given the choice by the war minister of becoming a member of the Legion staff in the strange position as General von Blomberg's personal representative to the Legion General Staff, or returning to Germany. Warlimont was not impressed with this sort of assignment and personally considered that his position on the Legion staff as a representative of the War Ministry would be totally untenable. As an Army General Staff and artillery officer, even though for some time he had functioned as the air commander in Spain, he felt that it would be best for all concerned if he returned to Germany as quickly as possible, but he was ordered to remain in Spain until General Faupel assumed his office as the representative of the Foreign Ministry in Salamanca.[5]

Hitler ordered that Faupel be accompanied to Spain by a member of the Nazi party who would be in the position of a propaganda aide. Willi Köhn of the A.O. was selected for this position and given the title of "general consul."[6] The Foreign Ministry did post the professional diplomat Karl Schwendemann as a diplomatic advisor to Faupel. However, conflict quickly rose between him and the man from the A.O.

Faupel arrived in Salamanca on 28 November 1936. Knowing in advance of Faupel's arrival, Colonel Warlimont had vacated his apartment, which would then become Faupel's residence.

After Faupel had been in the apartment a few hours, Warlimont made a call on him. When the colonel entered, he was surprised to find Faupel bending over a large map lying across a table and working out the details as to how the Spanish war could be brought to a quick conclusion. At that time, in a very polite manner, Warlimont attempted to caution Faupel to keep himself and his staff removed from Spanish military and internal political affairs. He had worked with General Franco and his staff long enough to recognize their sensitivities and that they definitely wanted to run their affairs without any foreign pressure.[7] But Faupel proceeded to ignore the colonel's suggestion. Two days later, Faupel met with General Franco for the first time, and Colonel Warlimont took leave of the small Spanish general whom he had come to respect greatly.

Warlimont, wanting to remove himself completely from what he saw was becoming a very complicated affair in Spain, quickly left Salamanca for Seville. When he arrived in Seville, he did not even report into the German headquarters located in the Hotel Cristina, but located a small hotel in the old *Santa Cruz* district. He was amused to see his countrymen of the Legion marching in formation through Seville singing German songs. "So much for security," he thought.[8] He wanted to stay in and near the hotel until he could make arrangements for transportation to Lisbon, where he hoped he would be able to find passage on a ship back to Germany. However, he had not been in the hotel long when he was located by an agent of Admiral Canaris. The colonel was disturbed to learn that he was to return to Salamanca as the military advisor to Faupel.

Much to his annoyance, Warlimont returned to Salamanca to assume the duties of which he wanted no part, nor did he exactly know what was expected of him. Warlimont was even more disturbed when he realized that Faupel was giving no consideration to the warnings that he had given him a few days earlier; also that Faupel was of the opinion that what was needed as a solution for the Nationalists' problems was more German direct military participation in the form of German ground forces. After two days Warlimont suggested to Faupel that there was really little that he could accomplish there, and besides, there were many "military attachés" on hand and that it would be best if he could ask General von Blomberg to be permitted to return to Germany. After he had been in Salamanca again for about ten disagreeable days, this permission came from Berlin.

It was with apprehension that Warlimont departed Salamanca for Germany, but this time it was by air via Rome:

> I felt that Faupel would get into trouble with everyone. That is, I felt he would play the role of the Nazi in Spain. He would quickly involve himself in Spanish military affairs directly with Franco, as well as in political matters which were strictly none of his business. There is a line in the affairs of others that one should not tread; but he did not understand.[9]

Warlimont returned to a Germany cloaked with snow and immediately was given command of an artillery regiment at Treves. But this did not end his involvement in Spanish affairs. After reporting to his regiment, he went for a short leave of absence with his family. Hardly was he home when on 20 December he was surprised to receive a telephone call from General Keitel in Berlin, who advised him that he was ordered to meet with Hitler the following day. Taken aback, Warlimont pressed for further information. Keitel would only advise him that he was to attend an important conference with Hitler and some of the ministers.

His train was already moving when he opened the door to his compartment, but he was stopped by the conductor. "Are you Warlimont?" he asked. When assured he was, the conductor continued: "Well, then, I have a telegram for you from the Reich Chancellery." Surprised, Warlimont entered the compartment, nodded to the passengers already seated, and placed his bag in the rack overhead. He sat down and opened the telegram. The message stated that he was to proceed on to Cologne and from there go to the airport where Hitler's personal aircraft would be waiting to fly him to Berlin. The conference would be held that same night. By now, the train was well under way. Warlimont worried for some time as to what this was all about and came to the conclusion that indeed General Faupel might be trying to convince Berlin to send additional German ground forces to Spain. Finally he stood up and retrieved his bag from the rack.

> I took my bag into the W.C. and changed from civilian clothing into my uniform. When I returned to the compartment I was amused at the startled glances from the other passengers to see me come in dressed in the uniform of a *Wehrmacht* colonel. But I could not help worrying about what Faupel was up to.[10]

When the train stopped at Cologne, Warlimont took a taxi directly to the airport, where he was met by Hitler's personal pilot Bower. They immediately boarded Hitler's aircraft and were quickly airborne with Warlimont as the only passenger. When they landed in Berlin, Warlimont was met by Colonel Friedrich Hossbach, Hitler's military adjutant, who advised him that the conference had been put off until the following day.[11] He learned now that Faupel indeed was in Berlin and had proposed that Germany increase its military commitment to Spain and that Hitler wanted to hear his, Warlimont's, views on the matter because of his experiences with the war and his personal knowledge of General Franco and his views.

Warlimont found quarters and continued to worry about exactly what Faupel might have in mind, and at the same time, if there was any way he could possibly prevent it, if it involved sending additional German ground forces to Spain. He felt that he could have little influence on General Goering and his Air Ministry, which was already so deeply involved. He knew that the War Ministry as well as "Special Staff W" were fully aware of his own position on such a matter because he had made this clear in his reports from Salamanca. He was aware that General Ludwig Beck, Army chief of staff, had opposed the initial German involvement in Spain and was determined to have a talk with the general before he attended the conference the next day.

When he called General Beck the following morning, the general agreed to see him immediately. Once Warlimont met with Beck, he learned that his suspicions were true. Faupel actually wanted to have three full German infantry divisions sent to Spain as a combat force. Warlimont then went over his personal objections and was pleased with the general's response:

> General Beck confirmed my own position, in detail, not to send any more German personnel. General Beck would agree to resupply, but definitely no more personnel. He then used the words: "It would be fatal for us to send whole divisions to Spain, along the *British Window* and the *French Door*."[12]

The colonel and general stood up and shook hands in their mutual agreement. The junior officer then saluted and departed with the general shaking his head. Warlimont rode to the Reich Chancellery in a staff car and after receiving the salute of the sentries, entered the building alone. He was surprised on entering to find Hitler standing there alone in the corridor. It was the first time that he had ever been in front of the German *Führer*, but it certainly would not be the last in the years to come.

> Hitler saluted me and then told me that the conference had been delayed for awhile. Then he excused himself and departed. This is the only time that I can remember a polite Hitler!

Warlimont noted that when the conference was finally called, besides Hitler and Faupel and himself, in attendance were: General von Blomberg of the War Ministry; General Goering, representing the Air Ministry and the *Luftwaffe*; Grand Admiral Erich Raeder of the German Navy; Colonel General Baron Werner von Fritsch, the commander in chief of the German Army; and Colonel Hossbach.

Warlimont was somewhat uncomfortable to be sitting with the highest members of the Third Reich and knew that his position, if Hitler called upon him to give it, was directly in opposition to what Faupel had in mind. Still, he knew that initially most of these people had been opposed to Germany becoming involved in Spain back in July.

Hitler began the conference by introducing Faupel to those who did not know him, and then asked Faupel to explain his proposals for the conduct of the Spanish Civil War. Faupel insisted what was needed was for Germany to send three full divisions to Spain. He then went into a lengthy explanation as to why they were needed and the inadequacy of the Nationalist forces as well as poor leadership on the part of the Spanish staff. If a German force of this size should be sent to Spain, the war would be over in only a matter of a few weeks. Warlimont told the writer many years later:

> This was a totally irresponsible recommendation! It came from a man who had only been in Spain for two or three weeks, and had never been to one of the many fighting fronts. It was impossible for me to understand how he could have come to these conclusions from bending over a map in my former apartment in Salamanca!

Hitler then turned to Colonel Warlimont and asked him for his views on the recommendations. The colonel explained his objections in detail, much of which he had already written to Berlin, but other reasons which he had not included in his memorandum. As best as he could later recall, this took about forty-five minutes. In that time, he attempted to explain the particular nature of the Spanish Civil War as he had experienced it. He was insistent that the appearance of German divisions would not materially change the situation in favor of the Nationalists. True, the

German divisions on a particular front at a given time might act like a "corset stay" but they would never be able to produce the crucial results needed for a Nationalist victory. The future in Spain would only be determined on the battlefield by the Spaniards themselves; and this was what General Franco and his generals wanted. Materially, Germany and the Soviet Union could support the side of their choice, but added troops were not the solution; this would have to come from within Spain for the side who would win. And this victory would be a long time in the future. An immediate deployment of three full German divisions to Spain and committing them to battle was not only unlikely but impossible. Such an act could not possibly remain a secret and the international repercussions, particularly from France and England, would be profound.[13]

Warlimont went into detail about the great problems of resupply for such a German force and the danger that these supply lines would be exposed to. Then he noted that it would be a great drain on the existing *Wehrmacht* to commit a force of such magnitude. It would be at least 60,000 men and all the required equipment. He pointed out that the German Army, in reality, was still just the shadow of an army and that Germany could, in his view, ill afford to squander so much of its strength. In Germany's own national interest, no matter how sympathetic he might feel to the Nationalist cause, this would be a gross mistake. He then suggested that France might respond in a like manner, and German troops would soon be fighting French forces in Spain. He then strongly voiced his personal knowledge of General Franco's opposition to such a move. Franco was adamant that his success in the conflict must be determined by the use of Spanish troops and the deployment of German forces was fundamentally not desirable. Franco believed that such an idea would have little support from the Spanish people and that was what he needed to overcome the Popular Front: the support of the Spanish people. Warlimont then attempted to explain that the great difference in military customs and the grave cruelty of the war would have a detrimental effect upon the German troops. These factors he had discussed in his memorandums to the war minister:

> I could sense the hostility from General Faupel because my position was so adamantly opposed to his. I knew that I had the support of General Beck, and thereby I assumed also General von Blomberg. I suspected that General Fritsch was in agreement, but I had not had the opportunity to talk with him.

General von Blomberg finally interrupted Warlimont's narrative: "*Führer*, we cannot possibly spare these Divisions! We would have to send to Spain not only our best trained officers and men but our limited amount of equipment to properly support them. This would in fact destroy the German Army." As Warlimont suspected, Baron von Fritsch supported this position.

Hitler now took over the discussion:

> I have listened to both of you and I understand each of your points of view. But, my decision is founded on another train of thought, our only interest in Spain is that Franco should not lose. On the other hand, I am not interested in that he should finish it quickly. With the continued conflict in Spain, Europe will be interested in events there and be less concerned with Germany and my objectives.[14]

Warlimont was pleased that there would be no German divisions sent to Spain, but at the same time he was greatly distressed at the reason Hitler gave for not sending them. That is, Hitler's rationale was that by not sending them, he would be prolonging the Spanish Civil War for his own reasons. Hitler was agreeable to continued material support, as well as the men and aircraft of the Condor Legion, but it was obvious that these were merely pawns in his own scheme of things. Warlimont later commented, "In all my meetings with Hitler later, and there were many that were terribly disagreeable, I always could recall this cruel callousness he demonstrated that day in December 1936."

Warlimont left the Chancellery pleased that in some way he might have assisted in subverting General Faupel's intentions, but it was with grave apprehension for the future of Germany that he returned to his family and his regiment. This finally ended his mission to Spain. Phase Six of German involvement in Spain was stillborn.

General Faupel returned to Salamanca, but it seems he had not learned his lesson in Berlin. Immediately he began to involve himself directly in Spanish military matters, very much to the annoyance of Franco and other Spanish generals. But he did not seem satisfied to stop there and very quickly ran head-on into the strong-willed gigantic Sperrle. Faupel never did learn the lesson described by General Warlimont as: "There is a line in the affairs of other men that one should not tread."

Notes

1. *GD*, Series D, Vol. III, Doc. No. 103.

2. R. Hidalgo Salazar, *La ayuda alemana a España 1936-39*, p. 89, notes that during World War I, Faupel was the colonel of the same regiment in which Hitler was a corporal.

3. Clarence D. Beck, "A Study of German Involvement in Spain 1936-1939," unpublished doctoral dissertation (University of New Mexico, 1972), pp. 104-107, and *GD*, Series D, Vol. III, Doc. No. 125.

4. *GD*, Series D, Vol. III, Doc. No. 125, Editor's footnote.

5. Warlimont's memorandum of 22 September 1945. In a conversation with

this writer, Warlimont noted that the position offered him in the Legion was a vague sort of "second chief of staff." He wanted no part of it.

6. *GD*, Series D, Vol. III, Doc. No. 125, and Beck, "A Study of German Involvement in Spain 1936-1939," p. 106.

7. Warlimont's comment to the writer.

8. Ibid. Warlimont was also concerned that Faupel was surrounded by so many outspoken members of the Nazi party who he felt would quickly cause friction between the German military personnel and the Spanish leadership, who he knew for the most part had little patience for German national socialism.

9. Ibid.

10. Ibid.

11. Colonel Friedrich Hossbach was the author of the famous "Hossbach Minutes" and also wrote *Zwischen Wehrmacht und Hitler* (Hannover, 1949).

12. Warlimont's comment to the writer.

13. The views expressed to the writer by General Warlimont were largely an expansion of those written in his memorandum of 22 September 1945.

14. In his discussion of these events with the writer, Warlimont said he could not recall every word of Hitler's comments, but in essence this is what he said.

7

Combat, Problems, and Reorganizations

Through Colonel Warlimont in Berlin, General Franco had a spokesman to give voice to his personal objections to further deployment of German soldiers to Spain, but this was not the case in Rome. Where General Faupel felt that three German divisions would bring a rapid end to the war, Benito Mussolini was of the opinion that a few Italian divisions could solve the Nationalists' problems.[1] Greatly dissatisfied with the Nationalist failure to take Madrid in November 1936, he took the view: "They [Nationalists] were obviously lacking in offensive spirit and also in personal bravery. There were evidently very few real men in Spain."[2]

The following day Count Ciano, Italian foreign minister, advised the German ambassador that: "Italy was determined to send to Spain a whole division of Black Shirts, of whom 4,000 men were already organized in four battalions. . . ."[3] Dr. Hans Dieckhoff of the Reich Political Department in the Foreign Office appears not to have been any more enthusiastic about this than he was for Faupel's suggestion to send German divisions to Spain.[4]

Franco, however, was not aware that the *Duce* had such a low opinion of his Nationalist soldiery and that he was planning to come to his rescue with his Black Shirt militiamen and "put some backbone into the Spanish National formations."[5] Finally on 14 December, Franco was advised by the Italian Colonel Emilio Faldella that soon 3,000 Black Shirts would be arriving at Cádiz. Franco had not approved of any such move, nor had it been discussed with him, and he quickly showed his annoyance to the colonel with his response: "Who asked for them?"[6]

A very ill-selected and hastily organized Italian force departed for Cádiz on 18 December, and by 10 January 1937, Italy had a 15,529-man force forming in southern Spain. They were 60 percent Black Shirt militiamen and 40 percent troops from the Italian army. By mid-February, the force had grown to about 49,000 with the ratio of militiamen to army remaining the same.[7] The Italians were then formed into four divisions. Three divisions were of militiamen with the names *"Dio lo Vuole"* (God Wills It), *"Fiamme Nere"* (Black Flame), and the *"Penne Nere"* (Black Feather). The Italian army unit was the "Littorio Division." The Italian motorized infantry units "were an innovation in the commitment of infantry forces. In Spain, those units were tried out for the first time in a European theater of war."[8]

On the Madrid front, in December 1936, the Nationalist ground forces faced most difficult military odds. Some observers feel that had the Madrid forces concentrated strong attacks on both Nationalist flanks, the Army of Africa could have been encircled and destroyed in detail. Both sides now began to reinforce and reorganize their committed formations. The Madrid forces regrouped into "Mixed Brigades" and divisions; the Nationalist battle-columns began to re-form into brigades, but for some time they continued to use battle-column tactics. These brigades became known as the "Madrid Reinforced Division." In their rear areas both sides were in the process of raising tens of thousands of troops, which before long would grow into hundreds of thousands. Colonel Warlimont was correct when he predicted that the conflict would be a lengthy one.

General Franco conceded his direct assault on Madrid was a failure and agreed with General Sperrle that Madrid should be brought under siege by a double envelopment and thereby cut off from Valencia and Catalonia. If he could join the Army of Africa with the Army of the North near Alcalá de Henares east of Madrid, this could be accomplished. But first General Varela was ordered to secure his forces in the University City and *Casa de Campo* by straightening his lines west of Madrid from Húmera to Pozuelo, and at the same time to cut the Madrid-to-La Coruña highway. In an attempt to accomplish this with 7,000 men, Varela ran directly into a government force twice that size (with heavy Soviet armor) attacking the same area. One government brigade broke and fled the battlefield when faced with the cool professionalism of the *banderas* of the Foreign Legion, but the few Nationalist light tanks that engaged the Soviet T-26s were outclassed. Some were destroyed and the survivors quickly withdrew. In support, when the weather permitted, German and Spanish-flown Ju-52 bombers struck at enemy positions around Madrid and along the Coruña road. Even though the bombers were under the protection of German and Italian fighters, the bomber formations were repeatedly broken up by the Soviet interceptors. General Varela could accomplish little but hold his ground and regroup his forces until 16 December.

On that day, with his losses replaced, Varela initiated a vicious attack which destroyed a full Madrid brigade and carried Boadilla del Monte with German and Spanish air support. The battle raged without interruption until 20 December, when Varela was forced to give up all positions won except Brunete, directly west of Madrid. General Varela was wounded and had to be relieved of his command.

Meanwhile, the German fighter squadrons recently committed to Spain were assuming combat status. The 1st Squadron (under Captain Lehmann) was based at the airfield of León, the 2nd Squadron (of Captain Lützow) flew into one of the airfields at Vitoria, the 3rd Squadron (with Captain Harder) moved to Escalona (twelve kilometers north of Maqueda on the Madrid-Talavera de la Reina road), and the 4th Squadron was at the old facility of Ávila where it absorbed the remaining aircraft and personnel of the original He-51 flight of Captain Houwald. The entire Fighter Group (J/88) was commanded by Major Merhard.[9] Also located at Ávila was the General Staff of the Condor Legion.

The air crews and ground personnel already at Ávila were billeted in houses, and the Command Staff moved into a castle. However, the newly arrived squadron personnel were quartered in the unique facility they called a *Wohnzug*, or "housing train."

This *Wohnzug* was a train which consisted of about nine cars with a steam engine at each end. There were three cars for quarters in which each officer pilot had a sleeping compartment and the enlisted men were two to a compartment. There were two cars which served as mess halls and a cantina and then a kitchen car. There was a car for the headquarters and as many as two cars which were used for maintenance and spare parts storage. Steam was maintained on the engines to provide power and heat. It is very cold during the winter in Castile in the area of Ávila with the heavy snows and biting winds. The Germans found their *Wohnzug* very comfortable under the circumstances. Men working on the aircraft in the open, however, had to guard against frostbite of fingers and ears.[10]

An advantage of the *Wohnzug* was that it not only functioned as living quarters and a headquarters facility but that it was mobile. In a matter of minutes all cars could be under way with all equipment and support personnel while the flight crews flew their aircraft to another airfield to support operations in an adjacent area. The *Wohnzug* was used to support Lieutenant Pitcairn's squadron until late 1937.

Before Christmas 1936, the Communications Group had established its central communications section in Salamanca and was connected to all the widely separated units of the Legion, Spanish commands, and the

Italian Central Staff. The Ln/88 *War Diary* relates their preparations for the holidays in wartime:

> Christmas and the New Year are coming in Spain. We are working very hard to make ready for Christmas. The biggest problem this year is a Christmas tree because we have not been able to find them in Spain, and what we want is a *tannenbaum*. At the last moment some arrived from Germany. Also, the packages from relatives arrived, which were mailed in Berlin 3 December. Each man received a small package from our government containing chocolates, marzipan, etc. (tobacco not included!).
>
> In Salamanca, the children of the needy were given gifts on Christmas Eve. Major Schubert then gave a speech to the people gathered in the market place. He explained how the Germans celebrated Christmas and how we are always thinking of the poorest of the poor at this time of year. In the evening, Christmas was celebrated at all stations of Ln/88 from Vigo to Salamanca and Madrid to Seville. One tries to help the soldiers over being homesick because they cannot be with their families. As was the case of Christmas in the last war, the telegraph was the means of passing messages from company to company and station to station. They were greetings of poetical outpouring.

Then the *War Diary* recites a long poem transmitted by the Seville station to Major Schubert and all other stations.

Also based at Ávila was the band of the Condor Legion, which was welcomed by the Spaniards when it played concerts in the ancient square of the city of St. Theresa. The German airmen found the medieval city, with its walls and historic sites, a delightful place to explore in their free moments. Their major concern was not about their comforts but the poor reaction of their He-51 fighters when faced with the high-performing Soviet planes flown by very capable pilots.

It was in December 1936 that General Sperrle made the decision, in sharp contrast to the desires of the Nationalists, that because of the continually increasing danger of enemy fighters, the Legion would only support the battle for Madrid during hours of darkness. To accomplish this, the Legion would concentrate its attacks against the traffic on the roads leading into Madrid. The railroad to Valencia had been cut near Aranjuez, and the capital was dependent on truck traffic to a distance of fifty kilometers from the city. At night the bomber flights could determine the amount of traffic from truck headlights in a given sector. They learned that the truck traffic was bothered with traffic jams at bridges and the narrow streets of small towns. If the weather permitted, one or two squadrons would fly nightly attacks along these roads. A squadron would bomb the traffic congested at one or two small towns and then bomb the road areas and bridges with single aircraft. They quickly learned that it was extremely hard if not impossible to hit the small bridges with their bombing systems. In addition, the stone bridges of Spain were most difficult to destroy completely. The lack of visible results was discouraging to the crews. But it was later learned that these missions did make things very difficult for the forces within the city.[11]

At the same time, the Legion desperately attempted, within the limits of its technical inferiority, to destroy the enemy aircraft on the ground. For their own protection, the reconnaissance planes would search the known landing strips shortly before dusk. The "Evaluation Rügen" report notes that the constant watching for enemy fighters had reached "the condition of a phobia" that greatly reduced the effectiveness of the re-connaissance crews.[12] Furthermore, the enemy proved himself very clever with camouflage and the use of dummy aircraft. In addition, the planes would be dispersed to fields which, to the observers, appeared as nothing more than empty farm fields. The planes were hidden under trees, in old buildings, or camouflaged, and could be located only through the close study of aerial photography. Photography in the hours of flight was most difficult or impossible. The reconnaissance planes had no night recon-naissance capability and had to return to their own bases before dark because of the conditions of the fields and lack of night landing aids.[13] If at dusk a field was found to have aircraft, weather permitting, the bomb-ers would be over the target at early dawn, only to find that the planes usually had been moved during the night. And, as in the case of the reconnaissance planes, there was always the concern that enemy fighters might be lurking in the skies above to dive on the slow bombers as they approached the target area.

If all conditions were perfect, and an actual night bomber attack could be made, the bombers had great difficulty locating the enemy airfields because there were limited ground points to aid in navigation. There were few roads, and as soon as ground traffic heard the engines of the bombers all lights would go out. If the bombers were able to locate the airfield, the aircraft on the ground were always widely dispersed and the possibility of their destruction or damage was remote unless the strike force consisted of a full squadron bombing. Again the lack of visible results was very discouraging to the flight crews. Still, it was determined to be a necessary operation; it did harass the enemy and provided valuable experience for the crewmen. At this time, additional machine guns were installed in the bombers. They may not have been very effective, but they did give the crews a little more feeling of security.

For a while the German flights were able to destroy a few enemy aircraft on the ground by sending some of their planes into the skies near the enemy airfields. When the Soviet fighters took to the air, the German planes would remain out of range until the interceptors had to return and land for refueling. A second German flight would be timed so it would be over the airfield while the refueling was in progress and would bomb and machine-gun the refueling aircraft. This was a delicate operation, and when the Soviets soon took countermeasures, it had to be stopped. "The Soviets were very clever. At times we could not locate their aircraft on airfields, such as Cuatro Vientos, because they had trucked them into Madrid where they used the wide streets for take-off. Then we would have the uncomfortable experience of encountering them in the air."[14]

The crews of all units were frustrated because enemy planes had almost unlimited domination of the skies over friendly ground forces; even their own airfields were not safe. Enemy pilots, however, did show respect for the Legion airfields protected by the rapid-firing 88mm antiaircraft cannons. Frantic Spanish commanders still requested Legion support for hard-pressed units or aerial preparation for a ground attack. Sperrle and von Richthofen had to weigh each request in the light of their capability and the possible cost to the Legion. Whenever possible, Sperrle would respond. He would be advised of the details for a ground attack and asked to strike strong points and pockets of resistance. If the bombers did not have to break off their attack because of fighter interception, strikes against heavily fortified positions usually produced measurable results. At such times, the enemy would flee the positions or would be badly stunned by the bombardment. However, the Germans repeatedly complained because friendly infantry would not press the attack immediately following the bombardment. This was an operational problem that had to be resolved between the air and ground commanders, but it was a situation that remained annoying to the Legion staff for many months to come. Too frequently "friendly troops would come out of their trenches and applaud their comrades-in-arms in the air who were flying over their heads. Only in one case was the enemy so shocked that when the position was attacked by friendly forces, hours later, it was found the enemy had surrendered the positions without a fight."[15]

For the Ju-52s, and the bombers which were soon to replace them (as well as all the aircraft), a major problem in Spain was to be, and still is for any aircraft, the varying topography of the country with its many high mountain ranges and the resulting rapidly changing weather conditions. Bombers flying from Salamanca have to cross the Sierra de Gredos to reach the Madrid area. These mountains, along with the Sierra de Guadarrama lying to the west and north, form a natural barrier to Madrid. The barrier is not only the mountains, but also the variable weather conditions created by the ranges. Most of the time, particularly in the winter, the weather will differ completely on the two slopes of the sierras. At times of icing conditions, which are frequent, it was impossible for the Ju-52 (with its limited ceiling) to be able to top the mountains, as was the case of the Sierra Nevada in Andalusia.

"The different weather conditions between their bases and the target areas came as a complete surprise to the airmen and almost drove them out of their minds."[16] Practically all flights had to be flown through dense clouds, and the ever-present fear of icing conditions was putting a great strain on the air crews. "Particularly trying to the nerves was the fact that no visible results could be seen."[17]

The Spanish Nationalists had practically no meteorological service, and the German weather sections did not have the experience that could be adapted to conditions in Spain. The Legion frantically attempted to find at least a partial solution by putting the weather sections through several reorganizations and establishing weather reporting stations throughout Nationalist Spain. Spain was divided into six weather zones tied together by radio and teletype. It was to be several months before any notable improvement in weather forecasting could be realized, and even then it was very limited because "sometimes it was impossible to have the several weathermen agree on a weather prediction."[18]

Sperrle and von Richthofen felt that the nature of the missions and repeated flying were reducing the efficiency of the bomber crews. They became very reluctant, except under gravest circumstances, to commit the same crew for a second flight on the same day. They attempted to relieve this pressure by transferring the crews and aircraft from one operating base to another, but found that this was self-defeating. They did attempt to ensure that the personnel had proper clothing and adequate quarters well removed from the airfield. "They made certain that the crews had good food and the amenities of life that made living a little easier."[19] Eventually to be included in the latter was a sponsored and medically examined brothel.

In December 1936, to eliminate the icing problems, a combined Spanish-Italian bomber squadron moved to one of the few airstrips on the Madrid side of the sierras not in enemy hands. The airfield was only fifteen kilometers from Madrid and the squadron, hardly deployed, was completely destroyed in the early dawn.[20] This convinced the Germans to give up the idea, at this time, of moving over the mountains.

Like the American Douglas-built C-47 transports of World War II (and many years after), the Ju-52 built by Junkers of Germany was one of the greatest aircraft in flight history. It was originally designed and built as a commercial transport for *Lufthansa* and made its first flight in October 1930. As a transport it could accommodate seventeen passengers and some cargo. Because of their dependability and flight safety record the planes were adopted by different countries and companies. With the birth of the *Luftwaffe* in 1935, some of the Ju-52s were configured as bombers for the first *Luftwaffe* bomber squadrons. Like the legendary American Ford tri-motor transport, the Ju-52 had a reciprocating engine in each wing and one in the nose. Its fuselage was of a corrugated metal construction. By most airmen it was considered ugly; at the same time it was highly respected for its reliability. There were many different models built in different countries which will not be discussed here. The first ten transports and bombers sent to Spain in July 1936 were of both the commercial and military models. In November, with the creation of the Condor Legion, thirty-six bomber models constituted its heavy bomber force.

The maximum operational ceiling of the Ju-52 bomber, with a full load, was approximately 11,500 feet. Its best speed at low altitude was 150 miles per hour (mph). Radio communications were limited to air-to-ground; it carried no direction-finding instruments or intercommunication system.

For armaments, it had two vertical bomb racks that could accommodate 3,307 pounds of bombs—the maximum size being the 250-kilo bomb. Because of the short and rough landing fields in Spain, the bomb load rarely exceeded 2,500 pounds. It had a very primitive bomb sight and release mechanism, and the bombardier was far removed from the pilot, which made an accurate target approach difficult, although the bombardier did have limited rudder control.

For defense, the original models carried two machine guns; one gun was in the tail assembly and the other in a pod that could be lowered from the fuselage. Both guns fired to the rear with a limited field of fire. In Spain, more guns were to be added—up to five—including one in a forward turret, two waist guns, and two guns fixed, firing forward on the wings between the engines and the fuselage.

Carrying maximum fuel, its flight duration was approximately five hours at 9,500 feet with a flight radius of 310 miles. With no bombs, but added fuel tanks, the transport models could fly up to eleven hours. Both models could be flown by instruments.[21] The plane had excellent flight characteristics. But it was very awkward for a combat plane.

In early January 1937, the Legion had to divide its operation between the Madrid front and the Basque region in the north. The He-51s with their fragmentation bombs and machine guns, from Vitoria, were committed as aerial artillery against strong enemy forces attempting to open a path to Villarreal (in the province of Álava). Their attack was intercepted by enemy fighters, and one He-51 was shot down and others damaged, but the pilot of the lost plane was able to parachute into friendly territory. A few days later (4 January) one of the Ju-52 bombers was shot down over Bilbao. Flight Sergeant Adolf Hermann and his crew, Herbert Barowski, Paul Zieppe, and Hans Schüll, were killed in the crash.[22]

On the Madrid front, General Franco had appointed General Luis Orgaz as field commander, and Orgaz was determined to crush the superior forces that had stalled the assault of General Varela in December. At the same time he was determined to cut the Madrid-Coruña road. His offensive started on 3 January 1937, with German, Spanish, and Italian air support. Again, a spectacular aerial battle developed over the western outskirts of Madrid where the Ju-52 bombers were committed under protection of Fiat and He-51 flights. The Italian fighters were able, to a measure, to hold their own against the Soviet interceptors which swarmed in to break up the bomber formations, but the Germans watched two of their own fighters, with their pilots Lieutenant Hans-Peter Gallera and Warrant Officer Kurt Kneiding, shot down in flames.[23]

The mass and ferocity of the Nationalist ground and air attack shattered the defenses all along the front where three Communist brigades crumbled and the Thaelmann Battalion of the XI International Brigade was destroyed near Las Rozas. The German Legion contributed greatly to this success. But now the battlefield was enveloped with a thick fog, which made aerial operations impossible. On the ground, however, a fierce battle continued to rage in the extreme cold and zero visibility. By 9 January, General Orgaz held ten kilometers of the Coruña road (see map 4), but General Miaja, in Madrid, committed two fresh International Brigades, which had just arrived from the Granada sector, as well as additional battalions from Madrid, supported by three squadrons of heavy Soviet tanks. The counterattack, led by the tanks, smashed through Orgaz's positions west of Las Rozas, reaping a terrible toll of *banderas*, *tabores*, and equipment. But once again the Soviet armor was not properly coordinated with infantry. Orgaz now launched a vicious counterattack into the enemy mass.

Because of the dense fog, air support was impossible. All the airmen could do was to follow the bitter struggle through reports that filtered through to their headquarters. A Nationalist battalion became lost in the mist and stumbled into enemy positions and was destroyed. On the other side, a unit of the International Brigade disappeared into the fog and was never seen again.[24] Both sides, totally exhausted, dug in their positions on 16 January. The Nationalists had advanced twenty kilometers and regained ten kilometers of the Coruña road but at a very high cost. The enemy had also secured his front, and what was important was that Madrid was safe from encirclement from the north and east. The cost for the Madrid army is calculated at half again the losses of the Nationalists. The price for the Condor Legion could be measured in the loss of prestige and morale of the fighter squadrons. Besides the two planes and pilots who went down in flames, other aircraft were damaged. It was the loss of the two highly trained pilots and not counting even a single "possible victory" that became the most damaging. The Italian Fiats had realized limited success.

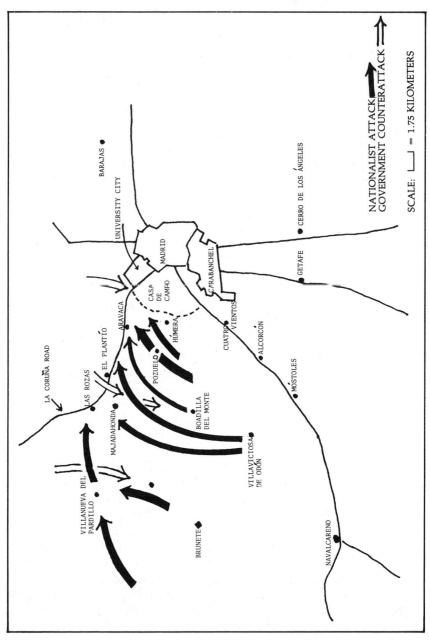

Map 4. Battle of La Coruña Road, January 1937.

NATIONALIST ATTACK
GOVERNMENT COUNTERATTACK

SCALE: ⌐⌐ = 1.75 KILOMETERS

BARAJAS

UNIVERSITY CITY

CERRO DE LOS ÁNGELES

MADRID

GETAFE

CASA DE CAMPO

C. RABANCHEL

ARAVACA

VIENTOS

EL PLANTÍO

HUMERA

CUATRO

ALCORCÓN

LA CORUÑA ROAD

LAS ROZAS

POZUELO

MÓSTOLES

MAJADAHONDA

BOADILLA DEL MONTE

VILLANUEVA DEL PARDILLO

VILLAVICIOSA DE ODÓN

BRUNETE

NAVALCARENO

The German open-cockpit biplane with its fixed landing gear, in relation to the Soviet fighters, held no comparison in speed, armament, rate of climb, and maneuverability. Its maximum speed was 205 mph. The absolute altitude was a little over 24,000 feet and the flight range was 242 miles. The two machine guns had to be charged manually after each burst of fire. Because they had no radios, the Germans had to communicate by hand signals. Furthermore, the squadrons were not receiving replacement crews, aircraft, or badly needed spare parts for damaged planes.[25]

Distressed by the impossible technical odds his men faced, Major Merhard sent a message to General Sperrle stating that he would no longer commit his planes and pilots as interceptors against the Soviet craft. The Legion commander flew to the fighter base and was met by Merhard as he climbed from the plane. It was an unpleasant scene.

> Our commander told Sperrle, to his face, that he absolutely refused to send his people into the air anymore against such an utterly hopeless situation. Furthermore, if he was directly ordered to do so, he would demand to be relieved and returned to Germany! Sperrle looked at the Major in surprise and anger, but he did not say a word. He turned his massive bulk on his heel, climbed into his plane and took off.[26]

The German pilots felt that if they could have some of the new Bf-109s, which were in an early stage of production by the Messerschmitt firm, they might have a chance against the Soviet craft. There were three very early model Bf-109s that were in the Experimental Flight of the Legion, but as in the case of the early dive-bombers, they had never been committed to combat because of material difficulties.[27]

Sperrle had taken up the fighter, as well as all the other problems, with Berlin. "Special Staff W" was fully aware that

> because of Red fighter superiority, the attempted fighter protection for the bombers ended in a "farce." The fighter squadrons could not put themselves between the bombers and the attacking enemy; in fact, the German fighters had to take refuge with the bomber formations where they hoped to seek the protection of the bombers' machine guns. They had to do this in order to fly at all.[28]

In an effort to correct this the Legion was directed to discontinue all fighter protection flights. "The fighter planes were now ordered to fly low-level attacks against enemy front lines."[29]

This change in operations required the Legion to revise completely its battle tactics for not only the fighter squadrons but for the bomber and reconnaissance squadrons as well. Very few of the fighter pilots had experience with such low-level tactics. Even pilots such as Pitcairn, who had been trained in Russia, had only flown one or two simulated missions. "We learned the low-level ground support operation in combat as 'On-the-Job-Training.'"[30] Initially, the fighter squadrons began flying single missions in the sectors near Madrid, where they hoped to avoid enemy fighters. They would bomb and strafe enemy positions and quickly flee the area. They developed hand signals for plane-to-plane communications, and panels, flares, and smoke pots for ground-to-air communications. The pilots quickly learned they had to avoid their own bomb blasts and adjust themselves to the idea of flying a few feet above the trees and brush. In addition, there was the necessary respect due the small arms and machine gun fire that could be put in the air by ground troops. Still, it was some time before the German flyers were able to readjust themselves to these tactics and to accept the new role in which they had been cast.[31]

"Special Staff W" moved to have new and better aircraft sent to Spain as soon as possible. For the Fighter Group (J/88) it was hoped to equip at least one squadron with the new, but still-to-be-proven, Bf-109s. Early in 1937, some of the Bf-109s were being reassembled and flown in Spain; however, as is generally the rule with new aircraft, they realized operational and maintenance problems.

Originally, the Messerschmitt-built Bf-109 assumed its letter designation "Bf" from the factory Bayerische Flugzeugwerke. Sometimes the early models were identified as "BFW," but after 1938, when the company was renamed Messerschmitt AG, the aircraft was known worldwide as the Me-109.

It was a single-place, low-wing monoplane of metal construction with enclosed cockpit and retractable landing gear that folded into the wings. Powered by a single liquid-cooled engine, the flight characteristics and performance varied depending on the particular engine installed and the many different models eventually to be built. The first test flight of the Bf-109 was in early September 1935. A year later the first prototype models sent to the "Experimental Flight" of the Legion were the Bf-109 V5 and V6. They were plagued with vibration and major engine-cooling problems. The production model Bf-109 B-1 was sent to Spain early in 1937. The main difference was in the aircraft power plant and a variable pitch propeller. The first production models in Spain had a maximum speed of 292 mph at sea level and a cruising speed of 236 mph. The operational ceiling was 30,000 feet. At 20,000 feet, the flight duration was one and a half hours.

In 1938, these models were replaced with the Me-109 D, which had a flight duration of two hours and a maximum speed of 323 mph. This extended the range of bomber protection. All models were equipped with air-to-air and air-to-ground radios. For armament, the first models had three machine guns synchronized through the propeller. As time went on, additional machine guns were installed in the wings, and eventually two 20mm cannons. There was a bomb-release mechanism for five small fragmentation bombs.[32] No models carried armor plating. Later versions, such as the Me-109 E, became available to the *Luftwaffe* at the start of World War II, and for many years remained the backbone of the *Luftwaffe* Fighter Arm.

It was a delicate aircraft to fly. In some aspects it could be unforgiving of pilot error. The narrow landing gear required alertness on landing, and the plane had a dangerous roll or swing on takeoff under full power. It had poor control in high-speed turns, which would throw even an alert pilot off his target. In spite of these factors, it quickly proved superior to the Soviet planes and remained a dangerous and highly respected fighter plane. When the first models arrived in Spain, as could be expected, they could not be flown in combat immediately because of the time required for transition training for the pilots of the old He-51s.

In January 1937 the original bomber squadron, consisting of the converted transports under Captain Moreau, was dissolved. Some of its planes replaced losses in the other squadrons, and the balance were turned over to the Spaniards. The personnel, along with the captain, were sent back to Germany where they were given well-earned furloughs. Later they were regrouped into an "Experimental Bomber Squadron" of three flights, equipped with He-111s, Ju-86s, and Do-17s. Here the combat experience of the veterans from Spain was put to good use.

About the same time, the crews of the short range tactical reconnaissance flight, who had been the first to arrive in Spain, were also sent back to Germany and their aircraft turned over to the Spaniards.[33] General Sperrle felt that the long hours of dangerous flying, with the resulting physical and nervous stresses, had exhausted these men and they had become dangerous to themselves.

Aerial reconnaissance is an exact science, from the accomplishment of aerial photography to the processing of raw materials and final production of the photographic mosaics or maps. This is too often not understood by operational commanders, who generally are oriented to direct tactical or strategic operations. When reconnaissance planes are not able to produce instant desired results, the combat commanders too frequently will immediately divert the armed reconnaissance planes to a direct tactical mission. From the evidence that exists, this was the case with the Condor Legion. Comments in Evaluation Rügen "Reconnaissance" are very typical of this view:

> Reconnaissance is only useful when it brings in the results which are important for the War Command. The intelligence obtained by our reconnaissance flights could not be utilized fully because of the limited force available. To directly support the ground armies, it was felt that it was no longer necessary to have the intelligence from an entire reconnaissance squadron. *It was more important to wear the enemy down through continued bombing by bomber forces.*[34]

Even though General Sperrle in his later writings did show concern for aerial reconnaissance, he repeatedly committed these aircraft directly to ground support. For this, the automatic cameras had to be removed and the camera compartment converted into a bomb bay. With this, the aircraft lost its reconnaissance capability. But by spring of 1937, the Legion learned that for their direct support of ground forces immediate intelligence was required of the target areas, and it was necessary to reestablish the He-45 flight. But only four aircraft were assigned, and they frequently were also committed as ground support aircraft.

The Heinkel-designed and built He-45 was introduced in 1933 as the first airplane specifically designed as a combat aircraft for what was to become the *Luftwaffe*. It was originally designed as a reconnaissance plane but also configured to be used as a light daylight bomber. In 1936 it was deployed as a close-range armed reconnaissance plane for the German army. It was a two-place, open cockpit, biwing plane with a fixed landing gear. It was powered by a single internal liquid-cooled engine. The metal tubular fuselage and wooden framed wings were fabric covered. It had no armor plating. Its armament consisted of a fixed machine gun fired forward by the pilot and a flexible gun in the rear operated by the observer. When cameras were removed, it could carry eighteen 10-kilo bombs. It had a mechanical bomb sight.[35]

In the early period of the Reconnaissance Squadron, its long-range aircraft was the He-70, also designed and built by Heinkel. The aircraft was designed in the amazing short time of thirty days as a commercial aircraft to compete with American-built planes for the European market. In only twenty-one weeks after design, the first "Blitz," as it was to be known, was test-flown 1 December 1932. It was put into production in 1934. For the time, it was a spectacular aircraft. The fuselage of dur-alumin was aerodynamically smooth. Further drag was eliminated by a retractable landing gear. Powered by a single engine, it carried a crew of two, four passengers, and limited cargo.

The Blitz created a sensation because of its clean lines and speed, which captured many international records at 234 mph. Its conversion to a combat military aircraft greatly reduced both its speed and altitude. There were many different models with different performance characteristics. Some were configured for the dual role of armed reconnaissance, but others lacked the reconnaissance capability. The military versions carried a crew of pilot, observer, and radio operator. The armament was two flexible machine guns, firing to the rear and down. With cameras removed, it carried either six 50-kilo or twenty-four 10-kilo bombs. The gross weight was increased to 7,630 pounds and its maximum speed at sea level dropped to 199 mph. The ceiling was 18,040 feet and the flight range 310 miles. It was the first reconnaissance plane of Germany that could be flown by instruments.

As is frequently the case in converting good civilian aircraft to a military role, its performance did not come up to expectations. It was greatly restricted for reconnaissance because of poor visibility for the observer, and the lack of speed, limited altitude, and rate of climb made it an easy target for the fighters.[36] Some of the reasons for this poor performance were: addition of camouflage paint (which became damaged in transit); wartime maintenance facilities; machine guns were always in the firing position; antennas for the air-to-ground radios were always out; and all windows and flaps were in the open position. Even minor problems would put it in the maintenance shop for days, resulting in a very low in-commission rate.

Berlin decided to replace all of the He-70s with the Do-17s. By the spring of 1937, the Reconnaissance Squadron became a multipurpose squadron with both reconnaissance and bomber aircraft in three flights. One flight was equipped with nine of the bomber versions of the Do-17s, the second flight had four Do-17s as armed reconnaissance, and the third flight flew four He-45s as short-ranged armed reconnaissance.[37] Before the conversion was complete, one He-70 was shot down by the Italians by mistake.[38] It was quickly proven, however, that the Do-17 was not able to protect itself against fighters any better than the He-70 Blitz.

Only in rare instances, even after the Fighter Group (J/88) was equipped with some of the new Bf-109 fighters, were the reconnaissance planes protected by fighters. The long-range reconnaissance planes, operating deep in enemy territory for the most part of their missions, exceeded the range of their own fighters. When attacked by enemy fighters, German aircraft would break off their missions, and "in all cases try to save themselves by flying into the clouds. If the clouds were below the mountain tops, or there were no clouds available, the planes would try to escape by going into a steep dive to gain enough speed so that the fighter would be able to make only one attack."[39] In addition, they learned to open their own machine gun fire against the enemy fighters, at extreme range, as the attack started. "The fact that the enemy would usually break off his attack at about 200 meters was a tactical error on his part and explains why, considering its technical disadvantage, the Legion still lost few reconnaissance planes."[40]

There is no doubt that the Germans were very disappointed with the performance of the Do-17s which replaced the Me-70 Blitz. Again this was a case of a commercially designed aircraft that was transformed into a military plane. In late 1933, Dornier had received a contract from *Lufthansa* for a fast mail plane that could carry six passengers to the cities throughout Europe, thus speed was considered more important than range.

Dornier produced a beautifully designed aerodynamically smooth aircraft. Its long slim fuselage and bullet-shaped nose gave it the name

"Flying Pencil." The single high wing was ingeniously designed into the air flow of the fuselage, and the wide-track landing gear, as well as the tail wheel, neatly retracted to eliminate drag. Powered by two twelve-cylinder BMW6 liquid-cooled engines (the most powerful of the time), the plane exceeded the *Lufthansa* speed specification of 200 mph. However, *Lufthansa* rejected the design because of the restricted space of the slim fuselage.[41]

The Reich Air Ministry was of the opinion that with some modifications, which cannot be considered minor, the Do-17 could be converted to a light, fast bomber. After several prototypes, late in 1935, one model (in speed trials) performed at 243 mph at sea level, and the "Flying Pencil" was ordered into production. As in the case of most aircraft, many models were to be produced with varying equipment, performance, and flight characteristics. The Do-17 models E, F, Fl, and P were to see service in Spain. They carried a crew of pilot, observer, and radio operator. The armament was one machine gun fired forward, one downward, and a third to the rear. There was no protecting armament. All models were equipped for instrument flight and carried air-to-ground communications.

The reconnaissance model "Flying Pencil" carried 210mm and 500mm cameras. The bomber versions of the same aircraft varied in capacity, depending on the model. The maximum speed of the E and F models was 220 mph. The Do-17 P model was powered by two BMW(132N) nine-cylinder reciprocating engines that developed 1,000 horsepower on take-off. These engines were equipped with superchargers and variable pitch propellers. This gave the model P a maximum speed of 249 mph. The service ceiling of the E model was 16,730 feet, but the P model increased to 20,340.[42]

Again, as in the case of the He-70, unexpected maintenance problems developed because of the conditions in Spain. Grounded aircraft sitting for several days in muddy, wet, and icy parking areas required a noticeable amount of maintenance hours to make the aircraft combat ready.

At this time, the Air Ministry concluded it must do something about the inadequacy of the Ju-52 bombers. There was no aircraft in Germany that could be designed to replace them except the very new He-111s, which were hardly coming off the assembly lines. Where the early bomber planes of the *Luftwaffe* were modified civilian transports, the He-111 was designed by Ernst Heinkel specifically as a bomber, but also at the same time a commercial transport model. It was built on the pattern employed in the development of the He-70 Blitz and frequently is known as the He-70's big brother.[43] It was much larger and was powered by two engines. The transport model carried ten passengers, four forward and six aft, who were separated by a "smoking compartment," which in reality was a bomb bay.[44] The first test flight was 24 February 1935, where it produced a speed of 217 mph, and its flight characteristics were judged to be superior to its little brother, the Blitz.[45]

The first ten military models built were rejected because the military equipment increased the gross weight of the aircraft to the degree that it could not come up to the desired specifications. With some design changes and the installation of more powerful engines, the test model of the He-111 bomber was ordered into production. This was the first modern bomber of the *Luftwaffe*, and its speed was such it was mistakenly thought it would be immune to fighter interception; thus no armor plating was installed.

The first thirty He-111s (Model B-1) began arriving in Spain in February 1937. They had to be reassembled, test-flown, and then turned over to the Ju-52 crews for transition flying. But it would be the first week in March before they would begin to replace the old tri-motor plane and to fly their first combat mission, which was a bomber strike against the airfields of Alcalá de Henares and Barajas.

There were several different models used in Spain before the end of the Spanish conflict. Each model varied in its flight characteristics and performance according to the modifications made and the installed power plants. They all carried a crew of pilot, bombardier, radio operator, and tail machine-gunner. For defense they had three flexible machine guns. One fired forward, one to the rear and upward, and the third downward and to the rear. The maximum speed of the He-111 B at sea level was 186 mph; at 13,000 feet its maximum speed was 230 mph, and the cruise speed was 214 mph at this altitude with a flight range of 276 miles.[46] The operational ceiling was 23,000 feet, and the maximum bomb load (which was rarely used because of runway conditions) was 3,307 pounds.[47]

When this aircraft joined the first squadron in the Condor Legion, Bomb Group K/88, in the early spring of 1937, and the Bf-109s were to be seen in one of the fighter squadrons, it was obvious that the entire air war of the Spanish conflict would witness a rapid change. Where the Me-109 was to perform a major role in the *Luftwaffe* Fighter Arm for much of World War II, the He-111 was to become the mainstay of the *Luftwaffe* Bomber Force (with a great many modifications) throughout the war.

Before the year 1936 ended, the Germans of the Legion recognized that not only would they have to improve greatly the quality of their aircraft but they would have to undertake a general reorganization of the entire Legion and their operational procedures, from the General Staff through all tactical and support forces. There were far too many things encountered which had never been thought of, or dreamed of, in Berlin. Many things came not only as a surprise, but as a complete shock to the Germans.

Hardly had the Legion passed the middle of December when it was recognized that they had not only underestimated the combat deficiency of their battle forces but also the maintenance, replacement parts, and facilities that would be required to maintain a respectable number of their aircraft suitable for flying. The rapidly shifting battle fronts placed a great strain on the Legion's transportation. The Germans themselves aggravated this problem by sending many different types and models (over 100) of vehicles. Maintenance became a major problem.

The steep, narrow, winding roads through the mountains quickly took their toll of German transports. The hard-surfaced roads were so narrow that if a truck was crowded off the surface, it would become mired in thick, sticky mud. Rapidly the number of men killed and injured in accidents became a command nightmare.[48] They found that some engines lacked the power to drive from Seville to Cáceres; many trucks that did climb the steep roads moved slower than a person walking. Engines burned out, generators exploded, and gear chains shattered. Soon transports were scattered from Seville to Vitoria awaiting replacement parts and major overhaul.[49] "The movement of a complete squadron at the same time was impossible with the number of vehicles available. Up to fifty percent of the trucks fell out because of the shortage of replacement parts, due to the great number of types and models involved."[50]

In an attempt to solve the replacement parts problem for the many types of ground vehicles, a train was organized which operated as a mobile resupply depot. Replacement parts were carefully identified by type and model and stored in specially designed shelves and bins in boxcars. The train would move from one organization or centralized location to another where vehicles could be gathered for maintenance. The Legion attempted to help resolve the issue by assigning the same types and models of equipment to specific units, but with the many different types involved this was never fully successful. The lack of standardization remained a problem through the entire war and into World War II.[51]

One bright side was the quickly proven capability of the German heavy 88mm antiaircraft guns. They also proved their devastating effectiveness as field artillery against fortified positions and as antitank cannons. Their rapid deployment from one sector to another, as well as shifting the batteries' fire during battle, gave confidence in their vehicles which exceeded what had been expected in Germany. The battery moved by mules did not do as well.[52]

The reorganization of the flight elements of the battle squadrons and their ground support personnel was very important, not only for what was accomplished in Spain, but for its great impact on the future, because the accepted organization developed there became standard for the *Luftwaffe*. In addition, many of the operational procedures adopted became the battle tactics and formations used by Germany through most of World War II.

A great burden was imposed upon the Communications Group with the dispersal of its sections to the Command Staff, Spanish Headquarters, Italian Command Staff, Legion maintenance facilities, and weather reporting stations, and the constant movement of the battle command posts and combat units. Its problems were added to by the deteriorated condition of the Spanish communications system and desperate lack of communications personnel in the Nationalist forces. The Legion Communications Group realized several reorganizations to meet the changing requirements and established an intense training program for its personnel.

Sperrle and von Richthofen not only remodeled all of the units of the Condor Legion but their General Staff as well. It was expanded to work with the problems of liaison with the Spaniards and Italians and their own combat and support units. At the same time there was a reevaluation, which resulted in major modifications of their operational procedures, aerial tactics, and ground support functions. This did not happen immediately but was a step-by-step change. Importantly, again, much of what they adopted under the stress of combat became standard procedures for the *Luftwaffe*.

Since it was obvious that the Spanish conflict was going to be long and bitter, "Special Staff W" was working not only on trying to improve the combat aircraft but also on solving the problems of logistics. Other than for the most basic items, such as food, their men in Spain had to be supported by everything from munitions to fuels and lubricants. All had to be shipped 1,200 miles by sea. There were four air transports that weekly flew between Berlin and Spain, but they could carry only a few key personnel. Most of the space was for small but very critical parts, official dispatches, inspection personnel, and the mail addressed to the post office box of Max Winkler in Berlin.

After the original shipment of the Legion from the Stettin area, the Special Staff moved the shipping operation back to the facilities first used in the port of Hamburg. The selected replacement personnel, usually in groups of 300 to 500 of all specialties, from pilots to service, communications, medical, clerks, and cooks, were drawn from existing units. Supposedly well trained, they were assembled at a *Luftwaffe* facility near Gatow, not far from Berlin. In the case of these men the story is different than it was in the early months. Many of these men were true "volunteers" who had learned of the operation in Spain and, for whatever their personal reasons, wanted to be a part of it. As before, others were "selected to volunteer."[53]

At Gatow they were issued civilian clothing, given the Max Winkler post office box number S.W. 68, and advised of what was expected of them. During the night they moved by bus to Hamburg. Still in the dark hours, they boarded launches and were taken to a ship anchored in a remote part of the harbor. The ship would already be loaded with weapons, munitions, and supplies. All troops were quartered below decks, and the hatches were carefully closed. The ship would then up anchor and slip from the harbor. "During the entire voyage no one was allowed on deck as long as there was even a remote chance that a passing vessel might come close enough to get a good look."[54]

Efforts were made to change the visible identity of the ships after they passed Dover. This would be done by painting an additional ring around the smoke stack, adding a fake smoke stack, changing the name of the ship, or then completely repainting the vessel.[55]

Following these procedures, the fighter pilot (then a lieutenant), Adolf Galland, boarded his ship "a rotten old tub of 3,000 tons, [which] was more like a slave trader and flew the Panama flag."[56] This ship earlier had been used to ship Soviet arms into Spain but had been seized by the Nationalists. Galland describes the deplorable, primitive conditions of the ship which were demoralizing to the troops. Finally the ship's captain appointed him to maintain order which he notes as "by no means a pleasant task."[57] On his ship, as on others, it was exceptionally unpleasant when all passengers were confined below deck. This was aggravated by a reduction of fresh water and food. Galland comments that their morale deteriorated to the degree that "there was a danger of open mutiny."[58] This he suppressed with harsh measures even though his personal sympathy lay with his countrymen. The voyage was one of indescribable chaos, particularly after they were struck by gales in the Bay of Biscay. The severity of the storm was such that they were surprised to see "the old tub" was able to emerge from the deep sea troughs. Most of the troops became violently seasick but could not lie on their bunks because they had crashed down during the storm.[59]

Finally they dropped anchor, on 8 May 1937, at the port El Ferrol on the tip of Galicia. Once on Spanish soil they were promoted one grade; Galland became a captain, and most men probably felt they deserved the promotion for merely surviving the journey.

It was standard procedure for the resupply ships to be intercepted and escorted by a Nationalist warship once they approached the Spanish coast. They would, generally, move into the harbor of El Ferrol at night. At the far end of the bay was the arsenal which was hidden by the terrain. Not far away would be a troop train waiting to transport the troops, in their ill-fitting civilian clothing—but still wearing their military boots—to the Legion's main facility established now at León. Here they would be issued Legion uniforms and dispersed to their respective units.[60]

During the early weeks of 1937, as the Legion was being reorganized and reequipped, there was a decided curtailment in its combat operations. In part, this was due to the superiority of the enemy aircraft but also to the difficult weather conditions. The ground operations slowed to a degree, but still the combatants traded sanguinary blows with each other.

Notes

1. *GD*, Series D, Vol. III, Doc. No. 148. In his message to Berlin of 10 December 1936, Faupel stated that Franco had asked for one German and one Italian division to be sent to Spain. One really must question the accuracy of

Faupel's report in the face of Franco's continued opposition to having either German or Italian ground forces fighting in his country. When asked about this by the writer, General Warlimont stated that he could not believe it. The most detailed study of the Italian involvement in Spain is the very fine work by John F. Coverdale, *Italian Intervention in the Spanish Civil War* (Princeton, N.J., 1975).

2. *GD*, Series D, Vol. III, Doc. No. 129, Mussolini's comment to the German ambassador.

3. Ibid., Doc. No. 130.

4. Ibid., Doc. No. 145.

5. Coverdale, *Italian Intervention*, p. 167.

6. Ibid., p. 168.

7. Ibid., pp. 171-175.

8. General Karl Drum, "The German Luftwaffe in the Spanish Civil War (Condor Legion)," p. 59.

9. R. Hidalgo Salazar, *La ayuda alemana a España 1936-39*, p. 126, and comments of Colonel Pitcairn.

10. Letter from Colonel Pitcairn, 25 March 1975, in which he sketched the *Wohnzug* as he remembered it.

11. Freiburg, Evaluation Rügen, RL 7/57a, p. 28, hereafter cited as Freiburg, Evaluation Rügen.

12. Freiburg, Evaluation Rügen, "Reconnaissance," RL 7/57a, p. 8, hereafter cited as Freiburg, Evaluation Rügen, "Reconnaissance."

13. Ibid.

14. Pitcairn's comments to the writer.

15. Freiburg, Evaluation Rügen, p. 25.

16. Ibid., p. 37.

17. Ibid., p. 28.

18. Ibid., p. 25.

19. Ibid., pp. 37-38.

20. Ibid., p. 25. The location of the airfield is not given.

21. Drum, "The German Luftwaffe," pp. 24-26. The data were reduced from the "Table of Performance Characteristics of German Military Aircraft," 1 December 1938 (Karlsruhe Document Collection).

22. Salazar, *La ayuda alemana*, p. 132 and Appendix 1.

23. Ibid., p. 133 and Appendix 1.

24. Robert G. Colodny, *The Struggle for Madrid* (New York, 1958), p. 105.

25. Comments to the writer by Colonel Pitcairn and Lt. General Galland. Also see General Adolf Galland, *The First and the Last* (London, 1955), pp. 28-30, and Drum, "The German Luftwaffe," pp. 28-29.

26. Pitcairn's comment to the writer. He could not recall the exact date.

27. Freiburg, Evaluation Rügen, p. 10.

28. Ibid., p. 33.

29. Ibid.

30. Pitcairn's comment to the writer.

31. Freiburg, Evaluation Rügen, p. 33.

32. Tony Wood and Bill Gunston, *Hitler's Luftwaffe*, 3d ed. (New York, 1979), pp. 219-223; Salvador Rello, *La aviación en la guerra de España* (Madrid, 1969), pp. 62-68; and Drum, "The German Luftwaffe," pp. 30-31.

33. Freiburg, Evaluation Rügen, p. 10.

34. Freiburg, Evaluation Rügen, "Reconnaissance," p. 2. Italics added.

35. Drum, "The German Luftwaffe," pp. 32-33; Wood and Gunston, *Hitler's Luftwaffe*, p. 175; and Rello, *La aviación en la guerra*, pp. 17-20.

36. Freiburg, Evaluation Rügen, pp. 16-17; Herbert Molloy Mason, Jr., *The Rise of the Luftwaffe* (New York, 1975), pp. 175-176; Wood and Gunston, *Hitler's Luftwaffe*, p. 178; Rello, *La aviación en la guerra*, pp. 31-34; and Drum, "The German Luftwaffe," pp. 33-35.

37. Freiburg, Evaluation Rügen, "Reconnaissance," p. 3, Sperrle's Memorandum signed in rough draft.

38. Ibid., p. 3.

39. Ibid., p. 10.

40. Ibid.

41. Mason, *The Rise of the Luftwaffe*, pp. 188-189.

42. Drum, "The German Luftwaffe," p. 35; Rello, *La aviación en la guerra*, pp. 11-13; and Wood and Gunston, *Hitler's Luftwaffe*, pp. 144-145. There are slight differences in the specific data given.

43. Wood and Gunston, *Hitler's Luftwaffe*, p. 180.

44. Mason, *The Rise of the Luftwaffe*, p. 191.

45. Ibid.

46. Drum, "The German Luftwaffe," pp. 26-27.

47. Ibid. Rello *La aviación en la guerra*, pp. 34-38, gives the different models and their performance. Also see Wood and Gunston, *Hitler's Luftwaffe*, pp. 180-184.

48. Colonel Pitcairn states that, in part, the great number of accidents occurred because the majority of his fellow soldiers were very young and did not know how to drive very well and that the road conditions added to the problem.

49. Freiburg, Ln/88 *War Diary* has a detailed account of some of these problems.

50. Freiburg, Evaluation Rügen, "Movement of Combat Forces," p. 5.

51. Drum, "The German Luftwaffe," pp. 49-50.

52. Freiburg, Evaluation Rügen, pp. 41-42.

53. Comments to the writer by General Plocher and Lt. General Martin Harlinghausen who, as a major, was the second commander of the Legion Seaplane Squadron, AS/88.

54. Drum, "The German Luftwaffe," p. 47.

55. Ibid., pp.47-47a.

56. Lt. General Galland's comments to the writer, and Galland, *The First and the Last*, p. 24.

57. Ibid. Galland's added comment to the writer: "It was decidedly unpleasant."

58. Ibid., pp. 24-25.

59. Ibid., p. 25.

60. Drum, "The German Luftwaffe," p. 48.

8

Málaga, Jarama, and Guadalajara

In early January 1937, the bomber force of the Condor Legion, in squadron strength, struck at the port facilities of Málaga and the rail connections to Granada. Against their better judgment they also committed daylight flights in direct support of ground operations near Madrid. Some squadrons operating from Salamanca also bombed enemy concentrations at Bilbao. It was on one of these missions that Flight Sergeant Adolf Hermann and his crew were shot down. Another bomber had an engine shot out over Madrid but managed to crash-land in friendly territory near Mérida, and the crew was rescued. From 8 through 15 January, there were heavy air raids directed against Alcalá de Henares and the roads leading to Madrid. Ground fires were used in an attempt to direct aircraft to the targets, but they were hardly successful. Using cross references and operating under radio control by the ground communications section, most flights were able to find their target.[1]

Because of the continual bad weather, recovery fields were readied in southern Spain to accommodate aircraft that were unable to return to their original station. At times, complete squadrons had to be recovered in this manner. One bomber made a bad approach to the airfield of San Fernando (near Salamanca) where it landed short, crashing through tents and destroying reserve transmitters. This was but one of the many problems that plagued the Communications Group Ln/88.

The communications lines were repeatedly cut by saboteurs operating in friendly territory. Lines were tapped by enemy agents to the degree that Captain Roskothen and a special detail were assigned to correct the problem and establish security measures. Other lines were continually shorted out, particularly telegraph lines, by the heavy rains. The Communications Group had to move several of its Air Watch stations, which were situated near the front, because they had been located by the enemy and had come under heavy air attacks. Vehicle accidents, some of which were the result of sheer carelessness, continued to put men in the hospitals. For example, two enlisted men took a vehicle for a joyride and stopped at several bars where they had more than one drink. Returning to the station, the driver lost control and crashed. The car then burst into flames and burned the other man to death. The driver of the vehicle was court-martialled for manslaughter.

Many of the Communications men were sent back to Germany very early, some because of family problems and others for health reasons. The latter ranged from nervous breakdowns to ulcers. But it was the ever-increasing vehicle accidents that took the heaviest toll of personnel. Men were scattered in field hospitals with broken arms, legs, shoulders, collarbones, and brain concussions.

Bad weather grounded all combat aircraft after 15 January. Between 23 and 31 January there was a series of heavy storms which caused a loss of all the land communications systems. Having only one uniform and being continually wet, the troops began to suffer from flu and pneumonia. The weather made the airfield near Salamanca unusable, and the Ju-52s were temporarily moved to Burgos. Still no combat missions could be flown because of the storms, and most aircraft were grounded until 10 February. A courier aircraft attempted to brave the weather on 4 February but crashed in the Béjar mountains. The German search crew under Herr Munz did not locate the wreckage until 18 February. The crew was dead.[2]

With the bad weather hampering military operations on the Madrid front, both sides now strengthened and realigned their ground forces. The Nationalists, with their left flank straightened and secured on the Coruña road, began to regroup their forces for an attempt to encircle the city from the south. Their cause in Andalusia now realized a notable success. General Queipo de Llano and his so-called South Army were reinforced by the motorized units of the Italian Corpo Truppe Volontarie (C.T.V.) under General Mario Roatta.[3]

Italy very much wanted to have a safe port on the Mediterranean so its ships would not have to risk the narrows of the Straits of Gibraltar to reach the Nationalist-controlled ports on the Atlantic. The port of Málaga, with its fine harbor, located at the base of the Sierra Nevada, was the obvious choice. The defenders had the advantage of the terrain, control of the mountain passes, and heights which could easily have been fortified and would have been most costly to carry in a frontal assault.

There were to be five main thrusts of the Nationalist forces. The Spaniards under Colonel Borbón (Duke of Seville) were to attack from Ronda to the coast and up the coastline under protective fire from Nationalist warships through Estepona and Marbella. The Italians numbered between 6,000 and 10,000 and were divided into three assault columns.[4] They were to drive south through the mountains from Anteguera, Loja, and Alhama.

A Condor Legion liaison officer was assigned to the Italian Staff, and a reconnaissance plane with its crew was attached for the use of General Roatta. The Legion also provided a 100-watt transmitter and crew for the German officer to maintain instant communications with General Sperrle and the Spanish Command Staff in Salamanca. Another Legion transmitter and receiving section were sent to Granada to provide ground-to-air communications with the reconnaissance plane. One section was to support the advance. These were the only Germans committed to the Málaga operation.

The Duke of Seville started his offensive on 3 February and initially met strong resistance, which began to crumble under naval fire. The Italians started their attack early 5 February. By the following day, the defending forces were fleeing up the coastal road which had been left open deliberately. The Spaniards and Italians joined columns on 7 February, entered Málaga, and continued to press the enemy up the coast to Motril. The total Nationalist advance was over 160 kilometers, and a Mediterranean port was now accessible to friendly shipping. The Italian fighter planes, in the process, largely eliminated André Malraux's French squadron that flew for the Valencia command.

As noted, German aircraft and crews of the Condor Legion took no active part in this operation, but it was with interest that the German staff watched the use of the Italian mobile forces. For the Italians, the ease of the victory was mistakenly viewed as proof of the superior quality of their troops, equipment, and tactics. In not too many weeks to come, their confidence would be mired in the mud of Castile.

The Nationalists now pushed their planning to encircle Madrid in the east. This was to be accomplished by two forces which were supposed to converge in the vicinity of Alcalá de Henares, some thirty kilometers east of Madrid on the Saragossa road. One force was built on a line due south of Madrid from Cerro de los Ángeles to Seseña (about a twenty-five-kilometer front). It was to drive due east over the Río Jarama to Arganda and Valdilecha. Its left flank was to attack over Loeches to Villalbilla and Alcalá de Henares. This attack, if successful, would sever the important Valencia-Madrid road, cut off the Popular Front government which had fled to Valencia the first week of November 1936, and bring about the surrender of the forces in Madrid.

At the same time, elements of General Mola's Army North were to attack southward from the cathedral city of Sigüenza over Brihuega,

Torija, and Guadalajara to make the juncture with the Army of Africa
that had crossed the Jarama. The Army North, however, was far too
weak for such an ambitious operation, with its forces strung out on a
front hundreds of kilometers wide through Aragón and the northern
provinces. To make up for this deficiency, the General Staff initially
wanted to make use of the unasked-for Italian C.T.V. units that had been
committed to the Málaga operation and the other Italian units being
assembled in southern Spain. According to German documents, the offensive was planned for the first week in March, but the timing for the
two operations was completely off.

One factor which should be recognized relative to the planned pincers
movement is that the operation would very likely have been denied major
air support. Madrid, with its Soviet aircraft, controlled the air space, and
the German Legion could not be considered an effective force with its
antiquated equipment; at the same time it was in the throes of reor-
ganizing its forces on hand. Importantly, the mass of the Nationalist and
Allied aircraft were deployed to the north and west slopes of the Gredos
and Guadarrama mountains. With the prevailing winter weather conditions the icing problem alone could deny access to the attack sector. Planes
deployed on the upper Río Ebro flew off of grass fields which were in-
operable in wet weather. On the other hand, the enemy had the hard-
surfaced airfields near Madrid. Still, in the face of these problems and
with limited reserves, the planning for the offensive proceeded.

The Nationalist commander was General Orgaz and his field army was
divided, with General Varela (who had recovered from his wounds) commanding three brigades, and Colonel García Escámez y Iniesta commanding two brigades. *Banderas* of the Legion and *tabores* of Moroccans
were distributed throughout the regiments of the brigades. Included in
the assault were 45 German light tanks, 15 horse cavalry squadrons, and
101 pieces of artillery. A battery of the Condor Legion heavy 88mm guns
was assigned to one brigade.[5] The assault force numbered 18,000 men
with 4,000 in reserve.

Ironically, the enemy forces were being deployed for an offensive into
the same sector. The Madrid force of fifteen Mixed Brigades greatly
outnumbered the Nationalists, and they could count on an armored brigade of 120 heavy Soviet tanks and two score of armored cars.[6]

Orgaz repeatedly set back the date of his assault because of heavy
rains. Finally, by 5 February (during the early phase of the Málaga
operation), the rains stopped and the fields had dried enough to order
the assault battalions to initiate the first phase of the offensive. From
aerial reconnaissance each side realized that the other was poised for an
attack. But bad weather on the other side of the mountains kept the main
bomber force of the Legion on the ground. Still, the front ruptured under
heavy artillery fire which was measurably added to by the devastating

barrages from the battery of the Condor Legion 88mm guns.[7] It was not until 10 February that the weather permitted mass deployment of the Legion combat force, with the bombers striking Villarejo de Salvanés and the area of Alcalá de Henares-Guadalajara. This was followed by daily bombings of the roads leading from Madrid to the battle zone. Their efforts did not go uncontested because the bomber formations, at times, would be broken up by the enemy fighters.[8]

With the first onslaught, some of the Madrid fine brigades and battalions were demolished. Madrid now frantically pulled in additional battalions from the city, disengaged brigades from other sectors, and committed fifty heavy tanks in a massive counterblow. Some were able to break through the Nationalist lead brigades, taking a heavy toll of infantry and cavalry squadrons. Eventually they were contained and forced to withdraw by heavy artillery fire and concentrated bombing from German aircraft. Several tanks were captured, along with a large number of prisoners, and the offensive continued.

It was a terrible battle that developed along the banks of the Jarama (see map 5) with hundreds and thousands of men on both sides falling. The story was one of wild attacks into concentrated and determined defenses with defenders dying to the last man. Then counterattacks, first by one side and then the other. Grenades, knives, and bayonets (as well as artillery and machine guns) were the order of the day as Spaniards, Legionaries, and Moroccans locked in gory hand-to-hand combat with other Spaniards and the men of the International Brigades, representing dozens of countries and speaking as many languages. There were spectacular cavalry charges of screaming Moroccan horsemen with great gaps cut in their ranks by raking fire from French machine guns of the International Brigades. Still, the cavalry charged across the plains and up the slopes to ravage the infantry in position after position. ⟵

The Nationalists established bridgeheads across the swollen Jarama and carried heights which were quickly turned into artillery platforms from which they decimated enemy battalions thrown into counterattack after counterattack. At times the river crossings would be brought under enemy machine gun fire which took a terrible toll of the *banderas* and *tabores*. General Varela repeatedly called for air support to break up the mass concentration of armor and troops, but the Soviet fighters controlled the air space and made it very difficult for the Nationalist bomber forces to respond. On 12 February, the German Ju-52 squadrons were scattered by forty Soviet fighter planes. A communications Air Watch section on the front did see one enemy fighter shot down.[9] Two days later the Ju-52s, protected by He-51 fighters, attempted to bomb enemy concentrations at Arganda but again had to break off their attack because of the ferocity of the Soviet fighter interception.[10] The Legion, however, continued to respond to the requests of hard-pressed Nationalist ground

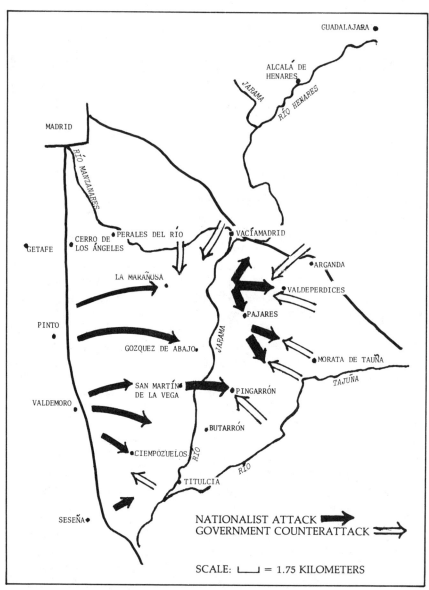

GUADALAJARA •

ALCALÁ DE
HENARES •

JARAMA

RÍO HENARES

MADRID

RÍO MANZANARES

• GETAFE

CERRO DE
LOS ÁNGELES •

• PERALES DEL RÍO

VACÍAMADRID •

• ARGANDA

LA MARAÑOSA •

• VALDEPERDICES

PINTO •

GOZQUEZ DE ABAJO •

• PAJARES

JARAMA

• MORATA DE TAUÑA

TAJUÑA

SAN MARTÍN •
DE LA VEGA

• PINGARRÓN

VALDEMORO •

• BUTARRÓN

RÍO

• CIEMPOZUELOS

RÍO

• TITULCIA

SESEÑA •

NATIONALIST ATTACK ➡
GOVERNMENT COUNTERATTACK ⇒

SCALE: ⊔ = 1.75 KILOMETERS

Map 5. Battle of the Jarama, 6-25 February 1937.

commanders. Daily flights of bombers, in squadron strength, struck at the roads leading from Madrid. One squadron flew out of the facility at Matachana.[11] By 16 February the Nationalist ground offensive was over. They had made a sizeable breakthrough, had crossed the Río Jarama and brought the Madrid/Valencia road under artillery fire, but they were many kilometers from their objective of Alcalá de Henares. The remnants of their forty battalions and fifteen cavalry squadrons in the sector now faced seventy-four enemy battalions, still supported by most of an armored brigade. The Nationalists dug in defensive positions and repulsed repeated enemy attacks until 24 February, when Madrid finally gave up the effort to dislodge them from their salient. Through the entire period the Condor Legion, as well as other Nationalist aircraft, struck at the communications leading from Madrid to the battle front to relieve the pressure. On 19 February, however, in early dawn the Legion struck, with twenty-four bombers, the enemy base of supply at Albacete. A smaller force repeated the attack the following day, but the mass of aircraft was again directed east of Madrid. The weather now again began to hamper operations, even with snow at Salamanca. In one of the few strategic missions to be flown during this period, fifteen bombers were staged out of Saragossa in a night bombing of the chemical plant located at Flix (Tarragona).[12] In the months to come there was to develop a bitter contest in this area.

The Battle of the Jarama was costly for both sides. The estimates of the losses vary, but it can be calculated that the Nationalists lost some 6,000 and Madrid, 10,000.[13] Little was accomplished. It was a stalemate similar to the battle that developed along the Coruña road. As near as this writer can determine, several of the German aircraft suffered damage, but the only loss was Lieutenant Paul Rehahn, who died in the crash of his fighter plane at Cáceres on 11 February.[14]

While the Army of Africa was locked in a desperate battle in the Jarama sector, the Italians were being disengaged from Málaga for the long trip to northern Spain. By now the Italian force could be considered an expeditionary army of 50,000, and at the *Duce*'s insistence was to make rapid attacks on the important objectives. General Roatta had returned to Rome to have his wound treated, and on 12 February his chief of staff, Colonel Emilio Faldella, arrived at the Nationalist headquarters in Salamanca. At that time the Nationalists still felt that they would be able to obtain their objectives across the Río Jarama.[15]

The Italian officer told Colonel Barroso (General Franco's chief of operations) that the Italians proposed an Italian offensive against Sagunto and Valencia on the coast. He was abruptly informed that General Franco would not permit the Italians to carry out an attack against the seat of his enemy's government. Colonel Faldella then made a modification in the Italian proposal for consideration of an offensive from Sigüenza toward Guadalajara, which could begin the end of February.[16] When Faldella finally met with Franco, he received a severe dressing-down from the Spanish general who viewed the Italian proposals as an imposition. He pointed out that Italian forces were in Spain without his permission and had grown to a force he had not conceived. Now he was being told this force was to fight under Roatta's orders and in a manner contrary to his own ideas.[17]

When Faldella pressed the issue for a rapid defeat of the enemy, Franco stood by the position he had frequently expressed, much to their agitation, to the German commanders. He viewed a civil war far differently from an international conflict. He wanted to make his advances methodically so he could guarantee the political security of conquered regions. For political reasons he was determined that Valencia would be captured by Spanish Nationalist troops, but he might consider using the C.T.V. for the attack on Guadalajara. This was within the framework of his general battle plan of the moment.

As his Nationalists' position continued to disintegrate along the Jarama, Franco made the decision to ask that the Italians act immediately to relieve the pressure. By now, 19 February, some eighteen Italian battalions were assembled along the Río Duero, but the Italians' stand was that they were not completely organized and could not be committed.[18] The relations between General Franco and the Italian command deteriorated to one of hostile cooperation. But Franco agreed to reinitiate the Jarama offensive to coincide with an Italian attack from Sigüenza. It is possible, however, that at the time he did not realize how badly his Jarama brigades had been mauled.

In the late days of February, events in the North interrupted the Nationalist plans even further. General Aranda, in Oviedo, had been reinforced by *banderas* and *tabores* in the fall of 1936, but the city was still being assaulted by superior forces of well-armed Asturian miners. At this time, the defending force came under a powerful and desperate attack. To reverse a dangerous situation, General Franco ordered Spanish troops assembled near Sigüenza to move immediately by truck to Asturias. Throwing their weight into the enemy flank and with determined counterattacks from the Oviedo garrison, the Asturians were pushed back to their original position after a bitter struggle. The relief force then moved back to its assembly position. This could be considered a side issue except it required delaying the offensive to Guadalajara for a week, and (as fate would have it) this week ushered in a period of severely bad weather which had a major impact on the pending operation.[19]

It was not until early March that the assault forces to be used against Madrid were finally assembled. The Italian right flank was covered by the Spanish Division Soria, reinforced with *banderas* and *tabores*, under General Moscardó (the hero of the Alcázar), now promoted to general.

General Roatta advised Franco that he would initiate the attack on 8 March. In his reply, General Franco warned the Italians of the condition of his troops on the Jarama.[20]

The C.T.V. now consisted of the three Black Shirt Divisions with 6,300 men per division, and the Littorio Division with 7,700. The Italian Corps had adequate artillery which was moved by trucks and tractors, but the infantry was not as motorized as is frequently thought. There were eighty-one light whippet tanks armed only with machine guns.[21] The Italian air squadron was under Roatta's control.

The combined Spanish/Italian attack force was 50,000. This was the largest force committed against Madrid until this time. They were, however, deficient in communications, and General Sperrle—in the Condor Legion headquarters—was asked to support the effort with signal sections from his Communications Group Ln/88.

General Sperrle responded and ordered Lieutenant Arend to create a special communications detail to support the entire operation. German liaison officers were also ordered to the C.T.V. headquarters and all Italian or Spanish divisions.[22] Arend assembled a force in Salamanca of eighty-three officers and men with several radio and wire sections. They were to be reinforced on the front by additional signal sections from Palencia and Saragossa. They joined the Italian headquarters at Arcos de Jalón on the Madrid-Saragossa highway not far to the east of Medinaceli.

Arend received his orders to install his communications net, but the details were left to his judgment. He was surprised to be ordered, unless informed otherwise, that he was to transmit all messages in clear text rather than code. Also, he was ordered to write all their messages with the Latin "E" rather than the German "E." Concerned about breaches of security, he instructed all his sections to send messages in code unless they were transmitted by an Italian.

Lieutenant Arend then established signal sections with each Italian assault and reserve division at Torremocha del Campo and Sigüenza; all were connected to the C.T.V. headquarters at Arcos de Jalón. Also, connections were made with the Condor Legion and the Italian mission in Salamanca. Then he established direct contact with the Italian air squadrons operating from Saragossa.

The C.T.V. ordered all troops to be in position by 5:00 p.m. on 7 March and the offensive to start at 6:30 the next morning (see map 6).[23] Schubert (now promoted to lieutenant colonel), as commander of the German Communications Group, arrived at the front the evening of 7 March and found all of his signal sections well positioned and working. The night turned very cold, giving an indication of things to come. Before the artillery preparations started, the rains, mixed with sleet and snow, began. Still, General Roatta ordered the infantry to advance despite the bad weather and the fact that he was denied air cover from his air arms because their improvised airfields were a mire of mud. On the other hand, the enemy, operating from Madrid, was at a lower altitude where the airstrips were hard-surfaced.

General Sperrle, in his Ju-52, landed at Almazán midmorning and visited the front. Sperrle was satisfied with the efforts of his Legion signalmen, but Arend made no notation in his record of remarks by the general relative to his views of the entire operation. Before leaving the front (3:00 p.m.), Sperrle ordered Arend to transmit a message to his headquarters in Salamanca: "Departing 1800 hours from Almazán. Turn on the night guiding lights at Salamanca! (Signed) Sander." However, when the general arrived at Almazán, he found his aircraft covered with ice. With flight impossible, he set out on the long, dangerous drive to Salamanca in the dark. When he did not arrive in Salamanca at the expected time, the Legion and Spanish commands had a near panic. Lieutenant Arend noted in his diary: "Therefore, during the evening there were a great many radio messages between Arcos and Salamanca."

The general advance was from four to eight miles in disagreeable weather. The enemy front was not completely shattered, but it had been well dented. The important element of surprise had been lost and the enemy, using his interlines of communications, dispatched reserve brigades from Madrid to the threatened sector and, at the same time, disengaged brigades facing the fronts about Madrid. That night Roatta asked Franco to order General Orgaz to commit his forces on the Jarama. But the latter did not move. Some observers believe that a little more determination by the Italians would have opened the front all the way to Guadalajara.[24]

The weather did not improve on 9 March, but the offensive resumed. The Condor Legion had begun receiving its new He-111 bombers in February, and these were quickly being transitioned into the Bomber Group. At this time, several flights were able to penetrate the weather and strike the enemy airfields at Alcalá de Henares. German crews were also phasing in the new Do-17 reconnaissance/bomber and bombed the enemy positions near Aranjuez.[25] Meanwhile, Colonel Schubert and Lieutenant Arend, with their signal sections, advanced with the lead elements of the Italian divisions. The enemy-deployed forces were in full retreat. The Italian officers were confident that they were on the way to victory, and their chiding of the Spanish Nationalists was not taken kindly.[26] By evening the men were wet, tired, and hungry, and the German signalmen were hardly in any better shape. By afternoon (9 March) the Italians had reached points approximately thirty kilometers from their starting point.

On 10 March, the Italian Attack Division began its advance down the Saragossa road to Torija, and from Brihuega along the short road joining it with Torija. The XII International Brigade battalions were located in

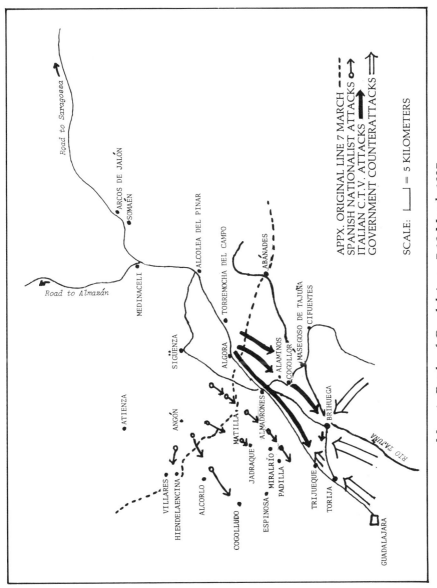

Map 6. Battle of Guadalajara, 7-18 March 1937.

111

the wooded area along this road, and here the Black Shirt militiamen ran head-on into their countrymen of the Garibaldi Battalion supported by the French André Marty Battalion. The light tanks of the militiamen could not penetrate the woods, and they lacked artillery to support their own infantry for an assault on the well-positioned defenders. A German signal section was transmitting the results of the stalled operation from Brihuega. With the right column, another German section accompanied the advance on the Saragossa highway where the Italians became engaged with battalions of the XI International Brigade. Roatta's troops stalled with both sides taking heavy losses.

The enemy continued its buildup of forces by pulling additional brigades and battalions from the Madrid sectors, and Roatta committed his 2nd Division into the Brihuega sector. With the Italian troops suffering from the wet cold weather and near exhaustion, operations were held back the morning of 11 March. Later in the day, the 2nd Division vainly tried to dislodge the Internationals from their positions along the Brihuega/Torija road. The 3rd Division on the Saragossa road shattered the Edgar André Battalion with flame throwers and pushed about two kilometers beyond Trijueque toward Torija.[27] There was little change on 11 March, but one German signal unit was advanced to kilometer stone 84. Through the night and early dawn of 12 February, Brihuega came under heavy artillery fire which lasted through the day. The German signalmen repeatedly had to change positions. Although there were near misses, no men were injured or equipment damaged. The section of Sergeant Krust, at kilometer stone 84, came under direct fire, and he had to change his position several times. The weather now improved to the degree that enemy aircraft operating from their surfaced runways added their weight to the artillery barrages. The 3rd Division and Krust's signal section came under aerial machine gun and bombing attacks. Friendly aircraft were stuck in the mud. The infantry of each side was attacking and counterattacking, and the front would move back and forth a kilometer or two at a time. When 12 March ended, the Italians were generally back in their morning positions. The losses were heavy and the troops exhausted, wet, and cold.

Lieutenant Arend wrote in his *War Diary* that the 2nd and 3rd Divisions were pulled from the line and replaced respectively by the 1st Division and the Littorio Division. With this move General Roatta had committed all his reserves. Although they had been under continual artillery fire, the two German signal sections remained in the line with the replacement divisions. They began to develop minor equipment problems, but they maintained their communications.

On 14 March, supported by heavy artillery, air power, and tanks, the enemy launched a powerful attack along the entire front. Arend wrote that twenty enemy fighters machine-gunned and bombed truck columns and artillery positions in his sector and some bombs landed very close to his communications section located immediately on the front. Nationalist planes were still stuck in the mud or covered with ice. The stalled Italian truck columns were easy targets for the machine guns and bombs of the enemy fighters. Arend viewed the situation as serious enough to pull Sergeant Krust's section back to kilometer stone 88 and move the signal section out of Brihuega to a point a few kilometers north. The Italians were driven out of their position between Brihuega and Torija and at the same time retreated back along the Saragossa road. The truck columns along the roads were under continual aerial attack. If drivers left the roads, they immediately mired in thick mud.

Lieutenant Gollmann of the Condor Legion was able to fly his He-70 reconnaissance plane out of Saragossa and avoid enemy fighters to obtain an aerial view of the front. By prior arrangement, he wrote out his findings and dropped his messages to the German signal section at Arcos de Jalón, where they were dispatched to all commands.

There was no change at the front on 15 March, but the next day the Italian line came under heavy artillery barrages and attacks from low-flying planes all along the roads. Some friendly aircraft were now in the battle area, and the two forward German signal sections were firsthand witnesses to several aerial dogfights. Operations slowed on 17 March, and Lieutenant Arend had to relieve some of his men with the forward units for evacuation to rear hospitals because they had come down with the flu.

While the Italian and Spanish generals were discussing their problems, the enemy initiated a massive offensive in that very sector. On 18 March flight after flight of aircraft pounded the Italians at Brihuega and on the Saragossa road. These were immediately followed by heavy Soviet tanks and infantry. The Italian lines broke.

Sergeant Knrawosky, commanding the forward German signal section, suspected the entire front might collapse and relocated his signal section. He showed good judgment because an enemy attack began up the Torija road, led by Soviet tanks commanded by the Soviet general himself, and the Garibaldi Internationals.[28] The Italian commander in the sector, Colonel Frezza, was killed by the first wave, and his troops were cut to pieces by the fire from the Soviet tanks. The light antitank guns of the Italians were useless. The defending forces now disintegrated with survivors fleeing in a disorganized mass toward a partially prepared secondary line of resistance west of Brihuega.

In his *War Diary*, Lieutenant Arend noted that General Roatta and Colonel Schubert arrived at the front in time to be advised of the fall of Brihuega. Arend described the Italian retreat as "a complete rout with no discipline whatsoever." Sergeant Knrawosky lost all connections with his division command and decided to withdraw his section to Alcolea.

Lieutenant Arend wrote that the Littorio Division withdrew during the night to kilometer stone 97, and Sergeant Krust's signal section was ordered back to Algora. It was not until after 8:00 p.m. that information began to trickle through to Arcos de Jalón telling of the mass confusion on the front and the lines of retreat. Arend had lost contact with his lead communications sections and feared they might have been overrun. He was about to return to the front when Colonel Schubert arrived and instructed him to locate the sections which were supposed to have withdrawn to Algora and get them to safety.

Arend located Sergeant Knrawosky's section at the south entrance to the village Alcolea del Pinar. The sergeant had already managed to contact the two sections that had been ordered withdrawn to Algora. They were stuck in a convoy of trucks fleeing the front that had completely blocked the roads, and it was not until 4:00 p.m. that the two sections managed to reach Algora and advise Arend, still in Alcolea, that they were safe.

Even though Brihuega had been lost and the retreat on the main road had reached kilometer stone 97, by dawn on 19 March, the German signalman's view was that "the extremely gloomy impressions of the night before were not completely justified." On 20 March, the German sections remaining in Algora came under an enemy low-level air attack. A vehicle in each section was damaged, but no one was wounded. Bad weather set in, and the following day the signal sections once again took up new positions with the various Italian divisions. Late in the afternoon Sergeant Thierfelder, the Ln/88 supply sergeant, arrived from Salamanca with replacement uniforms, spare parts, mail from "Max Winkler" in Berlin, and "what gave the whole command a great pleasure—German cigarettes!"

At 7:00 p.m. 23 March, Lieutenant Arend received orders from the Condor Legion that he was to disassemble all radio and teletype connections and prepare to move all sections. All sections were pulled from the line, and Lieutenant Arend left the Italian command with the last three radio sections, on 26 March, for operations in northern Spain. The so-called Battle of Guadalajara was over. The Battle of Guadalajara was now to be written into history books, with critics and pundits of all sides having a great time at the expense of the Italian humiliation. It does seem, however, that the battle was completely misnamed. It would have been more accurate to call it the Battle of Torija after the village seventeen kilometers up the highway from Guadalajara. It was the little village of Torija with its Renaissance church and ruined thirteenth century castle that was the objective of the drives down the Saragossa and Brihuega roads.

The Italian offensive was a failure and humiliation, but still it was not the complete military disaster it is frequently painted. Some of the C.T.V.

regiments had been badly mauled and, along with the divisions, had to be reorganized. Incompetent staffs had to be restructured and timid commanders replaced at all levels. These are not impossible tasks. Armies before and since have bounced back from a reversal when they have not been destroyed in detail, and lost equipment can be replaced as long as there is a source of supply.

There is no doubt, however, that the reversal was shattering to the Italians' morale and had provided a great propaganda victory for the enemy. Furthermore, there was a loss of confidence in the Italians by the Spaniards and Germans in the Nationalist headquarters and the troops in the field.

Colonel Jaenecke of the "Special Staff W" in Berlin did not take a very generous view of the Italian embarrassment. Shortly after the battle he visited Spain for several weeks and talked to all the major personalities involved, including Spanish, German, and Italian. From them he obtained a picture of the battle as they saw it. Back in Berlin, he prepared a detailed memorandum for Hitler (which has never been found) of what he learned in Spain. Hitler then called Jaenecke to his headquarters for further details. The discussion lasted two hours, and Hitler's first question was, "What do you think of the Italians?" From his later account it is obvious that Jaenecke gave Hitler a rather accurate account of the tactical problems and what had happened on the battlefield. But it does appear that he overplayed the "panic" that set in among the Italians when confronted by what he described as a few random shots from the enemy, and how some officers fell to their knees praying to the Virgin Mary and others told their troops to flee.[29]

The C.T.V. was completely reorganized and continued to participate in the Spanish conflict. But from that moment on it remained directly under the control of General Franco's High General Staff. Franco's decision was now to concentrate against the enemy in the North.

Notes

1. Freiburg, Ln/88 *War Diary*, entries for 8 through 15 January 1937.

2. R. Hidalgo Salazar, *La ayuda alemana a España 1936-39*, makes no note of this crash.

3. General Roatta used the pseudonym of "Mancini."

4. Luis Bolín, *Spain: The Vital Years*, pp. 237-253. The author was with the Nationalist assault on his home town. Bolín places the Italian force at 6,000 (p. 238). Thomas in *The Spanish Civil War*, 2d ed., p. 583, puts the Italian forces at more than 10,000, supported by 100 aircraft. John Coverdale, in *Italian Intervention in the Spanish Civil War*, pp. 207-209, does not give a total number of troops but identifies the number of battalions, tank companies, artillery, and engineers in the respective columns, as well as reserve battalions. The air support

consisted of fifty aircraft which included bombers, fighters, and reconnaissance planes flying out of Seville and Granada. The Condor Legion Ln/88 *War Diary*, 4 February 1937, puts the Italian strength at about 12,000.

5. George Hills, *The Battle for Madrid*, p. 119, and Colodny, *The Struggle for Madrid*, pp. 109-110. Colodny (p. 110), using Geoffrey Cox, *The Defence of Madrid* (London, 1937), p. 220, and Tom Wintringham, *English Captain* (London, 1939), pp. 194 and 234, states that operating in the Jarama offensive under separate command were two battalions of "heavy machine-gunners made up exclusively of German soldiers dressed in the uniform of the Foreign Legion." This writer has not been able to verify the existence of these battalions (if they did exist) from any other sources.

6. Hills, *The Battle for Madrid*, p. 117.

7. R. Hidalgo Salazar, *La ayuda alemana a España 1936-39*, p. 133.

8. Freiburg, Ln/88 *War Diary*, entries 10 through 14 February 1937.

9. Ibid., entry of 12 February 1937.

10. Salazar, *La ayuda alemana*, p. 133.

11. Freiburg, Ln/88 *War Diary*, entries of 15 through 24 February 1937.

12. Ibid.

13. Hills, *The Battle for Madrid*, pp. 123-124.

14. Salazar, *La ayuda alemana*, Appendix 1.

15. Coverdale, *Italian Intervention*, p. 213. Colonel Barroso told Faldella that they would be in Alcalá de Henares within five days.

16. Ibid., pp. 214-215.

17. For details of the exchange, see Coverdale, *Italian Intervention*, pp. 215-217.

18. Ibid., p. 218.

19. General Karl Drum, "The German Luftwaffe in the Spanish Civil War (Condor Legion)," pp. 80-81.

20. For details of this exchange, see Coverdale, *Italian Intervention*, p. 221.

21. A complete order of battle is in Coverdale, *Italian Intervention*, pp. 222-224. This differs somewhat from the order of battle in Colodny, *The Struggle for Madrid*, pp. 129-130. Colodny includes, with the Italian C.T.V., a brigade of German infantry and a brigade of mixed Italian and German infantry. This writer has not been able to identify these organizations in other sources.

22. The information of Lieutenant Arend's special command is drawn from his *War Diary*, which was attached to the Freiburg, Ln/88 *War Diary*.

23. Different works give different times for when the offensive was supposed to have started. The times given here are from Lieutenant Arend's *War Diary*.

24. This was the view of Colonel Vicente Rojo, the former chief of staff of the Madrid forces. See Colodny, *The Struggle for Madrid*, p. 2320, fn. 169.

25. Salazar, *La ayuda alemana*, p. 135, and Salvador Rello, *La aviación en la guerra de España*, p. 36.

26. Colodny, *The Struggle for Madrid*, p. 132.

27. Coverdale, *Italian Intervention*, p. 232.

28. The Soviet general was Dimitri Pavlov.

29. Colonel General Jaenecke's comments to General Karl Drum, which appear in the unpublished manuscript, "The German Luftwaffe," pp. 83-85.

9

Battle in the North

With the failure to close the pincers about Madrid, the Nationalists considered shifting their major effort from the capital to other sectors. For this, General Sperrle and Colonel von Richthofen strongly urged a decisive campaign to secure northern Spain. There had been a sizeable buildup of Nationalist troops under General Mola in the region of Vitoria which were, in the main, battalions and brigades filled by the enthusiastic but untrained Carlists from Navarre. The German record describes these forces, at this time, as having the characteristics of "free corps." The German study commented: The leadership of these [Navarre] forces actually camouflaged the strength of their reserves to keep it a secret from the Nationalist General Headquarters. There were units which had twice the battalions reported to Headquarters.[1]

Sperrle and Richthofen recognized the ultimate conclusion of the war would not be made in the North. Still, if Bilbao and Santander (and eventually Asturias) could be cleared, the Nationalists' central forces would be freed of possible threats from the rear, the front facing the enemy would be greatly reduced, and the divisions in the North could be made ready for operations in other sectors. Then the rich ore fields, which were a matter of major concern for Germany, would be available for exploitation. "At the same time, it might be possible to get the British to take a more neutral position by occupying the mines in which the British have a great interest."[2]

To this end, General Sperrle, for some time, had been putting notable pressure on General Franco to support General Mola and his Navarre forces. For this, Sperrle promised he would commit the entire Condor Legion. General Franco now ordered the preparation for the Bilbao offensive. Richthofen, with Lieutenant Wittmer (of his staff) and Major Sierra (Spanish liaison officer), went to Burgos to meet with Generals Pinto and Kindelán to learn the details of their proposed operation. He was insistent that while the enemy was still in a state of shock—after the Legion had bombed and strafed the front lines—the infantry must attack immediately. Colonel Vigón (Spanish chief of staff) made it clear that, above all, the Nationalist forces "absolutely were not to have heavy losses."[3] The enemy on the Vizcaya front had a force of forty battalions numbering 27,600 men and forty pieces of artillery with calibers up to 155mm. They had the advantage of position and controlled the fortified high ground. In the region were about thirty aircraft, some flown by Russians. Air superiority in the sector was decidedly with the Nationalists. On the ground the Nationalists had 25,000 men and thirty-four artillery batteries. Finally, the Spaniards agreed to Richthofen's tactical battle plan, along with the delicate methods of coordinating artillery and air strikes directly in front of advancing troops.

The German Legion was divided into two forces. One force operated out of the two airfields near Burgos, and the other from the two fields of Vitoria. At Burgos was the Bombardment Group K/88, reinforced with the "Experimental Flight" (VB/88), equipped with the new He-111 bombers. The group had a total of twenty-two aircraft. Also at Burgos was the Reconnaissance Squadron (A/88), with seven bomber versions of the He-70 and one reconnaissance He-45. When General Kindelán and Richthofen inspected the fields, they found the small field unusable because of mud and water. At Richthofen's suggestion, twenty dummy aircraft were installed on the small field, and the Legion aircraft were concentrated on the larger field.

The Legion Staff was headquartered in Vitoria. One field at Vitoria accommodated the Fighter Group (J/88). This group now had three squadrons: the 1st Squadron (*Marabou*) had ten He-51 fighters; the 2nd Squadron ("Top Hat") was equipped with seven prototype Bf-109s; the 3rd Squadron ("Mickey Mouse") of Lieutenant Pitcairn had ten He-51s.[4] The 4th Squadron ("Happy Hunter") had temporarily been disbanded. The other airfield supported the dive-bomber flight (three aircraft) of Hs-123s (under Fighter Control), and the Spanish Nationalist squadrons. All Italian and Spanish squadrons committed were put under the command of General Sperrle. Among these were two Spanish squadrons of He-45 light bombers (with twenty aircraft) and a few assorted antiquated aircraft that would fly out of Vitoria. In all, about 150 aircraft were available to the Condor Legion command. There was no question of air superiority in the sector.

The Germans considered the Italian fighter squadrons as being near equal to the Soviet planes, and the Italian bombers superior to the German Ju-52 and He-111, but the Italian crews were very poorly trained and were inclined to bomb the wrong targets.

Sperrle determined that the Battle Staff should be as close as possible to watch the results of the air strikes and artillery barrages. The Command Post (C.P.) overlooked the front and was to be moved forward as the offensive progressed. It was always to be in instant radio and teletype communications with both air and land battle forces.

On 26 March, the air squadrons were ordered to work—through the night if necessary—to have all aircraft available. The following day the gun batteries started moving into their positions.

General Sperrle was troubled because he believed there were not enough Nationalist brigades to carry out a double envelopment of the front and the Nationalists were definitely short of artillery for the task ahead. The Germans viewed this as "a major mistake, which was felt time and time again until Bilbao was finally captured."[5]

He-111 bombers began bombing the enemy airfields around Santander and reconnaissance planes started surveillance of the Santander-Bilbao-Durango roads. The liaison officers immediately took up their positions with the attack brigades.[6] By 30 March, all combat flights were in their forward bases. Ground crews were advised that they were expected to reservice their aircraft at least six times a day through the daylight hours, and also to be prepared to support night missions.

Richthofen spent much of the day (30 March) at the front. He calculated the enemy expected the attack and the only surprise would be the strength and exact time. To hide the strength, much of the friendly infantry was held back from the attack zone until the heavy bombers had struck the enemy rear areas and the artillery had started its fire on the front. Each infantryman was to wear a white panel on his back that could be seen from the air. White panels were to be laid out pointing to enemy positions that were to be struck by bombers and fighters. General Mola ordered the attack to start the following morning, 31 March (see map 7).

It was clear and bright when the attack started at 7:20 a.m. General Sperrle, General Velani (Italian air commander), Colonel Vigón, and Richthofen rode by horseback to the high Legion Command Post. Twenty Ju-52s bombed enemy positions. Another strike was directed at enemy concentrations near Ochandiano and the road and rail junctions of Durango. The artillery started its barrage, but the rate of fire was discouraging to the Germans because only thirty-four batteries were available. But then German aircraft struck fifty meters in front of the Nationalist infantry. At 9:50, the squadrons of He-51s bombed and strafed the enemy front positions and were immediately followed by the He-70s and Spanish flights with 50-kilo bombs. At 10:05 a.m., wearing easily seen white panels

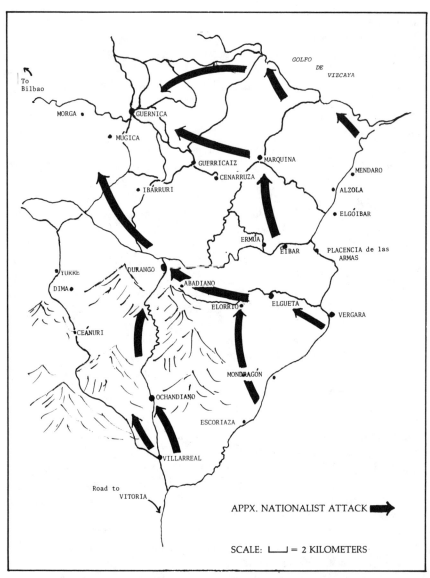

Map 7. Battle in the North, 30 March-30 April 1937.

on their backs, the infantry of the 4th Navarre Brigade stormed Mount Maroto.

The enemy was doggedly holding to its positions on the nearby Mount Jarinto. A German battery of 88mm guns directed its devastating rapid fire into the fortifications, and the He-51s struck again in force. By noon, the He-51s and 88mm guns had shot the enemy out of the fortifications, which were carried by the infantry.

The men in the C.P. were disgusted because, after all the preparation by air and artillery, the 3rd Brigade, on the right flank, had not made its attack. The brigade commander had left his communications post and could not be contacted and ordered to move forward. After that, the German liaison officers were ordered "to stick like glue" to the commanders to which they were attached. The He-51s were called in again to bomb and strafe before the 3rd Brigade's positions and the 88mm guns took up fire against the heights above. Medium and light Legion and Spanish planes pounded the positions again at 2:00 and 5:00 p.m. Still the 3rd Brigade did not attack. Even the scholarly and generally unruffled Colonel Vigón was annoyed. The German study noted: "Therefore the Brigade commander was relieved."[7] The offensive the first day, even though all the objectives were not attained, was a success.

That night the German, Italian, and Spanish commanders evaluated the day's operation. The enemy had proven very stubborn and had had to be blown out of its positions by artillery or aerial bombardment. Thus, the cost for the attacking forces would have been high without the proper aerial and artillery preparations. The performance of the low-flying He-51s was considered exceptional. Many times the troops were engaged within grenade-throwing range, and the He-51s sent in to machine-gun the enemy troops more than once were the deciding factor.

During the night the Command Post was advanced to the recently captured Mount Jarinto. Because of rain it was not until 10:00 a.m. the next day that the He-51s could bomb and strafe before the infantry. Lieutenant W. August Blankenagel's plane was shot down by ground fire and crashed and burned on a hill under attack. It was later learned he had been shot in the head. Six other He-51s received severe damage from the intense ground fire. The He-51s and Spanish Breguets repeatedly attacked the lines, but it was not until 6:00 p.m. that the bomber force, protected by Bf-109s and Fiats, was able to strike, with twenty-two aircraft. The light bombers, fighters, and 88mm batteries continued to bomb and shell enemy troops coming into Ochandiano. The Nationalist line, with flanks now parallel, had advanced, but the attack stalled because of the terrain.

Richthofen was furious that the 4th Brigade had not moved, and returned to Vitoria to urge Sperrle to have a confrontation with General Mola. But Sperrle decided to let his chief of staff do the dirty work.

Richthofen wrote in his diary 2 April: "I am in the right mood for it."[8] It was not a cordial meeting, with the German colonel charging the Spanish general sharply over the slowness of his ground forces and pointing out details and reasons for the failures. Richthofen "demanded stronger action and accused him [Mola] of want of energy." He pointed out that the flyers, "who had done all the work so far, will not work together with such a lack of leadership." Mola became very angry. At the same time his own chief of staff, Colonel Vigón, grinned in agreement with the German.

Mola's position was that the Spanish Civil War was different from what Germans knew of warfare. Success was not possible every day. The terrain was terribly difficult, and one could not ask more of the men. The troops were not well organized or highly trained, and one could not insist on imposing excessive demands on them. One had to pressure the enemy slowly, and he could be pushed back *poco a poco* (little by little).[9]

Mola then objected to the concentrated use of air power on the limited front. He wanted the squadrons to fly missions for a few days to destroy at least half of the factories in Bilbao. Richthofen was startled: "I emphasized that this idea was new to me, and I could not see destroying something which one was trying to occupy in the near future." The German was well aware that General Franco stood opposed to the destruction of industry, and not a single factory in Spain was to be destroyed by German aircraft without his specific permission. Mola's position was that: "It was unhealthy for Spain to be governed by industry in Catalonia and Bilbao."[10]

Richthofen hotly refused to carry out such attacks unless there was a direct request from Mola, and: "I made myself very clear that I had never heard such nonsense." They parted highly "unsatisfied."[11] Richthofen shortly received such an order through Colonel Vigón, but refused to accept it. Mola finally signed the order, and then Richthofen agreed to bomb a powder plant the first day his force could be freed from its assigned tactical support function.

Colonel von Richthofen was still in a fit of pique the morning of 3 April. He "demanded" an increase in the rate of artillery fire and that the artillery spotters must be moved farther forward. Colonel Vigón told him that they were all in agreement for the attack on the morning of 4 April. Feeling assured, he finally went to bed past midnight.

The next morning, General Sperrle, General Velani, Colonel von Richthofen, and Colonel Vigón made their way to the Command Post halfway up the slope of Mount Albertia. An intense artillery barrage started at 8:00 a.m., and Richthofen was pleased that it was at a much higher rate of fire. Then the German, Spanish, and Italian bomber squadrons were committed. The enemy now began to flee the positions en masse. The He-51s then appeared and struck the enemy columns with bombs and machine gun fire with impressive accuracy. Enemy forces attempting to reach Ochandiano were now caught by the Italian bombers, and the German 88mm guns blasted the enemy artillery to pieces. Finally the Nationalist infantry was ordered forward. Over 200 enemy dead were scattered over the slope of the mountain, and 400 prisoners were taken.

The enemy that managed to escape the aerial attacks, stopped at strongly fortified positions on Mount Monchetegui. The German Command Post now ordered a massive effort by their combined air squadrons. All units arrived at the same time and dealt a devastating blow. In the first two minutes, sixty tons of bombs were dropped. The mountain became a terrible sea of flame and smoke. When the smoke cleared, the men in the C.P. could see the enemy fleeing in a great mass to the forest behind. For the next eighteen minutes, twenty more tons of bombs rained from the sky. Richthofen wrote in his *Diary*: "The cleanup was terrible."[12] He continued to note that once again the infantry did not push immediately forward. However, toward evening they cautiously entered a badly battered Ochandiano and found many dead. From later interrogation of captured enemy leaders it was learned the bomb and strafing attacks had completely routed their forces. The Germans noted:

> Ochandiano was of great tactical importance. In the last century, during the Carlist Wars, the generals sacrificed other military advantages to capture the town. This town, with its mountain, is the gate to the Cantabrian mountains and dominates the passes and roads to Bilbao.[13]

Early the next morning, 5 April, Richthofen found a new location for the Command Post which overlooked the proposed battle area. He then climbed Mount Monchetegui to inspect the results of the previous day's operation. He arrived at the top in time to observe his Ju-52s bombing in front of the 1st Brigade, which was supposed to take Sebigan. The timing of the strike was off, for which he blamed his absence from the C.P., and some of the bombs fell on friendly troops. Such accidents do happen in close ground support, but this was doubly embarrassing because Generals Franco and Kindelán were observing the operation. Richthofen suddenly saw a parachute, with a lifeless body, come oscillating through the clouds and drop into the front lines. Who was it? He later learned that Lieutenant Gunther Lützow, in his Bf-109, had engaged four Soviet planes and shot one down. The others flew into the clouds. This was the first victory recorded for the new Bf-109 fighters. Lieutenant Lützow himself was to have five victories in Spain. He was the second German aerial ace to have over 100 aerial victories and a total of 103 during World War II.

Richthofen carefully inspected the enemy defensive positions on Monchetegui and found them strongly prepared with three rows of barbed wire and tank traps. He was convinced that without their aerial bombardment it would have taken days, and at a high cost, to dislodge the determined defenders. There was a ditch into which the defending forces ran for protection that was caught in the air raid. It made a "terrible picture!" It was filled with "terribly mutilated corpses."[14]

The Battle for Altun developed the following morning. The Command Post was established on Mount Monchetegui, which Sperrle insisted on calling "Mönchsberg." The preparatory artillery fire was weak, but the bomber planes were very effective. The infantry, however, remained crouched before the enemy trench positions and asked for additional air strikes. Annoyed, Richthofen called in the bombers again, and directed the German flak guns to fire on occupied houses and positions west of Altun. In cloudy weather, the Ju-52s dropped their bombs, and the infantry finally moved to occupy Altun with little resistance. But, the advance along the heights remained painfully slow. The battalion commander of the 4th Brigade's lead battalion still did not move. Richthofen managed to reach him by phone and then handed the phone to Vigón and insisted that the Spaniard order the battalion to attack. Colonel Vigón complied and the battalion moved out, under protection of the German flak batteries, to occupy the heights and the pass without a fight.

The decision was then made to break off the pursuit. Instead an attack would be directed at Vergara farther east. Some of the staff now visited the positions at Altun, and General Sperrle had a major problem. He was wearing civilian dress and was captured by Moroccan troops. After a few uncomfortable moments, he decided it was best to get into uniform.

Sperrle now decided to shift the remaining Legion personnel in Salamanca to Vitoria. This was greeted enthusiastically by Richthofen. The decision was probably prompted by Sperrle's bitter differences with the German ambassador, General Faupel.[15] There is little doubt the two men detested each other.

General Sperrle took advantage of a lull in operations because of weather to express his objections to the conduct of the campaign to Generals Franco and Kindelán. He complained because Franco had not provided the additional brigades he had recommended. The loss of time not only was giving the enemy the opportunity to build his defenses in the area, but as well allowed forces to strike in other sectors. Sufficient Nationalist forces should be gathered to attack the enemy from seven directions at the same time. If this was not done, it would be best to call off the offensive to conserve forces and prestige.[16] Franco was hardly more responsive to Sperrle's position than he had been to what he viewed as previous Italian interference in areas of his responsibility. It was to be several days before his official reply came to Sperrle. Franco thanked Sperrle for his help, and promised to follow his suggestions. Richthofen saw this as: "Probably out of politeness. Therefore we stay in the North, thank God, and wait, wait, wait."[17]

Rains continued to delay the offensive at Vergara. Suddenly the plans were interrupted on 13 April when the enemy, taking advantage of the bad weather grounding aircraft, opened a strong ground spoiling attack against the Nationalists on Mount Sebigan.[18] The planned offensive would now have to be delayed until this situation could be reversed.

It was impossible to fly the next morning because of fog and rain, but tha Battle Staff was in the flak Command Post at 8:00 a.m. to direct the artillery barrage. "When the artillery fire started against the slopes, the mountain suddenly began to move (people)."[19] The enemy, who were lying on the slopes, were stunned and tried to find cover from the shells bursting about them. Because of the wet ground it was possible to see white puffs each time the enemy fired. In one hour the batteries blasted the enemy from the slopes, and the Nationalists occupied the area without opposition. They found 200 dead, and captured 40 prisoners. Weather now grounded all aircraft.

On 18 April, for a short time, the Legion bombers penetrated the weather over Bilbao, where one of their Do-17s was shot down by enemy fighters that broke through the Bf-109 escort. Lieutenant Hans Sobotka, Sergeant Otto Hoffemeister, and Sergeant Friedrich Müller died in the crash.[20]

The same day, hoping the weather would clear, Colonel Richthofen climbed to the Command Post which was wrapped in the clouds. It was a futile effort, and after a few hours, soaked to the skin, he returned to Vitoria, where he found Sperrle in an ugly mood over the delay. "There is no reason to wait! We should go to the center, etc." The colonel suggested: "It is better to wait here and do nothing, than to go over there and do nothing."[21] In an effort to distract his frustrated general, knowing his taste for fine wines, he suggested a visit to the vineyards of the Marqués de Murieta near Logroño. With flying weather remaining impossible, they visited the vineyards the following day, but returned in time to be in the Command Post for the long-awaited breakthrough effort at Vergara.

Wanting to be assured that the infantry was ready, Richthofen (at 7:00 a.m.) contacted by phone the 1st and 4th Brigades, only to find that neither brigade knew anything. Frustrated, he ordered the communications men to locate Colonel Vigón by phone. "They found him in church!"[22] The Spaniard promised he would give the order to attack. Still no message came through from the 4th Brigade. The weather now cleared. The colonel then contacted General Sperrle in the rear zone and asked him to protest vigorously to Vigón.

Finally, the artillery started its barrage and the bombers were ordered into the air. Then the weather turned bad. It quickly worsened, causing the Ju-52s to become separated as they approached their targets. Some German and Italian planes once again dropped their bombs on friendly infantry. The Spanish and German artillery fire was poorly concentrated, and the He-51s were called in to try to pin the enemy down as their own infantry attacked. The infantry, however, having been stung by their own planes, hesitated to move forward. All of this could be seen from the C.P. Later they learned their center battalion was a Falange Battalion which, at that time, had lost all of its officers. Even though new officers were sent forward, under the circumstances it is not surprising that the battalion was not able to regroup properly. The Command Post itself now came directly under artillery fire. Prudently, some very prominent officers jumped into muddy water-filled ditches. As a result, it took two days to have their uniforms cleaned.

Hoping to have their infantry charge, the C.P. now concentrated all artillery fire on the first line of enemy trenches. The weather finally cleared and German and Italian bombers were ordered in for direct support. When it appeared the effort would be successful, the Italians again bombed friendly infantry. "With that, the last attack attempt was stopped right in the bud."[23] The entire day was a major disappointment. Richthofen properly noted: "The final meeting with Mola was very uncomfortable because all the men, however polite, were mad at us."[24] Weather again shut down operations.

On 22 April, the Battle Staff rode up the steep mountain on horseback to the C.P. and immediately came under artillery fire. All made a hasty departure. General Sperrle, on another height, watched the incident through glasses and "cracked up laughing" at the sight.[25] But with flak batteries and bomber squadrons cooperating, the enemy positions on the opposing height were reduced and the mountain was captured without a fight.

All bomber and fighter units, including Italian, were now deployed against the front and rear areas and Bilbao. Enemy fighters, over Bilbao, attacked the bomber formation but were intercepted by the Bf-109s. Lieutenant Radush and Sergeant Heilmayer each claimed a victory.[26] On the ground, although repeatedly pounded from the air and by artillery, the enemy infantry doggedly held their positions at Vergara. Still, the day's operation was largely successful, and the decision was made to postpone further efforts until morning.

The next day, six additional Nationalist batteries were on the line, and Colonel Vigón had the infantry ready. The Italian squadrons saturated Elgueta with bombs, but the German squadrons, apparently nervous after having bombed friendly troops, dropped their bombs on positions behind the lines. Artillery pounded the enemy front trenches, but once again the 4th Brigade did not move. Richthofen correctly assumed Mola and Vigón would be mad. "The battalion commander, as well as the Brigade, got chewed out."[27] All the while, the bombers and fighters kept the enemy pinned down. "Our complaints to Vigón stopped being diplomatic. He agrees with us, but cannot do anything."[28] Sperrle finally ordered the Legion to stand down at 6:00 p.m., and Richthofen returned to quarters angry and frustrated.

Progress was materially improved on 24 April. By noon, with air support, the 1st and 4th Brigades were well forward, with the 1st Brigade pushing toward Elorrio. The enemy was in flight from the Inchorta mountain range to the north. If there was a general withdrawal imminent, the obvious tactical move would be to try to cut off the retreating forces before they could seek security within the fortifications circling Bilbao. The German fighters were ordered to attack the retreating columns at low level, and the bomber squadrons were deployed against forces along the roads north of Elgueta-Elorrio. In the evening, Richthofen drove into Elorrio as the enemy was withdrawing. These forces tried to take up positions about 500 meters away but were dispersed, in the dusk, by fire from the 88mm guns.

Elorrio was badly damaged, and the Germans were very impressed with the Italian bombing patterns, which were much more concentrated and effective than their own.

On the morning of 25 April, communications broke down from the C.P. to the attack force, and Richthofen drove immediately to the front to determine the problem. As the colonel followed the advancing troops, he drove directly into well-placed machine gun fire, and had several uncomfortable moments. He found the 1st Brigade, of Valiño, with its left flank moving against Durango to the west. With the 4th Brigade still behind at Elgueta, he hoped to push the enemy farther north and catch the great enemy mass in the area of Marquina-Guernica. In a little over an hour, the Spanish artillery was properly placed. Richthofen then managed to contact Vigón by phone and have him order Valiño's brigade to move north. At the same time he ordered his own flak guns to move quickly into positions south of Elorrio. Very shortly they closed off the roads west of Éibar-Marquina and at the same time brought the retreating enemy columns under fire. Richthofen then ordered the Legion fighter squadrons against the same roads, and his Ju-52s and Italian bombers against the road division at Ermúa, west of Éibar, where all forces fleeing northwest had to pass. Blocked here, the enemy had to turn north in the direction of Marquina. Bombers and fighters were repeatedly called in on targets and the 1st Brigade pressed its advance. The Ju-52s successfully blocked the road junction at Ermúa with 250-kilo bombs. The Italians, however, missed the target and hit near Éibar.

Guernica was bombed on 26 April 1937. The story of the bombing of this previously little known Basque town of Guernica immediately developed its own library of material around the world. In the decades since, many tomes have been added. There hardly exists a basic history textbook that does not have reproduced in it the famous painting by Picasso. Even though only a few paragraphs may be devoted to the entire Spanish Civil War, the bombing of Guernica is always noted. Allegations, vituperations, and near slander have been cast into the winds.

This writer does not intend to enter the debate as to who was really responsible, how great was the damage, how many were killed and wounded. Was the town damaged as a deliberate, fiendish scheme of General Sperrle on orders from Berlin, that is, Goering, a test-bombing site deliberately engineered by Richthofen, was or was it not asked for (or approved) by the Nationalist command, was it destroyed by the anarchists to create a propaganda story, or was it deliberately fanned out of proportion by the propaganda agencies of the Popular Front?

The point is that Guernica was bombed. Of all the volumes written on the topic, the most detailed historical description is in Doctor Klaus A. Maier's *Guernica 26.4.1937*. Dr. Maier made use of the same material as this writer in tracing the "Battle in the North," located in the *Bundesarchiv Militärarchiv* in Freiburg. Importantly, his book also contains pertinent entries, made available to him, from the *Diary* of the late Field Marshal von Richthofen.

The researcher, studying the detailed German report, "Battle in the North," and expecting to find an account of the Guernica bombing, is disappointed. When one comes to this date the report states:

> In relation to the supposedly devastating bombardment of Guernica by the Nationalist Air Force, particularly the role of the German Air Force units, about whose dreadfulness and cruelty the whole world's press was filled with words of great disgust, like it was made to order, will be reported on in a special enclosure. It was found the flyers had spared the town and that it was, however, set on fire and exploded systematically by the Reds and changed into a mountain of rubble.[29]

In his *Diary* entry of 26 April, Richthofen made no reference to Guernica in excess of the general operations that were carried out that day. At 6:00 a.m. that morning, bombers were sent to block the retreating forces at Guerricaiz (fifteen kilometers southeast of Guernica) and two villages at the crossroads west of Marquina. The Bf-109 fighters shot down two enemy interceptors over Bilbao. An hour later he met with Colonel Vigón. The 1st Brigade of Valiño still occupied the east slopes of Monte Oiz, and was to press from there north toward Guernica and take Durango from the northeast. The 4th Brigade, on the right flank, was still stopped, and Richthofen hoped it would remain so, because with a short advance of the 1st Brigade battalions, the enemy could be trapped. These forces had pulled back from Éibar during the night, after setting it on fire, and it was now occupied by Nationalist troops who were to advance against Marquina and to the west. At that time, Richthofen ordered the squadrons readied for the attack, but after the Bomber Group had returned from Guerricaiz.

The Legion Bomber Group (K/88), Fighter Group J/88, "Experimental Squadron" VB/88, and the Italian squadrons were ordered against the "roads and bridge (including suburb) [Renteria and the bridge northeast of Guernica]. This *has* to be closed off if finally success against enemy personnel and materiel is to be achieved. Vigón promises that his troops will advance in such a manner that all roads south of Guernica will be closed."[30] The mission was flown as scheduled, but the bridge was missed.

In the rest of his lengthy entry for that day, von Richthofen made no reference to the Guernica operation. He wrote of his trip to the front through Éibar, where the Nationalists, using fire-fighting equipment that had been brought from San Sebastián, were trying to put out the fires that had been set by the withdrawing forces. These events he described in detail, as well as the drive on to Elgueta, where he examined how his bombers had caught an ammunition convoy. There is a lengthy description of the manner in which the Italian Mixed Brigades were supposed to be used shortly in the offensive, and how the Legion was expected to support these forces.

The next day most flights were ordered to stand down, but the fighters, He-70s, and He-45s were sent on armed search along the roads around Guernica. An He-45, with Lieutenant von Roon, received heavy ground fire but managed to land. Roon was slightly wounded but the pilot received serious head injuries. The Nationalist brigades pushed very slowly forward. Richthofen wrote: "I am concerned that Guernica is supposed to be burning and that traffic (very heavy) is going east from Guernica to the northwest."[31] He was furthermore disturbed that the 1st Brigade had not been able to block the roads, and the enemy was slipping through what he had hoped to be a trap. With this, the efforts of the flying units had gone for nothing. The 4th Brigade had hardly moved.

Detailed plans were discussed for the operation to start 28 April, but von Richthofen was very apprehensive as to what they could expect from the Italian Mixed Brigades, which were to attack into a relatively quiet sector with Legion support. The attack was held back because of weather until 11:00 a.m., and shortly Spanish forces occupied Ondárroa. Richthofen was gravely concerned because they had lost radio communications with both air and ground units and his bombers were on the way into the attack sector. He was fearful that they would again bomb their own forces. The flight commander, however, flying through heavy rain, decided to turn back. For this, the colonel was most grateful and gave thanks to *St. Petrus*.[32] Meanwhile, the enemy started to withdraw from Durango under fire from the Legion flak. That night Richthofen learned that Guernica had been heavily bombed.

The general offensive now went into a state of limbo. The next major objective would be to breach the fortifications ringing Bilbao. Most air units were ordered to rest, but a few fighters and bombers were committed against Bilbao and its fortifications. Early on 30 April, Richthofen drove the Verriz-Guerricaiz-Guernica-Durango road. He was pleased to see the new 5th Brigade relieving the 4th Brigade. He states the town of Guernica was practically leveled:

> The attack was with 250-kg bombs with fire bombs making about 1/3 of the load. When the first Ju [squadron] arrived there was already a lot of smoke (from VB, which attacked with 3 aircraft), nobody could recognize the streets, bridge, and suburb [targets] and therefore just dropped bombs anywhere. The 250-kg bombs destroyed a number of houses and the water supply lines. Now the fire bombs did their work. The kind of buildings: tile roofs, wooden beams, and wooden galleries, were the reason for the complete destruction.[33]

He then wrote (with which many writers would disagree), that the population was mostly out of town and the rest left when the bombing started, but that some people had died in the shelters which received direct hits: "Bomb holes can still be seen in the streets—unbelievable. Town was completely closed off for at least 24 hours and it gave the prerequisite for a success [closing the retreat] if the troops had followed."[34]

He then described the Guernica "Holy Oak" monument and its importance in Basque history and nationalism. He noted how it and the buildings in the city center had not been damaged. From Guernica he drove to Durango and was concerned about the destruction resulting from the two Italian bombing raids, the results of which he described in detail, noting "The Reds have not cleaned up anything for reasons of propaganda." His last comment for the day was: "Official invitation from Kindelán to us and Italians. He is with Franco in Vitoria. Oops!"[35]

The offensive was now thirty days old. The enemy outer defenses had been ruptured, and many kilometers of difficult, but vitally important, territory was in Nationalist hands. The enemy, who had suffered greatly in loss of men and materiel, showed great determination. They were not destroyed as a field force. The fact that the Nationalists, for the most part, had uncontested control of the air made up for the deficiency of artillery needed for an offensive through such difficult terrain. Besides the casualties noted, the Legion suffered three dead and five wounded in a flak battery when one of their own rounds exploded prematurely. An additional eight flak and communications troops and Captain Hansemann, liaison officer with the 4th Brigade, were wounded by artillery fire. Many fighters and bombers of all models were damaged by ground fire and enemy fighters and several planes were damaged in ground accidents. Lieutenant Balthasar seems to have had a tendency to crack up the He-51s. One day he ruined an He-51, but still went on to fly eleven missions that day and so was forgiven.

There was a lack of coordination between air and ground forces, and within the ground units many problems had yet to be resolved, but they were improving as they became battle-tested. The Nationalists won territory, but the enemy had won the war of propaganda with Guernica.

Some of the Nationalist commanders optimistically assumed they would be able to break the enemy's final defenses and be in Bilbao in a few days. The Germans, on the other hand, calculated it would be much longer. They were correct. The Bilbao offensive was to last well into June.

Notes

1. Freiburg, MF, RL 1/v. 3188, "Battle in the North," p. 2. Hereafter cited as Freiburg, "Battle in the North."

2. Ibid., p. 4.

3. Richthofen's *Diary* entry of 24 March 1937. Klaus A. Maier, *Guernica 26.4.1937. Die deutsche Intervention in Spanien und der "Fall Guernica"* (Freiburg, 1975), Appendix 1, and Freiburg, "Battle in the North," p. 6.

4. Captain Galland was later to assume command of this squadron, and writers comment that one always knew his aircraft because of the "Mickey Mouse" painted on the side. This writer, later, asked General (retired) Galland why he had his plane so identified. The general responded: "All of the planes of the squadron had the 'Mickey Mouse.' As for the reason, you will have to ask Colonel Pitcairn. I have no idea." Later the writer posed the question (why) to Colonel Pitcairn who answered: "One day, one of the mechanics asked if it would be all right to paint the 'Mickey Mouse' on the planes and I agreed. I have no idea why he wanted to do so."

5. Freiburg, "Battle in the North," pp. 27-28.

6. Ibid., p. 26. Major Seibert and Lieutenant Hasemann joined the two lead Spanish brigades and Lieutenants Schmidt and von Thilo the mixed Spanish-Italian brigades.

7. Ibid., p. 42. For Richthofen's comments, see his *Diary* entry 31 March 1937 in Maier's *Guernica*, Appendix 1.

8. Ibid., 2 April 1937.

9. Ibid., and Freiburg, "Battle in the North," p. 55.

10. Maier, *Guernica*, Appendix 1, Richthofen's *Diary*, 2 April 1937.

11. Ibid.

12. Ibid., 4 April 1937.

13. Freiburg, "Battle in the North," p. 60.

14. Maier, *Guernica*, Appendix 1, Richthofen's *Diary*, 5 April 1937.

15. Maier, *Guernica*, p. 93, fn. 48.

16. "Confidential" letter from Sperrle to Franco, dated 11 April 1937. Copy made available to the writer by the Spanish War Ministry and the *Archivo de la Guerra de 1936-39*. The letter was in Spanish and signed "Sander" (Sperrle's

pseudonym). Also see Freiburg, "Battle in the North," p. 70.

17. Maier, *Guernica*, Appendix 1, Richthofen's *Diary*, 18 April 1937.

18. Freiburg, "Battle in the North," p. 74, states the attack was on 14 April; however, Richthofen's *Diary* puts it on 13 April.

19. Maier, *Guernica*, Appendix 1, Richthofen's *Diary*, 14 April 1937.

20. Freiburg, "Battle in the North," p. 75.

21. Maier, *Guernica*, Appendix 1, Richthofen's *Diary*, 18 April 1937.

22. Ibid., 20 April 1937.

23. Ibid.

24. Ibid.

25. Ibid., 22 April 1937.

26. Freiburg, "Battle in the North," p. 76.

27. Maier, *Guernica*, Appendix 1, Richthofen's *Diary*, 23 April 1937.

28. Ibid.

29. Freiburg, "Battle in the North," p. 77. It is also reproduced in German in Maier's *Guernica*. The enclosure mentioned, if it exists, has never been found. Dr. Maier suspects it might never have been written.

30. Maier, *Guernica*, Appendix 1, Richthofen's *Diary*, 26 April 1937.

31. Ibid., 27 April 1937.

32. St. Peter of the Twelve Apostles. In Germany, besides being keeper of the keys to the Pearly Gates, he is also the keeper of the weather.

33. Maier, *Guernica*, Appendix 1, Richthofen's *Diary*, 30 April 1937.

34. Ibid.

35. Ibid.

10

Fall of Bilbao

Many days were still to pass before the Nationalists would realize the successful conclusion of the Bilbao campaign. The enemy had established strong pockets of resistance which they defended with determination. To the Germans, the Asturians were a tough mountain people who were farmers, shepherds, fishermen, and miners. "They are proud of their Celtic-Gothic blood which shows itself in their simple way of life. They are very courageous and well-known for their honesty."[1] The miners were "daredevils" who, with their dynamite, went about their task of mining roads, bridges, tunnels, and houses with great zest. The defending forces had the full advantage of position. Because they held the mountainous terrain, with its deep gorges and ravines, a single well-placed machine gun nest repeatedly held up the advancing forces. General Sperrle spoke highly of their foe:

> The enemy infantry showed as much backbone and courage as the Germans fighting in the battles of the Great War. Our repeated fire from 30 batteries of artillery, consisting of all calibers on a one-kilometer-wide front, and supported by 30 bomber aircraft and low-flying attack planes, did not make the Reds move. Only when they were attacked from the front and rear were they forced to leave their infantry positions. The Nationalist attacks were made easier because of the lack of Red artillery and aircraft. However, enemy bomber and fighter planes arrived at the front in the last few days in the area of Bilbao.[2]

Much the same feeling was expressed by Colonel Richthofen: "Have pushed the Reds back. They realize great losses in personnel and morale; however, little in materiel. The Reds hold and defend themselves tenaciously, every step has to be fought for."[3]

There is no doubt that Sperrle and his staff were highly pleased with the contribution of their Legion and other air forces to the Nationalist successes. Richthofen made a strong note of this on 1 May 1937:

> Spanish artillery is always late in arriving; it fires too slow and too bad to keep the enemy pinned down. The load of the battle rests with the flyers. First by inflicting casualties, second, by holding him down, making him run, destroying his spirit to fight, and hindering his resupply and reinforcements. A large load of the battle rests on our two flak batteries committed to the front. They shoot the enemy out of positions and scatter them when they run—we are able to do this because the enemy does not have an air force. Their fighters have been shot down or have been destroyed on the air strips.[4]

The long-suffering Spanish infantrymen in the cold, rain, and mud, and faced with seemingly impossible heights bristling with enemy fire, and the artillerymen straining every muscle to move their antiquated guns into position, undoubtedly recognized the importance of the air support; at the same time, they might take the view that the flyers overstated their case. Air power can prepare for the infantry assault; still, the position must be taken and held by the ground soldier.

The effectiveness of the German 88mm flak guns as artillery was proven without a doubt.

> The flak, to the horror of experts in Berlin, has consistently been used as the backbone of the ground artillery. We pulled the joke of sending a battery north of Guernica as coastal defense. If that battery would manage to sink a Red ship, the comedy of errors would really receive its crowning glory.[5]

It is obvious that the long hours and continual strain had made Richthofen very weary. He asked for and received permission for a leave to hunt the fabulous mountain sheep in the Gredos Mountains. But first, details were worked out with Colonel Vigón for the continuation of the offensive which it was hoped would break the "Iron Belt" defenses about Bilbao. Before this was possible, the Italians had to be extricated from a difficult situation.

Some C.T.V. battalions were placed under General Mola for the final aspect of the Bilbao operation. But, after the humiliation at Guadalajara, according to Colonel Richthofen, Mola did not want them. The Germans, on the other hand, did not want to lose the seven battalions, along with the support troops that had been made available. The Germans pressed General Mola to include these forces in the operation. Finally, Sperrle and Richthofen were able to convince Mola to have them replace three Spanish Defense Battalions on the north flank that was to reach the sea. Richthofen wrote: "Mola has repeatedly emphasized to me that he was doing this only to do us a favor and he would not be responsible, in any way, if something goes wrong."[6]

At noon on 30 April, battalions of the Italian Brigade "Frecce," on the left flank north of Guernica, started marching to Pedernales without making contact with the enemy and occupied Bermeo, on the coast. Sperrle remarked:

> "The Italian Brigade had been ordered to take Guernica, and the heights northwest of it, after the Reds had left their positions west of Deva. Instead of following these orders, the Italian Brigade marched from Guernica to Bermeo along a valley road which is only a little above sea level. They did this without securing the heights west of the road that extend up to 400 meters. Because of this, the Italian Brigade was in a critical situation for several days."[7]

The next day the enemy surrounded the brigade and brought it under heavy fire. At the same time, the enemy disrupted the communications to Guernica at Mundaca. The weather turned bad and the river mouth was enveloped by a thick cloud cover, making air support nearly impossible. General Mola made the decision to hold the Bermeo position and began to realign forces to free the Italians.

Richthofen was far more caustic in his view of these events than was Sperrle. He saw the Italians as "having gotten into trouble because of their own stupidity." On the other hand, "they [Spaniards] were afraid of a possible enemy success."[8] Sperrle and Richthofen responded with their fighters and bombers, which attempted to fly through the thick clouds.

Meanwhile, relief forces were being assembled, consisting of the C.T.V. "23 March" Group and the 4th and 5th Falange *Banderas*. The endangered force was finally relieved late 2 May. Meanwhile, the Nationalists learned that there were problems within the enemy camp. The Basque president, José Antonio Aguirre y Lecube, had pleaded for help. In a radio message to Valencia he stated his case clearly: "I have to admit our situation is more than difficult, it is serious. There are many people who urge for a capitulation because of the enemy's amount of artillery and aircraft. The only possibility to save us is the mobilization of all men to bear arms."[9]

In order to keep the enemy guessing as to the next point of the thrust, diversionary attacks were made near Miravalles, about seven kilometers due south from Bilbao, on the edge of its "Iron Belt" fortifications. The German bombers and other air groups dropped heavy bombs in daily attacks, from morning until night, on hill positions, tunnels, command posts, artillery positions, and troop concentrations. Also, they continually bombed the passes north of Miravalles to interrupt all traffic. All air groups were ordered not to bomb, under any circumstances, villages or populated areas.[10]

Although the Nationalist air arm was repeatedly committed, an impatient and critical General Sperrle was most succinct about the overall offensive:

> No command leadership. Things drift. Even though they try, there are no telephone connections. Inefficient coordination with artillery. Poor shooting from the Italian batteries. Poor artillery spotting. Wrong connections. Shells explode too early. They don't bring shells on targets. Barrels are shot out. They do not take advantage of air attacks. They do not move forward under air protection. On 6 and 7 May the diversionary attacks, even though they had been warned several times, frittered away their energy. Cooperation with the Italians is loose, thus forces are not very effective. Leaders of the Spanish brigades attack, according to their own ideas, in some directions without paying attention to orders.[11]

In spite of Sperrle's criticism, the offensive progressed methodically, although slowly, one kilometer at a time. Finally, on 11 May, a frontal area before the "Iron Belt" was occupied. On 13 May as the He-51s were bombing and strafing vehicle columns at Larrabezúa, Lieutenant Wandel's plane was caught by enemy flak; he managed to parachute from his burning aircraft and watched it explode on impact. He landed safely, but within enemy lines, and was taken prisoner.

The Legion bombers, protected by Bf-109 fighters, flew three or more missions a day with all aircraft. The He-51 fighters flew even more sorties in the hotly contested battle for the heights near Amorebieta and the height of Bizcargui, which topped the surrounding area by 200 meters. On 16 May, Richthofen sent a message of appreciation to all units of the Legion thanking them for their strong commitment.

During the period of 30 March until 10 May, the Legion had dropped 681 tons of bombs of all sizes. They noted that this was six times the total tonnage of bombs dropped on England during the Great War. On 16 May, 178,700 kilos were dropped.[12]

By now the Spanish Navarre Brigades had realized material successes. Vast stores of war materiel, as well as great numbers of prisoners and deserters, were falling into their hands. The advance stopped 17-18 May, because of bad weather, but on 19 May, there was a vicious, successful assault with all aircraft repeatedly committed in wave after wave.

The embattled Basques and their allies were beginning to receive some much needed material support from Valencia. As Richthofen noted, the efforts to supply their forces through France had failed; however, on 22 May, seven new fighters flew across Nationalist territory and landed at Bilbao. Shortly, forty-five aircraft were to arrive, which included I-15 (Curtiss) and I-16 (Rata) fighters and Katiuska SB-2 (Martin) bombers. A shipment of Czechoslovakian arms, including fifty-five flak guns, and thirty pieces of artillery, along with two squadrons of I-15 fighters, arrived in June 1937.[13] The Nationalist air arm would no longer have almost complete freedom of the skies.

The same day that the first seven fighters arrived in Bilbao, the 2nd Navarre Brigade, under massive air support, attacked from Durango-Ochandiano to Bilbao. The German bombers, protected by the Bf-109s, flew three missions. A bitter aerial battle developed between the Bf-109s and the enemy. One enemy Curtiss was seen to crash in flames, and the Germans listed two others as "probable" victories. During the battle, one He-112 destroyed two enemy tanks.[14]

The Nationalists continued to push slowly forward, under concentrated air power, from one peak to the next. Tons of bombs were dropped and hundreds of rounds of artillery shells paved the way. Amorebieta was taken on 29 May, assisted by Spanish, Italian, and German air squadrons. It was planned to attack the enemy's final line of fortifications, the "Iron Belt," on 31 May, but bad weather again canceled all ground operations.

The Nationalist command issued orders that under no circumstances was Bilbao to be destroyed. To ensure this, all air forces and artillery batteries were prohibited from bombarding the town, and a bomb safety zone was created three kilometers from Bilbao.[15] With his army held up by the weather, General Mola took off from his headquarters to fly to General Franco's Command Post. Due to dense fog, the general died in the crash of his plane on the slope of Mount Alcocer, not far from Bilbao. As could be expected then, and now, some people speculate that his death was brought about by sabotage, and even possibly by the Germans.[16] There has never been a shred of evidence to support these allegations.

True, as noted, there were incidents of differences of opinion between Generals Mola and Sperrle and Colonel Richthofen. These differences were not hostile, and a warm working relationship had developed among the three. The Germans felt his loss keenly and viewed him as the "spiritual leader of the whole Nationalist movement in the north since the very beginning. He was very knowledgeable of the conditions of the land and the people, a believing fighter, and a knowledgeable organizer." They saw him as a "knightly and gentlemanly soldier."[17]

Generalissimo Franco named Major General Fidel Dávila Arrondo as Mola's successor. General Dávila was chairman of the National *Junta*

Técnica (State Technical Committee) where he was charged with the finances, commerce, and labor, as well as cultural matters of Nationalist Spain. At the same time, he was chief of staff of the Nationalist Army. To the Germans he was not a well-known military figure, but they quickly came to believe that General Dávila brought even more direction, planning, and order into the Nationalist effort.

The day following the death of General Mola the enemy launched a strong counterattack near Peña Lemona, west of Amorebieta. The Nationalists were forced to withdraw with heavy losses. The weather cleared on 4 and 5 June, and the positions were recaptured with massive air support, but the Nationalists were now faced with a battle in the skies. On these two days, the Nationalists' planes were engaged by eighteen enemy fighters, with the Germans and Spaniards losing eleven aircraft. The German Legion claimed no victories.[18]

Bad weather once again settled over the battlefield. The Nationalists viewed the enemy as holding numerical superiority and the advantage of interior lines of communications. But through defectors, deserters, and aerial reconnaissance, the Nationalists had a fair knowledge of the fortifications known as the "Iron Belt." The "Belt" consisted of two lines of fortifications from 180 to 290 meters apart. Most of the fortifications were simple dirt parapets. However, many were built by engineers and architects and were well constructed at important defensive positions. The fortifications were built far enough from the city and harbor that it was hoped they would not be brought under fire from attacking forces in event of a siege.[19]

The system was a tight closing chain of trenches. Connecting trenches linked the main lines and were guarded by double rows of barbed wire entanglements. These entanglements were 1.20 meters high and 2.5 meters thick. A machine gun nest, depending upon the terrain, was deployed about every 500 meters. Generally the trenches were protected by large piles of logs, but some were fortified with thick concrete. Several places in the line, to be used as bases of operations, were very strongly fortified. Others were only watch towers and defensive posts at important road junctions. The concrete positions were well camouflaged. However, the regular shapes and straight lines cast shadows, which made them easily identifiable to aerial reconnaissance. The positions built of logs were also given away by their straight, unnatural lines.

The "Iron Belt" was a large loop with its two ends anchored on the Mar Cantábrico. The west end was anchored northwest of Bilbao, and the east end was anchored north and slightly east of the town. The two ends were separated by about twenty or more kilometers of the coastline. Depending upon the terrain, the loops extended southeasterly inland, with a width of about seventeen kilometers at the widest point directly east and west of Bilbao. The inland depth of the loop was about eighteen kilometers, terminating near Miravalles and Galdácano.

After repeated delays because of bad weather, the assault started 11 June (see map 8). The designated breakthrough area was at the southern end of the "Belt," which ran from northwest to southwest. The attack force was the 6th, 2nd, and 1st Navarre Brigades with thirty-seven batteries. The 4th and 5th Brigades were in contact with the attack force to their south. All air squadrons were ordered to prepare for a massive effort by air crews and ground personnel. They were to be ready to fly seven or more missions a day.

With concentrated close air and artillery fire, the first day's objectives were attained, with the Spanish infantry storming steep slopes against heavy fire. By evening they carried the heights only 1.5 kilometers in a line of flight from the "Iron Belt." From here they could look directly down into the enemy positions. However, on the right flank the enemy still held the advantage of position. The Legion's Communications Group frantically moved communications lines forward under enemy fire. In the process, Lieutenant Paul Fehlhaber, NCOs Wilhelm Aldag and Willi Oblau, and Radioman Oscar Wiegand died under enemy artillery fire. NCO August Wilmsen, of the Legion Fighter Group, was killed about the same time.[20]

Through the night the air squadrons' ground crews cleaned and reloaded guns, reloaded bombs and gas, patched damaged planes, and smoothed rough-running engines. By dawn, all aircraft possible were readied once again for a full day of frantic operation.

The weather was perfect on 12 June. First, there were concentrated artillery bombardments and aerial attacks by wave after wave of aircraft. These were followed by the infantry assault. The artillery and aerial attacks were so devastating that their infantry carried position after position with limited losses. The Nationalist breakthrough was made south of Fica. The enemy was in flight and pursued both from the air and by infantry.

Other Nationalist brigades made a breakthrough of the "Iron Belt" north of Amorebieta. Besides their direct support for the attacking brigades, the air squadrons bombed and strafed enemy columns along roads leading to the west from Bilbao. The Germans were disappointed that the C.T.V. did not attack north of Orduña. But in the area north of Bilbao to the sea, the Mixed Brigade (Black Arrows) attacked with little resistance. The Germans lost NCOs Felix Claus, Richard Steeg, and Friedrich Bauer, and Corporal Martin Hoffman when one of their flak batteries was hit during an aerial bombardment.[21]

For two days it had been a major effort supported by all air squadrons and ground service personnel. Aircraft would land, be reserviced, and be back in the air in a matter of minutes. It was not unusual that General Sperrle would issue a Special Order on 12 June:

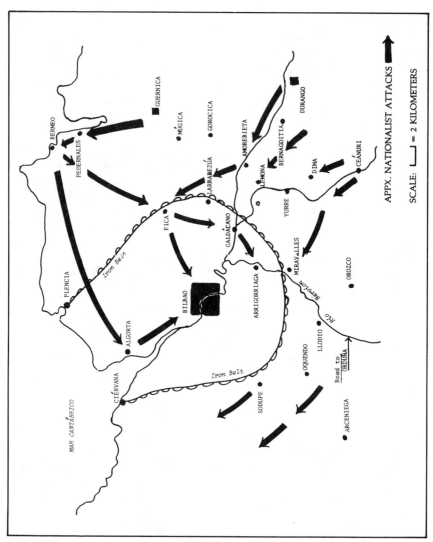

Map 8. Fall of Bilbao, June 1937.

I give my fullest recognition to the units, the flying, flak, and air communications on their achievements of yesterday and today. I also fully recognize the achievements of the ground personnel and flak crews.[22]

Three German flak batteries had assisted in the breakthrough as artillery, and the performance of the 5th Light Flak Battery was particularly notable. In an enemy counterattack, the German gun crews, with their light cannon and rifles, prevented a breakthrough.

Good weather held, and the following day the Nationalist breakthroughs were widened to an additional three kilometers and a depth of the same distance. This prompted General Sperrle to issue another order:

The impressions of today reveal a complete loss of planning by the leadership of the Reds.

The uninterrupted attack of air units, the effective fire of the flak batteries, and the smoothly working communications during these past days have broken the serious resistance of the Reds.

It is important in the next days that each flying unit be ready to attack with several missions throughout the day.

The defeat of the Reds has turned into a panic. I know that the flight, as well as ground personnel, are convinced as to the importance of their duties.

The highest measure of readiness for additional missions must be maintained in the coming days.[23]

The breach was widened even more on 14 June with the air squadrons flying up to seven missions. They continued to shatter enemy strong points and to pave the way for friendly infantry. At the same time, they attacked at low level, with bombs and machine guns, a fleeing and badly confused enemy. It was much the same story the following day with some of the Nationalist battalions reaching points one kilometer from Bilbao.

These days saw the largest concentration of air power used in the war to date. It did not go without cost. On 16 June, an He-70 reconnaissance bomber of A/88 was shot down by antiaircraft fire with the crew of Lieutenant Siegfried Gottanka (navigator), Lieutenant Helmut Hildemann (pilot), and Sergeant Feitz Heerschlag (engineer) dying in the crash.[24]

The 4th Navarre Brigade shattered enemy resistance before it, to advance the battle line south of Bilbao to about two kilometers from Miravalles. The Mixed Brigade in the north continued to advance, and the entrance to the harbor was taken under control. Other parts of the "Iron Belt" were now being deserted by a demoralized enemy. However, they continued to resist north and directly east of Bilbao, but now the Bilbao radio ceased broadcasting, and this was taken to mean that the enemy leadership was fleeing the city.

By 18 June, in the north the Nationalists were within two kilometers from the city; where the river bends in the east they had advanced to four kilometers; and in the south a brigade was two kilometers from the city gate. That night, 1,000 prisoners came over to the Nationalist side. Included was Lieutenant Wandel who had been shot down on 13 May. Powerful explosions could be heard as the defenders destroyed the bridges within the city.

By noon, 19 June, women, children, and prisoners were flooding over to the Nationalist side, and the 5th Brigade stood half a kilometer from the town, but had not received orders to move forward. At 3:00 p.m. the Condor Legion liaison officer, Lieutenant Gockel, with some tank crews, began to build a temporary bridge across the river into the city. Thirty minutes later he and the tank crews moved into Bilbao. Lieutenant Gockel moved to the western part of Bilbao and accepted the surrender of two barracks of police troops and a police motorized force. At 6:00 p.m. four battalions of the 4th Brigade moved into Bilbao from the southeast, and Lieutenant Gockel turned the police chief and the quartered police over to the Spanish battalions. Bilbao was occupied.

As the Nationalists secured Bilbao, NCOs Leo Gorski, Richard Link, and Fritz Götze, of the Legion Bomber Group, died in the hospital in Burgos as a result of mortal wounds received in a bomb explosion.[25]

The battle for Bilbao started 31 March, and it had taken eighty days for the Nationalists to enter the provincial capital. The distance was not great, but the terrain and weather were most difficult. The Germans, rightly or wrongly, believed that without the air power concentrated around the entire Condor Legion, the objective never would have been attained. From the very beginning, air power had proved repeatedly to be the deciding factor. Where at times they had been critical of their allies in the ground operations, the Germans now took the view: "We cannot fail to praise the proven comradeship of the Italian and Spanish Air Forces who fulfilled their duties here."[26] Importantly, the Nationalist North Army had proven itself in battle.

General Sperrle advised Generalissimo Franco, by telegram, of the fall of Bilbao and received in reply from Franco's headquarters:

> The Generalissimo sends his heartfelt greetings to E. E. and the glorious Condor Legion. Thank you for the expressive telegram which was sent in regards to the successes at Bilbao, a success to which this force has given so much. And, he [Franco] expresses his appreciation for the given effort and his continued remembrances for those heroic flyers who died for the defense of Spain and its civilization against Communist barbarity. He expresses his appreciation to E. E., Chiefs, Officers, Soldiers, and Mechanics.
>
> As ordered,
> 1st Lt. Adjutant and Secretary of the Generalissimo[27]

The air squadrons were ordered concentrated against the new defense line being prepared before Santander. General Franco now dispatched another telegram to General Sperrle, 27 June:

> My General,
> The completed operation which resulted in the capture of Bilbao and the occupation of nearly the entire province of Vizcaya, was a success crowned by the Air Force effectively and brilliantly under your command. I would like to thank your excellency with my best wishes and ask you to give my heartfelt thanks for the Bilbao operation to Chiefs, Officers, and Soldiers under your command, and particularly to Colonel von Richthofen who has worked with such great skill. At the same time, I want to take this opportunity to remember sadly the heroic Germans who died or were wounded defending the ideals to which we all adhere.[28]

The Germans calculated that it would take at least ten days to capture Santander. However, it proved to be much longer because government forces from Madrid launched a massive offensive against the Nationalists ringing the city in what was to be known as the sanguinary Battle of Brunete.

Notes

1. Freiburg, MF, RL 2/v. 3189, p. 7.
2. Ibid., p. 43.
3. Klaus A. Maier, *Guernica 26.4.1937. Die deutsche Intervention in Spanien und der "Fall Guernica"*, Appendix 1, Richthofen's *Diary*, 1 May 1937.
4. Ibid. The enemy was to receive additional air support, but it proved too late to turn the tide of battle.
5. Ibid.
6. Ibid., 26 April 1937.
7. Freiburg, MF, RL 2/v. 3189, p. 53.
8. Maier, *Guernica*, Appendix 1, Richthofen's *Diary*, 1 May 1937.
9. Freiburg, MF, RL 2/v. 3189, p. 52.
10. Ibid., p. 51.
11. Ibid., p. 58.
12. Ibid., p. 59.
13. Hugh Thomas, *The Spanish Civil War*, 2d ed., pp. 687-688.
14. Freiburg, MF, RL 2/v. 3189, p. 61.
15. Ibid., p. 63.
16. Thomas, *The Spanish Civil War*, 2d ed., p. 689, fn. 3.
17. Freiburg, MF, RL 2/v. 3189, p. 64.
18. Ibid., p. 65.
19. This narrative of the final battle for Bilbao is reduced from the Freiburg file MF, RL 2/v. 3189, pp. 65-77.
20. Ibid., p. 69, and Salazar, *La ayuda alemana*, Appendix 1.
21. Freiburg, MF, RL 2/v. 3189, p. 70.

22. Ibid.
23. Ibid., p. 71.
24. Ibid., p. 72, and Salazar, *La ayuda alemana*, Appendix 1.
25. Salazar, *La ayuda alemana*, Appendix 1.
26. Freiburg, MF, RL 2/v. 3189, p. 73.
27. Ibid., p. 75.
28. Ibid., p. 76.

11

Battle of Brunete

As the Nationalists prepared their assault on Santander, in the early hours of 6 July 1937 the quiet and sparsely-manned Nationalist front west of Madrid erupted with a massive assault of fifteen infantry brigades, divided into two army corps (5th and 18th). They were supported by 130 pieces of artillery, 70 tanks, 20 armored cars, and uncontested air superiority. This Nationalist front was defended by only 2,700 troops, with twelve antitank guns and six field pieces. This force included two *tabores* of Moroccans who had recently arrived as reinforcements.[1] The attack divisions were the right flank of a two-pincers enveloping attack to surround the Nationalist army deployed before Madrid.

The left flank of the attack struck from the southern suburbs of Madrid through Carabanchel with two divisions, thirty tanks, and twenty armored cars. There was a reserve force of twenty-four guns, forty tanks and armored cars, and eight brigades. The total attack force of twenty-eight brigades (including five International Brigades) constituted between 80,000 and 90,000 men. With its concentration of armor and artillery, it was the largest force to be deployed in an assault in the Spanish war up until this time.[2]

The left flank of the pincers was to link with the much larger right flank near the village of Móstoles, southeast of Brunete on the Madrid-Navalcarnero road. Then some 50,000 Nationalist troops would be trapped and could be destroyed in detail.

The Soviet general, Yakov Schmouskievich (General "Douglas"), who at the time controlled all the Valencia government air squadrons, provided a sizeable air armada to support the assault from Madrid.[3] Writers vary in their estimates of the size of the air force deployed by "Douglas."[4] However, there is a German study, dated 1 November 1940, which was based on all available documentary material at that time.[5] In that numbers and types of aircraft available to the enemy had to be determined through analysis of various intelligence sources, the Germans recognized that their figures could only be considered an estimate. A report dated 3 July 1937, "Mission of the Red Air Force," noted: "According to an estimate at the time of this report, it can be assumed that earlier there had been on hand 200 aircraft, but 80 of these were presumed to have been lost. The recent arrival of 100 planes would give the number now available as 220."[6]

At the time of this report, "Douglas" controlled the three air districts of Madrid, Valencia, and Albacete. He was assisted by Colonel Basart, inspector of the Air Force, and the Soviet Colonel Marovo, who was chief of staff of the Soviet Group. The Soviet Group was stationed mainly in the Madrid District, but did have some flights at Albacete. This group had fifty fighters (Ratas and Curtisses) and twenty bombers.[7] Flying generally in the Madrid District was a small Spanish group under Lt. Colonel Hidalgo de Cisneros.[8] The number and type of aircraft are not reported separately in the German study, but are combined with a French Group (*Wing España*) under Colonel Ecrivain which operated out of Valencia. It was calculated that these two groups had fifty fighters of different types, forty-five bombers, ten armed reconnaissance, and thirty training aircraft (some of which could be used in combat).[9] In Albacete, where the General Staff was located, there were about sixty aircraft. The German analysis, however, did not indicate the type of aircraft. The German staff was of the opinion that the enemy units at Valencia and Albacete were flown into the Madrid District as needed to concentrate in the attack area to support the assault and grasp air superiority. In the early period this was not a major task, with most of the Nationalist combat aircraft deployed in the north.[10]

After the initial aerial and artillery bombardment of early 6 July, the two wings of the attack pincers moved out (see map 9). The left pincers, from the southern suburbs of Madrid, quickly ran into General Yagüe's 14th Division. A dent was made in Yagüe's lines, but before long the Madrid force stalled and was then thrown into retreat and remained behind their fortifications. Brigades of the main thrust on the right flank, led by tanks, were shattered by a single Nationalist battalion at the village of Villanueva de la Cañada where the few antitank guns brought the Soviet armor to a halt. Finally the Corps cavalry and two International Brigades (XIII and XV with the American Lincoln and Washington Battalions) were committed. A frontal attack by the Lincoln Battalion was stalled by Nationalist machine guns.[11] Eventually the Washington Battalion was thrown into the battle and, although the Battalion suffered heavy losses, the defenders were finally overrun at 9:30 that night. Brunete was defended by only sixty troops and twenty medical corpsmen, who were subdued by battalions of the 5th Corps of the Communist Juan (Guilloto Leon) Modesto.

The Nationalist reaction to the attack was instant and determined. General Yagüe notified the small Nationalist force at Villaviciosa to hold their positions at all cost and sent a *tabor* to help. He alerted the General Headquarters of the Army Center, under General Saliquet, that they were faced with a massive and very dangerous situation. Saliquet immediately ordered in his reserve (13th Division). A small force moved frantically to a height less than a kilometer from Brunete, where they beat back an enemy brigade led by tanks. They were joined by the *tabor* sent by Yagüe. Soon additional *tabores* and *banderas* were being rushed to take up positions on the road leading from Brunete. They came under enemy artillery and aerial bombardment through the night, but could not be dislodged by the brigades thrown in by Lister.[12]

Undoubtedly there was confusion in the Nationalist General Headquarters. General Franco immediately sent a message to General Sperrle advising him that the enemy was operating with many fighters and bombers. He asked Sperrle to send one of his fighter squadrons to assist the Nationalist planes operating out of Ávila. The fact that he only asked for one squadron, and assumed that the critical situation could be corrected in twenty-four hours, shows that his headquarters did not yet fully appreciate the magnitude of the attack. Still, he ordered the two divisions *Cáceres* and *Galicia* to move to support the Army Center.[13]

The Condor Legion quickly responded by sending the Do-17 bombers and a Bf-109 fighter squadron, which were engaged 7 July. General Franco now put in the Spanish and Italian aircraft which were to be used against the breakthrough under General Sperrle, and the entire Condor Legion, about 80 aircraft, was ordered into the battle. Besides aircraft, soon flak batteries, service and maintenance crews, communications and transportation sections, and the Legion Staff were all dashing into Castile. For many weeks they had labored in the rain, fog, and mountains of the north, but they were now to be faced with operations in the scorching heat of a Castilian July. Also, the 4th Navarre Brigade (under Colonel Alonso Vega), and the 5th Navarre Brigade (of Colonel Bautista y Sánchez), were disengaged and were moved south.

Colonel Richthofen prepared a special report, "Battle of Brunete," which unfortunately—as is the case of the Legion *War Diaries* and the "Special Staff W" Summaries—has been lost. A few references are made to these writings in the later German study. Richthofen wrote: "Two Italian fighter units stationed directly north of Toledo, and one Spanish Ju-52 bomber squadron stationed at Talavera, were put under the Legion command beginning 7 July." The Condor Legion *Diary* for 9 July stated: "The Italian combat force stationed at Soria was ordered to fly two mis-

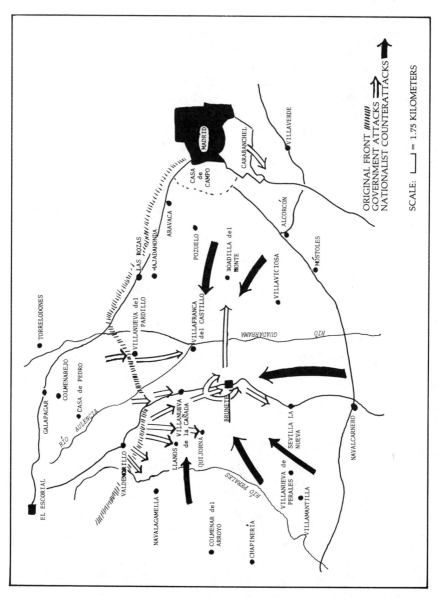

Map 9. Battle of Brunete, 7-26 July 1937.

ORIGINAL FRONT
GOVERNMENT ATTACKS
NATIONALIST COUNTERATTACKS

SCALE: ⎣___⎦ = 1.75 KILOMETERS

sions daily."[14] The *Diary* noted the Nationalists assigned a Spanish squadron of six Ju-52s (presumably this is the same squadron noted by Richthofen), eleven He-45s, eleven Pragas, and the fighter squadron (number of aircraft not given). At the same time, the Italians put under Sperrle's command thirty-seven Fiat fighters, two Romeos, and nine fast bombers (presumably Savoia-79s).[15]

As early as 7 July, some of the German squadrons were landing in, and operating out of, their old forward bases near the battle zone. Captain Lützow started flying out of the old Legion facilities at Villa del Prado, and others from Matacán. It was Captain Lützow who had claimed the first aerial victory with the Bf-109. He wrote: "Next to us is a reconnaissance squadron and on the other side of the airstrip are the Italians with 45 Fiat fighters."[16] General Sperrle established his Command Post at San Martín de Valdeiglesias where General Varela, field commander of the Army Center, had his headquarters.

Through the late winter and early spring of 1937, the Condor Legion received many replacement personnel from Germany. Among those who arrived in May had been Lieutenant (quickly promoted to Captain) Adolf Galland. He was assigned as a maintenance officer, but when the Legion moved to Castile, he hoped to fly with Captain Harder's He-51 squadron operating out of Villa del Prado.[17]

The enemy had concentrated many antiaircraft guns in the battle zone, and one of the first objectives of the He-51s—besides bombing and strafing enemy concentrations and close support of hard-pressed friendly infantry—was the destruction or neutralization of the enemy flak batteries. If not, the cumbersome Ju-52s would suffer heavy losses. Immediately, when fire from an enemy battery was sighted, the He-51s would swarm in with guns and bombs. The Germans also searched carefully for the flak Command Posts, which were the heart of the air defense. If these were located and destroyed, the batteries were neutralized.[18]

The heavy concentration of flak guns near Villanueva del Pardillo quickly became prime targets of the He-51 squadron of Captain Harder. Because of smoke and confusion it was difficult to spot the individual batteries, but once located, Harder would divide his squadron into four flights, with two planes per flight. Each flight was signaled the batteries it was to attack. They would sweep in abreast and open fire with their machine guns a good distance from the batteries. They would salvo their bombs over the guns and make a quick pull-up to avoid their own blast. One such attack lasted only eight minutes, and the pilots felt they were fortunate to escape. Captain Harder commented: "Our planes were shot to pieces."[19] Flying with Harder's squadron, Captain Galland realized his first hostile experience, which he considered "a terrific baptism of fire."[20] But the way was paved for the heavy bombers to fly in at low altitudes so as not to scatter their bombs on friendly forces.

As air and ground reinforcements rushed to meet the threat, the defenders of the villages of Quijorna, Villanueva del Pardillo, and Villafranca del Castillo, with great determination and at a terrible cost, were throwing back attack after attack of the Madrid brigades supported by artillery and air power. General Varela established a front by 7 July, and was bringing some degree of order into a confusing situation, as battalion after battalion and batteries poured into the area to take up positions before the enemy mass. At the same time, General Miaja, the supreme enemy commander, was committing brigade after brigade, and shifting the direction of others. For both forces there was terrible disorder and the fighting was incredibly cruel. Bombers of the Condor Legion struck Villanueva de la Cañada. The next day an enemy division was thrown against Quijorna and the defenders were overrun.

General Franco, on 8 July, established his field headquarters at the Command Post of Colonel Barrón's 13th Division near Sevilla la Nueva. All squadrons of the Condor Legion, and the Spanish and Italian flights, were now involved. The next day all bombers flew several missions, dropping tons of bombs on communications and enemy buildup areas with the He-51s, although constantly alert for enemy fighters, hammering at the front lines with their machine guns and light bombs. By this time Franco had twenty-six battalions engaged with twelve battalions formed as a reserve. Still Villafranca del Castillo was overrun, and bitter fighting raged around Villanueva del Pardillo. The ranks of the International Brigades were being thinned in the process. When a Nationalist observation plane sighted enemy concentrations, about thirty minutes later the bombers would strike en masse followed by strafing planes. What surprised many men of the International Brigades was, considering the ferocity of the air attacks, that they did not suffer more casualties. The artillery fire was far more devastating.[21] Madrid Brigades vainly tried to take Boadilla del Monte east of Brunete but were repeatedly hurled back by forces of Colonel José Asensio.

General Sperrle, on 10 July, ordered all the bomber squadrons into the air to strike all enemy airfields about Madrid to catch as many aircraft as possible on the ground. At the same time, they were to bomb en masse directly behind the front lines. Then Sperrle shifted his tactics. The bombers were ordered over the attack zone in smaller flights at ten-minute intervals. This procedure was to be followed for several days and well into the night. The enemy was to have no rest from the threat out of the skies. This was not without cost. One of the experimental He-112s crashed on landing at Escalona. Then Lieutenant Hans von Posser and crewman Roland Reinhold, in their He-70, were shot down near Brunete. They crashed into friendly territory, but died in the hospital.[22]

Initially, whereas the squadrons of General "Douglas" had dominated the skies, their superiority now quickly began to fade. The Bf-109 and

Fiat fighters began to take their toll, and more German pilots were on their way to becoming fighter aces. It is unfortunate that the daily records of the Fighter Group J/88, the Operational Reports of the Legion Headquarters, and "Special Staff W" Summaries for this period have been lost. Thus, an accurate picture cannot be drawn.

The He-51s, continually flying in direct infantry support, suffered much damage from ground fire.[23] Although their losses cannot be considered terribly high under the circumstances, there was hardly a plane that was not hit repeatedly, with some requiring extensive repairs, which removed them from service. Flight Sergeant Guido Honess in his He-51 (12 July) was hit over Villaverde and died in the crash.[24] Through it all, the efforts of the He-51 pilots and ground crews were considered spectacular.

At the same time Nationalist gunners did very well against the Soviet armor. By 11 July, only thirty-eight tanks and armored cars were operational in the assault force.[25] In spite of the great mass committed to such a limited and thinly held sector, the Madrid offensive was stalled by 13 July. The losses had been tremendous, and the men were exhausted by the heat. With only four days in the line, the XIII International Brigade, which had shattered itself at Villanueva del Pardillo, had to be replaced.[26]

The Nationalist aircraft, although not completely uncontested, were taking their toll of enemy ground forces, particularly of exhausted units which were being relieved. The Brigade Commander of the XV International Brigade, Major George Nathan, was killed in such an attack. Steve Nelson, commissar of the Brigade, states that he saw two of the bombers destroyed by antiaircraft fire and that the others were scattered.[27]

A big day for the Condor Legion was 18 July, with twenty-one enemy aircraft shot down.[28] Unfortunately there are no Legion documents available which pertain to this day's operation.

By now, the enemy had a salient into Nationalist territory of about eight miles deep and ten miles wide. But the Spanish, German, and Italian air squadrons had gained control of the air over the battlefield, and the Nationalist divisions from Cáceres and Galicia, and also the 4th and 5th Navarre Brigades, were taking up positions.[29]

The Nationalists now assumed the offensive with a concentration of artillery and air squadrons. They encountered resistance as determined as their own had been a few days earlier. The 4th Navarre Brigade gave a stunning blow to the enemy 46th Division, the 5th Brigade shocked another, but was damaged in the process, and Colonel Asensio's battalions visibly reduced the enemy bridgehead east of the Río Guadarrama held by one enemy division and three International Brigades (XIII, XV, and XVI). These Brigades were being plagued with desertions and mutiny. The remnants of the XIII broke completely and fled the field, only to be stopped in the rear by armored cars. The Brigade was dissolved, and the men who had not been shot were distributed to other brigades.[30]

The Nationalist command recognized that they did not have the strength
to cut off the bulge and trap the enemy as hoped. The decision was then
made to push the enemy back toward, and hopefully past, Brunete. For
this the two Navarre Brigades were disengaged and took up position on
each side of Colonel Barrón's 13th Division for a direct assault toward
Brunete.

The final phase of the Brunete struggle started 24 July. Following a
massive artillery barrage, including fire from the Condor Legion flak
batteries, on 25 July the German planes flew in three waves over the
attack zone.[31] They and other Nationalist bombers swept in at low altitudes to preclude scattering their bombs on friendly troops.[32] The highly
respected He-51 pilot, Lieutenant Ernst von Reuter, was shot down as
he strafed before Brunete and crashed into enemy territory.[33]

Besides strikes directly on the front, the Germans and other squadrons
heavily bombed enemy reserves assembled in narrow valleys. Troops of
the International Brigades were caught in such a bombing and shelling
which lasted three hours, with wave after wave of Ju-52s sweeping over
them. On one occasion part of the American Battalion (XV Brigade) was
trapped in a ravine by a single German plane which dropped its bombs,
killing eight of the Internationals by concussion.[34]

The 25th of July was a costly day for the Condor Legion Bomber Group
K/88. Two Ju-52s and one Do-17 were shot down by enemy fighters over
Valdemorillo. Their crews of Lieutenant Leo Falk and NCOs Georg
Ubelhack, Fritz Berndt, Walter Brötzmann, and August Heyer were
lost.[35]

By noon Barrón's troops had driven Lister's forces out of Brunete, but
Madrid rushed in reinforcements of two divisions. There were repeated
counterattacks until well into the afternoon of that day. The issue seemed
in doubt when the Nationalist infantry attacked, supported by aircraft
and artillery. The Madrid forces retreated first in disorder, then in a
panic, which became a rout. Their own tanks and cavalry could not stop
them.[36]

Nationalist tanks and cavalry pursued the disorganized mass until dusk,
when they stopped very close to the formerly bitterly contested Villanueva de la Cañada. The fact that General Franco did not permit Varela
to continue the pursuit of the defeated enemy by some critics is considered
to be a violation of one of the basic rules of war. However, Franco was
satisfied to let the enemy hold some of the former Nationalist lands of
Castile and ordered new defensive positions prepared, and his Navarre
brigades, artillery, and air squadrons (including the Condor Legion) back
north, to conclude the Santander-Asturias campaign.

Many Madrid commanders felt very bitter over the tremendous impact the Condor Legion and its supporting squadrons had on the battle. Juan Modesto, commander of the Madrid 5th Army Corps, was most acid in his description of the Legion's attacks on 7 and 8 July, which were followed by the attacks on his communications and concentrations both day and night. The Madrid chief of staff Colonel Rojo considered, from the third day of their offensive, the Nationalist air strikes as devastating, the likes of which had never been seen before. The machine gun fire kept their men pinned to the ground to the point where they could not man their guns, and the attacks in their rear caused great confusion. Enrique Jurado (the sole high-ranking non-communist Madrid commander), who commanded the 18th Army Corps, felt that the air attacks of 11 July were a disaster for them. He echoed Colonel Rojo's feelings about General Sperrle's revised tactics of sending over only a few aircraft, but continually, which not only destroyed equipment but was shattering to the morale of his forces. The low-level attacks with machine gun fire were paralyzing to their efforts. Colonel Segismundo Casado López, who was to relieve Jurado during the battle, seems to have summed up the sentiments of the Madrid field commanders by charging their own air force had failed them and had stopped coming to their aid when it was desperately needed.[37]

By some the battle plan for Brunete is considered sound and even brilliant; others consider its conduct stupid. Some believe that the Nationalists completely overreacted for the matter of a few kilometers of territory, which cost them dearly. The cost to each side for such a few kilometers of sandy soil was tremendous. As could be expected, analysts vary in their debate over the casualties. The figures of 23,000 casualties for Madrid and 17,000 for the Nationalists are frequently accepted. General "Douglas" lost some 100 aircraft and General Sperrle (in all Nationalist squadrons) probably lost 23.[38] The Italians had contributed notably to the combined effort by dropping 106,000 kilos of bombs, and their fighters flew 2,700 combat hours.[39]

The battle was ugly, many times hand-to-hand. It raged in over 100-degree heat. Men not only were blown to pieces by bombs and artillery, but were cut in two by machine gun fire, had their brains blown out by a sniper, or died crying for water. Some were to take their own lives. On both sides men fought bravely, but others fled the battlefield in terror.

The German Condor Legion, as noted, added to the list of casualties. Besides those already named, an interpreter for the Flak Group F/88, Felix Wolf (14 July) was killed in a vehicle accident. In the tank force *Imker* (24 July) NCO Walter Schaumburg was killed by a hand grenade and NCO Otto Balewski died the same day of a heart attack. A sergeant of the Communications Group Ln/88 (11 July) committed suicide.[40]

The Battle of Brunete was over. Later some of the Germans would come to the conclusion that, without knowing it at the time, General Franco had indeed won the Spanish Civil War there on the plains of Castile. Still, there were many battles yet to be fought, and the Condor Legion began packing to move back for the interrupted campaign in the North.

Notes

1. George Hills, *The Battle for Madrid*, pp. 143-146, and Hugh Thomas, *The Spanish Civil War*, 2d ed., pp. 710-711.

2. Hills, *The Battle for Madrid*, p. 143.

3. General Schmouskievich was known by the "Douglas" pseudonym.

4. For example, Gabriel Jackson, *The Spanish Republic and the Civil War, 1931-1939*, (Princeton, N.J., 1965), p. 349, suggests 70 planes; Hugh Thomas, *The Spanish Civil War*, 2d ed., p. 710, notes 300; and George Hills, *The Battle for Madrid*, p. 138, lists "Douglas" as having 320 aircraft available as of 14 May 1937, but with only 200 planes committed to the offensive (p. 143).

5. Freiburg, RL 2/v. 3191, "The Battle of Brunete, a Reevaluation of Documents."

6. Ibid., p. 46.

7. Ibid., pp. 47-48.

8. Ignacio Hidalgo de Cisneros y López de Montenegro was the commander of the government air force. His *Memorias*, 2 vols. (Paris, 1964), are an important view of the government air arm, as is General Andrés García Lacalle's, *Mitos y verdades, la aviación de caza en la guerra española* (Mexico City, 1973).

9. Freiburg, RL 2/v. 3191, p. 48.

10. Ibid., p. 49.

11. Edwin Rolfe, *The Lincoln Battalion* (New York, 1939), pp. 91-92. Another account of the battle is in Steve Nelson, *The Volunteers* (New York, 1953), pp. 145-163.

12. Hills, *The Battle for Madrid*, pp. 153-155.

13. R. Hidalgo Salazar, *La ayuda alemana a españa, 1936-39*, pp. 150-151. The message from Franco is quoted.

14. Freiburg, RL 2/v. 3191, p. 24. Unfortunately Field Marshal von Richthofen's personal diary for this period has not been made available. The Nationalist *Jefatura del Aire* (Chief of Air) Report No. 284 of 8 July 1937 lists additional aircraft committed to the Legion command and states that three squadrons of Italian fighters were assigned: "Fiats 38 in number (fighters), missions with 24 aircraft." (Ibid., p. 26). Captain Salazar in *La ayuda alemana*, p. 151, using Spanish War Ministry material, places the Spanish aircraft assigned to Sperrle as six Junker-52s, eleven Pragas, five Fiats, and eleven Heinkel-45s. From the Italian units were two Romeos, nine Savoias, and thirty-seven Fiats. These aircraft, along with the possible eighty Condor Legion planes, gave Sperrle an air fleet of about 150 aircraft, as opposed to about 200 for the enemy. Salazar notes that Colonel Rojo shows a greater difference, with 300 planes for "Douglas" and 200 for Sperrle.

15. Freiburg, RL 2/v. 3191, p. 25.

16. Ibid., p. 25. The Germans had some interesting observations about the Italian Fiats: "It is one of the most used and at the same time most criticized aircraft in Spain. It would be perfect were it not for the frontal location of the oil and water cooling systems and the position of the gas tank, which are vulnerable to enemy fire. The enemy always attacks from the front or below. All Fiats lost burn in the air. To give the enemy as poor a target as possible, the Italian pilots have demonstrated great knowledge of aerobatics and flight skills." Ibid., p. 18.

17. Adolf Galland, *The First and the Last*, p. 27, and comments to the writer.

18. Freiburg, RL 2/v. 3191, p. 52.

19. Quoted in Salazar, *La ayuda alemana*, p. 153.

20. Galland, *The First and the Last*, p. 27.

21. Rolfe, *The Lincoln Battalion*, pp. 94-96.

22. Salazar, *La ayuda alemana*, p. 152 and Appendix 1.

23. Comments to the writer by General Galland and Colonel Pitcairn.

24. Salazar, *La ayuda alemana*, p. 152 and Appendix 1.

25. Hills, *The Battle for Madrid*, p. 159.

26. Ibid.

27. Nelson, *The Volunteers*, pp. 165-167.

28. Thomas, *The Spanish Civil War*, 2d ed., p. 714.

29. These brigades were larger than normal, and General Franco was inclined (as often was the case) to refer to them as divisions and by the name of their commanders; in this case, *Division Bautista* (5th Brigade) and *Division Alonso* (4th Brigade).

30. Thomas, *The Spanish Civil War*, 2d ed., p. 716, and Hills, *The Battle for Madrid*, pp. 160-162.

31. General Karl Drum, "The German Luftwaffe in the Spanish Civil War (Condor Legion)," p. 98.

32. William Foss and Cecil Gerahy, *The Spanish Arena* (London, 1938), p. 344.

33. Salazar, *La ayuda alemana*, p. 152 and Appendix 1.

34. Rolfe, *The Lincoln Battalion*, p. 101.

35. Salazar, *La ayuda alemana*, p. 152 and Appendix 1.

36. General Drum, "The German Luftwaffe," p. 98, and Hills, *The Battle for Madrid*, p. 164.

37. The direct quotations of these Madrid commanders are in Salazar, *La ayuda alemana*, pp. 154-155.

38. Hills, *The Battle for Madrid*, p. 165. Thomas, *The Spanish Civil War*, 2d ed., p. 715, estimates the Madrid loss at 20,000, but closely agrees with Salazar, *La ayuda alemana*, p. 152, who estimates Madrid lost 104 aircraft and the Nationalists lost 23.

39. John F. Coverdale, *Italian Intervention in the Spanish Civil War*, p. 281. For his source Coverdale cites General Francisco Belforte, *La guerra civile in Spagna*, III, (n.p. 1938-1939), p. 172. The Italians were to realize aerial victories, but the number is not given. Belforte lists 105 Madrid planes destroyed. Coverdale, *Italian Intervention*, p. 281, fn. 53.

40. Salazar, *La ayuda alemana*, Appendix 1.

12

Termination in the North

While bitter fighting raged in Castile, in Salamanca there was another heated battle. Faupel's interference in military affairs caused him to clash head-on into the stubborn and outspoken Sperrle. His continual meddling in matters of internal politics in Spain also agitated General Franco.[1] The Spaniards were well aware of the battle raging between the two Germans, and no doubt felt one or the other might be inclined to play the Spaniards off against his antagonist.

Ambassador Faupel carried the battle between the two Germans directly to Berlin in a memorandum from Salamanca. He claimed Sperrle was critical about HISMA (the company charged with Spanish/German economic matters); Sperrle's remarks were denounced as "derogatory" and were spreading quickly to the Spaniards. Furthermore, a staff officer of General Kindelán had complained to him that Sperrle had "frequently made very pessimistic statements concerning the progress of the war and derogatory remarks concerning Spanish conditions. . . ."[2] Faupel went on to complain that the problems the German economic mission had encountered in Burgos were due to ". . .numerous careless and completely unfounded statements by General Sander [Sperrle]."[3]

Faupel followed this with a personal denunciation of Sperrle in a meeting with Hans von Mackensen of the German Foreign Ministry. Faupel was specific that his relations with Sperrle were "untenable," and that he had made this clear to Hitler several months before. He absolutely could not make a personal approach to Sperrle because the general refused to receive him when he visited Sperrle's hotel in Burgos. "This state of affairs could not continue." On the other hand, von Mackensen was aware that General Franco had approached Sperrle to use his influence in Berlin to have the ambassador recalled because Faupel was "no longer acceptable to him in any way. . . ."[4]

At the same time, War Minister Field Marshal von Blomberg, who had had a discussion with Admiral Canaris about Spain, had come to the conclusion he would replace Sperrle with General Kesselring.[5] The German Foreign Office itself had never been pleased with Hitler's posting Faupel to Spain and would have liked to see him relieved. It was obvious that Faupel was correct—something would have to be done.

Hitler finally made the decision to replace both Faupel and Sperrle, but he did not want to call further attention to an unpleasant matter by withdrawing both men at the same time. Before Sperrle returned to Germany, Hitler hoped there would be a change in the military situation in Spain. Faupel was recalled 20 August and replaced by Dr. Baron Eberhard von Stohrer, who had been named as ambassador to the Spanish Republic in July 1936 but had not taken up his post because of the outbreak of the war. Sperrle was to remain with his Condor Legion until 31 October 1937.[6]

Within hours after General Franco ordered his ground and air units to break off the counteroffensive effort at Brunete, the Condor Legion aircraft began redeploying to fields in the North. Their main forward bases were initially the airstrips of Herrera de Pisuerga and Calahorra de Boedo (Palencia). The offensive ground forces, including the C.T.V., amounted to about 90,000 men. Even though the air groups were to operate under their respective air commanders, they were closely attached to their respective Army Corps commanders.

The air order of battle for the Condor Legion at the time was: the Bomber Group (K/88) with one squadron of He-111s and two squadrons of the old Ju-52s; the Reconnaissance Squadron (A/88) had flights of the He-70s, Do-17s, and the short-range He-46s; and the Fighter Group (J/88) had one squadron of the Bf-109s and two of the He-51s. The entire force consisted of about seventy aircraft, many of which had to undergo extensive repairs after the large effort at Brunete. In addition, there was the Floatplane Squadron, (AS/88) which was operating out of Pollensa Bay, Mallorca. This squadron operated as a separate unit. Although under General Sperrle's direct command technically, it was under the operational control of the Nationalist *Comandancia Militar* and the *Jefatura del Aire* (Chief of Air) on Mallorca, who at the time was Lt. Colonel Ramón Franco, brother of the generalissimo. In practice the Squadron Commander of AS/88 actually was left to operate almost completely on his own judgment. Being far removed from the Condor Legion, the squadron took no part in the operations in the North.[7]

The Italian *Aviazione Legionaria* and the Nationalist Air Brigade each also committed about the same number of aircraft. There was no question but that the Nationalists would have air superiority in the North. During the period, the Condor Legion was still undergoing a change in its structure as more modern aircraft and replacement personnel were being phased into the squadrons. Older aircraft were taken over by Spanish squadrons. The Germans were assigned to support the six tested Navarre Brigades, including the 4th and 5th Brigades, which also had been disengaged from Brunete. These brigades were now grouped in the Corps Navarre under General Solchaga. Once again Sperrle and Richthofen would work closely with Solchaga's staff and Colonel Vigón.

Sperrle and Richthofen initially were concerned that Franco—faced with the rugged terrain of the North and memories of the painfully slow advance against Bilbao—might for an extended period of time be content to remain with the gains already realized. Consequently the two Germans put considerable pressure on their Spanish colleagues to conclude the interrupted campaign. Here they found an ally in the person of Colonel Vigón.[8] Thus, both Sperrle and Richthofen were pleased to learn that the operation would be resumed.

Facing the Nationalists was an enemy force of about 50,000 which was decidedly deficient in artillery, and had between seventy and eighty aircraft. Of the latter, about eighteen Soviet fighters could be considered first-line warplanes. Once again the defenders held the advantage of position by controlling the heights of the rugged Cantabrian mountains. The battle zone was characterized by steep mountains and deep canyons, defended by a people who had been a problem for the Romans, Arabs, and armies of Napoleon. The Germans predicted it would be the same for the Nationalists.

The Italians had managed to convince the Nationalists that they should permit their forces to have a more active role in the ground advance. The C.T.V. was now given the center of the attack with the Navarre Brigades advancing on the flanks. The "Black Arrows" were to advance along the coast.

As the ground forces deployed on 8 August, the air squadrons started their preparatory bombardments in the Reinosa sector, southwest of Santander (see map 10). The squadrons dropped tons of bombs daily. Finally on 14 August, the artillery and infantry brigades were in position and ready. The artillery pounded the defenders, to be followed by the heavy bombers and the vicious ground support planes. The tactics were identical to those that had been adopted and perfected through the agonizing weeks of their attacks through the Basque lands. The artillery and aerial bombardments shattered the enemy defenses; at the same time the He-111 bombers (with Bf-109 escort) flew deep into enemy territory, bombing one vital target area after another. They were intercepted by

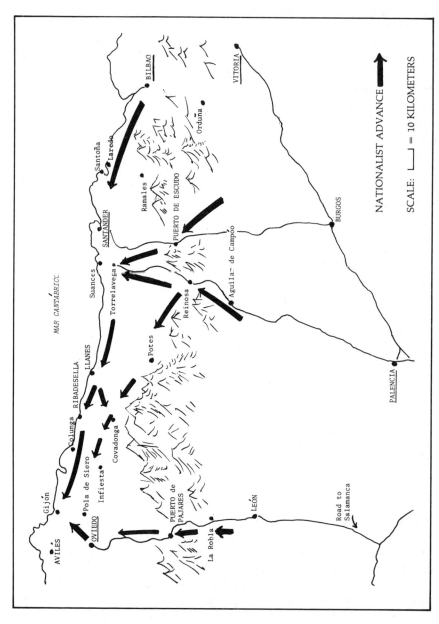

Map 10. Final Operation in the North, August–October 1937.

MAR CANTÁBRICO

AVILÉS
Gijón
OVIEDO
Pola de Siero
Infiesta
Covadonga
Colunga
RIBADESELLA
LLANES
Suances
Torrelavega
Potes
Reinosa
SANTANDER
Santoña
Laredo
Ramales
PUERTO DE ESCUDO
Aguilar de Campoo
Orduña
BILBAO
VITORIA
BURGOS
PALENCIA
PUERTO de PAJARES
La Robla
LEÓN
Road to Salamanca

NATIONALIST ADVANCE ◀━━

SCALE: |__| = 10 KILOMETERS

160

the remnants of the enemy fighters, which were now flown by Spanish pilots because the Soviets had decided to depart. The gritty Spanish pilots vainly tried to stem the Legion planes but were no match for the Bf-109s that shot them out of the sky.

It was hoped to trap much of the enemy force between the Río Ebro and the summit of the Cantabrian mountains. This would prevent thousands of enemy troops from escaping into Asturias, where it would be even more difficult to subdue them. To this end, the C.T.V. moved toward the important Escudo Pass, and the Navarrese drove toward Reinosa from the south. Colonel Alonso Vega's 4th Brigade took Reinosa on 15 August, the C.T.V. "23 March Division" moved well against the Escudo Pass, and the "Black Arrows" broke out along the coast. The enemy front was ruptured, with thousands of troops surrendering. Those in flight were pounded by bombs and machine guns from the air, with the Nationalist squadrons flying more than three missions a day trying to cut off as many of the enemy as possible from fleeing deep into Asturias. The commander of the enemy 15th Corps noted the air squadrons, in waves of forty to fifty planes, would attack his forces for up to an hour at a time.[9]

An attempted enemy counterattack was broken by Nationalist artillery, supported by the rapid-firing German 88mm flak guns and heavy blows from the air squadrons. This paved the way for Colonel García Valiño's 1st Brigade, 23 August, to drive to the sea past Torrelavega. Three enemy divisions were trapped. All possible escape routes were closed by 15 August, and the Basque troops surrendered to the C.T.V. at Santoña (east of Santander). The following day the troops in Santander gave up the fight.

The capture of Santander had taken less than two weeks. The effort cannot be considered a great aerial battle, with the defenders so hopelessly outclassed and outnumbered. It was, however, a well-executed advance closely coordinated with infantry, artillery, and air support. Even at that, after the painful experience of the eighty days to capture Bilbao, it did come as a surprise to many that the effort was not more difficult and more costly. Through it all, the German Condor Legion did not lose a single aircraft to enemy fighters, and what is equally interesting, none were lost to ground fire. There were personnel losses, however; Corporal Hermann Otto with a flak battery was killed (15 August) in direct contact with the enemy at Alar del Ray and NCO Fritz Mohlgemuth of the tank group *Imker* was killed (31 August) at Muñorrodero defending a tunnel. The Communications Group lost radioman Kurt Noack in a truck accident near Reinosa, and Corporal Richard Wolf of *Imker* died in Burgos of typhus.[10]

In a belated effort to disrupt the Nationalists in the North, the Valencia government initiated a large-scale offensive on the Aragón front on 24

August. The Army of Catalan was re-formed into the Army of the East under General Pozas and was reinforced with Modesto's 5th Corps with three divisions (including four International Brigades), which were disengaged from the Brunete sector. The Nationalist forces facing the offensive were thin and were scattered over many hundreds of kilometers from Teruel to the French border. It was not a continuous front of trenches and strong points, but a front in which high points were fortified with a field piece, mortars, and machine guns. The defending troops were quartered in a village to the rear with only part of the force manning the positions at any given time.

The Army of the East attacked at eight points from north of Teruel to the French border, with the main concentration against Saragossa. For this, it was necessary to carry the small town of Belchite, which had held back the armies of Napoleon in another age. The offensive opened without aerial and artillery preparation and the main thrust swept past Belchite, which was surrounded but refused to surrender to the International Brigades. The town came under siege and was pounded by artillery mortars and antitank guns. General Franco quickly responded by pulling General Barrón's 13th Division and General Saénz de Buruaga's 150th Division from west of Madrid (with the 105th Division as a reserve), which were rushed from around Madrid to meet the threat. Franco did not disrupt his ground forces deployed in the North, but elements of the Condor Legion were disengaged from the Santander sector. They flew to Saragossa where they operated against the enemy breakthrough at Belchite. But the main forces remained in the North.

Barrón was able to contain the threat against Saragossa; however, the 150th Division was unable to fight through to relieve the beleaguered but heroic defenders of Belchite before, after fourteen days of siege, it had to surrender. The heroism of their defense was something that the members of the Internationals had to admire. In fact, the Army of the East leadership was taken aback by the determined resistance of the few defenders all along the front. Still the Army of the East had pressed forward on a front extending on a line from Villanueva to Fuentes de Ebro, and eventually it was to make a small pocket south of the French border, as well as south of Huesca near Zuera, but the assault army was now thrown on the defensive.

In Asturias, the defenders were demoralized by the surprisingly rapid conquest of Santander, the loss of thousands of troops, and vast stores of materiel. After the Nationalists consolidated their newly won positions, the preparations were made for the final operation into Asturias to complete the conquest of the north. The Nationalists and Germans recognized that to gain control of Asturias, even though the enemy had no offensive capability, would be very difficult because of the rugged terrain. If the conquest of the region could not be completed prior to the rains of late fall and the snows of early winter, it would not be possible until the following spring. It was calculated that they were faced with some 50,000 defenders who, once again, were decidedly inferior in artillery and aircraft. At the same time the Nationalists knew that there were many internal difficulties in the enemy ranks, particularly in the leadership. It had been learned from prisoners taken at Santander that many of the troops were unwilling conscripts whose sympathies actually lay with the Nationalists. Still, from past experience it was determined that the effort would be difficult. The Germans were concerned that the struggle might deteriorate into a guerrilla-type war which would negate the effectiveness of their air superiority.

General Dávila was still the supreme commander, but the field commanders were General Solchaga (with his six Navarre Brigades now organized into the Corps Navarre) and General Aranda to operate out of the long-beleaguered Oviedo. The Italian C.T.V. was not to be used, but there were several Spanish battalions from Castile. The Nationalists were to attack west from along the coast, north from León, and east from Oviedo. The Condor Legion, with both aircraft and flak cannon as artillery, remained in support of the Corps Navarre. This was but natural because of the many months the German and Navarrese commanders had worked together in developing their close coordination between air and ground units.

The Condor Legion bombers, protected by the Bf-109s, several days before the offensive, started striking hard at the enemy areas and communications such as Gijón. When the general offensive began, on 1 September, the Legion heavily bombed mountain passes, ports, and all airfields. The He-51 fighters worked directly in front of the advancing battalions, as did the flak cannons. As expected, strong points of resistance quickly developed. The German liaison officers with the brigades called to the Legion Command Post and requested additional air strikes, which rapidly appeared. When the position was neutralized or stunned by the air attack, the infantrymen advanced wearing their white panels and were easily seen by the pilots. Slowly one strong point after another was destroyed.

Heated air battles developed between the far-outnumbered defenders who were Spaniards flying the Russian-made fighters. In a hopeless situation, these few pilots hurled their fighters out of the sky through the protecting Bf-109s to attack or disrupt the bomber formations. The German pilots held more than a little respect for these Spanish airmen who demonstrated not only outstanding aerial skills, but a heroic determination. However, these factors were not enough, and many outstanding enemy pilots were shot down. The enemy air force had a few old mixed bomber planes formed into a group known at the "*Circo Krone*," which showed as much determination in a difficult situation as their comrades in the fighters. The enemy flights operated mainly out of the airfields Colunga and Carreño, which were prime targets for the bombers of the Condor Legion.

The German air crews quickly learned the enemy flak gunners were surprisingly accurate. On 4 September, over Llanes (on the coast), the enemy aircraft guns shot down an He-70 and a Do-17 of the Reconnaissance Squadron. To die in the crash was Lieutenant Hans Detler von Kessel, who was so highly respected by the Spaniards because of his heroic efforts, many months before, to help the beleaguered and tragic defenders of Santa María de la Cabeza. Also to die were Lieutenant Gerhard Krocker, NCOs Ernst Hein, Waldemar Schnell, and Hermann Heil, and Corporal Waldemar Kruger.[11]

Also at Llanes, the enemy fighters broke up a formation of the He-51s now commanded by Captain Galland. The He-51 pilots could not always avoid the enemy fighters and had adopted the procedure of forming a protective circle. However, on this occasion the planes scattered, with the pilots attempting to flee individually by seeking the protection of the deep valleys. Captain Galland found himself with two fighters on the tail of his aircraft but managed to escape. In the excitement, he noted the smoke from a burning plane that had crashed on the airfield. He assumed it was one of his flight and landed at his base angered that his pilots had broken formation. When he gathered the squadron about him (for a dressing down) one of the pilots, Lieutenant Eduard Neumann, arrived late and tried to interrupt his irate commander. But it was not until Galland had given vent to his anger that Neumann was able to tell him that the plane he saw burning was an enemy Curtiss that he had shot down.[12]

When the Navarre infantrymen, under close air support, occupied Llanes (north of the fabulous Picos de Europa) on 5 September, they were able to recover the bodies of German crewmen who had been shot down the day before. Immediately General Dávila went to Llanes to award the Spanish Military Medal to the remains of Lieutenant von Kessel.[13]

German planes and flak batteries continued to support the infantrymen as they pressed past Llanes, and at the same time the Legion began to redeploy some of its fighters to the former enemy airstrip. An unusual airstrip it was. The landing field was very small with three sides towering above with extremely steep slopes. The remaining side was a sheer drop into the sea. Solid wire mesh fences were constructed all around the field to catch aircraft that would overshoot the landing. The importance of the field was its proximity to the battle front. From it the He-51 pilots were able to fly as many as seven sorties a day. They would have to refuel only on every other landing. The other landings were to replenish their ammunition and bombs, and many times this would be done without shutting down the engine. Quickly they would be back in the thick of battle. During hot weather the pilots usually would fly dressed only in shorts or swim trunks, boots, and goggles. Quickly they were covered with sweat and oil, and blackened by smoke from gunpowder.[14]

Solchaga's infantrymen were now moving toward the important communications center in Ribadesella, twenty-eight kilometers on the coast, due west of Llanes. In face of even greater determined resistance, more and more aerial flights were deployed in front of the Navarre brigades. The pilots flying the He-51 fighters found they had to revise their tactics against the enemy strong points, which were well fortified. An attack of one or two aircraft with their machine guns and light bombs would not reduce the position because the defenders would quickly withdraw into safe dugouts and reappear after the planes passed overhead. The pilots named these positions "coffin lids" because from above they looked like the ornamentation on a coffin. The He-51 squadrons reverted to attacking these positions in a mass formation which would fly at very low altitudes up the valleys to the rear of the positions. Over the target they dropped their bombs en masse. They called this "the little man's bomb-carpet."[15]

The mechanics of the He-51 squadron lent their ingenuity to the effort by developing an early version of a napalm bomb. It was a gas can filled with fuel and oil and with a fragmentation and incendiary bomb attached. Although very crude, it was effective and proved even more so as the pilots developed their delivery techniques.[16]

The Condor Legion fighters and bombers continued to fly sortie after sortie directly on the front and deep into enemy territory, but it was not without cost. On 11 September, Corporal Stanislaus Leske was shot down and killed in his He-51. That same day enemy bombers struck at the Germans who had moved into Llanes. During the bombing raid Corporal Georg Kohlheim, of the Flak Group, was killed as he manned a machine gun. Then on 21 September, a Ju-52 of the Bomber Group crashed and exploded on Mount Reinosa. Killed in the explosion were NCO Claus Held and Corporals Bruno Ness and Franz Nokier. That same day Lieutenant Friedrich Schwanengel of the Reconnaissance Squadron was shot down by antiaircraft fire and killed in his He-45 over Avilés. On 22 September, Lieutenant Hans Kemper, taking off in his He-51, crashed into a He-70 and died in the explosion.[17]

The following day General Solchaga's infantry finally moved into Ribadesella, twenty-eight miles due west of Llanes on the coast. The enemy was well positioned on the other side of the Río Sella, but under protective air support and fire from the German flak guns, the infantry forced a bridgehead and attacked the entrenched enemy from the rear. The Legion Bomber Group struck the enemy very hard again on 24 September, but Lieutenants Ernst König and Heinrich Meyer, along with NCO Franz Niebuhr and Corporal Karl Brettmeier, developed serious problems with their Ju-52. They tried to make an emergency landing at Pontejos (Zamora), but all died in the crash. Another bomber of the Group was attacked by enemy fighters but managed to escape. However, one of the crew, Corporal Willi Sembach, died shortly thereafter from his wounds.[18]

The planes of the Condor Legion never let up their pressure on Gijón and its environs. On 27 September there developed a hot aerial battle between five Soviet Ratas and five Bf-109s over the city. Captain Harder and Lieutenant Wötke both shot down a Rata, and Captain Harder forced another down on the landing field, which he strafed in several passes. The following day five Bf-109s engaged four enemy fighters, and once again, over Gijón, Captain Harder shot one down in flames. This was his seventh victory in Asturias and his ninth since he had arrived in Spain. Eventually Harder was to have a total of eleven victories in Spain and eleven more during World War II.[19] Then on 30 September, Lieutenant Wötke, flying his Bf-109 with the 1st Squadron (J/88) engaged three Ratas and five Curtiss fighters over Gijón. Wötke shot down his second Rata and Lieutenant Flegel, flying with the 2nd Squadron, was given credit for a "probable" victory. During this same period Lieutenant Bodden was given credit for two victories. Bodden and Flegel earlier had been credited with two victories each on the same day during the later phase of the Battle of Santander."[20]

But 30 September proved to be a difficult day for the Condor Legion. An He-111 bomber had an engine failure and attempted a forced landing. The plane was completely destroyed and the crew badly injured. The pilot of a Bf-109 returning from a mission was unable to lower his landing gear and slid the aircraft down the landing field on its undercarriage. The plane was badly damaged, but the pilot walked away from the crash, no doubt thinking under the circumstances "any landing you walk away from is a good landing." Two other He-111s were also forced to crash-land, but the crews were not badly injured.[21] Other planes were badly damaged by enemy fire.

The Nationalist soldiers received a great boost in morale on 1 October, when troops of the 5th Navarre Brigade, supported by the Legion, captured the historic Covadonga deep in the Picos de Europa. It was here in A.D. 718 that a small group of Spaniards under Pelayo inflicted the first reverse on the Moorish outriders during the Islamic conquest. Pelayo was shortly proclaimed king, and his tomb and that of his wife, as well as other early medieval Spanish royalty, are located at this historic and legendary site.

But the enemy still had not been shot out of the sky. On 5 October the Bf-109s protecting the bombers engaged seven enemy fighters again over Gijón. There were no losses or victories claimed but for moments it was uncomfortable. The following day two men of one of the German flak batteries were badly wounded supporting the advance of the 5th Brigade.[22]

On 7 October, a Ju-52 from the Bomber Group was hit by antiaircraft fire over Gijón. Its crew of Lieutenant Heinrich Stallamann (observer), Sergeants Ogaza (pilot) and Rudolph Hartig (bombardier), Brodnike (radioman), and Karl Ulirmeister (mechanic) were seen to parachute into enemy territory. All were killed except the pilot Ogaza, who was taken prisoner.[23]

The Germans working directly with the Spanish Brigades on the ground did not escape the danger. Corporal Walter Grempel of the Headquarters Staff was shot in the stomach and died quickly. Also Sergeant Matschinske with the Communications Group was badly wounded in the chest by a rifle bullet on 10 October, and two days later Sergeant Krempel, firing his flak gun in support of the 5th Brigade, was also gravely wounded by a bullet. Both men were to survive and eventually return to Germany.[24]

On 13 October, when the Legion bombers were over their targets, the enemy fighters attempted to break through the protective screen of Bf-109 fighters. Captain Harder now claimed his tenth victory, as an enemy fighter went down in flames. This was followed shortly by a Curtiss shot down by Alferez Siegmund. Their comrades on the ground were not so fortunate. Sergeant Scheurer was badly wounded by a rifle bullet, and Sergeant Schlotthauer, along with Corporals Felle, Schober, and Dolling fell victim to the plague of the Legion—a vehicle accident—and were seriously injured.[25]

The Nationalists had good news on 15 October when troops of General Solchaga and General Aranda's forces joined at the town of Infiesta. General Sperrle and Colonel von Richthofen could now see the final end in sight of the long, bitter, and frustrating operation in the North. The enemy forces were disintegrating as a field army. Nationalist sympathizers in Gijón managed to seize the city on 20 October, and the next day the Nationalist troops moved into the city; then with the capture of Avilés, due west of Gijón, the Nationalists had Asturias in their hands.

There were enemy redoubts that had to be reduced in the months to come, and guerrilla bands which were a thorny problem for even longer. But the operation in the North was over. A long and dangerous front had been eliminated. The Nationalists now controlled the entire North, and importantly, the great store of resources and arms industry of the region made the Nationalists, to a measure, a little more self-reliant.

On the Nationalist side there was unity of command, and close coordination between air power, artillery, and spirited ground troops. Colonel Adolfo Prada, who commanded the Asturian forces, noted the great impact of the Condor Legion and its incessant bombing of his forces. He reported these bombings would bury complete units in their trenches, and that many times 10 percent of a force would be lost without ever having come in contact with enemy ground forces.[26]

The Nationalists and Germans claimed fifty-one enemy aircraft shot down or destroyed on the ground. Some enemy planes were abandoned on the airfields in the last hectic days. Those that were reparable were soon back in commission wearing the Nationalist colors.

The infantry had hardly moved into Gijón and Avilés when many of the Condor Legion unit commanders and staff officers visited the cities to examine the effectiveness of their operation. Detailed studies were made of the successes and failures and forwarded to "Special Staff W" in Berlin. This was, however, the last such inspection to be made by the massive General Sperrle. After eleven months in the Spanish war, he received, at the end of October, orders from the Reich War Ministry to return to Germany. Other personnel that had departed the ports on the Baltic Sea almost a year before were soon to follow him, and new "Blond Moors" from Germany would take their places.[27]

Notes

1. Hugh Thomas, *The Spanish Civil War*, 2d ed., p. 772.
2. *GD*, Series D, Vol. III, Doc. No. 386, dated 7 July 1937.
3. Ibid.
4. *GD*, Series D, Vol. III, Doc. No. 399, dated 20 July 1937 Hans von Mackensen was state secretary in the Foreign Ministry.
5. Ibid. In his memorandum on the matter Mackensen did not explain what Canaris might have said to make Blomberg come to this decision.
6. Von Stohrer assumed his post in September 1937 and remained in Spain until January 1943.
7. R. L. Proctor, "They Flew from Pollensa Bay," *Aerospace Historian* 24, No. 4 (Winter/December 1977), pp. 196-202.
8. General Karl Drum, "The German Luftwaffe in the Spanish Civil War (Condor Legion)," p. 99. Also, in *The Republic and the Spanish Civil War in Spain*, ed. Raymond Carr (London, 1971), Ricardo de la Cierva y de Hoces, "The Nationalist Army in the Spanish Civil War," p. 207.
9. Directly quoted in R. Hidalgo Salazar, *La ayuda alemana a España 1936-39*, p. 156.
10. Salazar, *La ayuda alemana*, Appendix 1.
11. Ibid.
12. General Adolf Galland, *The First and the Last*, pp. 28-29, and discussion with the writer. Also see Trevor J. Constable and Colonel Raymond F. Toliver, *Horrido!* (New York, 1970), p. 390.
13. Condor Legion Headquarters Staff Report dated 26 September 1937, *Archivos Militar* (Madrid). The original copies of the daily reports of the Condor Legion for this period have been lost, as well as the later summaries prepared by "Special Staff W." However, the Legion did send copies, in Spanish, of these reports to the Spanish Command. For the most part these have been lost also, but there are some reports for this period in the *Archivos Militar* in Madrid. Also see Salazar, *La ayuda alemana*, p. 162.
14. Galland, *The First and the Last*, pp. 30-31, and the writer's discussions

with General Galland and Colonel Pitcairn. Pitcairn complained that very soon their boots acquired a very unpleasant odor.

15. Galland, *The First and the Last*, p. 30.

16. Ibid.

17. Salazar, *La ayuda alemana*, p. 162.

18. Ibid., Appendix 1.

19. Condor Legion Hqs. Staff Report of 27 and 28 September 1937. Sergeant Schalm of F/88 was gravely wounded by a premature explosion of a shell in a Spanish battery. See also Salazar, *La ayuda alemana*, p. 162.

20. Condor Legion Hqs. Staff Report of 13 September 1937, and Salazar, *La ayuda alemana*, p. 162.

21. Condor Legion Hqs. Staff Report of 30 September 1937, and Salazar, *La ayuda alemana*, p. 162.

22. Condor Legion Hqs. Staff Report, dated 5 October 1937.

23. Ibid. Also see Salazar, *La ayuda alemana*, pp. 162-163 and Appendix 1. This writer has located some of the interrogation reports of a few of the Germans who were captured and then later released. Although they named all of their fellow German prisoners they came in contact with, no reference was made to Pilot Ogaza. His fate is unknown to the writer. Captain Salazar in his totals of fatalities makes no note of Sergeant Brodnike.

24. Condor Legion Hqs. Staff Report, dated 1-12 October 1937, and Salazar, *La ayuda alemana*, Appendix 1.

25. Condor Legion Hqs. Staff Report, dated 13 October 1937. The report did not indicate the organization of the men injured.

26. Quoted in Salazar, *La ayuda alemana*, p. 161.

27. In *The Distant Drum: Reflections on the Spanish Civil War*, ed. Philip Toynbee (New York, 1976), Alfred Lent, "The Blond Moors are Coming!" pp. 95-104.

13

New Commander
and Teruel

There was a change of command ceremony on 30 October in the Condor Legion Command Staff at Salamanca as Sperrle turned his Legion over to General Helmuth Volkmann. With this there was a temporary lull in the fighting, which was welcomed by the flying squadrons and exhausted ground support units. The Legion had been battered by the continuous operation over the past months and there were many repairs to be made both to aircraft and to ground equipment. They were still having problems with a lack of spare parts for both aircraft and vehicles. This was not only because of a lack of standardization, but because of neglect by Berlin. To overcome the current problems, all maintenance crews had to salvage parts from damaged vehicles and aircraft. Colonel Pitcairn was candid in his remarks about these problems: "We really wondered about our government. We had the feeling we had been sent to Spain and then deserted. We had to bail ourselves out of a generally forgotten war. Our ground crews, who were the very best of the new German Air Force, worked very hard."[1]

At the same time, new aircraft continued to arrive from Germany that had to be reassembled and phased into the squadrons. The new people were confronted with problems and procedures of which they had never dreamed—many of which were directly opposite of what they had been taught and could be considered a violation of regulations.

The new Legion commander, General Volkmann, labored to learn the unique functions of his unusual command. Temporarily he retained the services of Colonel Richthofen as his chief of staff, which eased the transition. Volkmann, like Sperrle, was given a pseudonym and to many, as well as in correspondence, he was known as General Veith.[2]

General Volkmann was born in 1889 in Diedenhofen, Germany. He entered the German service as an ensign of Pioneers in 1908. In 1914, he transferred to the air arm and became a fighter pilot. He chose to remain in the *Reichswehr* of the German Republic, but as Germany was denied an air force, he served in the infantry, artillery, and cavalry. In 1934 he was a colonel. By 1937 he was a major general in command of the *Luftwaffe* Service Department. He was promoted to lieutenant general upon assuming command of the Condor Legion.[3]

Volkmann was considered a very good, honest, and hard-working commander, highly respected by his officers and men. As events proved, this honesty was to create problems for him in Berlin.

Volkmann re-formed the fighter group under Major Handrick into four squadrons. There were two squadrons of He-51 close support fighters, and two squadrons of Bf-109 fighters.

The Bomber Group, now commanded by Captain Neudörffer, soon had all four squadrons equipped with the decidedly higher performance He-111s. The old Ju-52s were turned over to the Nationalist Air Brigade, along with the He-70s from the Reconnaissance Squadron which were replaced by the Do-17s; but the unit retained the single flight of the short-range He-45s.

The Seaplane Squadron on Mallorca bid farewell to its commander Major Hefele and welcomed the dynamic Major Martin Harlinghausen, known by the nickname *"Eiserner Gustav."* Originally a torpedo officer of the German Navy, Martin Harlinghausen was to become one of the most noted bomber flyers and respected commanders of the *Luftwaffe*. Short in stature, slim of build, and with nerves of steel, he was a kind and sensitive man with a sparkling sense of humor. He asked no man to perform a task he would not do himself. Being highly professional, he was held in admiration by his officers and men and greatly respected by his superiors for not only his professional skills, intelligence, and ability, but for his candid honesty.

The Flak Group (F/88) was now composed of four heavy batteries of 88mm cannons, two batteries of 20mm, and one battery of 37mm guns. The air depot facility which had been near Seville was moved to León.

Now that the north of Spain had been secured and the Nationalists controlled about two-thirds of Spain, General Franco planned his next military move. The Nationalist army had been increased to 500,000 men, but was still less than the enemy with 750,000 men and 1,500 pieces of artillery. Of this force, the enemy Army Center (Madrid) was still under General Miaja, Army of the Levante (Valencia) was commanded by General Hernández Saravia, and the Army of the East (Catalonia) was under General Pozas. The combined enemy air strength was calculated at about 100 bombers, 200 fighters, and 100 reconnaissance and other aircraft. The Nationalists had an edge in numbers of bombers but the enemy held the advantage in fighter planes. From this point on, however, other than for a given sector at a specific moment, the air superiority shifted in favor of the Nationalists.

In his very first meeting with the Spanish and Italian staffs, General Volkmann noted all were in agreement that the next main Nationalist thrust would be toward the Mediterranean through Aragón with ten divisions to be covered by all air groups.[4] Thus, from the existing German evidence, it came as a surprise when Franco changed his mind and ordered the Aragón offensive discontinued and made plans for a drive against Madrid.

For some time the Condor Legion Command Staff had been equipped with a *Wohnzug* (housing train) as Command quarters, consisting of about twelve cars which were used for sleeping, eating, conference rooms, and a communications section. Protected by a flak battery, it could move quickly from one point to another with relative safety. It was decided to move the complete Operational Staff to the medieval walled-fortified market town of Almazán on the Río Duero, north of the Guadarrama mountains, halfway between Soria and Medinaceli. Flights of the Bomber Group and the Reconnaissance Squadron took up station at the airfield of El Burgo de Osma, and the fighter squadrons moved into Torresaviñan. The Legion was now stationed so it could support either a drive against Madrid or from Saragossa to the Mediterranean Sea. All facilities were very primitive.[5]

All air groups were ordered to strike deep into enemy territory to the south and hit enemy airfields behind the front in Aragón along the Río Ebro. Strong raids were made against Sariñena, Puebla de Hijar, Balaguer, Lérida, and other concentrations. Because of limited fuel, even with extra tanks, many of the Nationalist planes were able to remain in the target areas only for a very short time. Colonel Pitcairn explained:

> Fuel was always a problem; that is why we had to change our bases of operation so many times. We had extra tanks which were susceptible to ground fire during our attack but we could not afford to drop them because of the limited supply, unless we were attacked by enemy fighters. To extend our fuel as much as possible, we started engines, ran them up, checked them out, and shut them down. Then we filled the tanks and made an immediate take-off. For fuel economy, we usually approached the target area at 2,000 meters altitude, then dropped to our attack altitude of between 50

and 100 meters. It was very carefully calculated with 50 minutes to the target, 10 minutes over the target, and 55 minutes back to base. We generally flew in squadron strength of 10 to 12 aircraft.[6]

Even though all air units were concentrated against enemy positions for three days, the Legion staff calculated they were not able to accomplish their missions as desired. They were surprised at the resiliency and reserves of the enemy.[7] While hitting enemy facilities (10 December) near Fraga (Huesca), Lieutenant Gerhard Klein was shot down and died in the explosion of his He-51. Killed at the same time was the crew of a He-111, which was also shot down. The crewmen were Lieutenant Friedrich Karl Beuke, Sergeants Anton Bergmann and Fritz Bruhl, and Corporal Alois Ehlen.[8]

General Volkmann continued to hold his squadrons at their bases. From there he could strike along the Guadalajara-Madrid front or the middle of the Ebro. By 15 December, the Nationalist forces were ready. But, on that day the Nationalists were faced with a massive enemy assault out of Aragón to Teruel, which by all accounts caught the Nationalist command by surprise.

Since the beginning of the Civil War, the front line in this sector followed the mountains west, south, and east of Teruel. The city on its hill was a salient into government territory, and the only communications link between it and Nationalist Spain was across the high plateau and valley of the Río Jiloca, which flows past Calamocha and Daroca. It was here that the longest and most vicious battle of the Spanish conflict until now developed.

Teruel, like Brunete, was only lightly held by the Nationalists. The forces of the city and its environs numbered but 3,000 and were augmented by 2,000 volunteers from within the city. There were makeshift trenches and dugouts about the city at tactical positions but with limited artillery. The attack force of the Army of the Levante comprised about 60,000 men with an additional 40,000 reserves. They were supported by 120 fighter planes and 80 bombers, with an additional 100 aircraft of different types, including armed reconnaissance. It later proved they were supported by a surprising number of flak guns, including some very effective new weapons which had just arrived from the Soviet Union. The attack ground force was divided into three Army Corps and included the 22nd Corps of Colonel Juan Ibarrola (Lister's 11th Division was attached to spearhead the assault), the 18th Corps of Colonel Fernández Heredia, and the 20th Corps of Colonel, later General, Leopoldo Menéndez López.

Teruel (population 20,000) is the capital of the southernmost of the three provinces that made up the ancient kingdom of Aragón. Located at 3,000 feet, overlooking the confluence of the Turia and Alfambra rivers, it is built mostly of brick with remains of castellated walls and fantastically beautiful Mudéjar towers. Teruel is notorious for its bad winter weather, with the lowest temperatures in Spain.

Without artillery or aerial bombardment to betray the intention, the assault started 15 December in a snowstorm. Shortly the Nationalist command realized it was faced with a massive assault in a very poorly defended area.

Franco determined that the enemy must be halted, and for this he would have to scrap his intended attack against Madrid. The decision should have come as no surprise to the Germans, after watching Franco's earlier responses to concentrated enemy offensives that had realized initial success. To the German military men, this came about because of the general conduct of the Spanish conflict. They saw the war as being concentrated around specific targets. These might be a city, a village, a hill, or a bridge. The Germans were repeatedly disturbed that the Spaniards did not seem to consider a flanking or diversionary attack in another sector, and despite their suggestions, the Spaniards repeatedly insisted on meeting any threat head-on. In part, the Germans took the view that this was explained by the Spanish character which ". . .regards it as a matter of course to meet the enemy at a point where he attacks and finds it unnecessary and not quite honorable to avoid him by attacking somewhere else."[9]

General Volkmann and his staff believed the best course of action was: if the Nationalists immediately continued their planned attack toward Madrid, it would relieve the pressure against Teruel. Their opinion was shared by the Italians, but Franco was determined. Reluctantly, the Italians assigned most of their artillery to support his plans; but Volkmann, at this point, agreed only to commit two of his 88mm batteries. By 17 December, however, he concluded the initiative lay with the enemy and ordered his air units moved to fields near the battle zone to contain the advance. The headquarters *Wohnzug* left Almazán and descended into the Jiloca valley to Calamocha, seventy kilometers north of Teruel. Flights of the Reconnaissance Squadron He-45s flew into its landing strip and were quickly dispatched into the battle zone. Other flights and fighter squadrons flew into the fields of Saragossa and Valenzuela, and the long-range bombers took up station at Alfaro and Gallur in the Ebro valley north of Saragossa. All support functions were again on the move with the communications sections frantically working to establish wire and radio communications to all organizations and allied command staffs.

The combat squadrons immediately encountered severe weather. Snowstorms increased and the temperature continued to slide below freezing to restrict air operation on both sides. By 18 December, the Army of Levante divisions occupied the ridge called Muela de Teruel (Teruel's Tooth) overlooking the city from the southwest. The defending

Nationalist commander, Colonel Rey d'Harcourt, realized his limited force could not hold the outer defenses and withdrew his troops for consolidation behind the city walls. The enemy divisions encircled the city by double envelopment east of the villages of San Blas and Campillo, and parts of the two attack divisions could now be turned into the city from two different directions.

Finally, on 22 December, General Franco called Colonel Richthofen to his headquarters to meet with the Spanish and Italian staffs. Franco was determined to concentrate his Corps Galicia (of General Aranda) and Corps Castile (of General Varela) south for a counterblow, no matter how high the cost. He established a new command under General Dávila to carry out the task, and appointed Vigón, now a general, as chief of staff. To start, Richthofen was to have the German Legion support Varela's Corps Castile, and the Italian air group to cover Aranda's Corps Galicia. Including the Italian artillery, Franco ordered 400 guns moved to the battle zone. He set the day for the counterattack as 29 December.

General Volkmann ordered all fighter squadrons into Calamocha, to be closer to the operation. He moved his Command quarters to the little village of Bronchales in the Sierra de Albarracín, northwest of Teruel. The Legion Command Post (C.P.) was established in a group of farm buildings called La Magdalena on the battlefield near the Command Post of General Varela.[10]

Furious battles developed around Teruel as one Nationalist position after the other had to be reduced. The deteriorating weather restricted aerial operations, but whenever possible all Nationalist squadrons were in the air as direct support and at the same time trying to destroy enemy reserves and concentrations.

By Christmas, enemy assault forces were in the narrow streets of Teruel and a battle developed block by block, building by building, and floor by floor. Once again the Spanish war had degenerated into hand-to-hand battles with fire bombs, grenades, bayonets, and knives. The defenders piled the streets deep with enemy bodies, which quickly froze stiff. But, one by one, the defenders' positions of resistance fell to the attack forces.

The German Legion and Nationalist Air Brigade committed all aircraft possible over San Blas, Concud, and Alfambra as the fighting raged in the city. The Nationalist ground relief force was ready on 29 December, and once again bombers and strafing planes were paving the way as the attack swept over Morrones. The enemy line was broken, causing reinforcements to be rushed forward to try to seal the breaches. They too were attacked from the air as the advance rolled forward, with the planes opening the route for General Varela's battalions to dislodge the enemy from La Pedriza and La Muela de Teruel (only two kilometers from Teruel). On 31 December, there was a panic within the city in the ranks of the enemy, who was now on the defensive and still fighting the remnants of Colonel Rey d'Harcourt's force. For a few hours, the city could have been grasped by the Nationalists, but government discipline was restored.[11]

Now there was a terrible change in the weather. High winds and heavy snow turned into a raging blizzard as temperatures dropped far below zero. Vehicles by the hundreds were stranded in deep snowdrifts on each side for miles behind the front. The suffering troops of both sides were completely cut off from their bases of supply. Air operations came to a halt, as well as the Nationalist counterattack, but the battle continued to rage within Teruel.

The Legion mechanics found they were unable to start their aircraft engines. The low temperature congealed the oil to the point where the propellers could not be turned through. They had encountered this problem during the previous winter and had learned to build hoods around the engines to contain heaters. When the metal and oil warmed, the engines fired. They were able to get their aircraft in the air the last day of 1937. But it was a futile and almost costly effort. A bomber formation of twenty-three aircraft encountered strong winds with snow and turned south where it was scattered by enemy fighters. For many hours, it was a worried staff in the Legion Command Post. Seven aircraft were missing. It was not until late that night that Volkmann learned his missing bombers had landed at Ávila, Escalona, and Talavera.[12]

On New Year's Day 1938, within Teruel one Nationalist strong point after another fell to the assault. Outside the city, heavy snows and freezing cold across the mountains and windswept plateaus gave birth to a battle of attrition as each side threw in new forces that somehow managed to push their way through the high drifts.[13] To the Germans, it was a battle that made its own rules and the Command Staffs had no recourse but to follow, as one minor terrible battle after another developed. Battalions on each side were left on their own initiative with little or no knowledge of what was transpiring on their flanks.

The blizzard raged for four days, completely immobilizing ground and air forces on both sides. The government assault forces now devoted their efforts to holding their positions. Finally, on 8 January, Nationalist Colonel Rey d'Harcourt surrendered his remaining troops in the ruins of his city.

The Barcelona government and its supporters gained a great propaganda victory with the capture of Teruel and the failure of the Nationalist counterattack. Many in Rome and Berlin also saw Teruel as a major victory for the enemy and seriously questioned whether the Nationalists would ever be able to succeed. Through January 1938, each side traded blows with the other as they rebuilt their forces, supplies, and equipment ravaged by war and blizzards. Weather permitting, each air force struck at its enemy.

There were additional changes in the Condor Legion staff during this period. Captain Christ arrived as the new operations officer (16 January) and started the daily *Diary* he maintained through 23 December 1938.[14] Colonel Richthofen bade farewell to the officers and men of the *Wohnzug* and made his last official visit to the Spaniards. Before the farewell, it was necessary to discuss in detail the proposed major offensive against the enemy located west of the Río Alfambra. General Franco had disengaged the divisions from Madrid grouped in the newly formed Corps *Marroquí* under General Yagüe, and was deploying them north of Aranda's Corps Galicia. Franco concluded it would be more advisable at this time to clear the enemy from the bulge extending from the area of Singra to the Río Alfambra. Singra is a very small village (it does not appear on many road maps of Spain) located west of the Río Alfambra and south of Calamocha. Besides supporting the assault forces, the Legion was to hit hard into the enemy rear areas.

General Volkmann drove to the front on 17 January, and joined General Aranda in his Command Post at Cerro Gordo to observe an offensive by the Navarre Units directly supported by the Condor Legion (see map 11). Both were pleased with the progress and air-to-ground coordination. Then Volkmann suggested the Corps *Marroquí*'s attack around Monreal del Campo be directed between the villages of Perales and Alfambra.

The following day the entire German General Staff at Almazán started its move to Baños de Fitero. Baños de Fitero is a very charming hot springs resort deep in the valley of the Río Linares, not far from where it flows into the Río Ebro.

Major Hermann Plocher, who had been instrumental in organizing the first units of the Legion, now assumed the position of chief of staff. Berlin was still playing the game of secrecy, and Plocher was amused when he received his orders for Spain to hear on the Stuttgart radio: "Major Plocher is going to Spain. Now he will have the opportunity to prove what he arranged in Berlin."[15]

The Nationalists advanced slowly north of Teruel from 20 through 24 January with all forces supported by the air squadrons. This changed abruptly 25 January when, with discipline restored, the government divisions of General Hernández Saravia launched a spoiling attack all along the Monreal del Campo-Teruel front. Nationalist units quickly deployed in defensive formations and rushed strong reinforcements into the line, and the entire German Legion was thrown against the assault divisions. Captain Christ wrote: "Only with the assistance of the Condor Legion was it possible to stop the Red attack. Particularly helpful were the attacks of the He-51 fighters."[16] Enemy fighters tried to scatter the Legion bombers. Although no bombers were lost, some were damaged; navigator Corporal Thomas Wartner was seriously wounded in his He-111. Under continual air and artillery bombardment, the enemy broke off pressure on 27 January and started to withdraw.[17]

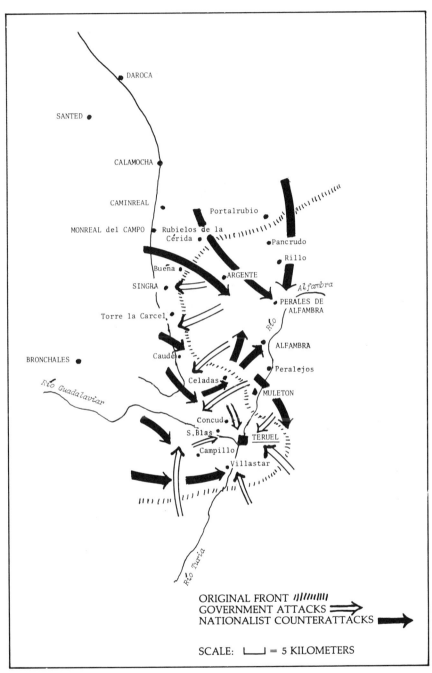

DAROCA

SANTED

CALAMOCHA

CAMINREAL

MONREAL del CAMPO

Portalrubio

Rubielos de la
Cérida

Pancrudo

Rillo

Buena

ARGENTE

Alfambra

SINGRA

PERALES DE
ALFAMBRA

Torre la Carcel

Río

ALFAMBRA

BRONCHALES

Caudé

Peralejos

Río Guadalaviar

Celadas

MULETON

Concud

S.Blas

TERUEL

Campillo

Villastar

Río Turia

ORIGINAL FRONT)ıl/ıllıllı
GOVERNMENT ATTACKS
NATIONALIST COUNTERATTACKS

SCALE: ⌴ = 5 KILOMETERS

Map 11. Battle of Teruel and Alfambra, January and February 1938.

Volkmann knew Franco would resume the offensive with renewed vigor and sent Lieutenant Gabriel of the Legion staff to fly in his light liaison plane (Storch) in search of a more suitable location to move the Command quarters closer to the battle zone.[18] All major commanders met on 28 January to determine the next phase of the offensive. Volkmann again suggested the forces concentrated for an attack against the enemy west of the Río Alfambra be aimed between the towns Alfambra and Perales de Alfambra. General Vigón agreed and issued the proper orders. D-Day was set for 4 February. In the meantime, the He-51 fighters again helped repulse another enemy attack at Singra. The Legion Battle Staff was alerted to prepare to move directly to the Legion Command Post being established on the battlefield.

On 3 February 1938, the Nationalists started an intensive artillery and aerial bombardment along the front. The enemy, well aware of what was to happen, sent aircraft over the buildup area and struck hard at the Condor Legion base at Almazán, where many of the German planes were caught on the ground. The Germans were distressed to see many of their aircraft damaged, but no personnel were lost.

Lieutenant Gabriel in his Storch finally located a suitable site for the Command quarters at the small village of Santed, sixteen kilometers southwest of the ancient Moorish stronghold of Daroca on the road to Molina. From there they had easy access to Hondo de Mas, which had been selected as the Legion forward Command Post (C.P.). To reach the C.P., the staff had to go by horseback. This was fitting, in that from there they would be able to watch a spectacular charge of General Monasterio's cavalry, attached to Yagüe's Corps *Marroquí*. The entire Legion Battle Staff moved from Baños de Fitero to Santed on 4 February. During the night, all units made a last inspection of aircraft and the crews were again instructed in detail as to what was expected from them the next day.

The Legion Staff was in the C.P. the next morning and pleased with the deployment of forces, along with the attacks of Spanish, Italian, and German squadrons. They were surprised at the limited counteraction by enemy aircraft or artillery; at the same time disappointed that their own ground objectives were not fully attained. They were distressed when one of their Do-17 bombers crash-landed behind friendly lines. It had been caught in its own bomb blast, which illustrates the very low altitude of the Legion attacks. Two airmen were seriously wounded by bomb splinters.[19]

An incident happened that day which is not reflected in Captain Christ's *Diary*, although subsequently he did make note of such occurrences. The 5th Spanish Division was mistakenly attacked by twelve German planes. The Division lost 400 dead and wounded. Among the wounded was a young lieutenant, José Aramburu de Topete. During the entire Alfambra operation, this division lost only thirty men to enemy action.[20]

That evening the Legion Staff rode down the hill on their horses to spend a restless night in the Command quarters at Santed. They were back in the C.P. early the next morning. Volkmann, Plocher, and Captain Christ were pleased to see the way their bomber and strafing planes pinned down the enemy and how the cavalrymen advanced to throw the enemy in retreat.

To keep up with the battle, they hurried down the mountain to move their C.P. forward to Monte de San Cristóbal for 7 February. After the artillery and bombers stopped their bombardment and the strafing planes cleared the front, the much-mustachioed General Monasterio's cavalry made a spectacular charge reminiscent of another age. The aircraft then continued to pound the enemy in retreat toward the Río Alfambra.[21]

Enemy aircraft swarmed in to bomb and strafe the Nationalist infantry and horsemen, but they were intercepted by the German Bf-109 fighter squadrons. A spectacular aerial battle developed in the sky to match the scene on the ground. The German fighters raged in on the enemy planes and twelve Martin bombers were blown to pieces in the sky or shot down in flames to explode along the Río Alfambra, where Christian and Moslem knights had charged each other centuries before.

Lieutenant Wilhelm Balthasar, in his Bf-109, accounted for three of the bombers but his plane was damaged in the exchange of fire. He broke off his attack and turned to nurse his crippled aircraft back to base, only to be intercepted by an enemy Rata. He managed to turn inside the enemy and catch him in a killing blast from his machine guns. When the Rata crashed in flames, Balthasar counted his seventh and last victory in Spain.[22]

By evening the Nationalists had reached the villages of Perales-Alfambra and the enemy was in full retreat across the Río Alfambra. Many enemy units were a disorganized mass to be pursued by the ground support planes. The offensive was a major success. The enemy had been driven back over thirty kilometers and suffered some 15,000 casualties; thousands had been taken prisoner, and vast stores of war materiel waited to be collected by the victors. Importantly, the Nationalist flanks could not be turned and their rear was safe for the eventual push to Teruel. The river crossings would be prime targets for the air squadrons the next day; but that night the Legion staff closed its C.P. and returned to Baños de Fitero to take advantage of the steam baths and a relaxing meal.

Accompanied by his immediate staff, on 9 February, Volkmann visited General Vigón's headquarters at Caminreal to discuss the next phase of operation. Volkmann suggested that much more could be gained by ignoring the enemy in Teruel, completely abandoning the Madrid plans, and regrouping the Nationalist divisions for an offensive down both sides of the Río Ebro to the Mediterranean Sea. This was flatly rejected. Captain Christ, in attendance, wrote later that day; "The efforts of General Veith [Volkmann] to convince the Spaniards of the stupidity of further attacks on Teruel is hopeless. To the Spaniards, the relief of Teruel is a moral necessity."

The Spanish staff was annoyed with General Volkmann at this time for another reason. They were of the opinion he had recommended the Condor Legion be returned to Germany. The reason Volkmann put forth was that he had heard rumors that Hitler was about to occupy Austria. If this were the case, he was concerned it might provoke a European conflict and his Legion would be trapped in Spain at a time it would be desperately needed in Germany. The Spaniards, however, saw his position more as one of stubbornness because they had not followed his suggestion to continue the Madrid offensive at the time of the Teruel breakthrough. His recommendation that Teruel be ignored now made the Spanish tempers grow. They considered his position as one of meddling and being intolerant of orders from the Nationalist command. Eventually the disagreement was smoothed over. When the final phase of the Battle of Teruel started, the German Legion was fully committed with all squadrons and flak guns.[23]

Volkmann returned to his forward Command quarters at Santed on 11 February. The attack was to start the next morning. Plocher and Christ remained in Baños de Fitero and worked very late preparing combat orders which were transmitted to all combat commanders. They were about to leave for Santed when word came from General Kindelán that the attack would have to be delayed because of deteriorating weather. The poor weather lasted for several days, which gave the enemy the opportunity to initiate a strong spoiling attack with some gains in the direction of the Caminreal-Montalbán road. This almost upset the Nationalist plans.

After frustrating delays, the offensive was finally set for 17 February. Major Plocher and Captain Christ were in the Command Post located on a hill near Muleton. For additional air support, the Legion now had three of the new Ju-87 Stuka dive-bombers. They had arrived a few weeks before, been reassembled, test-flown, and were now loaded with 250-kilo bombs.

Hoping to catch the enemy in Teruel and along the Turia and Alfambra rivers, the offensive opened with heavy artillery, aided by the Legion flak batteries, and aerial bombardment all along the front. The enemy stood firm along the line except at Villalba Baja, ten kilometers north of Teruel on the Río Alfambra. The Ju-87s, as well as the He-51 fighters, were used to pound the way for the infantry, and Plocher was most impressed with the results.[24] The enemy line had not been completely shattered, but there were high hopes for the next day.

General Volkmann was in the C.P. for the operation on 18 February to witness the breakthrough by Yagüe's Corps *Marroquí* on the left flank of General Aranda's Corps Galicia. The Río Alfambra was crossed in several places, and the Nationalists started their encirclement, which would bypass Teruel from the north. In the excitement a Ju-52 became lost and landed in Portugal. The battle was most intense with squadron after squadron making repeated sorties both along the front and into the enemy rear areas to add to the general confusion.

The next morning the Germans were still in their C.P. directing their squadrons against specific target areas. Captain Christ wrote that day: "The enemy fights very hard! In no way has his determination decreased. Even after they have been pounded by artillery and aerial bombardment, every position has to be stormed by infantry." Also, the enemy was still contesting in the air and shot down Sergeant Heinrich Torner, who died in the crash of his fighter plane.[25]

The Germans could see the battle turning decidedly in favor of the Nationalist ground forces. On 20 February, the C.P. was still in the same location when Captain Christ wrote: "The town of Teruel is completely surrounded with the Nationalists crossing the Río Turia in the south. It was now possible to overrun the feared cemetery north of Teruel. The surrounded enemy defended himself with great determination, but Teruel was penetrated." As the Nationalist infantry poured in, terrible street fighting once again raged in the city of the "Lovers of Teruel." The He-51s added their blows to the confusion. Major Plocher, at the same time, called in the Ju-87 Stukas with their heavy bombs to strike heavily fortified points of resistance. Still Captain Christ noted: "The situation remained unclear until evening."

General Hernández Saravia realized his forces' escape route toward Valencia was in grave danger of being severed from both flanks and gave the order for his army to withdraw from the battle. Quickly units disengaged and fled the battlefield before the Nationalists could close their trap. A large part of his army was unable to avoid the encirclement.

The following day Volkmann and Plocher were back in their C.P. directing their flak guns and aircraft at pockets of resistance. Suddenly enemy fighters appeared over the city and battlefield. A spectacular aerial battle developed between Ratas and the German Bf-109s. When the rattle of machine gun fire and screaming of engines faded away, the Germans counted seven victories and no losses. Captain Christ noted that day: "The capture of Teruel is soon possible. Many prisoners are being brought in, our losses are minimal." The next day, after heavy fighting, the Nationalist infantry cleared the enemy from the large plateau Castellar, and the end of the Battle of Teruel was in sight. General Volkmann, along with Lieutenant Gabriel, left the Command Post and went down into the city to examine their efforts firsthand. They came under enemy artillery fire and discreetly withdrew to the Command Post of General Varela for a warm welcome.

Captain Christ wrote in his *Diary* for 23 February: "No one in the Command Post. The final offensive goals have been attained. The recapture of Teruel is now brought to a successful conclusion." The same day, Major Plocher, Captain Christ, and Lieutenant Schwartz made an extensive tour along the entire battle front. A very tired General Volkmann repaired to Baños de Fitero but only for a few hours of rest.

The Battle of Teruel lasted for two months, and it is most difficult to determine the cost for both sides. It is possible the Nationalists lost between 9,000 and 10,000 soldiers and civilians within the city as dead or taken prisoner. The cost to the relief force has been put at 14,000 dead and 33,000 wounded, frostbitten, and sick. Few writers will make an estimate of the cost for the Army of the Levante other than to presume it might have been at least half as much again as those of the Nationalists.[26] The cost for the Condor Legion was far less than in the effort in northern Spain. Besides the airmen already noted, the Flak Group (F/88) lost NCO Ludwig Florezack who was killed on 28 December 1937, in an aerial bombardment. Corporal Heinrich Fingor, on 30 December, was shot in the head, and NCO Arno Lampe was killed by the premature explosion of an artillery shell.

On 23 December, NCO Anton Kurz, of K/88, died as a result of an aircraft accident in León. Then on 8 January 1938, NCO Paul Schick and Corporal Erwin Hoster died at Lerma when their aircraft from the Bomber Group K/88 struck a mountain. Corporal Ludwig Ottzen of Ln/88 was killed by a hand grenade while building a bunker at Teruel. Other Germans were lost to ground accidents.[27]

The Germans now expected Franco to deploy his forces for the assault against Madrid.

Notes

1. Colonel Pitcairn's comments to the writer.
2. This went as far as Captain Christ, who very shortly became his new operations officer, always referring to Volkmann in his *Daily Diary* as General Veith.
3. Material was reduced from General Volkmann's service record.
4. General Karl Drum, "The German Luftwaffe in the Spanish Civil War (Condor Legion)," p. 107, and the writer's discussion with Major General Plocher, who shortly became General Volkmann's chief of staff.
5. Drum, "The German Luftwaffe," p. 107, and writer's discussion with General Plocher. Colonel Pitcairn when describing the *Wohnzug* used by the fighter

squadrons noted they were surprised it was not repeatedly attacked by enemy aircraft. There were many leaks in the connecting steam fittings between cars, and in cold weather the *Wohnzug* could be seen for miles. Letter from Colonel Pitcairn to the writer.

6. Colonel Pitcairn's comments to the writer.

7. Drum, "The German Luftwaffe," p. 108.

8. R. Hidalgo Salazar, *La ayuda alemana a España 1936-39*, p. 164 and Appendix 1.

9. Drum, "The German Luftwaffe," p. 110.

10. Ibid., p. 113a.

11. Pierre Broué and Emile Témime, *The Revolution and the Civil War in Spain* (Cambridge, Mass., 1970), p. 482, fn. 8.

12. Drum, "The German Luftwaffe," p. 112, and Salazar, *La ayuda alemana*, p. 167.

13. Drum, "The German Luftwaffe," p. 112.

14. Captain Christ's *Diary*, Freiburg. Hereafter cited as Capt. Christ's *Diary*. If the date is in the text, no citation will be made.

15. The late General Plocher's comment to the writer.

16. Captain Christ's *Diary* entry of 25 January 1938.

17. Ibid., entry of 26 January 1938.

18. The Storch (Fieseler-156) was an observation monoplane used for many different purposes. The prototype was flown in 1936 and the production models a year later. In a slight wind it could hover at fantastically low speeds. The takeoff was about seventy meters and the landing twenty meters. It had two seats, but six people could crowd into the cabin. It carried one machine gun, firing up and to the rear. Tony Wood and Bill Gunston, *Hitler's Luftwaffe*, pp. 156-157.

19. Capt. Christ's *Diary*, entry of 5 February 1938. Many writers of the Spanish conflict state this offensive started 7 February; that was the day of its greatest successes. It started 3 February as noted.

20. Writer's discussion with Lt. General José Aramburu de Topete, director general of the Spanish *Guardia Civil*. Aramburu distinguished himself during the Battle of Krasny-Bor in Russia, when as a captain he commanded a company of combat engineers of the Spanish Blue Division.

21. Drum, "The German Luftwaffe," p. 114, and General Plocher's comments to the writer.

22. Drum, "The German Luftwaffe," p. 114; Salazar, *La ayuda alemana*, p. 169, and Trevor J. Constable and Colonel Raymond F. Toliver, *Horrido!* (New York, 1970), pp. 296-297.

23. Salazar, *La ayuda alemana*, pp. 169-170, and General Plocher's comments to the writer. General Plocher continued: "We were firmly convinced the Spanish reaction at Teruel was wrong, and made this specifically clear. Later when the Spaniards said they were merely going to readjust their front in the Belchite sector General Volkmann was specific. We absolutely would not commit the Condor Legion to anything other than a drive to the sea. Even though there was this disagreement on the matter of strategy, the relationship between Volkmann and the Spaniards always remained cordial. General Kindelán was a very intelligent, kind, understanding, and capable man."

24. General Plocher's comments to the writer.

25. Captain Christ's *Diary*, entry of 19 February 1938, and Salazar, *La ayuda alemana*, Appendix 1.

26. Thomas, *The Spanish Civil War*, 2d. ed., p. 794.

27. Captain Christ's *Diary*, and Salazar, *La ayuda alemana*, Appendix 1.

14

The Aragón
Offensive

General Franco, on 24 February 1938, had his Field Headquarters at Morata de Jiloca, south of Calatayud on the Daroca-Teruel road, and requested that General Volkmann, his Chief of Staff Plocher, and Operations Officer Christ meet with the Spaniards and allied field commanders. The Germans expected Franco would detail his plans for a renewed offensive against Madrid. None of the Germans were in favor of the operation and for some time had urged Franco to make a concentrated drive through Aragón to the Mediterranean Sea which would divide the enemy forces in Catalonia from Valencia.

In this meeting, the Germans were startled by Franco's comments. Plocher later commented: "I was most surprised the Spaniards had agreed, at least in principle, to our repeated recommendations."[1] Captain Christ was moved to write in his *Diary*: "Amazingly, Franco has given up on his objective of an offensive to Madrid! Instead he has decided to initiate an offensive to the Levante coast south of the Río Ebro."

As Franco met with his generals and allies, the front line of Aragón ran east of Teruel in a general northerly direction (see map 12). First it went along the Río Alfambra, and then toward Vivel del Río Martín. From there it made a wide bow to the west to the Río Huerva. It followed this river to Villanueva de Huerva where it turned north. Then it made a turn to the northeast and followed over Puebla de Albortón to Fuentes de Ebro. The line then crossed the Río Ebro at Osera, and there changed in a westerly direction to Saragossa. To the south, the terrain is a slowly climbing plateau crossed by several arid and barren mountain chains which run from northwest to southwest from the Sierra de Cucalón, south of Montalbán, and north to the Sierra de San Just, which terminates the high plateau. The elevation climbs to 2,000 meters. In the summer, little water is to be found. The mountain chains then change into the coastal mountain range, which extends from north to south in the direction of Valencia and divides inner Spain from the coastal stretch of the Mediterranean.

Franco's proposed battle area is crossed by several rivers flowing generally in a northerly direction to the Río Ebro. The attack was to be from three directions into the enemy bulge between Vivel del Río Martín and Fuentes de Ebro, and would be followed by a quick dash to the Mediterranean Sea.

Captain Christ noted in his *Diary* that a force from Cariñena was to direct its main effort against the enemy at Alcañiz, on the Río Guadalope and to Caspe at the confluence of the Río Guadalope and the Río Ebro. The generalissimo proposed that his offensive be carried out by his newly created Army North of three army corps under command of General Fidel Dávila Arrondo. This was the largest concentration of Nationalist forces up until this time during the war. There was the Corps Galicia under General Antonio Aranda Mata which was to attack in a direction over Alcorisa and converge upon Alcañiz. The Italian C.T.V. of General Berti was to attack over Rudilla to Albalate del Arzobispo. The Corps *Marroquí* under General Yagüe Blanco was to attack from the southeast of Cariñena over Villanueva del Huerva. From there it would take Azaila, Escatrón, and then with a quick dash seize Caspe. To accomplish this, Yagüe would have to recapture the lost Belchite. The reinforced Cavalry Division of General Monasterio Ituarte would cover Yagüe's flank. The three Nationalist Air Forces would support the entire operation with the Germans covering the Corps *Marroquí* and the Cavalry Division. Captain Christ noted that General Berti proposed that he attack with his Corps from the area around Teruel to Sagunto. This would have resulted in the Italians being the first to reach the Mediterranean. This Franco flatly rejected. Many years later the late General Plocher commented with a smile:

> General Monasterio pointed out that the area of attack given his cavalry was lacking water and forage. Franco looked at the General, and without changing his expression said: "You must ride faster than you have ever ridden before. If you do so it will not be necessary to have so much water. Less time—less water." However, 100 or more trucks were ordered collected from other divisions to support the horses. The enemy did not believe such a cavalry move possible. It was a great surprise!

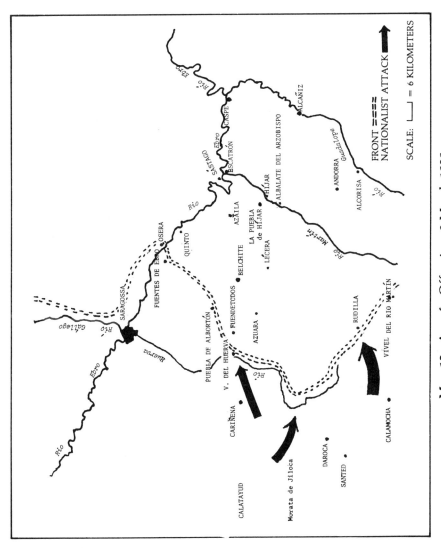

Map 12. Aragón Offensive, 9 March 1938.

189

The Nationalists calculated that the foe had about 550 aircraft, of which about 300 new models could be deployed to the attack area. They were not concerned about obtaining air superiority because the Nationalist squadrons had about 140 planes, the Italians 220, and the Germans could provide about 100. All air and ground units were ordered deployed and to make ready for the attack, which would be on 9 March. As the Legion units began their redeployment, Major Plocher and Captain Christ made an extensive drive along the frontal area. They examined the terrain with care and compared it with the maps and photographs provided by the Reconnaissance Squadron. Finally they called upon General Yagüe to discuss their aerial support of his Corps *Marroquí* and how they would coordinate their actions.

Later General Plocher explained that General Yagüe was concerned because the brunt of the offensive would have to be carried by his Corps *Marroquí*. Plocher was of the opinion that Yagüe believed his Corps was lacking in forces adequate for the mission. General Plocher continued:

> Our position was that we would only support an offensive through Belchite. "The enemy line must be broken! If you do not attack Belchite we will not support the offensive with the Legion!" General Vigón accepted our position, and General Yagüe was ordered to commit his force against Belchite. I think that it is because of this that the Germans are frequently blamed for the destruction of Belchite. Of course this does not consider the great destruction of the town when it was captured by the Internationals back in September.

There was much to be done in a few days. All aircraft and vehicles possible had to be brought in commission, vast stockpiling of materials from munitions to fuel at the separated strike strips, detailed briefings of many air crews, and very importantly the communications sections preparing a complete communications net for support of what was hoped to be a rapid advance. General Volkmann, accompanied by the German ambassador von Stohrer, made a two-day inspection tour of all units and the front lines. The Bomber Group was preparing at Alfaro, the Fighter Group at Gallur, and the Reconnaissance flights at Buñuel (halfway between Tudela and Gallur). The Command Staff was located at Baños de Fitero. All ground and air units were in position the night of 8 March. The offensive would start in the early hours the next day.

Throughout the initial preparations the Legion flew extensive reconnaissance, which reported that the enemy front was continually being fortified but there was no unusual activity. The defenses were in depth with four possible lines of resistance. German flak batteries were placed at each of the German air strips and two heavy and one light battery took up positions to support the assault division of General Yagüe as field artillery. The Legion Command Post was located on a height directly on the front which provided a commanding view of the attack area. The Legion air squadrons, however, actually started their first phase of the operation on 6 March with massive bombing and strafing of enemy air strips and concentration centers. Four enemy planes were destroyed on the ground at Caspe and Bujaraloz. The Bf-109s shot down one fighter plane in an aerial dogfight. At the same time the Seaplane Squadron of Major Harlinghausen flying out of its base at Mallorca stepped up its night attacks against enemy shipping and transportation facilities along the coast between Valencia and the French border.

Two days before the grand offensive the entire Legion was again in the air. The reconnaissance flights again reported no unusual enemy activity. The bomber planes struck in a mass attack the transportation facilities and munitions factory at La Puebla de Híjar. For the second time, Volkmann sent the dive-bombers in, in an attempt to remove the annoying bridge at Sástago, and once again the Stukas failed. The issue of the bridge at Sástago had become such an annoyance to General Volkmann that on the morning of 8 March he ordered it to be destroyed by two full He-111 bomber squadrons. To ensure success, he instructed the attack be flown at the unusually low altitude of fifty meters. The mission again was a complete failure and Volkmann was exasperated. The protecting Bf-109s shot down two enemy fighters.

The offensive was to start at 6:00 a.m.; however, it had to be delayed because the mass movements of troops and equipment had raised great clouds of dust which, along with the bright rays of the rising sun, greatly restricted visibility.

Where the dust and strong oblique rays of the rising sun had delayed the attack of the ground forces, the conditions were perfect for the initiation of the first air strikes. The air attacks started at 6:40 a.m. with mass flights of all four bomber squadrons, protected by two squadrons of Bf-109s. Their targets were enemy front-line positions at Huerva within sight of the Legion Command Post, and directly in front of the 5th Division. The squadrons dropped 42.5 tons of bombs about the same time the Do-17 squadron bombed the enemy front before the 1st Division in the Herrera mountains.

Surprisingly, the 150th Division of Muñoz Grandes made a sizeable advance even before its way could be prepared by an artillery barrage from Spanish guns and German flak batteries, which were still having problems with dust and bright sun. Eventually all batteries were to place their fire in front of the advancing infantry, which was now also being assisted from the air by two low-flying squadrons of He-51s making repeated bombing and strafing attacks directly before the advancing Nationalist lines.

After the 5th Division had moved into position to attack by storm, the

Ju-87s and Do-17s struck directly at the enemy positions at Fuendetodos. Then, as the infantry ran forward, their way was paved by bombing and strafing from another He-51 squadron.

The 13th Division now advanced directly behind the mass bombing attack of thirty-five bombers of He-111 squadrons which dropped 45.5 tons of bombs directly on the enemy lines. The Legion Command Post now received word that the enemy front was crumbling in all sectors under concentrated artillery, aerial bombardment, and the determined attack of the Nationalist infantry and cavalry. To prevent enemy reinforcements from being moved into the attack zone, General Volkmann once again directed his dive-bombers against enemy concentrations at Híjar. He also sent one of the reserviced He-111 squadrons against enemy positions at Cruz, seven kilometers west of Belchite.

At 2:00 p.m., Volkmann again ordered his two He-51 squadrons to bomb and strafe directly before the advancing Spanish infantry. The effort of the German ground crews in reservicing their aircraft for new strikes was truly remarkable.

Volkmann and Plocher now diverted more of their strike force against the enemy around Belchite, but at the same time they still maintained a rain of bombs against the enemy at Híjar. The enemy attempted to establish a new defense line seven kilometers west of Belchite. Immediately Volkmann ordered all bombers to strike in this quarter. This was accomplished by thirty-five bombers and ten fighters blasting the area with 45.5 tons of bombs. At the same time the Stuka dive-bombers, flying their fourth mission of the day, struck the enemy position six kilometers west of Belchite. The Nationalist infantry was rapidly closing on Belchite, and all He-51 squadrons continued to pave their way with bombs and machine gun fire. This was the fourth mission for these squadrons, and the maximum effort was beginning to tell on the exhausted flight and ground crews.

The rapid advance of the Nationalist infantry made it difficult for the air support units, because of the continuous movement of the front line, to recognize friendly forces, and the Legion Command Post was now left behind by the advance. The communications sections now lay wire eighteen kilometers forward, under artillery fire from the retreating enemy.

The enemy fought bitter holding actions as they retreated in the direction of Belchite. Through it all, they were under a rain of bombs from the air, as well as direct artillery fire and pressure from a determined infantry. It is little wonder that they began deserting their positions. One enemy artillery battery after another stopped firing and frantically tried to withdraw its guns. The resulting lack of artillery support added to the despair of the retreating infantry.

By evening, the three assault divisions of the Corps *Marroquí* had advanced with surprising speed. In support of their efforts the Legion had expended 160 tons of bombs and 639 rounds of flak ammunition. Through it all, not a single German aircraft was lost. Early strikes at enemy airfields had paid off, and the Nationalists controlled the air over the attack zone.

In the attack areas of the other two corps of Army North, the offensive had progressed with varying results. Captain Christ, however, noted in his *Diary* that the Corps Galicia under General Aranda had encountered very stiff resistance.

During the night the ground elements of the Legion worked frantically to prepare the strike forces for what they knew was to be a continuation of the maximum effort of their units the following morning. Many aircraft had sustained damage from ground fire. The Legion Command Staff moved the Command Post to Cruz (altitude 988 meters), which is six kilometers west of Belchite. Exhausted infantrymen slept on the open battlefield, and weary cannoneers lay by their guns. On the other side of the lines the situation must have been desperate, for nothing is more demoralizing than retreat accompanied by a constant pounding of artillery and a rain of bombs from the skies.

The very early reconnaissance flights of the Legion the next morning, 10 March, gave an encouraging picture of the results of the first day's efforts. The enemy line had been so dispersed that the Legion did not have targets of enemy forces against which the bomber squadrons could be economically deployed. Reconnaissance, however, did reveal that the enemy was frantically trying to redeploy its air force into the combat zone. Many of the enemy airstrips had been occupied during the night, and aircraft were still being brought in. Thus the entire Legion, at 6:00 a.m., was committed in a violent strike against the enemy airfields. At Caspe alone, five planes were seen to burst into flames. At the enemy strip of Jatiel, three Curtiss fighters were also set afire by bombing and strafing, and the 2nd Bf-109 fighter squadron in a hot aerial battle shot down two Rata fighters. This was not without cost, however. Some enemy fighters managed to get into the air before all of their bases were bombed and shot down one He-111 bomber over Candasnos. The Legion Staff learned much later that the crew had been captured.

On the ground, the objective was still Belchite. And, as on the day before, the attacking Nationalist infantry was covered by waves of bombing and strafing aircraft. At 10:00 a.m. squadrons attacked, at low level, street targets in Belchite itself. Belchite ironically was again occupied by American, British, and Slavs of the XV International Brigade which had captured it after its two-week siege the previous summer.

General Muñoz Grandes continued to push his division against enemy-held Azuara, behind bombing and strafing from low-flying Legion aircraft, Spanish artillery, and the fire of the Legion 88mm batteries.

The 6th Heavy Battery of the Legion under Captain Wäntig was firing on enemy movements northwest of Belchite, when he suddenly was confronted with a formation of five Soviet tanks blazing away at friendly infantry. He quickly redirected his fire and destroyed three tanks by direct hits.

Later in the afternoon the Flak Battalion commander, Major Lichtenberber, noted heavy fire from an enemy artillery battery which had taken position only two kilometers southeast of Belchite. It was putting a dent into the infantry advance, and none of the German or Spanish guns were in a position to bring the enemy battery under fire. The major dashed to the 6th Battery and pulled out two of its 88mm cannons. The gun crews moved their pieces into firing position at kilometer stone 35 on the direct road to Belchite, and quickly directed heavy rapid fire against the enemy battery. The enemy guns were soon silenced, and the infantry advance continued. When the enemy battery position was overrun, the Germans learned they had destroyed Soviet guns manned by French crews.

The infantry continued to close in on Belchite and the XV International Brigade. Lieutenant Lohse, who commanded the 4th Light Battery, now deployed his guns on the road leading directly into town. From his positions he could fire on enemy groups who were fortified in houses.

The 5th Division, accompanied by tanks and under cover of low-flying fighters of the Legion, closed rapidly on Belchite. Volkmann now learned that the enemy was committing its reserve forces to the battle. These consisted mainly of the International Brigades which had among them at least one German battalion. German records curtly note: "They were completely destroyed by effective missions of the He-51 squadrons!" Some of these Germans of the International Brigades were captured and brought to the Legion Command Post for interrogation by Lieutenant Asmus, the assistant Legion operations officer.

As the 5th Division drew into position for its final assault on Belchite, the Ju-87 dive-bombers and He-51 fighters once again were directed to strike at strong points in the town. In an air battle south of Jatiel, a Bf-109 shot down one Rata fighter. To maintain direct support, General Volkmann again moved his Command Post forward five kilometers. Finally, the infantry, supported by Spanish artillery and rapid fire from the German flak batteries, began its final thrust into Belchite. As in the first battle for Belchite, there was bitter house-to-house fighting with its expected losses in dead and wounded. Volkmann again directed new attacks by low-flying planes against strong points of resistance. Finally friendly tanks appeared in the narrow streets and brought the enemy under point-blank fire. The enemy forces surrendered Belchite to the Nationalists at 4:30 p.m. The main body of the retreating enemy was moving down the road to Azaila and Caspe, but they were under continual attack by the Legion from the air. According to the accounts of this day by the Americans who were in the retreating enemy columns of the XV International Brigade, it is evident that it was a total rout.

On this second day of the offensive, the flying units of the Legion had each flown from three to five missions. They expended 151 tons of bombs and 1,059 rounds of flak ammunition.

The following day the respected Lieutenant Count von Dohna was shot down in his fighter plane into the Río Ebro. Shortly afterwards, an He-59 (floatplane) was shot down near Tortosa and its crew captured. Two days after the fall of Belchite Captain Christ wrote in his *Diary*:

> During the entire day the Legion Command Post was surrounded by masses of infantry constantly being brought forward. The continuing problems of the movement, changing of artillery positions, and the marching of troops bring back memories to the old soldiers of the march of 1914.

As the sound of cannon faded across the plateaus and mountains in Aragón, Generalissimo Franco arrived at Belchite. Without question, he was genuinely moved by the destruction of the town which had been defended in the name of the Nationalists, and then recaptured for this same cause. As he viewed the ravages of war, he said to the people of Belchite: "I swear to you that on these ruins of Belchite I will build a new and beautiful city as homage to your unequaled heroism." And this promise was fulfilled; however, the new city was not built on the ruins of the old, but on the slope leading up to the ancient walls. It is a fine modern town laid out by modern engineers and architects. Besides new and comfortable homes it has a merchant section, schools, tree-lined *paseos*, *plazas*, and a new church on a large landscaped square, in which there is a monument that carries the words of Franco's promise. But Franco directed that the old town of Belchite should remain, just as it stood as he saw it, to be a lasting monument to civil war. This is the way you see Belchite today. As one drives through Aragón now and passes through the towns and villages that were fought over so bitterly, it is difficult to realize that this now peaceful land had once been so violently disrupted by war. But when one walks through the lonely, sad, and ghostly streets of "Old Belchite," it all becomes very real indeed. However, in March 1938 savage fighting continued to the sea.

The C.T.V. was given a day of rest, but General Aranda's Corps Galicia surrounded Montalbán while the Corps *Marroqui* was still smashing down from Belchite. The German He-51s and flak batteries opened their way with devastating attacks, and Yagüe's troops stormed into Escatrón (see map 13).

To stay with the advance, the Legion frantically relocated its Command Post on 13 March, on a hill near the Azaila-Escatrón road. Captain Christ commented that all infantry units were advancing so fast that the Germans were not able to follow with their C.P. communications. Montalbán was now overrun by Aranda; the C.T.V., Cavalry, and 1st Division Na-

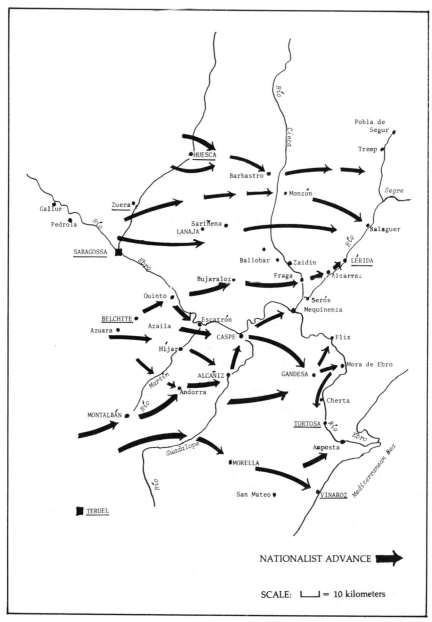

Map 13. From Belchite to the Sea, 11 March-15 April 1938.

varre were at the small village of Andorra and expected soon to reach Alcañiz. Yagüe's force now stood at the Ríos Martín and Ebro. The next morning Volkmann and Plocher were surprised, after they had prepared the way with bomber and strafing planes, when Yagüe hesitated to press on with his motorized columns and tanks with mixed Spanish and German crews against the important town of Caspe. They called on him in his C.P. to urge him on, but not until afternoon did he order his forces forward. Captain Christ wrote: "The enemy had a breathing space in which he was able to regroup and establish positions from which he could offer strong resistance; as a result the Nationalist advance from Escatrón to Caspe became 'stuck.' " Meanwhile, the Navarre 1st Division and C.T.V. reached picturesque Alcañiz.

By 15 March, the front before Caspe was the scene of hard fighting. Even though the Nationalist tanks, supported by the Legion bombing and strafing squadrons, had entered the town, the infantry was repeatedly halted or thrown back by strong counterattacks and counted heavy losses. The entire advance along the front slowed as other divisions had to clear bypassed pockets of resistance. It was obvious there had to be a consolidation of forces and revised planning. The Legion staff moved back to Baños de Fitero, but left behind General Volkmann and Plocher (now promoted to lieutenant colonel) who drove to Fuentes de Jiloca to meet with General Kindelán and revise the entire battle plan for the continuation of the offensive after the Alcañiz-Caspe line was stabilized.

All did not go well with the Legion this day. Major Harlinghausen notified the staff, from his seaplane base, that he had lost an He-59 and its crew. It was learned later the plane was shot down by antiaircraft fire near Tortosa. After the war, when the Legion assembled for a big parade in Berlin, Harlinghausen was stunned to meet again the plane's pilot Alfred Tonollo, and to learn that the crew had been taken prisoner. Months later Tonollo had been exchanged, but Harlinghausen had no idea as to the fate of the rest of the crew.

General Yagüe's battalions continued to attack the enemy west of the Río Guadalope with determination. But the foe doggedly threw back their costly assaults. Captain Christ noted on 16 March: "All of this could have been prevented earlier by a determined and rapid pursuit of the enemy." The Legion committed the He-51s to break the costly deadlock, and Caspe was finally taken, with some of the International Brigades being badly battered in the process. An entirely new Nationalist front was established 100 kilometers from the starting point eight days earlier.

Colonel Plocher drove to intercept General Vigón's train and discuss future plans. Franco now had eight Army Corps between the Pyrenees and Teruel, and the renewed offensive would be a drive on a wide front to the sea.

The enemy's major concentration was in the area between Caspe and

Alcañiz, but the Nationalists would first strike in the north, hoping the enemy would divert forces into that sector as well as dissipate his reserves. In the north, the key was the cathedral city of Huesca. Since the beginning of the war it had been a salient into the enemy front. Corps Navarre and Aragón were ordered to assemble in the Huesca sector to break the front and advance on Barbastro from both north and south of Huesca, and then drive to the Río Segre between Lérida and Tremp. At the same time, Yagüe's Corps *Marroquí* would attack the front line across the Río Ebro between Caspe and Quinto in a northeasterly direction—over the Sierra Monegros—to Bujaraloz. From there he would advance east through Fraga to Lérida. Plocher agreed to the request that the Germans support the Corps Navarre and Aragón between the Río Ebro and the Pyrenees, but with the major concentration at the Huesca salient.

It was assumed the Nationalist Army Corps south of Yagüe would soon reach the Río Guadalope between Alcañiz and Caspe. These were the reinforced 1st Navarre Division, the C.T.V., and Corps Galicia. The Navarre Division would deploy left of the C.T.V. and right of Yagüe's corps. The C.T.V. would move on Gandesa, then east to the Ebro and down to the sea through Tortosa. The Corps Galicia on the right wing, would drive south to the medieval walled town of Morella, in the heart of the wild and picturesque Sierra Maestrazgo, and push on to the sea. This would be an offensive through terribly difficult mountainous terrain which is largely barren, dry, and in the summer inconceivably hot. The route down the banks of the Río Ebro, although fantastically beautiful, with high mountains, deep canyons, and twisting loops of the river, is a military nightmare. The Corps Castile (Varela) was to stand by on the southernmost flank for possible deployment toward Castellón and Sagunto, twenty-three kilometers north of Valencia.

By 17 March, the enemy was pushed east of Caspe but still launched violent counterattacks against Yagüe's Corps. This again brought in the Legion bomber and strafing squadrons, while the Legion staff prepared operational plans, orders, and relocation of the combat units for what was hoped to be a big push to the sea. Volkmann wired Major Harlinghausen, at Mallorca, he was to step up immediately the attacks by his Seaplane Squadron against enemy coastal facilities, troop concentrations, and communications, and be prepared to support directly the ground forces when they reached the zone of his operation. The next day Caspe was secured.

The next few days were hectic with the Legion's units being realigned. Lieutenant Gabriel again flew his Storch to try to find a suitable location for the *Wohnzug* somewhere near Huesca. The Flak Group was instructed to support the Corps Navarre and Aragón with two heavy 88mm batteries and a single light battery for each Corps. Unknown to the staff—at the moment—Corporal Alois Schuller of their Headquarters squadron, who had been captured, was executed by the enemy.

Lieutenant Gabriel found a site for the *Wohnzug* in the only wooded area in the region of Zuera. The workers moved the living quarters in by 21 March, only to learn that they had had some problems that day. Lieutenant Wolfgang Schiller, of the 4th Bomber Squadron, liaison officer to the Corps Navarre, was killed riding his motorcycle from Huesca to Zuera, and the Seaplane Squadron reported from Mallorca the loss of another He-59 floatplane. For reasons unknown, the plane exploded in the air near Cambrils (Tarragona), killing Lieutenants Hayo Jurgens and Karl Zunker, and NCO Kurt Keitzel. Major Harlinghausen was distressed at losing two planes and fine crews within a few days. That night all air squadrons, support units, and infantry battalions were readied for the offensive to start the next morning.

The Battle Staff gathered, early on 22 March, in the Legion C.P. on a hill north of Huesca which gave a commanding view of the battlefield. Bomber and fighter planes struck the enemy on time and the infantry moved forward, supported by the strafing He-51 squadrons and fire from Corps Artillery and German flak batteries. The advance was generally limited. The weather then deteriorated and almost completely restricted air activity through 23 March. That day Corps Aragón managed to break open the front and moved forward so fast the Legion C.P. lost its observation of the front. To the south, after heavy fighting near Quinto, Yagüe's Corps forged the Río Ebro under heavy fire to build an extensive bridgehead. The German staff had hoped for better progress but were not greatly disappointed as they repaired to the *Wohnzug* for the night. Captain Hubertus Hering now reported to Plocher as the replacement for Captain Galland commanding the 3rd Fighter Squadron. Galland had previously refused to accept replacements recommended from Berlin on the grounds the individuals were not adequately experienced to command a low-level combat force such as his "Mickey Mouse" Squadron and he had reservations now as well.

The next day Corps Aragón advanced with difficulty. The divisions of Corps Navarre, Captain Christ noted, "were fighting desperately for every inch. They were able to gain only small areas in face of enemy resistance even with very strong support from our air squadrons." Still the advance moved to where the Legion had to move its C.P. (25 March) to the belfry of a church in Huesca. It was most crowded with officers and soldiers from several staffs jammed together. They became alarmed when word came that thirty-seven enemy aircraft were approaching the city from the north, but the formation did not attack the city. The two Nationalist Army Corps still had not managed to break the enemy front completely, but by that evening they had pushed the lines back three kilometers east of Huesca. In the south, Corps *Marroquí* finally ruptured enemy defenses during the night and advanced northeasterly toward Lérida. Corporal Karl Geisel of the Panzer (*Imker*) Group operating with one of Yagüe's battalions was killed in a bombardment as his troops closed in on Bujaraloz, north of the Ebro.

By evening of 26 March, the Huesca sector was secured, and Yagüe's motorized battalions were dashing toward the strongly fortified positions at Candasnos, west of Fraga; farther to the south, Aranda's Corps Galicia and the C.T.V. were prepared to attack. This required an immediate change of plans. The next morning Legion bombers dropped tons of bombs in the same sector. Volkmann then called on General Vigón in his mobile headquarters to reassess the operations. After an appraisal, Volkmann suggested his Legion move its major concentration from Huesca to support Yagüe's advance. Vigón agreed.

Volkmann ordered his flak batteries moved from Huesca in the direction of Bujaraloz-Candasnos. To enable the fighter planes to remain over the target areas longer, they were moved from near Saragossa to a combat field at Bujaraloz, on the road halfway between Saragossa and Lérida. All were concerned that a determined and strong defense would be encountered in the region west of Fraga. But Captain Christ wrote in his *Diary*, 27 March: "In the evening, General Yagüe overran the feared enemy positions without making a fuss about it." At the same time, Corps Aragón and Navarre reached the Río Cinca and occupied the communications center of Barbastro on the road south to Lérida.

It was obvious to all commanders that an important and major battle would develop over Lérida, and the Legion diverted all aircraft in direct support of Yagüe's forces, which encountered strong resistance east of Alcarraz, ten kilometers west of Lérida. The advance made it necessary to move the location of the Legion C.P. (30 March) to east of the Río Cinca near Fraga. However, during the night the enemy blew up the dam north of Barbastro and the river rose to where it was impossible for the combat forces to cross. The C.P. had to be pulled back to its last position, six kilometers west of Fraga.

Volkmann, on 30 March, instructed all his air squadrons and flak batteries to open the way for Yagüe to storm Lérida, but frustratingly for the Germans, Yagüe did not give the order to assault. Flights of the 3rd Squadron of He-51 fighters were returning to base after bombing and strafing east of Alcarraz when a major loss was realized. Captain Hering (who had just arrived to be the new commander of the squadron) and Lieutenant Manfred Michaelis collided in midair, and both aircraft crashed east of the Río Cinca. Lieutenant Gabriel and the doctor from the Flak Group immediately took off in the Storch and flew across the Cinca to help the crash victims, but both men were dead. Captain Galland would remain with the "Mickey Mouse" Squadron for a while longer.

The advance on Lérida was stalled until 2 April. During this time, the

C.T.V. and 1st Navarre Division were in a race for Gandesa, west of the great bend of the Río Ebro. This was a busy and trying day for the Condor Legion. The Bomber Group returned from a mission against the front, and as the flights made a circle of the airfield at Alfaro, two He-111s collided in the air. One crashed in flames into the town, killing the crew of Lieutenant Herbert Hoyer, NCOs Herbert Bruggemann and Walter Hoyer, and Corporal Kurt Kondziela. The other plane made an emergency landing with a badly shaken but unhurt crew. It was a gloomy evening in the hotel at Baños de Fitero, but the staff did welcome Lieutenant Colonel Kressmann as the replacement commander for Major Lichtenberber of the Flak Group.

Matters did not improve the next two days. Admiral Canaris (chief of *Abwehr*) made one of his frequent visits and had a private talk with General Volkmann. In his *Diary*, on 4 April, Captain Christ made no reference to what was discussed, and Plocher stated that Volkmann spoke to him only of vague generalities. The meeting was interrupted by a message from the Legion Operations Section. Two Bf-109s of the 1st Squadron flying from Saragossa to the fighter field at Lanaja collided in the air and were completely destroyed. Rescue crews rushed to the scene but found Lieutenant Awe, who had shot down three enemy planes, dead in the mangled wreckage. They found Sergeant Borchers still alive in the tangled mess of his aircraft and, after much difficulty, were able to pull him out. He was terribly shaken but not seriously injured. Colonel Plocher was most distressed because there had been such a number of these incidents in a few days, and knew there would be repercussions from Berlin. They were quickly coming.

Lérida finally succumbed to charges by Yagüe's infantrymen 3 April. There was a general slowing of the ground advance, but the air squadrons maintained their strikes daily against the enemy. Vast stores of enemy supplies had arrived at Cartagena and Almería, and the limited number of search planes in Harlinghausen's Seaplane Squadron could not shut off the flow. General Kindelán now called Volkmann and Plocher to Saragossa on 7 April to consider what he viewed as a grave matter. That night, however, many of the German staff joined the Bomber Group for a farewell party in honor of Captain Hentschel and Lieutenant Klinkicht, who had orders to return to Germany. The party was dampened by news that one of their aircraft was missing. Word came over the enemy radio at 11:00 p.m.; it had been shot down by flak near Artesa de Segre. The aircraft and crew burned. To die were Lieutenant Max Kendel, NCOs Paul Birkhofen and Willi v.d. Driesch, and Corporal Erich Fiedler.

Good news arrived from the front on 8 April, when Corps Galicia in a surprisingly short time had pushed to within six kilometers of Cherta, upstream from Tortosa on the Río Ebro. This made General Aranda's battalions closest to the sea.

Volkmann decided to move the *Wohnzug*, and sent Commander Bendler

(German Navy liaison officer with the Legion) and Captain Christ to find a key location in the area of Alcañiz—at the time the Italian headquarters. Volkmann and Plocher then met with General Franco and General Berti. According to Captain Christ on 9 April, "There was a discussion between Franco and Berti in which the competition in the push towards the sea was discussed. Berti pleaded to have the Corps Aranda stopped and let him have the honors. Franco refused." Plocher then gave the Spanish generalissimo 150,000 pesetas which had been collected by the men of the Legion for a Spanish charity. He received warm thanks in return, and Franco invited both the Germans and the Italians to join him for lunch. As usual, Captain Christ added his little personal comments to events that day: "Otherwise it is very hot. The Staff cooled off by taking a bath." That night the Staff listened on the radio to the news of Hitler's seizure of Austria. Volkmann's concern of the weeks before was fully justified, and he was genuinely concerned about the consequences.

Through 11 April, the front had changed little. Two of the He-51s were hit by enemy fire while making strafing attacks. Both crash-landed; one exploded and burned completely, and the other was almost totally destroyed. However, both pilots managed to escape unhurt.

The next day the enemy launched strong counterattacks against Corps Aragón on the bridgehead of Balaguer. The Legion flak batteries and He-51 flights turned back the assault, but one fighter plane was badly crippled by ground fire. The pilot, Sergeant Gerstmann, managed to fly his plane to a recovery base for a successful crash-landing with a bullet in his shoulder.

Colonel Plocher, Captain Christ, and other members of the operational staff made an inspection, 13 April, of the area in the north just recently captured by the Nationalist battalions they had supported with their aircraft and flak batteries. First they drove to Huesca and visited the cemetery which had been the scene of much bitter fighting since the beginning of the war.[2] They then took the road to Barbastro and were impressed to see the Nationalists were already repairing damaged bridges. From there, they continued to Tremp and through the beautiful valley of Desfiladero.

Captain Christ wrote on 14 April in his *Diary*: "The following message reached the Command quarters: 'The troops of General Aranda's Corps have reached Vinaroz on the Mediterranean.' This gave cause for a small celebration in the canteen." The enemy was divided.

Years later General Plocher commented: "We were elated when we heard the news that General Vega's 4th Division had broken out at Vinaroz. We knew there still would be some difficult fighting ahead. But not one of us could have envisioned that it would be a full year that the fighting would continue and before the Germans of the Condor Legion would return to Germany."

The immediate concern of the combat crews was "Operation Neptune." This was a major air strike against the enemy buildup at Cartagena and Almería which had been in the planning since 3 April.

Notes

1. The material for the Aragón Offensive was compiled from Captain Christ's *Diary*, Freiburg File No. RL/35-1, and interviews with the late Major General Plocher, Lt. General Harlinghausen, Lt. General Aramburu Topete, Lt. General Galland, *Oberst* Franz Brey, and others. The Condor Legion records in Freiburg File, RL 2/v. 3195, "First Ebro Offensive," were used as supporting evidence. In general, they all agree with Captain Christ's *Diary*. The writer drove the route of the Condor Legion from its Headquarters at Baños de Fitero through all of the staging bases and then the battlefields from the beginning of the offensive through Belchite, Alcañiz, Caspe, and Gandesa to the breakout on the Mediterranean Sea. The terrain was studied in detail and many people were located who lived through the battles. To them the writer expresses many thanks for their assistance. Unfortunately, all their stories cannot be related here.

2. The writer asked General Plocher about the grim scene painted by Julian Amery in *Approach March* (London, 1973), p. 92, that the Nationalists found skeletons, rotting bodies, and recently killed men arranged in a dance of death to welcome the enemy. Also see Hugh Thomas, *The Spanish Civil War*, 2d ed., fn. 2, p. 800. The general responded: "I saw no such thing! But with the character of the Spanish struggle, it would not have been at all surprising."

15

The Levante
Offensive

"Operation Neptune" started early dawn, 16 April, when forty He-111s took off from their airfields in the battle zone. They were to land at Salamanca and Ávila for fuel and then fly to Seville and from there to gather on their forward base at Granada for the air strike the following morning. The mission encountered problems from the start. Because of low clouds and a navigational error, one He-111 crashed into a mountain near Cabeza la Vaca (Badajoz). Killed were Lieutenant Andreas Siemsen (observer), NCOs Oswald Kruschbersky (pilot), Rudolph Spieler (radio operator), and Corporals Erich Frielingsdorf and Fritz Schmalfuss (both mechanics).[1]

Another bomber had engine problems and made an emergency landing, in which the landing gear was badly damaged but the crew escaped injury. Two other planes returned to their base because of mechanical problems and two more were not able to fly on to Granada. Finally that evening, thirty-four bombers assembled at Granada, with the Group Commander and all crews gloomy because of the problems they had encountered that day.

The next morning the bombers took off without fighter escort and cleared the Sierra Nevada. In two waves they swooped over the harbor of Cartagena, where they encountered very heavy antiaircraft fire. They bombed the harbor facilities, ships in the harbor, railroad supply areas, and the oil refinery. Then they returned to Granada for refueling and new bombs, and twenty-five planes again struck Cartagena to sink a torpedo boat and strike the battleship *Jaime I*. At the same time, the balance of the Bomber Group dropped its bombs on Almería, causing considerable damage. In all, eighty-two tons of bombs were dropped. One of the planes over Cartagena was hit by ground fire, and the pilot, knowing he would never be able to clear the Sierra Nevada, turned south along the coast hoping to reach a friendly airdrome. As the bomber passed Almería, it was hit again and had to make a crash letdown at sea near Motril. The crew was saved. Because of flak damage three other aircraft landed at Málaga. Although others were also hit, they were able to return to Granada. On 18 April, only twenty-seven aircraft were able to return to their northern bases.

Colonel Plocher was very concerned about the reduced combat capability of his force and the negative impact the mission had on the morale of the ground and flight crews.[2] The Flak Group had problems the same day when there was an accident with one of the 20mm guns and its crew on the Lérida-Fraga road. Three cannoneers were badly injured, and the gun with its carrier was totally destroyed.

The decision was made to relocate the Legion Command Staff to the Mediterranean. They chose to establish the Command quarters a few kilometers to the south at Benicarló. Captain Christ described Benicarló as ". . .a nice little village on the Mediterranean which unfortunately has suffered much from the war."

Ground and aerial action declined as both sides reappraised their positions, regrouped their forces, and determined the next course of action. General Volkmann and Colonel Plocher were in complete disagreement with the Nationalist Command's decision not to continue the pursuit of the enemy's shattered forces on into Catalonia, but instead insisted on a concentrated attack against Valencia. General Plocher later commented:

> The drive should have continued with all determination into Catalonia! I am still convinced we could have rolled past Barcelona up to the border of France. The enemy divisions were completely disorganized. As much as possible, we continued to pound the enemy, with our ground support and bomber planes being used as airborne artillery. Our pilots reported the enemy fleeing in all directions. Also, reports were coming to our Intelligence that on more than one occasion enemy officers had been shot in front of their own troops, and the Communist and Anarchist leadership was torn with distrust and were accusing each other of treason. Furthermore, the International Brigades had been shattered as a combat force.[3]

These were not unfounded rumors that the general recounted. The enemy leadership was in fact in absolute disarray.[4]

General Plocher continued:

By concentrating our attack against the still organized and well established forces to the south, and coupled with inclement weather, many weeks were to pass which gave the enemy in Catalonia the opportunity to become completely reorganized. They were also re-equipped because France opened its border to a vast flow of war materiel.

It can be suggested that Franco was concerned that if he moved close to the French border at that time (particularly with the German Legion), it might bring France into the Spanish war on the side of his enemies. In any event, he decided to concentrate his attack to the south from Teruel across the Maestrazgo with Corps Castile (Varela), and Corps Galicia (Aranda) to attack south on a line parallel to the coast and along the coastal plain. Volkmann and Plocher were asked to have the Legion support Corps Galicia.

The Bomber Group remained initially to operate out of Saragossa and the long-range reconnaissance/bombers from Bruñel. The fighters and short-range He-45s were moved to the fields of La Cenia, northwest of Vinaroz, and Zaidín, due west of Lérida. These fields were also designated as recovery bases for the bomber planes. La Cenia also supported the Legion staff and courier flights to Germany.

The Flak Group detached three heavy 88mm batteries and a single light battery to augment General Aranda's Corps Artillery. One heavy and light battery took up stations at La Cenia and a single heavy battery and light guns were deployed to protect the Command quarters established at Benicarló. The Flak headquarters was located at the small village of Santa Magdalena de Pulpis, south from picturesque Peñíscola jutting out to sea.[5] By 24 April, the communications were tied to all stations but were repeatedly being sabotaged. The night before, at 11:30 p.m., communications man Martin Franke was shot and killed by a sniper as he drove the line from General Aranda's headquarters established at San Mateo on the road west of Benicarló leading south to Castellón de la Plana.

The Legion was now positioned to support what the Germans called the "Mediterranean Offensive" (see map 14), and it would prove to be the most frustrating to the Legion staff, combat crews, and ground support functions. Torrential rains and high winds restricted air operations for days and mired the ground forces in mud. The well-positioned enemy had skillfully placed artillery and was resolute in his defense. Then when weather permitted, the advance was painfully slow and costly. Enemy air squadrons, bomber and fighter, were committed to contest the Nationalists in the skies and in permissible weather would strike the Nationalist assault forces and rear areas. One after another bitter air battle developed. The Legion was to claim many aerial victories but at the same

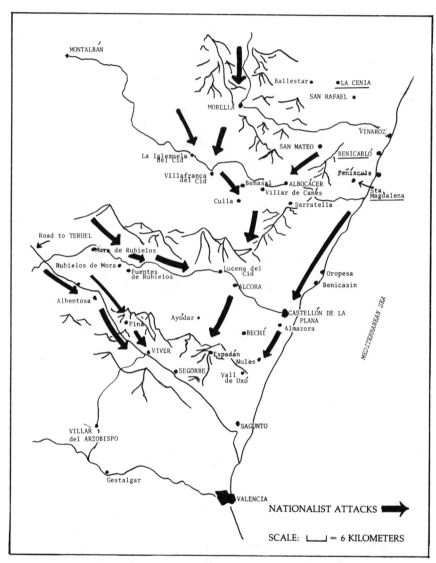

Map 14. Mediterranean Offensive, April-July 1938.

time to realize losses and a continual deterioration of equipment.

Volkmann, Plocher, and other staff officers rode horses and mules to the C.P. high on a hill the morning of 25 April to direct the offensive. Plocher commented later: "We had no idea of all the problems we would have for such a small stretch of territory. All of our bombers and fighters were deployed but the enemy counterattacked with great force." The following day the enemy was thrown back by the bombing and strafing planes and fire from the German flak batteries which silenced an enemy field battery. But in a matter of moments another enemy battery found the Legion C.P. and it came under direct artillery fire. Captain Christ wrote: "With this consideration and a very unfriendly rain an end was put to the battle." The rains continued to hamper all operations, and the Navarre Division of General Valiño was committed between Aranda's and Varela's Corps. It was not until 4 May that the He-51 fighters could fly over the front. One was immediately shot down by ground fire over Albocácer with its pilot Sergeant Andreas Hester dying in the explosion. At the same time the German flak batteries came under heavy artillery fire and had to be withdrawn.[6]

Heavy rains and strong winds continued for several days, and the Command quarters was moved southwest of Benicarló to the Villa Lolita with charming gardens and surroundings. The front exploded again on 11 May, and the Legion encountered large enemy air formations. Sergeant Herbert Ihlefeld, in an exciting aerial dogfight, added to his mounting score of victories by shooting down another Rata.

The Fighter Group had to commit all aircraft for bomber protection but at the same time divert some flights in an attempt to intercept enemy bomber formations. The Legion headquarters itself became the target of frequent enemy bombing attacks. Enemy bombers continually harassed the areas at night and were entitled "Night Ghosts." The Legion bombers opened the way for General Alonso's 4th Division on 18 May, but the He-51s could not lead the assault because of high surface winds. High above, the Bf-109s became engaged in a heated battle with enemy Ratas. The new Fighter Group commander, Captain Hermann, scored his first victory and Sergeants Ihlefeld, Rochel, and Seufert each gained a victory. But again the weather closed in on the battlefield. General Volkmann was called to Berlin but was trapped at Mallorca for several days.

To direct the assault, Colonel Plocher moved the temporary headquarters on 28 May over the mountains to Iglesuela del Cid (thirty-five kilometers southwest of Morella) and put the C.P. on a peak at nearby Villafranca del Cid which they had to ascend by horses and mules. Their aircraft performed well, and the next day they moved the C.P. to Picazo. Unable to obtain mounts, the staff found it was a most difficult climb to the top, and Captain Christ had some caustic remarks to make in his

Diary. The next day an He-111 was hit by antiaircraft fire over Castellón, and Lieutenant Karl Kostlin was killed, but the pilot managed to land the badly crippled plane at its recovery base. Constantly moving the C.P., the Legion closely followed the advance. On 31 May, Lieutenant Losigkeit, flying with the 3rd Squadron, was shot down by ground fire as he made a strafing attack. He was seen to parachute into no-man's-land and to set fire to his He-51. But Lieutenants Werner and Plaas, who went immediately to his rescue, were not able to find him anywhere between Benasal and Villar de Canes. It was later learned that he had been taken prisoner.[7]

On 1 June, the Legion C.P., high in the Sierra de San Cristóbal, came under artillery and machine gun fire. The next day enemy bombers struck hard at the fighter base of La Cenia. Five Martin bombers were shot down by the Bf-109s and one Martin exploded when hit by German flak. Captain Christ in his *Diary* on this occasion did not list who gained the victories. But the Germans lost Lieutenant Martin Haup, who was shot down in flames by antiaircraft fire north of Villar de Canes. Hermann Goering wired his congratulations from Berlin for the aerial victories.

The enemy squadrons were not dissuaded. On 3 June they struck the German C.P. with nine bombers and thirty-one fighters that raked the mountain with machine gun fire. There were no German casualties, nor was the Fighter Group able to intercept the enemy formation. The C.P. was now moved to Culla.

General Aranda's infantry and the 4th Navarre Division continued to push forward against strong opposition. On 8 June, the He-51 4th Squadron was strafing enemy truck columns when Lieutenant Erich Beyer was caught by ground fire. He crashed in flames at Sarratella. The next day the enemy air squadrons were back in force, but the German flak batteries scattered the formations and the planes dropped bombs on their own troops. The Bf-109s also made contact with thirty-one enemy fighters, but the formation broke up with no German victories or losses.

It was different two days later. Captain Christ and Lieutenant Werner made their way under heavy artillery fire and aerial bombardment to the Command Post of the 4th Division. They again came under air attack late that afternoon by two flights of six enemy bombers. When the first flight reached the zone of fire of the 6th German Flak Battery, the battery opened fire and the guns were perfectly directed. Captain Christ described it in detail in a "Special Letter" to Berlin:

> I had the strongest impression that three enemy planes were caught in the middle of our flak zone. By dividing and turning first to one side and then the other, the aircraft managed to turn around and jettison their bombs. One machine disappeared in the direction of the coast, and the other two planes, after losing much altitude,

turned first towards the west and finally flew in a southerly direction. Suddenly I saw smoke streaming from the right aircraft and then the left plane was on fire. Both planes started to come apart in the air and then went into a vertical dive, to crash in flames.[8]

The German fighters then became involved, and Lieutenant Meyer shot down a Martin bomber in flames. Lieutenant Neumann shot down a protecting Rata fighter, but the pilot saved himself by parachuting and was captured. He was later interrogated by Lieutenant Asmus of the Legion Staff. Sergeants Seufert and Rochel again each shot down a Rata. One Curtiss was blown up by the 4th Flak Battery. It was a busy day.

Weather slowed operations until 13 June, when the German fighter planes intercepted enemy fighter squadrons in large formations. The Bf-109s shot down seven enemy planes. Lieutenants Schellmann (commander of the 1st Squadron) and Ewald each shot down a Rata, and five Curtisses were shot down in flames by Lieutenants Müller, Maurer, and Keller, and Sergeants Stege and once again, Seufert. The 6th Flak Battery shot down one Martin bomber and was listed with another as "probable."

The Legion entire bomber force heavily bombed the enemy front but received intense and accurate antiaircraft fire. Six of the He-111s were badly damaged and two had to make emergency landings at La Cenia.

The enemy struck back hard at the bomber formations the following day with between forty and sixty fighters. An exciting aerial battle developed as they in turn were intercepted by the protecting Bf-109s. This time Sergeant Kuhlmann definitely scored a victory as he shot down a Rata in flames. One Bf-109 was shot down south of Castellón. The pilot, Lieutenant Henz, was able to crash-land north of the Río Mijares and was seen to set his plane on fire. Much later it was learned that he had been taken prisoner. Lieutenant Priebe, in his fighter, was shot in the shoulder but managed to bring his plane back to La Cenia. On the ground the battle moved slowly forward. Captain Christ wrote in his *Diary* on 14 June: "In the evening the following message was received: 'North and east entrance to Castellón and the harbor have been captured. The town Villarreal was captured by the 4th Division.' "

Volkmann returned from Germany late on 15 June, and the next morning his flak guns shot down two enemy bombers and possibly a third. Captain Christ wrote: "At 1030 hours, the Commander related the events of his trip to Berlin at an officers' meeting in the Command quarters." Then Christ made the unusual comment: "One cannot say don't be mad, just wonder." General Plocher later suggested the comment was referring to the fact that Volkmann felt Germany was headed for a European war. Also, he had asked Berlin for much-needed replacement aircraft and crews, but was able to gain little satisfaction, and indeed the Legion might be forced to operate on a reduced scale. He had attended a meeting in Berlin, 10 June, where he complained about the combat status of the Legion. The flak guns were completely worn out and had to be reconditioned. "The combat power of the combat planes had been reduced by one-half (16 out of 30 fighter planes were unusable)." The enemy had superiority in numbers "often three to four times as great. . . ." The He-51 support planes "could no longer be sent into action because of their poor condition, which recently resulted in very high losses." When asked if the Legion could be reduced in size to a point where it could function with the existing materials, Volkmann considered this impossible. The Legion structure was such that its effectiveness would be destroyed. His position was "that only two possibilities were open: either restore the Legion to its original effectiveness by resupplying materials and maintaining it at this level, or to withdraw it." When asked about the military effect of its withdrawal, Volkmann noted this would be a great boost to the enemy's morale, and the recent shipments of materials from France and the Soviet Union had already shifted the ratio of air strength in favor of the enemy. He already had pointed out that if resupply was to come from Germany, it would be four to six weeks before it would be seen on the battlefield.[9] Berlin concluded that for political as well as military reasons the Condor Legion would be brought back to strength, but this decision was not made until the day Volkmann was meeting with his staff.

The ground advance continued south as did the Legion Command quarters. The staff made detailed inspections of conquered regions, and on 22 June, the entire staff along with the Legion band assembled in San Rafael. They were warmly received by the civilians who entertained them with food, wine, and punch. But the war went on. Major Harlinghausen's seaplanes had been raiding nightly along the coast, and on this night one seaplane sank an enemy ship in the harbor of Sagunto.

Enemy resistance stiffened south of Castellón and a bitter aerial battle developed on 15 June, with Lieutenant Schellmann scoring another victory. Gunner Freibel with the 5th Flak Battery was shot through the upper arm by a sniper while his battery was involved in an artillery duel with the enemy. This duel continued on into the next day when one of the German guns received a death blow from the enemy, killing Corporal Ehrhardt Horn instantly and badly wounding two other gunners, one of whom, Erich Vandrey, died of his wounds on 8 July.

The offensive took on new dimensions on 1 July, when Solchaga's Corps, which had moved into the Teruel area, struck south toward Turia. The objective was to surround the enemy's main strength at Valencia and destroy the forces in detail. The Germans tagged Solchaga's divisions as "Corps Turia" and quickly established communications and liaison with his Command Post.

The Legion now began to receive some of the new Me-109s from Germany.[10] General Volkmann made the decision to convert Lieutenant Mölders's (who had replaced Captain Galland) 3rd Squadron from their He-51s back to the fighter mission and equip it with the new aircraft. As could be expected, this news was received with great enthusiasm by the men cast into the ground support role because of the inadequacy of their airplane. Mölders immediately sent his engineering officer, Lieutenant Goy, to León with several mechanics, and in only a few days they had the planes put together. The first four were divided between the 1st and 2nd Squadrons, and some of Mölders's pilots started their transition flying, which lasted only a few days.[11]

As time permitted, the officers and men of the Legion entertained themselves with sporting events, which were very competitive not only between individuals but organizations. In the evenings, there were at times movies which had been flown from Germany, such as *Allaortia* with the popular Heinz Rühmann.[12] Many trips were made to the beaches for swimming in the sea. Other Legionaries were very interested in the scenic and historical towns and villages of Spain and played the role of excited tourists. Whenever possible they would join in the local village *fiestas* and were particularly popular with the young people. The Legion band was continually invited to put on a lively concert, which was the signal to dispense food, wine, and punch. The Germans were very fond of the strawberry punch popular in the region. There were also the maintenance duties and unpleasant tasks connected with military life, such as inoculations which had to be kept current. Captain Christ looked upon the inoculations as an excuse for a *doppelaopf* (double drink). It did not help him, however; he became quite ill.

The interruptions in war were momentary. Cannoneer Walter Müller was shot through the heart on 2 July, as he fired his flak gun at Bechí.[13] Solchaga's Corps crossed the Río Turia and Aranda's Corps crossed the Río Nules with the Legion bombing and strafing enemy positions before them. On 5 July, in three missions, the Bomber Group dropped fifty-six tons of bombs.[14] Major Harlinghausen's seaplanes continued to strike the coastal communications from Pollensa Bay. Because of engine failure, one of his He-59s had to make an emergency letdown on the sea twenty miles off the coast at Vinaroz. He brought it under tow with one of his emergency crash boats and pulled it all the way to Pollensa Bay where it was soon repaired.

Between 3 and 6 July the ground fighting was very bitter before the Corps Turia. Solchaga's lead division lost 693 dead and wounded. The enemy at the same time lost 1,500 dead and wounded, and 1,200 were taken prisoner.[15] Cannoneer Wolfgang Bauer of the 5th Flak Battery was shot in the head by a 2cm shell. He was carried to Castellón but died quickly.[16] The same day the Legion learned that twenty of its flyers who had been taken prisoner had been assembled in Barcelona. Since there were not enough captured enemy airmen to make an even exchange,

General Franco agreed to recover them with captured enemy political commissars.

The Legion bomber planes, in formations of from thirty to forty aircraft and carrying up to thirty-five tons of bombs, started a series of heavy bombardments, assisted by the Stuka flight, of enemy positions before the Nationalist battalions fighting their way through the Sierra de Espadán. The results were devastating. Other missions were flown against Vall de Uxó. But the flak batteries had to raise their barrels to scatter fifteen Curtiss and six Martin bombers which attempted to strike the assault divisions.[17]

German reconnaissance planes had noticed a rise in enemy activity north of the Río Ebro, and Volkmann ordered increased surveillance in the area. They quickly encountered heavy antiaircraft fire and fighter interception. Captain Christ wrote (9 July 1938) that Nules on the coast, twenty-five kilometers north of Sagunto, was captured, but the town had been completely destroyed by the retreating enemy.

General Berti's C.T.V., plus the 5th Division, was now moving down both sides of the road to Sagunto against strong resistance, but Valiño's division was suffering heavy losses to counterattacks. Night after night, the Seaplane Squadron, in repeated missions, continued to bomb and strafe (with machine guns and cannon) trains and shipping and supply areas along the coast, taking a heavy toll from north of Barcelona to Cartagena. One warship was beached at Barcelona and the Cruiser *Libertad* was hit with four bombs at Cartagena.

The Me-109s flying protection for repeated bomber sorties continued to intercept enemy fighters trying to break up the bomber formations. On 13 July, in the 2nd Squadron, Lieutenant Keidel and Sergeant Ihlefeld each shot down one Curtiss.[18]

On 15 July, the 1st Squadron, with seven fighters, over Segorbe-Sagunto tangled with forty enemy Curtisses. This time Lieutenants Müller and Keller and NCOs Kuhlmann and Quasinowski each shot down one Curtiss and the others scattered. The 2nd Squadron, flying ten planes as escort over Almedijar, fought with fifteen to twenty Curtisses, and once again Sergeant Ihlefeld shot two more out of the sky. These were his eighth and ninth victories in Spain.[19]

That same day the 3rd Squadron ("Mickey Mouse") flew its first mission as a fighter squadron, with six of the new Me-109s, led by the new commander, Lieutenant Mölders, over Villamalur. Mölders saw small specks in the distant sky and suspected they were approaching enemy fighters. When the specks grew larger, he gave the signal for his squadron to attack. The Me-109s stormed into what proved to be between twenty-five and thirty enemy fighters. Mölders picked one plane and maneuvered for his attack, but in his excitement opened fire far too early. The enemy made a sharp turn and the first thing Mölders knew he was looking at fire flashes from the enemy's machine guns directed at him, but he pulled out of the line of fire. He now questioned his wisdom of the odds he had wished on his squadron of six planes. Then he saw two Curtisses coming toward him. "Sweating like a bull" he drove his Me-109 between them to safety. Then suddenly he became very calm and could see the entire battle unfolding before him and at the same time his role in it. He watched one Curtiss take a steep dive, trailing smoke and then flames, as its pilot jumped out with his parachute to safety. He knew one of his comrades had scored a kill. Then two enemy fighters were before him. He dove his plane to come up under them; one pilot saw him and broke off in a violent maneuver, but Mölders now saw the other filling his gun sight. This time he held his fire until he closed to within fifty meters, and his guns fired on time. The enemy seemed to jolt and then winged over with Mölders following him down with his guns still firing. This was Mölders's first victory. He was pleased but worried about the remainder of his small squadron.

The enemy now scattered and he turned toward his base to be joined by four other planes. His major concern now was—who had been lost? The worry turned into relief when all six Me-109s landed at their station.[20] There was great jubilation among the pilots and ground crews to learn that on their very first mission as a fighter squadron they had scored three victories without a loss against overwhelming odds. The first to hold honors was Lieutenant Wolfgang Lippert and another was Lieutenant Walter Oesau.

On the ground at Sierra de Espadán, Valiño's divisions were repeatedly thrown back by violent counterattacks from firm defensive positions. Volkmann repeatedly concentrated his bombers against the enemy threatening Valiño's flank. Difficult as the offensive was, the Germans were encouraged to the degree they felt the contest would soon be decided at Valencia. But the enemy in the air was still as determined as on the ground in the Sierra de Espadán.

By 16 July, Solchaga's Corps had stormed past Sierra del Toro, and the C.T.V. battered its way through strong defenses to occupy Barracas and Pina, and General Varela's divisions had reached Mora de Rubielos and Rubielos de Mora. That night there was a celebration in the Legion Command quarters in honor of Herbert Ihlefeld who, because of his spectacular demonstration of his skills as a fighter pilot, was promoted to lieutenant.

On repeated missions the following day, the bombers of the Legion dropped fifty tons of bombs on enemy concentrations before the advancing divisions. But, concerned about what he considered as ominous enemy activity north of the Río Ebro, Volkmann ordered four photographic reconnaissance missions into the area. At the same time, he again committed the Stuka flight against enemy concentrations before General Valiño in the Sierra de Espadán. The Italian C.T.V. and Solchaga's divisions were again in a race to Sagunto with Solchaga's force taking 850 prisoners and deserters and General Berti's taking 300.

Despite their losses, thirty enemy fighters again challenged eight Me-109s of the 1st Squadron over Soneja. NCO Quasinowski shot down a Curtiss for his second victory, and the others scattered without making interception with the bombers. Flying escort for the bombers over Villamalur-Ayódar, with six Me-109s, the 2nd Squadron was attacked by twenty Curtisses. Lieutenant Resch watched one shattered by his guns.

The 3rd Fighter Squadron protecting bombers with eight planes over Segorbe-Soneja also engaged a superior enemy fighter force. Again Lieutenants Mölders and Oesau proved their skills by each shooting down a Curtiss. This time they were joined by NCO Bauer who scored his first victory.

Generalissimo Franco was now understandably moved to recognize the brilliant aerial performance of the Condor Legion, and the same day General Volkmann received the following message:

To: General Veith [Volkmann]
      C.O. Commander, Legion Condor
      I congratulate your excellency, as well as the brilliant forces under your command, in regards to the victories they have gained during these last few days. Here the pilots and crews of the Condor Legion again have won the victor's laurels.
      Burgos
      17 July 1938
                              /s/   General Moreno C/S

The bombers flew five missions 18 July, and the 1st Fighter Squadron protecting on one mission fought with an enemy Curtiss squadron. NCOs Kuhlmann and Quasinowski each gained another victory and were joined by Lieutenant Schellmann also scoring one.

The following day it was again the turn of the 3rd Squadron ("Mickey Mouse"), when on escort over Segorbe-Viver, to intercept three Rata squadrons. Lieutenant Mölders now scored his third victory. Lieutenants Goy, Tietzen, Ebbinghausen, and NCO Hien were also victorious with one Rata each. The "Special Staff W" Situation Report Number 541, 20 July, made the special comment: "In a five day period, since the arrival of the new Me-109s, the German fighter squadrons shot down 22 Red fighters without a single loss to themselves."

The battle continued to rage on the ground and in the air. The night of 19-20 July saw the floatplanes of Major Harlinghausen making their usual low-level penetration against enemy positions along the coast, shattering enemy buildup areas with bombs, machine guns, and cannon. During the daylight hours, Corps Varela captured 250 prisoners, and Corps Valiño, counting severe losses, recaptured lost heights in the Sierra de Espadán. This effort was supported by thirty-one bombers from the Legion. Despite their losses of the past few days, which must have been shattering to their morale, from fifteen to twenty Rata and Curtiss pilots tried to break through the German fighter screen of eleven Me-109s over Sierra de Espadán, only to have Lieutenant Wolfgang Schellmann blast two more Ratas from the sky in a demonstration that he had learned his lesson well. These were his seventh and eighth victories. At the same time NCO Brucks was credited with a victory. The following day the bombers dropped tons of bombs without interception.

On 23 July, the enemy aircraft were back in the air with both fighters and bombers. Six enemy bombers attempted to strike the Nationalist division before the 5th German heavy flak battery but the cannons knocked one down in flames and another was hit but managed to stagger out of the battle area. Very quickly the 5th Battery came under artillery fire, which wounded Corporal Steisle.[21]

In three sweeps of the battlefield, all three Me-109 squadrons with a total of thirty-two aircraft engaged between sixty and eighty Curtiss and Rata fighters. The heaviest enemy concentration attempted to break up the German bomber formation over Sierra de Espadán. Lieutenant Lippert sent another enemy fighter down in flames over Nules, and Sergeant Braunshirn of the 2nd Squadron scored his first victory. Once again not a single German fighter or bomber was lost.

The great importance of the German sorties this day was the intelligence gathered by the Reconnaissance Group during its missions north of the Río Ebro. This material was correlated with the data gathered from 14 through 23 July. It was studied in detail by Captain Christ and the operational staff. It was seen that during the first few days the enemy truck convoys would pull off the roads into the shade at the approach of aircraft. But Captain Christ commented in his *Diary* on 23 July:

> In the past few days it has been noted the traffic continues without interruption. This could be for two reasons—one, the Reds feel it is necessary to take the risk and directed it accordingly; second, it could be ordered as a temporary expediency to be able to realign their forces quickly. I personally believe the latter is the reason.

The German Intelligence gave an accurate description of the enemy movements, and Captain Christ explained in his *Diary* what he considered the reason:

> When considering the tactical solution, one can assume the Reds will attempt to break the Nationalist line of Benifallet-Mora la Nueva.

Before this frontal area is the town Gandesa which is a vital road junction. This is the area in which the enemy might possibly launch a successful attack to reach the roads Alcañiz-Morella-San Mateo-Castellón. With such a maneuver the main artery to Castellón would be cut. These possibilities coincide with statements made by Red deserters. Thus, one can expect an attack on this part of the front.

Captain Christ came close to reading the enemy's intentions. The very first sentence in his *Diary* for 25 July 1938 reads: "The enemy in a surprise offensive crossed the Río Ebro at dawn in the areas Amposta-Mora de Ebro, Vinebre, Flix, Fayón, and Mequinenza."

It is often written that the enemy's Río Ebro offensive came as a major surprise. But as noted from Captain Christ's *Diary* it came as no surprise to the Legion staff.[22] When later asked about this, General Plocher responded:

From all our intelligence the offensive came as no great surprise to us. The scope, however, exceeded what I had anticipated. I did feel the enemy would try something, such as in the case of Brunete and Teruel, because the Mediterranean offensive, although progressing slowly through the Sierra de Espadán, appeared it might be successful. We, of course, had forwarded all our intelligence to the Nationalist command and it is difficult for me now to comprehend why people would write it was not expected. When it came, there was little doubt, in my mind, how General Franco would respond.

Surprise or not, the enemy's Ebro offensive was one of major proportions which proved to be costly to both belligerents.

Notes

1. Captain Christ's *Diary*, 16-17 April 1938, and R. Hidalgo Salazar, *La ayuda alemana a España 1936-39*, p. 178 and Appendix 1.
2. General Plocher's comment to the writer.
3. Ibid.
4. See Hugh Thomas, *The Spanish Civil War*, 2d ed., pp. 801-802.
5. Forty-five years later in the *bodegas*, the older people recalled the Germans of the Legion and spoke well of them to the writer.
6. Captain Christ's *Diary*, 4 May 1938.
7. Captain Christ's *Diary*, 28 May through 31 May 1938.
8. Captain Christ's *Diary*, Special Letter, 29 June 1938.
9. *GD*, Series D, Vol. III, Doc. 604, and General Plocher's comments to the writer.
10. To eliminate confusion, the Bf-109 designation will be dropped from this narrative in that from this point forward it is impossible, from the documents available, to keep the Bf and Me designations separate.

11. *Oberstleutant* Fritz von Forell, *Mölders und seine Manner*, (Graz, Austria, 1941), entry of 15 July 1938, p. 40. This is basically Mölders's *Diary* edited by *Oberstleutant* von Forell. Hereafter cited as Mölders's *Diary*.

12. Captain Christ's *Diary*, 3 July 1938.

13. Ibid., 2 July 1938.

14. "Special Staff W" Report No. 13750/38 Ia, Situation Report No. 529, dated 6 July 1938. In the Freiburg Files, there are some daily summaries of the aerial and ground action, as well as political and intelligence data prepared by the "Special Staff" in Berlin. These summaries are based on the daily Operational Reports for the Condor Legion General Staff which are attached to the summaries. They will be cited here by the "Situation Report" number. These reports, along with Captain Christ's *Diary*, give a clear picture of the progress of the war during this period.

15. Situation Report No. 532.

16. Situation Report No. 530.

17. Situation Report No. 532.

18. Situation Report No. 535.

19. Situation Report No. 550, "Weekly Summary of J/88."

20. Mölders's *Diary*, 15 July 1938, p. 41.

21. Situation Report No. 545.

22. See "Special Staff W" Summary 15450/38 Ia.

16

Battle of the Ebro

During the early hours of 24-25 July 1938, rubber boats silently slipped onto the dark waters of the Río Ebro. They carried troops of the 5th Army Corps under Lister. This was but one of the four Army Corps constituting the newly formed Army of the Ebro commanded by Modesto. The force numbered between 80,000 and 100,000 men, well supported by artillery, tanks, and armored cars. In the air, they were covered by the new high-performance models of Rata and Curtiss fighters. This was the beginning of the great Battle of the Ebro (see map 15).

Lister's 5th Corps made its main crossing along the curve of the Ebro at Flix, Ascó, the deep gorge at Mora la Nueva, Miravet, and Amposta. The 14th International Brigade crossed upstream at Mora la Nueva to surround most of the battalions of Yagüe's 50th Division. Farther upstream the enemy's 15th Corps crossed between Fayón and Mequinenza. Thus, Yagüe's Corps *Marroquí* was to absorb the entire blow of the enemy attack.

When the Legion Command Staff learned of the breakthrough, General Volkmann immediately went to Caspe where Yagüe had his headquarters. The German offered Yagüe the full support of his Legion. At the same time General Franco was ordering five divisions moved quickly to meet the threat. The locks of the power plants along the Río Segre were opened to sweep away temporary bridges—or at least to raise the waters of the Ebro to make crossings more difficult. All Nationalist air squadrons were instructed to concentrate against advancing columns, bridgeheads, crossings, and enemy buildup areas east of the river.

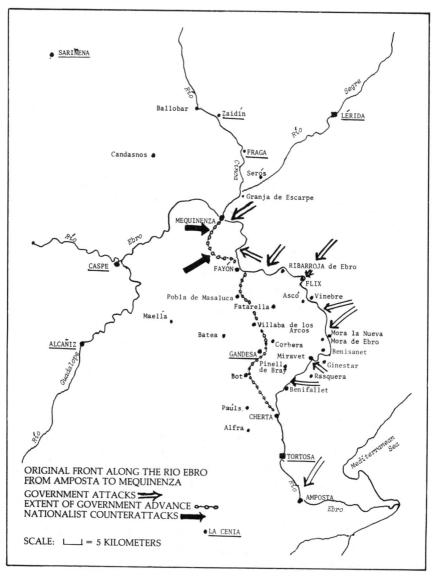

SARIÑENA

Rio

Segre

Ballobar   Zaidín   LÉRIDA

Rio

Candasnos   FRAGA

Rio Cinca

Serós

Granja de Escarpe

MEQUINENZA

Rio   Ebro

CASPE   FAYÓN   RIBARROJA de Ebro

FLIX

Pobla de Masaluca   Ascó   Vinebre

Fatarella

Maella   Villaba de los Arcos

Batea   Mora la Nueva
Mora de Ebro

ALCAÑIZ   Corbera   Benisanet

GANDESA   Miravet

Pinell   Ginestar
de Brai

Bot   Rasquera

Benifallet

Rio Guadalope

Pauls   CHERTA

Alfra

Mediterranean Sea

TORTOSA

ORIGINAL FRONT ALONG THE RIO EBRO
FROM AMPOSTA TO MEQUINENZA

GOVERNMENT ATTACKS

EXTENT OF GOVERNMENT ADVANCE

NATIONALIST COUNTERATTACKS

Rio   AMPOSTA

Ebro

SCALE: = 5 KILOMETERS

LA CENIA

Map 15. Battle of the Ebro, 25 July-6 August 1938.

Before midday the Legion bomber planes were airborne and over their targets. This was the beginning of a series of missions which would be flown daily for over three months. On this first day the Bomber Group, on two missions, dropped fifty-two tons of bombs. Direct hits were made on river crossings and troop columns. The Reconnaissance bombers, with from seven to nine aircraft, flew four missions and dropped sixteen tons of bombs on enemy forces at Venta de Camposines, Mora la Nueva, Ginestar, and Ribarroja; the Stukas, in four missions, dive-bombed the enemy at Mora de Ebro and Ginestar with seven tons. Surprisingly no intercepts by the enemy were attempted. Air crews, however, reported intense antiaircraft fire. The Seaplane Squadron struck twice at Gandía and sank one ship. The Reconnaissance flight flew eleven missions along the breakthrough area and into the enemy rear zone.

With air strikes and the determined resistance of General Yagüe's forces at Amposta, by noon, the enemy assault in that area was thrown back across the river. Over 600 enemy were killed, and the 14th International Brigade was badly damaged. Still, by that evening the enemy had penetrated three miles between Mequinenza and Fayón, and Lister's advance had carried to capture the heights of Sierra de Caballs and Sierra de Pandols, as well as controlling positions east of the important communications town of Gandesa. Several thousand Nationalist troops were captured. Captain Christ was proven very accurate in his prediction.

Before support could arrive, the Nationalist air squadrons had to hold back the mass of the enemy attack. The Legion had approximately seventy operational aircraft in its squadrons. The Spanish Nationalists had about 170 planes, and the Italians had 194.[1]

Volkmann dispatched two heavy and one light flak batteries to reinforce Yagüe's hard-pressed artillery at Gandesa. Being highly mobile, the batteries were soon taking up firing positions. It was obvious this was the main point of the enemy retreat. Captain Christ now estimated the enemy had four divisions across the river and four more ready to move. The opening of the gates of the Río Segre helped to a measure by the second evening. Pontoons, rowboats, building materials, and bodies were being swept out to sea past Amposta. German Intelligence reported that papers found on the dead revealed that the entire officer corps, half the NCOs, and 8 percent of the troops of the 14th International Brigade were Frenchmen.[2]

Through the remainder of the month of July, Lister's battalions repeatedly attempted to seize the town of Gandesa, but were hurled back by Yagüe's determined defenders, devastating artillery fire supported by the German flak guns, and constant air assault by the Nationalist air squadrons dropping tons of bombs. On 27 July, NCO Jaenisch had to crash-land his Me-109 southwest of Tortosa. The plane was a complete wreck, but Jaenisch was not injured. In a few days he was back in the air with another fighter. Major Harlinghausen's Seaplane Squadron sank another ship at Gandía.

General Volkmann wanted his Command quarters closer to the battle-field and moved from Benicarló to Alcañiz. By the evening of 29 July, they were well established. Meanwhile, Lister issued a series of excited bulletins describing the great success of his 5th Corps. His fourth bulletin, dated 29 July, noted that Yagüe's resistance had stiffened.[3]

By 30 July, the pattern was established by the Condor Legion which would be its story for the next three months. It was one of repeated missions by the same aircraft and crews against enemy positions, always trying to knock out the river crossings (which were rebuilt during the night), striking assault forces and disrupting the enemy's rear commu-nications. The missions were costly in expenditure of materials and wear on aircraft, and were trying to the flight and ground crews. Plocher and his ordnance section were hard-pressed to have adequate munitions on hand, and the engineering services labored hard to keep the aircraft serviceable. The bomber crews were frustrated in having to fly through hostile fighters and heavy antiaircraft fire to bomb the same targets over and over again. This operation may be illustrated by repeating here the "Special Staff W" Summary for 30 July 1938:

Special Staff W
  No. 15950/38 Ia.

ENCLOSURE 1 TO SITUATION REPORT NO. 551
(Details of Legion Missions 30 July 1938)

K/88 Bomber Group
  First Mission: 12 aircraft, 15 tons, from 2,300 meters. Bombed Cor-
                    bera and heights to the southeast. Good results. En-
                    emy flak defense.
  Second Mission: 9 aircraft, 11.25 tons, from 4,100 meters. Bombed Ebro
                    crossings between Miravet and Mora de Ebro. Direct
                    hits on bridge at Miravet and ferry at Mora de Ebro.
                    Enemy flak defense.
  Third Mission: 21 aircraft, 26.25 tons, from 3,700 meters. Attacked
                    crossings at Flix and Ascó. Several direct hits on bridge
                    at Flix.
  Fourth Mission: 21 aircraft, 11.25 tons, from 2,400 meters. Attacked
                    positions at Corbera and Villalba. Good bomb patterns.
  Fifth Mission: 21 aircraft, 26.25 tons, from 3,800 meters. Bombed
                    crossings at Vinebre and Flix. Both bridges hit. Traffic
                    interrupted. Flak defense.

Sixth Mission: 9 aircraft, 11.25 tons, from 2,500 meters. Bombed heights east of Villalba de los Arcos. Bombs fall in own area. Reason will be found.

A/88 Bomber Flight Reconnaissance Squadron
First Mission: 6 aircraft, 3 tons, from 4,000 meters. Bombed Ebro crossing between Ascó and Flix. Hits on bridge at Ginestar and Ascó, as well as bridgehead. Enemy flak defense.
Second Mission: 2 aircraft, 2 tons, from 3,500 meters. Bombed crossing between Mora de Ebro and Miravet. Hits on bridgeheads. Enemy flak defense.
Third Mission: 5 aircraft, 2.5 tons, from 3,500 meters. Target same as second mission. Hits on flak battery.

A/88 Reconnaissance Flight
Flew six missions in the Ebro area.

J/88 Fighter Group
Flew fighter cover for bomber and Stuka flights on 5 missions. Also flew 2 search and destroy missions in Flix area. No intercepts.

Stuka Flight
Flew 2 missions against positions in area Corbera, and against bridges at Ascó and Vinebre. 4 tons dropped. A direct hit on bridge at Vinebre.

AS/88 Seaplane Squadron
On night of 29 July, 3 aircraft attacked positions Ampolla with 3 tons from 1,200 meters. On night of 29-30 July, 5 aircraft attacked railroad, Cambrils-Hospitalet-Ampolla with 6.5 tons from 100 to 1,200 meters. Hits on buildings and tracks. Explosions and strong fires. Defense by fighters.

F/88 Flak Group
No action.

Many reports carried a section titled "Special Events." Report Number 552, dated 2 August, noted: "One section of the 5th Flak Battery received direct hits from enemy artillery. Corporal Gärtmer was lightly wounded."

If there was an engagement with enemy fighters, the losses, victories, and names of the pilots scored with the victory are normally listed. Also, Report Number 522 noted under "Air Situation":

The missions of the bomber units against the Ebro crossings have continued with good results. The bridge at Ginestar was destroyed with several hits, and traffic is once again interrupted. The Fighter Group, besides flying bomber protection, flew three "free hunt" missions. During an aerial battle with twenty-five enemy Curtisses, three kills were made. The pilots with the victories were Lieutenant Ebbinghausen and NCOs Jaenisch and Bauer. Lieutenant Tietzen had to make an emergency landing in the Nationalist area near Batea (twelve kilometers northwest of Gandesa) and is currently missing. The flak batteries in the area Corbera-Pinell took up fire against twelve enemy bombers and six Rata fighters.

By 2 August, the front was stabilized. The enemy had made a sizeable bulge west of the Río Ebro, but the offensive failed to obtain its military objectives. The success of the first few days, into the weakly defended area, did give the enemy a great international propaganda victory, and it assuredly disrupted the Nationalist advance against Valencia. The front between Mequinenza and Fayón was about ten miles at its deepest point of penetration. To the south, the front from Fayón to Cherta on the Ebro was almost a straight line—but with the Nationalists holding Villalba de los Arcos and Gandesa. Both sides began digging defensive positions, and General Franco was building up battalions and artillery.

That day saw an increase in enemy air activity with fifteen bombers and twenty Ratas coming within the cone of fire of the German flak batteries at Gandesa. One Martin bomber was shot down by the 6th Battery. On a "free hunt," an Me-109 flight intercepted three Ratas and Lieutenant Kröck scored his first victory. One of Harlinghausen's He-59s received a hit over Paitrosos, and the pilot, NCO Euen, was wounded. He managed to land safely at Vinaroz. The Bomber Group lost an He-111 which crash-landed near the airfield Sanjurjo because of engine failure, but no crewmen were injured. In his usual thoroughness Captain Christ commented: "The engine had 202 hours and 7 minutes flying time. It was last inspected at 72 hours and 2 minutes."

Lieutenant Werner of the Legion staff was promoted that day to first lieutenant. Captain Christ wrote: "The whole Command quarters is drowning in the aftermath of this happy occasion."

The Nationalists were bringing six divisions and a cavalry brigade into positions along the front. The speed with which this was accomplished may be noted in the case of the 102nd Division, of General Castejón, which had been committed in Estremadura. It departed by train from Mérida on 27 July, and in the early dawn of 30 July was building fortifications on the line between Villalba de los Arcos and Pobla de Masaluca.

On 3 August, enemy bombers struck hard at Gandesa, but one German flak battery scored a kill and the others scattered. In his sixth bulletin, dated 3 August, Lister noted the Nationalists' "aerial action is terrifying and deadly."[4]

The Legion Reconnaissance Flight increased its surveillance over the front to support the Nationalist counteraction, which was expected to start on 6 August. On the day before, however, one of the Do-17s did not return from its mission. It was later learned it had been hit by enemy flak and crashed in flames into the Río Ebro near Flix. Two parachutes were seen to float down. The crew was Lieutenant Wolf Fach (observer), and NCOs Friedrich Mende (pilot) and Otto Lehmann (radio operator). Lehmann was killed in the flaming crash and the other two were taken prisoner.[5]

As planned, planes of the Legion covered General Delgado Serrano's two divisions, supported by two companies of tanks, when they smashed into the enemy, on 6 August, between Mequinenza and Fayón (see map 16). The enemy was sent reeling back across the Río Ebro, leaving 900 dead and 2,000 prisoners along with vast stores of war booty. The losses to the Nationalists were very limited. The original front in this area was now reestablished.[6] Ground action slowed, but the air squadrons continued daily to saturate the enemy positions with bombs.

During the next few days, the enemy made limited attacks in various sectors, which were generally contained very quickly. During this period there were repeated meetings between the Legion General Staff and Generals Franco, Kindelán, Vigón, and the Italian Garda at their various headquarters. There, detailed plans were made for future operations. Meanwhile their air squadrons were continually over the targets.

On 10 August, on the right flank southeast of Gandesa, General Alonso Vega with the 4th and 84th Divisions advanced into the Sierra de Pandols and made a gain in the direction of Pinell. They were strongly supported by the Legion's planes and flak batteries used as field artillery.[7] The Germans were confused as to why Modesto had not made a larger contest in the air, as their own planes repeatedly dropped tons of bombs on his forces. However, on 12 August, enemy planes were over the front in force. One Me-109 squadron quickly engaged an enemy formation of nine Martin bombers protected by twenty-five Rata fighters. The nine German planes broke through the enemy fighter screen with Lieutenant Bertram shooting down one Rata. Captain Schellmann added to his list of kills by shooting down two of the bombers and was joined by NCO Brucks who destroyed a third bomber.[8]

The Legion Command quarters started celebrating Commander Bendler's birthday at midnight, 13 August. It must have been an interesting party because Captain Christ commented: "It was not until 0600 hours that Major Menhert was on his way back to base at Saragossa." It was probably fortunate for the major that he was not involved in the very high-level meetings that same morning. Besides several members of the

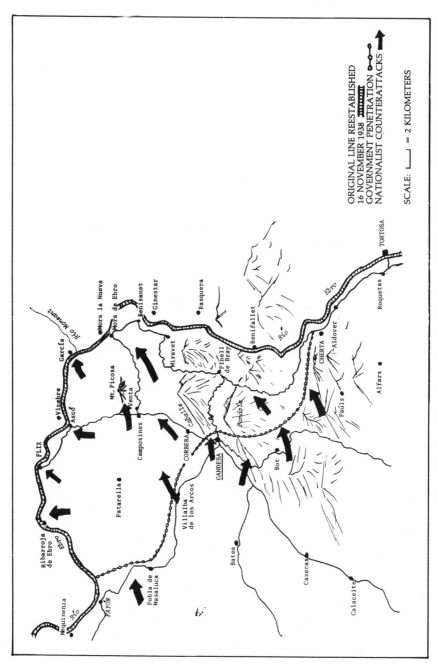

Map 16. The Ebro Bulge, 7 August-16 November 1938.

Legion Staff (some not feeling well) there were six generals from three nations. The Generals were: Volkmann, Dávila, Vigón, Yagüe, Garda, and Manca. They were standing together having their photograph taken from all directions when there developed in the distance an exiting aerial dogfight between Italian Fiats and enemy Ratas. On arriving back at the Command quarters, the Germans learned their Me-109s had shot down six Ratas. Again Captain Schellmann had one kill, NCO Hiehn scored two, Lieutenant Lippert added to his count with one, Lieutenant Bertram also had one kill, and NCO Szuggar had the sixth victory.[9]

The Battle of the Ebro now deteriorated into a war of attrition along the great bend of the river. Daily, aircraft intensely bombed the river crossings and enemy positions. But the bridges would be rebuilt the very same night. Artillery concentrated heavy barrages along a narrow front and the infantry would attack in one- to three-battalion strength. There would be short but intense encounters, and the positions frequently returned to the enemy by evening. In this, each side suffered heavy losses, and it was a question in the minds of Volkmann and Plocher which side could afford to sacrifice the most. Plocher commented: "On a small scale, it reminded one of the battles along the Western Front during the Great War."[10]

Volkmann, supported by General Garda, suggested to Franco that the Nationalists should merely hold along the river's bend and launch a strong attack to the north, with five divisions available, along either side of Lérida to relieve pressure all along the Río Ebro. Franco would not consider such an offensive until the Ebro bulge was eliminated.[11] At the same time, it must be remembered that Franco was greatly concerned with international events and how these events, in the long run, might possibly affect affairs in Spain. Europe's attention was now directed to the Czech crisis, and if this should develop into a general European war,— and many thought it possible—Franco could envision France entering the Spanish conflict on the side of Barcelona with the excuse that it was necessary to protect the French southern flank. France had advised Count Jordana, Nationalist foreign minister, that it contemplated in the event of a European war ". . .one of its first measures an invasion of Catalonia and the seizure of the harbors of the Red zone in southern Spain."[12]

Enemy fighter planes now began to make a repeated appearance to try to break through the German fighter screens. On 15 August, Lieutenants Oesau and Bertram and NCO Küll dived into an enemy formation, and each scored a victory.[13] Then on 19 August, four more Ratas were shot down. NCO Küll had another victory as did his squadron commander, Lieutenant Mölders. Lieutenants Scholz and Keller each made a kill. At the same time the flak guns at Gandesa drove off fifteen Ratas.[14]

The next day Captain Schellmann again shot down another Rata. The flak guns at Gandesa also had to raise their gun barrels to scatter nine bombers and twenty fighters. On a bombing mission against enemy positions near Gandesa one He-111 was shot down by enemy flak, and the crew parachuted down northwest of the town. The pilot, Lieutenant Hans Willer, died of a skull fracture and NCOs Schwarz (observer) and Frischling (radio operator) were slightly wounded. But NCO Naumann (engineer) was not located. Several days later the enemy radio broadcast that winds had carried his parachute into their territory and he had been taken prisoner.[15]

By 23 August the enemy had begun to make repeated bomber strikes against the Nationalist positions. Captain Christ felt there must have been differences within the enemy command on the use of air power which were now partly rectified. And he was correct. But this time their effort proved costly. One Martin bomber and three Ratas were shot down by the Me-109s. Lieutenants Bertram, Müller, and Ensslen each shot down a Rata, and Lieutenant Mölders caught the bomber with his guns. The flak guns at Gandesa again fired on eight bombers, nine Ratas, and twenty-one Curtisses. One bomber was caught in the firing zone and exploded.[16]

Enemy fighters and bombers escaped the Me-109 patrols to attack General Yagüe's troops at Gandesa (25 August), and once again German flak guns shot down one Rata. The Legion Staff learned that NCO Liebig with the tanks (*Drohne*) had been wounded in a strong tank engagement on 22 August near Villalba. And, surprisingly, Corporal Werner Koch of the Fighter Group, who had been taken prisoner (14 June), managed to escape and work his way to Nationalist lines.[17]

The Seaplane Squadron had been continually raiding along the coast in several sorties nightly. On 29 August, one He-59 float plane was totally destroyed on landing. Critically injured was Lieutenant Römisch (observer). The same day a cannoneer with the 4th Flak Battery was wounded in an artillery exchange. That night high buffeting winds struck the Legion airfield at La Cenia and badly damaged several Legion planes.[18] Because of the storm, the bomber flights were grounded for a few days. But protective fighter patrols and reconnaissance flights continued. One of the fighter patrols intercepted an enemy fighter formation, and NCO Hiehn shot down a Rata. On 1 September, a Do-17 was hit by enemy flak. Although badly damaged, the plane managed to land at a recovery field. The flak batteries at Gandesa repeatedly came under accurate artillery fire. There were no casualties, but the guns had to be relocated. During this period the Legion Command quarters moved back to Benicarló.

The Nationalist and German Intelligence had a clear picture of conditions behind the enemy lines. Deserters, prisoners, and captured documents revealed harsh measures being taken to keep the enemy troops on the line. Shooting of officers and troops by their own men was not uncommon.[19]

An He-111, on 3 September, bombing an Ebro crossing, was caught by a 3.7cm shell. The pilot was not hurt and managed to land his crippled aircraft at a recovery station. Then on 5 September, 246 German troops departed Vigo on a transport bound for Germany. They included eighteen crews from the Bomber Group, eighteen crews from the Fighter Group, three crews from the Reconnaissance Group, and three crews from the Seaplane Squadron. General Plocher commented:

> With our aircraft and combat losses we were in a difficult position. We had not received adequate replacement of either aircraft or for the crews returning to Germany. This made it very difficult for those who remained. Our combat capability was seriously affected and the enemy was still very strong with his fighters.

This was proven that very day when a bomber squadron, protected by Me-109s, was struck by fifty Curtiss and Rata fighters. The gunners on the bombers shot down one Rata, and Lieutenant Ensslen in his Me-109, brought down a Curtiss. Lieutenant Lutz had a desperate fight northeast of La Cenia, and his aircraft was badly damaged. Although wounded, he managed to break off the engagement and landed his plane at a recovery field. Then the flak at Gandesa fired on twenty-five more fighters.

It was at this time that General Kindelán assigned Spanish crews to the German Legion. By the end of the first week of September, nine Spanish crews were flying with the Bomber Group in the number 3 and 4 positions. The Germans were delighted with the Spaniards' performance. "These crews adjusted surprisingly fast, and the German commanders are very pleased with their performance. As yet, however, they are not ready for 'blind flying.' "[20] Not long after, Spanish crews were also assigned to fly some of the Do-17s of the Reconnaissance Squadron. Hardly a day passed without the flak batteries at Gandesa firing on from twenty-five to fifty enemy aircraft.

A one-sided aerial battle developed on 7 September, when an Me-109 squadron on a "free hunt" engaged sixty Curtisses and Ratas. This time Lieutenant Mölders found himself the target of a Curtiss and a Rata at the same time. Using his skill to the utmost, he caught the Rata with his guns and sent it crashing to the earth. Another Me-109 was not so fortunate. It was hit in the engine by machine gun fire, and the pilot was fortunate to dive it out of the battle. His engine then failed and he crash-landed, almost completely destroying the plane. Surprisingly, he was only badly shaken.[21]

At this time, Captain Christ commented about all the farewell parties and birthday celebrations they had had recently in the Command quarters. "Because of the repeated farewell and birthday parties, Lieutenant Asmus is in a state—in which up to now—he has never before been seen."

This was added to the next night because the entire staff, less the general, drove to La Cenia for another farewell party in honor of Captains Hermann and Schellmann. Both gentlemen were now highly recognized fighter pilots. This was repeated the following evening, again in La Cenia, with a party in which Major Mehnert was included. This time: "According to witnesses, Lieutenant Asmus really crowned himself, and in an unpredictable condition flew, with the returnees, to Palma for a holiday."[22]

The next day, 13 September, Lieutenant Mölders's squadron engaged nine bombers protected by twenty-five Ratas. In the melee, Mölders added another Rata to his list of kills. The flak guns were very busy with first thirty and then fourteen more Curtisses, and an 88mm battery blasted two Curtisses that flew into its firing cone out of the sky. On 18 September, an He-111 was hit in its control system by enemy flak. The pilot ordered all crewmen to parachute to safety and then brought the crippled plane in for a delicate emergency landing.

The intensity of the ground fighting is revealed in "Special Staff W" Summary No. 594, which noted that since 25 July, the Nationalists had lost 26,000 men on the Ebro bulge. "Particularly high losses are in the officer ranks. The attack divisions have received the highest casualties and are generally the best divisions of the Nationalist Army. At this time, one can say that these divisions are overburdened and burned out." The Germans commented with interest that since 19 August the Italian artillery batteries at Gandesa had fired 109,000 rounds from thirty-eight artillery positions.

Lieutenant Ensslen's fighter squadron engaged twenty Ratas on 20 September, and Ensslen scored another victory. But Lieutenant von Kügelgen, flying in his He-45, was attacked by an enemy fighter. Although his boots were filled with blood from bullets in his legs, one of which was broken, and another bullet in his hip, he managed to escape by flying low to the ground and nursed his crippled plane to a Nationalist base. That night there was a celebration in the Command quarters for von Kügelgen's escape, Ensslen's victory, and for Lieutenant Asmus (he had returned from Palma), who now had his orders to return to Germany.[23]

On 23 September the "Mickey Mouse" Squadron again distinguished itself with three enemy planes confirmed as victories and five more listed as "probable." Lieutenant Mölders had another Rata victory, and NCO Braunshirn shot down a Martin.[24]

The Legion now prepared to move the Command quarters into winter facilities at Sobradiel. Those Germans not returning to Germany were not too pleased with the prospect of spending another winter in Spain.

Another German fighter squadron encountered serious odds when it challenged a superior enemy force on 27 September. No definite victories were confirmed, but three were listed as "probable." Lieutenant Tietzen received the worst of it during a dogfight with a Rata. The enemy pilot managed to turn in on Tietzen and rake his plane with machine guns. Tietzen was hit twice in the shoulder but managed to break off the fight and, bleeding badly, made an emergency landing in a farmer's field not far from Gandesa.[25]

Because of heavy rains and thick mud the surface transport of the Command quarters to Sobradiel was most difficult. The night after their arrival they heard over the radio that the Czech crisis had been settled. This was undoubtedly a relief to General Franco, because offensive ground action on his part began to take a more determined form. The enemy responded by striking hard, early on 4 October, with bombers and fighters, the Legion airfield at La Cenia. One Me-109 was totally destroyed and four others damaged. Later in the same day some of the Me-109s engaged enemy fighters with Lieutenant Lippert scoring another victory. But Lieutenant Bertram now ran into serious trouble. His plane was caught in a deadly burst by an enemy pilot, and he had to take to his parachute which carried him into enemy territory.[26] One of the He-111 bombers was also shot through by an enemy pilot and had to crash-land. No crewmen were injured. The next morning another He-111 took a direct hit from enemy flak over Corbera and burst into flames. All but one of the crew, Radioman Gerhardt Pach, managed to parachute out before the plane exploded. The pilot, Lieutenant Hogeback, was seriously injured and badly burnt in the eyes.

The fighter planes again battled over the Ebro on 8 October with Lieutenant Ehrig and NCO Menge each scoring a Rata kill. But one enemy pilot broke through the fighter screen to engage in a firing exchange with the gunners of an He-111. The bomber managed to escape, but Radioman Ernst Eichelbaum received a crippling leg wound. Two days later the "Mickey Mouse" Squadron again had a furious battle with enemy fighters and bombers. Lieutenant Mölders once more shot down a Rata, and Captain Grabmann and Lieutenant Gamringer each shot down a bomber. Then Gamringer got into trouble and had to defend himself against a vicious attack by an enemy pilot. Gamringer was hit in the arm and dove to safety out of the line of fire to make an emergency landing. NCO Schob was more fortunate, on 13 October, when he blasted a Curtiss with his guns for a clear victory. For several days now, the Spanish-flown Do-17 bombers were flying in formation with the He-111s.[27] Another He-111 was hit by enemy flak and exploded in the air over Fatarella on 16 October. Lieutenant Thilo von Janson (observer), Lieutenant Emil Roedel (pilot), and NCO Heinrich Hoevener (student pilot) died in the flaming wreckage. NCOs Keppler (radio operator) and Ernst (engineer) managed to escape with their parachutes but landed in enemy territory.

Lieutenant Mölders and his squadron were in the air again on 18 October. This time Mölders counted two Rata kills; Captain Grabmann and Lieutenant Oesau had one each. Aerial interceptions then diminished for several days but the bombings remained constant. Then on 24 October, the Legion lost one of the courier planes flying out of Saragossa but none of the passengers or crew were killed.

After many frustrating weeks, the Ebro battlefield exploded on the ground and in the skies 30 October. General Franco had committed two Army Corps to the attack. The northern group was General Yagüe's Corps *Marroquí* which held the line between Mequinenza and Gandesa. The southern group was General García Valiño's Corps *Maestrazgo* with five divisions, two tank groups, and seventy artillery batteries augmented by Italian and German cannon. Valiño had the main thrust between Gandesa and Cherta. All available Spanish, Italian, and German planes supported the attack with repeated missions flown daily. The enemy had seven divisions in the attack zone and three brigades east of the river. These divisions were smaller than the Nationalists', and their ranks had been thinned further by having lost 30,000 men since the beginning of the Ebro battle. They still had possibly 100 fighter planes but very few bombers. There was no question about air superiority. A massive three-hour artillery barrage from all guns and tons of aerial bombs struck the barren ridges of the Caballs and Pandols ranges, which were soon covered by a blanket of smoke from exploding shells and bombs. Then the infantry of a Navarre Division started its advance directly behind a rolling barrage from the Spanish, Italian, and German batteries. Fighting every step of the way against determined resistance, the Navarre battalions struggled up the northern slope of the Sierra de Pandols and finally reached the crest. The enemy began to fall back to the village of Pinell under a rain of bombs.

Enemy fighter planes took to the air and tried to penetrate the Nationalist protective Me-109 and Fiat fighter screens. It was a costly effort with the Me-109s shooting six out of the sky and being listed with five more "possible." Mölders, now promoted to captain, added two Ratas to his ever-growing score. Lieutenant Schumann exploded one Curtiss, NCO Fleischmann shot down two Ratas, and NCO Kieling scored with a single Rata.[28]

The fighting raged into 1 November; there was no letup in the bloodbath as the enemy stubbornly tried to hold the eastern and southern slopes of the Sierra de Caballs. Enemy fighters again tried to dive through the Me-109s to get at the bombers, which were making the earth tremble with their bomb loads. NCO Menge shot down one Rata in flames. German and Spanish-manned tanks led the way for the infantry, and by 2 November the Navarre Division advanced to within two kilometers of Pinell as the fighting continued to rage in the Sierra de Caballs. Desperate enemy counterattacks were thrown back with severe losses. Corporal George Scharl with a communications section was killed by machine gun fire as he advanced his communications line toward Corbera. Then the next day the Nationalists ruptured the enemy fortifications in the Sierra de Pandols. Pinell was then captured as the Legion dropped tons of bombs on river crossings and on troops fleeing back to the bridgeheads. Once again enemy fighters tried to break through the Me-109 protective screen and lost five planes. Again Captain Mölders shot down a Rata. NCO Braunshirn caught another with his guns; Lieutenant Oesau and NCOs Schon and Freund each shot down a Curtiss. NCO Nirminger's Me-109 was trapped by a burst of machine gun fire, and Nirminger was wounded but he managed to land his plane safely. One enemy pilot closed in on an He-111 bomber and raked it with his guns. It was able to make it back to its base, but NCO Lutz was wounded.[29]

By 7 November, Mora de Ebro was in Nationalist hands, and their troops were storming Mount Picosa to the west. The German staff viewed the offensive as a major success, although it would be a few days before the enemy was completely cleared from west of the Río Ebro. The enemy attempted strong diversionary attacks in the south but were hurled back with serious losses. Then on 12 November, German Me-109s intercepted an enemy fighter squadron, and NCO Fleischmann shot down a Curtiss. Lieutenant Gustav Trippe standing up in the turret of his tank as it advanced with Yagüe's troops north of Fatarella, on 15 November, was shot through the heart by an enemy patrol. The next day Flix and Ribarroja were captured. The old line at the Río Ebro between Cherta and Fayón was reestablished. This same day, 16 November, was the second anniversary of the arrival of the Condor Legion. That morning the Legion band woke the Legion staff with a loud reveille and then gave a band concert. All squadrons were ordered to stand down except for one bomber and fighter squadron and a flight of reconnaissance planes. The Battle of the Ebro was over.

The Battle of the Ebro, initially claimed as a great victory by the enemy, proved to be a great mistake. The Army of the Ebro losses in men and materiel could not be replaced. As usual the personnel losses are difficult to determine, but the Army of the Ebro is figured to have lost 70,000 men, of which 20,000 were taken prisoner and 15,000 were left dead on the battlefield. They also lost 60 artillery pieces, 1,800 machine guns, 24,000 rifles, 35 tanks, and possibly 150 aircraft. The Nationalist losses in personnel have been put at between 50,000 and 60,000, with the dead possibly at 6,000. The important factor was that, despite their losses, the Nationalist forces (with the exception of certain units) had not suffered structural damage. On the other hand, many of the forces of the Army of the Ebro were shattered. This was one battle of the Spanish war in which artillery was used on a massive scale. In a 114-day period, from 336 guns the Nationalists fired close to 14,000 rounds daily. The Italians alone, between 19 August and 9 October, fired 250,000.[30]

Some analysts are of the opinion that the outcome of the Spanish conflict was determined along the west bank of the Ebro. Still, there were many more battles to be fought and, as in the past, the German Condor Legion was to play an important role.

Notes

1. Freiburg Files, Situation Report No. 541.
2. Captain Christ's *Diary*, 26 July 1938.
3. R. Hidalgo Salazar, *La ayuda alemana a España 1936-39*, p. 183.
4. Ibid.
5. Situation Report No. 556, and Christ's *Diary*, 5 August 1938.
6. Christ's *Diary*, 7 August 1938; Situation Report No. 557; and Hugh Thomas, *The Spanish Civil War*, 2d ed., p. 843.
7. Situation Report Nos. 560 and 561.
8. Situation Report No. 562, and Christ's *Diary*, 12 August 1938.
9. Christ's *Diary*, 13-14 August 1938, and Situation Report No. 563.
10. General Plocher's comment to the writer.
11. General Karl Drum, "The German Luftwaffe in the Spanish Civil War (Condor Legion)," p. 136, and General Plocher's comments to the writer.
12. *GD* Series D, Vol. III, Doc. No. 658. For further information see R.L. Proctor, *Agony of a Neutral: Spanish-German Wartime Relations and the "Blue Division"* (Moscow, Idaho, 1974), pp. 27-30.
13. Christ's *Diary*, 15 August 1938, and Situation Report No. 564.
14. Christ's *Diary*, 19 August 1938, and Situation Report No. 568.
15. Christ's *Diary*, 20 August 1938, and Situation Report No. 568.
16. Christ's *Diary*, 23 August 1938, and Situation Report No. 571.
17. His interrogation reports are in Situation Report No. 579.
18. General Plocher commented to the writer that the storm made a terrible mess.
19. Situation Report No. 579, Enclosure No. 3.
20. Situation Report No. 582.
21. Christ's *Diary*, 9 September 1938, and Situation Report No. 585.
22. Christ's *Diary*, 10-12 September 1938.
23. Situation Report No. 595, and Christ's *Diary*, 20 September 1938.
24. Christ's *Diary*, 23 September 1938.
25. Ibid., 27 September 1938.
26. Ibid., 4 October 1938.
27. Ibid., 10-13 October 1938.
28. Ibid., 30 October 1938. There was a Lt. Colonel Theodor Rossiwall who had seventeen victories in World War II, and a Major Heinz Schumann who had eighteen victories. This writer is not able to determine if these are the same two officers who were in Spain.
29. Christ's *Diary*, 1-5 November 1938.
30. Drum, "The German Luftwaffe," p. 139; John F. Coverdale, *Italian Intervention in the Spanish Civil War*, p. 357; and Thomas, *The Spanish Civil War*, 2d ed., p. 855.

17

Catalonia to
Döberitz

The day the Nationalists started their counterattack against the Ebro bulge, Volkmann received orders to return to Berlin. This was not entirely unexpected because he had been in Spain for a year and at the same time had had some unpleasant differences with Berlin because of lack of support for the Legion. Then, on 14 September, in a lengthy letter to Berlin he complained about the general conduct of the war. He described:

> The best thing the Nationalists had going for them was the spirit of their infantry which now has been used up, and it appears that there is nothing to bring it back to life. The best of the old soldiers have fallen. The officers corps in the ranks from lieutenant through captain have been decimated by losses and partly watered down by the quality of replacements.

He then went on to complain that the older officers emphasized their "colonial experiences and are not open to suggestions." His comments were most blunt about some of the high-ranking Nationalist generals whom he considered as basically incompetent. Even though the enemy leadership had also made mistakes, he considered it was more "energetic and resolute."[1] Indeed, the tone of the letter leads one to believe that he did not hold much faith for a Nationalist victory.

Plocher later commented: "I was aware of the communications with Berlin, and this letter specifically. In general, I was in full agreement. I knew General Volkmann was not happy with what was going on in Berlin and I was not surprised when he left the *Luftwaffe* and returned to the infantry as a division commander. The *Luftwaffe* lost a very fine commander."[2]

After visiting with Generals Kindelán and Vigón, accompanied by Colonel Plocher, Volkmann drove on 5 November, for his final meeting with Generalissimo Franco. It was a solemn occasion as the Spanish generalissimo decorated the German with the *Medalla Militar* with diamonds. Captain Christ wrote in his *Diary*: "The fact that the diamonds would have to be delivered later did not dim the occasion." Volkmann and some of his immediate staff then flew to Tetuán for a vacation as guests of the high commissioner. There they were decorated with the Order of the Rising Sun by the Caliph of Tetuán. Plocher, however, had a special mission of his own. He drove his staff car to Escatrón for the solemn ceremony of unveiling a memorial stone in honor of Corporal Schuller of the Legion staff, who had been captured and executed on 20 March 1938, while a prisoner of war.

Dressed in mufti, General Volkmann had his final meeting on 12 November with the Legion staff; it was described as a melancholy occasion.[3] The following day, accompanied by Lieutenants Gabriel and Schwartz (who also had been recalled to Germany), the general flew to Lisbon to take a ship home.

The Legion Command Staff was invited by General Garda to join with the Italian Air Staff at a cafe in Alcañiz for a dinner in honor of the Legion's second anniversary in Spain. An unusual evening it was. It is best described in the words of Captain Christ:

> After the usual speeches, the Chief of Staff [Plocher] was decorated with the *Aurelio Order* which weighed nine kilos. As we were about to eat, a plate, thrown from somewhere, crashed to the floor. After that, within a half hour, all glasses, plates, cups, etc., were broken. Also smashed were tables, chairs, and benches. Water was sprayed, and all bald heads were treated with grated cheese, mayonnaise, and red wine. It finally dawned on us why the Italians had worn their oldest uniforms to this official meeting. After the restaurant was a complete wreck, all adjourned to the Command quarters. Gin, rum, and cognac were drunk straight from the bottles. At 2330 hours the feast had to be ended.[4]

The next day Plocher had to meet with the generalissimo for a discussion relative to the next operation.

The decision was that the next offensive action would be into Catalonia against the shattered enemy divisions, a drive to Barcelona, and then up to the French border. Franco wanted this accomplished without delay to prevent the enemy from being able to recover his strength after the staggering reverse on the bend of the Río Ebro. Fourteen days were given to regroup the Nationalist ground and air forces, but bad weather delayed the offensive until 23 December.

Colonel Plocher flew to Palma to intercept the new Legion commander, no less a person than its former chief of staff, von Richthofen, now a lieutenant general. On 1 December von Richthofen's plane was joined en route by a squadron of He-111 bombers, which escorted it to a landing at the airfield of Sanjurjo, near Saragossa. While the band played "The Presentation March," Richthofen descended from his aircraft, followed by Colonel Plocher and Major Seidemann, to receive the Legion from Lt. Colonel Franz. The general then made a commander's inspection of the force which he had left a year before. All unit commanders arrived at the Command quarters to pay their respects and to learn what was happening at home. On 4 December Richthofen flew to Burgos to renew his relationship with Generalissimo Franco and to learn the details of the pending offensive. He then returned to Saragossa and made an extended inspection of the entire battle front and locations of the Legion units' Command Posts.

There was a farewell ceremony in San Sebastián for Colonel von Scheele, who was on his way back to Germany. It was Scheele who commanded the first few Germans sent to Spain in the summer of 1936. For two years he had been the military attaché to the German ambassador. Colonel Plocher surrendered his duties as chief of staff to Major Seidemann and attended a farewell party in his honor on 7 December, which was accompanied by the Legion band. There was a great feast of fine food and wine, in which Plocher delighted, and then a spectacular fireworks display. This was followed by a smaller celebration in the Command quarters in which the Legion staff band took over the entertainment. This band consisted of Plocher playing the drums, Lieutenant Phillips the saxophone, Captain Lienekampf the cello, and Major Kumme the bagpipes. An exciting evening was had by all, except Captain Christ, who was in the hospital with hepatitis.[5]

Major Harlinghausen flew in from Pollensa Bay on 10 December, to say goodbye because he, too, was going home. From all commanders he received warm congratulations for the brilliant performance of his Seaplane Squadron. Those staff members not returning to Germany knew they would miss the "Iron *Gustav*." That evening the staff learned the details of the coming offensive.

General Franco was dividing his force into two army groups, the North Army under General Dávila and the southern group, the Army of the Levante, under General Orgaz. The North Army was charged to break through to Catalonia. For this, Dávila had the six Army Corps of the Corps Navarre, under Solchaga; the C.T.V., now commanded by Gambara; Corps Aragón, under Moscardó; Corps *Marroquí*, with its long-time commander, Yagüe; Corps *Maestrazgo*, of García Valiño; and the new Corps *Urgel*, under the capable General Muñoz Grandes.[6]

The Corps Navarre and the C.T.V. were to assume the major assault south on both sides of Lérida and unite at Serós. The Corps Aragón would attack from between Lérida and Balaguer. Yagüe's Corps, on the bend of the Ebro between Tortosa and Mequinenza would drive across the Río Ebro to cut off the enemy in the Tortosa area. Dávila's northernmost forces were the Corps *Maestrazgo* deployed along the Río Segre and the Noguera Pallaresa to La Barona, and the Corps *Urgel* from La Barona to the Pyrenees. Franco intended to divide the enemy front into three parts: *Alto* Segre (Pyrenees), Middle Segre, and the Ebro Front. The first objective was the Middle Segre. The enemy had superiority in numbers, and again had the advantage of position and terrain. The total enemy strength was put at 220,000, with forty tanks and eighty armored cars. For air defense they had eighty fighters, but only twenty-six bombers.[7] There was no question of air superiority. The Italian squadrons, with 134 planes, covered the C.T.V., the Nationalist squadrons supported the Corps *Urgel*, Aragón, and *Maestrazgo* with 146 planes, and Richthofen realigned his squadrons of ninety-six aircraft to support the Corps *Marroquí* and Corps Navarre. Some of the newer Me-109 fighters, besides their machine guns, were armed with cannons.

Richthofen moved his Command quarters to the railroad station of Tamarite de Litera (on the Monzón-Lérida road). Because he had to support two specific attack forces, he established two Command Posts. The northern C.P. was located north of Balaguer on the Río Segre, and the southern C.P. southeast of Fraga. The Bomber Group was assigned to operate out of Sanjurjo but after the first mission each day would land at La Cenia for refueling and bombs. The reconnaissance bombers took up station at Tauste and later would fly from Sanjurjo. At first the He-45s and Me-109s operated from Zaidín and then La Cenia. A heavy and a light flak battery was assigned to the assault divisions.

The Legion began, on 17 December, a series of heavy and continuing bombing raids in the area before Yagüe's Corps *Marroquí* along the lower Río Ebro with the hope that the enemy would assume a major attack was pending from this area. The bluff was successful because the enemy pulled two divisions from the first attack zone and moved them south on the Ebro.

The offensive started 23 December (see map 17). The Legion headquarters came to life at 4:30 a.m., and by 6:00 a.m. the Battle Staff was on its way to the C.P. southeast of Fraga. There were terribly cold winds blowing frost, which later became snow. The artillery barrage of seventy-seven batteries started at 8:00 a.m., and the Legion Bomber Group hit the target area southeast of Serós on the Río Segre between 9:45 and

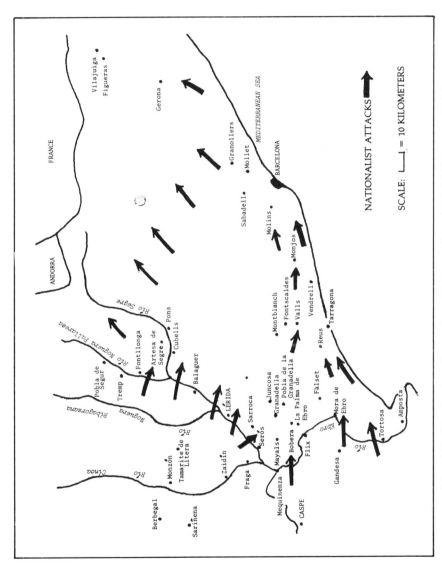

Map 17. Catalonian Campaign, 23 December 1938-10 February 1939.

NATIONALIST ATTACKS

SCALE: └──┘ = 10 KILOMETERS

10:45. At 10:30 a.m. the C.T.V. attacked to the east, and fifteen minutes later the Corps Navarre started its attack behind the bombing and strafing German aircraft and fire from the German flak guns. These were the same tactics that the men of the lead divisions had used so many times before with the Condor Legion. On the left flank, Nationalist batteries shelled enemy positions for three hours and then the lead divisions of the Corps *Maestrazgo* moved out. Farther north, two divisions of Corps *Urgel*, hampered by blowing snow, attacked to the south. Its other divisions pinned the enemy down from La Barona to the French border.

The entire Legion bomber force flew three missions before they had to stand down because of weather, but that night they started single aircraft harassment of the front. Throughout the day not a single enemy plane was seen. Captain Christ wrote in his *Diary*, 23 December:

> The weather improved about 1600 hours and K/88 started bombing Mayals, Llardecáns, and Granadella. Slowly it started to get dark. In the areas of the infantry one could already see the campfires, and only from time to time could one hear scattered artillery fire. Very much pleased with the beginning of the offensive we broke down the Command Post and returned very tired to the Command quarters. In the north we had reached Fontllonga, and in the south to the west of Sarroca-Mayals.

This was the last entry in Captain Christ's *Diary*. He, too, was soon on his way back to Germany.

As in the case of the first day's operation against the Ebro bulge, the Legion established the pattern that it would follow throughout the Catalonian offensive. Because of their mobility, the German flak guns repeatedly led the artillery advance, to be followed by the entire bomber and dive-bomber force pounding the enemy positions with terrifying results. The infantry fought forward behind the low-flying bombing and strafing planes. It was not a parade; the enemy fought doggedly. Some positions were carried in terrible hand-to-hand fighting. Others were blasted to oblivion by the German 88mm cannons, and Nationalist and Italian artillery. Most of the air squadrons flew three to five missions, but at times as many as seven. Initially enemy air defense was very weak. On 25 December, Lister threw his divisions, with Soviet tanks, against the C.T.V. flank, but had to withdraw before withering fire from the German 88mm cannons and aerial bombs. The Stukas on their seventh mission of the day made direct hits on Lister's retreating tank columns.[8] In an effort to stem the tide, enemy bombers tried to strike the Legion base at La Cenia but were driven off by the flak batteries.

On 27 December, the Bomber Group striking near Artesa de Segre encountered heavy enemy antiaircraft fire. A Do-17 flying with the He-

111 formation took a direct hit. As the crippled plane was blown out of the formation, it struck a Do-17 on its wing. Both planes exploded on impact, killing the Spanish crews.[9]

Richthofen on 28 December had to divide his battle staff to man the C.P. located seventy kilometers to the south. The enemy finally increased his air operations with both fighters and bombers. The Me-109s battled an enemy formation in a heated dogfight and shot down three bombers and a fighter.[10] The following day the Me-109s shot down four enemy fighters. Then on 30 December they scattered another enemy fighter formation over Cubells and Artesa de Segre. This time four more enemy fighters were shot down with no German losses. The Corps Navarre, battling against strong resistance, reached Pobla de la Granadella, Bobera, and La Palma de Ebro the last day of 1938. While flying their fourth mission of the day, the German bombers were again challenged by enemy fighters over Artesa de Segre. The protecting German planes scattered the attacking formation and shot one down in flames. On the ground the Legion northern C.P. had to be abandoned because it came under accurate artillery fire. No one was injured. Meanwhile, Richthofen moved the southern Command Post to near Pobla de la Granadella. Also, on the last day of the year, the Seaplane Squadron had a major loss with one of its He-59s shot down at Valls (Tarragona). Killed in the crash were Lieutenant Carl-Friedrich Printz, Lieutenant Otto Schmidt, NCOs Paul Jeck and Walter Bulling, and Inspector Ludwig Müller.

On New Year's Day 1939, the Navarre divisions continued to roll forward as an irresistible force. All operations in the north, however, were practically paralyzed because of bad weather with dense fog. The 84th Division did manage to connect with the 1st Navarre Division at Alós de Balaguer. The weather now cleared and the ground forces came under heavy enemy air attacks, but Valiño's Corps *Maestrazgo* continued to advance well north of the Río Segre. By 3 January 1939, the Legion Command Post in the north was advanced east of Cubells and the C.P. in the south moved to a hill southeast of Juncosa. The Command Post at Cubells quickly came under attack by low-flying planes and three communications men were killed. The dead were Corporals Liebreich Uhlig and Helmut Markus, and interpreter Hermann Buntrock. The Seaplane Squadron also lost another He-59 en route to the target because of ice. Killed in the crash were Lieutenant Poeschel, Lieutenant Schöbel, and NCOs Zervas and Hereld.[11]

Artesa de Segre was now closed by the infantry from the south, west, and north. Then General Muñoz Grandes's Corps *Urgel* crossed the Río Segre and the Canal de Urgel, and Artesa de Segre was completely surrounded. Legion fighters protecting the German bombers in the area shot down two enemy fighters.

The enemy tried to relieve the pressure on its beleaguered forces by landing troops from Valencia at Tarragona under air support. Thus all Legion bombers and Stukas, protected by Me-109s, were diverted south in a vicious attack. Enemy fighters broke through the German fighter cover and shot down one German plane, killing NCOs Bruno Albrecht and Horst von Prondzynski.[12] But in the exchange the Me-109s shot down two of the intercepting fighters. The German bombers hit the targets with a powerful blow, and the Stukas also made direct hits on ships in the harbor. Meanwhile the Spanish and C.T.V. divisions were advancing well. The following day, 5 January, the Legion bombers were again attacked by enemy fighters, but the flights were again scattered by the Me-109s with one enemy plane exploding on impact near Reus. The Nationalist fighters were taking a devastating toll of the enemy aircraft.

By 6 January, the Legion's northern C.P. was on a hill northeast of Moncla and the attack progressed well. The Seaplane Squadron had a problem when one of its He-59s was badly damaged by an enemy fighter, but no crewmen were lost. The Legion Intelligence passed information to Richthofen that enemy resistance was notably weaker and that they had brought two new divisions into the southern sector which were poorly armed and untrained and which quickly folded under fire from the flak batteries. "This is a sign the 'Reds' reserves are coming to an end."[13] Richthofen shifted the main strength of his Legion to the front of Corps Navarre for 8 January. The German flak guns shot down one enemy plane and shattered an attempted enemy tank attack. General Yagüe's Corps *Marroquí* was advancing well and by 10 January had secured the right flank of Corps Navarre. The next day the 3rd Flak Battery, at 10:20 a.m., had a vicious fight with an enemy tank column. Two of the Soviet machines were destroyed on the Espluga de Francoli road, but one of the flak cannons suffered a direct hit. NCOs Erwin Plewe, Georg Sordon, and Herbert-Joachim Knhr were killed and another cannoneer was wounded.[14]

That afternoon, twenty enemy Curtisses attacked in the area of Espluga de Francoli, and although scattered by the German gun batteries, they slowed the infantry assault. Richthofen was determined to destroy the enemy aircraft at their source, but his reconnaissance planes had difficulty locating the fields from which they operated, and at the same time many of the enemy fields were protected by weather. The enemy would take off from one field and—the same as the Legion—land at another. He learned that a number of enemy aircraft had gathered at Monjos and Pate, but it was not until 12 January that the weather cleared to permit a German attack. He directed his strike force to fly out to sea and approach the enemy fields from the rear. They caught the enemy planes on the ground and set ten on fire, as well as fuel service trucks. At the same time other German planes hit hard at the enemy air facility at Sabadell, near Barcelona.[15]

By 13 January, General Yagüe's divisions crossed the Río Ebro at Tortosa and were in hot pursuit of the fleeing enemy. Yagüe continued to the sea and then turned northeast. The next day the German C.P. was moved to Fontscaldes with all squadrons repeatedly bombing and strafing the retreating enemy and Stukas concentrating on enemy heavy fortifications. The way to Tarragona was open. A race now developed between the German flak crews and battalions of the 5th Navarre Division to see who would first reach the Mediterranean. The heavy German 88-batteries soon dropped out of the race, but Lieutenant Deventer hooked the guns of his 4th Light Battery to tanks and trucks and dashed the twelve miles past Spanish troops and ruined bridges, and around bomb-cratered roads. He placed his guns in firing position in time to shatter an attempted enemy counterattack, and then with the leading Navarre battalions made a spirited dash into Tarragona. After violent struggles, which in places were bitterly fought hand to hand, he and the Spanish troops reached the harbor. Yagüe's battalions also closed in on Tarragona at dusk. One third of the enemy army was trapped! While the Navarre Divisions regrouped, the Fighter Group was moved from Zaidín to Lérida. Meanwhile, Corps *Marroquí* rounded up thousands of prisoners.[16]

The Legion Bomber Group was repeatedly committed again on 17 January, and its protecting fighters shot down three enemy planes. The Nationalist northernmost divisions were now driving to cut off the enemy columns from reaching the French border, but unseasonably bad weather hampered all operations. Richthofen now moved his Command quarters to Valls, and all his aircraft continued to harass the enemy. Another enemy fighter was shot down on 18 January as the attack continued forward on all sectors. The next morning the C.P. was established to support again the 5th Navarre Division, and the infantry hit the enemy's third defense line near Barcelona which was supposed to be impregnable. However, German reconnaissance crews had reported that the defenses amounted to little more than normal field fortifications.[17] Wherever the enemy tried to hold, his resistance was quickly broken. As the southern divisions moved forward on 20 January, the remnants of the enemy air force and tanks vainly tried to slow the advance, but an Me-109 shot down a fighter and the flak cannons concentrated on the tanks. Enemy bombers tried again the following morning, but three were to crash in flames as victims of the machine guns and cannons of the Me-109s. The German Stukas, however, encountered serious antiaircraft fire as they pulled out of their steep dives over Barcelona harbor and were ordered to remain out of the area.

Later in the day the Legion bombers were again the targets of enemy fighters, but the Me-109s came to the rescue and shot down four. Almost at the same time Martin bombers tried to strike the advancing Navarre

Division's columns, and two were shot down in flames by the German fighters. The advancing German flak guns were very effective as usual. In only three minutes of fire a heavy enemy battery was destroyed, and then the flak guns directed their fire on truck columns which caught fire and completely closed off the line of retreat. With the fleeing enemy constantly being pounded from the air by the German bombers and Stukas, as well as the He-51s raking their columns with machine guns and light bombs, the retreat was turning into a complete rout. Richthofen now ordered his fighter and armed reconnaissance planes to operate out of Valls. They were all in position by the following morning.

On 22 January, the Bomber Group flew six missions concentrating on the enemy flak defense positions about Barcelona, and reported great success. At the same time, the light bombers operated directly before the advancing infantry in repeated flights. The enemy still tried to strike back in the air, but again a Curtiss fell as victim of an Me-109's guns. The ground advance slowed because of the destruction of roads and bridges, but it continued to move forward. Enemy sappers tried to destroy the stone bridge across the Río Llobregat at Molíns del Rey but came under attack from the German 88mm guns and fled the terrible fire. Aerial attacks continued with the same intensity through 23 January, and one enemy fighter that tried to intercept the Stuka flight was shot down.

By 24 January, the outskirts of Barcelona were in range of the 88mm batteries operating with the Corps Navarre, and the 3rd Battery took up fire against enemy defensive positions. All air squadrons were committed and enemy fighters quickly scattered. By 1:00 p.m., 26 January, General Yagüe's troops were in the suburbs of Barcelona and were faced with little resistance. By 4:00 p.m. Solchaga's Navarre battalions were pouring into the city and were quickly joined by the C.T.V. From then on it was a march into Barcelona, and the troops received an ovation from their supporters in the town who greeted them as liberators. The Condor Legion remained outside the city. Richthofen now moved his Command quarters to the former enemy facility at Sabadell to support the continuation of the attack north. He placed his flak batteries to support the Corps Navarre and *Maestrazgo*. While one of his communications sections was laying a cable from Mollet to Granollers on 28 January, it was taken prisoner. A few hours later all the German communications men were shot. Killed were Lieutenant Karl-Heinz Jochmann, interpreter Johann Berhmann, and NCO Walter Eckert.[18]

Heavy rains now turned the roads and airfields into seas of mud, and in the area of Corps *Urgel* heavy snows hampered all operations. Not until 3 February could air and ground action continue. On that day, Me-109s protecting German bombers shot down two Curtisses of the dwindling enemy air force. They scored another Curtiss the following day while escorting reconnaissance planes. Other enemy fighters tried to attack the flak batteries at low level, and the 4th Battery was listed with three "probable" victories. Then on 5 February, the Me-109s again engaged enemy interceptors and confirmed three more Curtisses shot down. Determined to eliminate enemy air resistance, Richthofen had his fighters attack the enemy field at Vilajuiga at 7:00 a.m., 6 February. It was a great success with eleven enemy planes set on fire and another shot out of the sky as it took off. Fifteen other planes were so badly damaged that they could not be repaired. However, one of his Me-109s was shot down with its pilot NCO Heinrich Windemuth dying in the crash.[19]

The Legion now struck the communications facilities through which the enemy fleeing north had to pass at Figueras. The German planes hit the area with bombs and strafing machine gun fire in waves of one-hour intervals for their last mission in Catalonia on 6 February. By 9 February, the Nationalist divisions reached the French border at several points. The Catalonian Offensive was over! Richthofen now ordered the Condor Legion to stand down temporarily. Because of possible international complications resulting from his flak battery being so close to the French border, he ordered them pulled far back from the frontier. The Legion now began to move back to its old familiar facilities at Avila, Salamanca, and Escalona.

With the fall of Barcelona, deterioration rapidly set in throughout the remainder of enemy-occupied Spain. The enemy leadership was fighting among themselves with many fleeing Spain. Once again non-Nationalist Spain was ravished by a civil war within a civil war. The Legion General Staff had only a limited idea of what was taking place within the enemy camp; because events were moving so rapidly, Richthofen could only make puzzled guesses. A new Legion Command quarters was established at Toledo for—and they hoped it would not be necessary—possibly the final offensive of the long war.

While fighting raged near and in Madrid between the varying enemy factions, the Legion fighter squadrons flew four sweeps over the city, on 13 March, as a demonstration of Nationalist strength and by intimidation added to the confusion within the enemy ranks. Enemy artillery and fighter aircraft were still active in the area, but the fighter pilots chose not to join in combat. Richthofen met with General Franco at Burgos on 16 March to learn of his final intentions. Franco said that he had decided on a final offensive and wanted all Legion squadrons deployed on the Toledo sector.

The Nationalist Southern Army began its attack early on 26 March and met with only scattered resistance, which was quickly overrun. Prisoners and deserters were gathered by the thousands, and the enemy leadership was in flight. All German squadrons were deployed the morning of 27 March, and all Spanish attack forces reported the enemy front completely broken at Toledo. White flags were appearing all through the enemy zone, including Madrid and Valencia. At 10:00 a.m. Richthofen sent the long-awaited message to his squadrons: "All German units will cease operation!" The enemy Army of the Center dissolved as whole units went over to the Nationalist side and soldiers of both sides exchanged strong *brazos* (embraces) on the blood-soaked soil of the *Casa de Campo*. The remaining Army of the Center was then surrendered by Colonel Prada at 11:00 a.m. Other Nationalist forces ripped through the front on the Sierra de Guadalajara and linked with the troops advancing from Toledo. By noon, forces under General Espinosa de los Monteros were occupying the center of Madrid to the riotous joy of the Nationalist supporters in the city. The German staff watched with interest and relief. On 31 March, the generalissimo was informed that all of Spain was controlled by his forces. In his usual unruffled manner, and anticlimatically, his response was a mild *"Muy bien, muchas gracias"* (Very good, many thanks).

The last flight of the Condor Legion was a mass formation of all squadrons flying in close formation over Madrid, Aranjuez, and Toledo in a salute to the Nationalist ground forces. Even though their combat was limited from the end of the offensive into Catalonia until the flight of 27 March, the Legion continued to lose men and planes. A bomber of the K/88 apparently caught fire and exploded with its own bombs over Madrid on 12 March. Killed was the Bomber Group commander Major Haerle and Lieutenant Hans Pawelcik, along with NCOs Rudolf Kollenda, Walter Lange, Hans Schrodel, and Harry Buttner. The Bomber Group also lost NCOs Kurt Langrock and Günther Mais killed in a vehicle accident. The Flak Group lost NCO Heinrich Remke when a vehicle carrying explosives blew up. The Ln/88 Communications Group added to its list of losses Lieutenant Dickore, Lieutenant Weyer, and NCOs Gall and Kaluza in the crash of a courier plane on 8 April at Saragossa. The *Imker* (Tank Group) lost four NCOs in a vehicle accident at Monasterio on 7 April. As near as can be determined the last German to die in Spain was NCO Hans Nirminger, 11 May, who (when flying his fighter in aerobatics over León) crashed as the Legion was being assembled to prepare for the journey home.[20]

There were several farewell ceremonies and parades of the Condor Legion, such as at Saragossa, Barajas, and Madrid. The last was held at León on 22 May. Generalissimo Franco was present with all the senior officers of the Nationalist Command, the Italian and German ambassadors, and Italian air and ground commanders. Franco gave a warm speech of appreciation and farewell, General von Richthofen responded and presented the generalissimo with a donation of one million *pesetas* collected by the men of the Condor Legion for the families of Spanish airmen who had fallen. Then the troops passed in parade. This was followed by a spirited luncheon with Spaniards, Italians, and Germans bidding cheerful farewells.

On 28 May 1939, the entire Condor Legion of "Blond Moors" departed Vigo by ship for Germany. When they arrived at Hamburg, they were greeted by Field Marshal Goering. He informed them they would assemble at Döberitz, outside Berlin, with all of the other German veterans, both military and civilian technicians, of the Spanish war. There would be a massive parade in Berlin for the *Führer*. It would be known as "Operation Döberitz." It went as planned. All veterans from Spain marched in review in German uniform, from General Warlimont, General Sperrle, and Baron von Richthofen, to cooks and bakers. Several men collapsed and died of heat stroke.[21] The men of the Condor Legion did not march at that time into the pages of history, but they marched into World War II.

Notes

1. Volkmann's letter dated 14 September 1938, which is attached as Enclosure 1, "Special Staff W" Situation Report No. 591.
2. General Plocher's comment to the writer.
3. Captain Christ's *Diary*, 12 November 1938.
4. Ibid., 18 November 1938.
5. Ibid., 7 December 1938.
6. These data are generally drawn from a detailed study prepared by the staff in Berlin entitled "Catalonian Offensive 23 December 1938—9 February 1939." It is located in the Freiburg Files under RL 2/v. 3198.
7. Ibid., p. 3.
8. Ibid., pp. 13-20.
9. Ibid., p. 18, and General Karl Drum, "The German Luftwaffe in the Spanish Civil War (Condor Legion)," p. 147.
10. Freiburg File, RL 2/v. 3198, p. 19. In many instances the Berlin study does not identify the types of aircraft shot down, nor the names of the pilots involved.
11. Freiburg File, RL 2/v. 3198, p. 24, and R. Hidalgo Salazar, *La ayuda alemana a España 1936-39*, Appendix 1. The first names of these men are not given.
12. Freiburg File, RL 2/v. 3198, p. 26, and Salazar, *La ayuda alemana*, Appendix 1.
13. Freiburg File, RL 2/v. 3198, p. 29.
14. Ibid., p. 33, and Salazar, *La ayuda alemana*, Appendix 1.
15. Freiburg File, RL 2/v. 3198, p. 34.
16. Ibid., pp. 36-40, and Drum, "The German Luftwaffe," p. 153.
17. Freiburg File, RL 2/v. 3198, p. 43.
18. Ibid., p. 54, and Salazar, *La ayuda alemana*, Appendix 1. The Berlin study listed only one man killed but did not give his name.
19. Freiburg File, RL 2/v. 3198, p. 62; Drum, "The German Luftwaffe," p. 156; and Salazar, *La ayuda alemana*, Appendix 1.
20. Salazar, *La ayuda alemana*, p. 159 and Appendix 1.
21. Colonel Pitcairn's comment to the writer.

Consequences

It has been seen that the moment the Nationalist call for revolt went out from Tetuán, Germany did not spring into the Spanish conflict with devastating weaponry surpassing Zeus's thunderbolts. Hitler alone made the decision for *Luftwaffe* support of the Nationalists over the objections of every ministry of his government, and this first assistance was very restricted in both men and aircraft.

Germany's early limited material and personnel commitment grew, however, as the conflict assumed new proportions and eventually resulted in permitting the few German personnel to become directly involved in hostilities. With the assignment of Colonel Warlimont to General Franco's headquarters another dimension was added to German involvement. Still, direct commitment of German military personnel was limited and haphazard. The unilateral decision of Berlin to augment its assistance with a specially created active military force in the form of the Condor Legion, early in November 1936, added width and depth to the German involvement. With the creation of the Condor Legion it absorbed all of the men and materiel already in Spain.

The earlier committed handful of airmen and aircraft probably did not determine the course of the Spanish conflict, but their efforts and accomplishments do warrant respect. The airlift of a large part of the Army of Africa to Andalusia was the first military airlift in the history of warfare, and it was at a time when these troops were desperately needed on the mainland. That so many thousands of troops and tons of equipment could be moved with the limited number of aircraft was truly a remarkable feat. It must be remembered that the *Luftwaffe*, as such, was but a few months old. No detailed staff studies or plans had ever been made for such a venture. Indeed, there was no precedent to borrow from. The few air and ground personnel, including the reluctant Flight Captain Henke, were thrown on their own limited resources, augmented by their great ingenuity. Between the end of July 1936 and 11 October 1936, they transported, with but nine aircraft, over 13,000 men and 270,199 kilos of equipment to the mainland. Their six (quickly reduced to four) He-51 fighters would have been an exciting plane in the days of the "Red Baron" but were as antiquated as the World War I tactics and organizational and maintenance structure given to the first units of the Condor Legion.

When the men of the Condor Legion arrived, they illustrated the professionalism, dedication, and resolve to adapt to the demands imposed on them as those who had preceded them. At times, their responses bordered on open insubordination. They were the first group of men to be involved in modern aerial warfare as a cohesive air unit operating under a single commander, but at the same time one who not only had inferior equipment but frequently was at odds with the host nation as to how the force should be utilized.

Differences between allied forces on the battlefield are not an uncommon phenomenon. They may be as varied as the nationalities involved. They frequently stem from opposing military philosophies, national temperament, lack of understanding of physical problems facing one or more of the allies, and an insensitivity for political ramifications. These problems can be enhanced in the case of involvement in a civil war. One ally might feel that too much is asked of his forces, or insist they are not being used properly. The forces native to the land might be inclined to blame their friends of the moment for excessive destruction of areas which resulted from the ally's action during a particular operation. The host may, rightly or wrongly, take the view that his ally is insensitive to the land and lives of the population.

There is no doubt that some problems did arise between the Germans and the Spaniards. This is revealed in the existing German documents, Captain Christ's *Diary*, and interviews with both Spanish and German officers. At the same time both of the latter are specific that no matter how wide the gap might have been at a given moment, the problems were not insurmountable. In the great war yet to come there developed many differences between the allies of both sides. Winston Churchill is credited with saying something like: "It is difficult to fight with allies, but harder to fight without them."

Frequently the Germans were critical of the Spaniards for not being ready or failing to press the offensive after the Legion had already flown extensive saturation bombing and strafing attacks against a designated attack zone; also, that the Spaniards at times did not fully apply the basic principle of hot pursuit when the front had been broken. This would permit the enemy to regroup, with the result the strikes would have to be flown again. The Spaniards would counter that the German flyers did not appreciate the sacrifices demanded of their ground forces, and the extent of their resources, both men and material. Shortly after the first phase of the Aragón offensive, General Yagüe gave a speech at a rally of the Falange in which he praised the valor of his enemy, but termed the Germans and Italians as "beasts of prey." Later General Plocher explained it was probably because: "We had insisted that the drive should be continued to the Mediterranean." General Plocher continued:

> The "beasts of prey" comment was not out of character for General Yagüe. He often exploded—he said what he thought at the moment. He was always very direct! We were not offended by him, we always knew where he stood. He was a great commander, very brave, and very tough. He commanded a fine corps.

With the Condor Legion the German Combat commitment in Spain increased to a little over 5,000 men. When the Legion returned to Germany, it had 281 officers, 4,383 men, and 472 civilian technicians. In all, about 19,000 Germans served in Spain.[1]

The Legion aircraft strength only at times exceeded 100 planes of all types, including transport and administrative. A total of 386 enemy aircraft were shot down; of these 59 were destroyed by the antiaircraft batteries. For their 386 aerial victories—313 were shot down by fighters—the Germans lost 72 aircraft shot down by enemy fighters or antiaircraft fire. Through accidents they lost 160 planes of all types.

The Seaplane Squadron destroyed fifty-two ships, and eight were destroyed by the Stukas. The seaplanes also made a complete wreck of the enemy communications facilities along the coast. The Legion bombers dropped 21,045.758 metric tons of bombs of all sizes. This figure does not include the bombs dropped by fighters and armed reconnaissance planes. From 1 January 1938 to the end of the war, the flak guns fired (in all calibers) 325,734 rounds from fifty-four guns, mostly used as ground support artillery.

The cost to the Germans in lives was 298; of these 131 were killed directly by enemy action, and 167 died from sickness and vehicle accidents. The latter claimed the highest total. Wounded through enemy action, aerial and ground, were 139. Injured by other causes were 449, with vehicle accidents again counting the largest number. The highest number, by units, of dead and injured (from all causes) was the bomber force with 205, the flak batteries with 173, and the communications sections with 131.

When one considers the combat and operational losses in relation to the number of missions flown and the successes obtained, the German losses were relatively low. Men such as *General der Flieger* Karl Drum, *Generaloberst* Jaenecke, and *Oberst Freiherr* von Beust (who flew bombers in Spain) note that the losses were far lower than the estimates made by the staffs in Berlin.[2] Without exception, the men of the Legion believe that their relatively low combat loss was due to the training and high caliber of the personnel. At the same time, they recognize that many of their missions, particularly the very close ground support, were of very short duration over the target areas, and frequently their sorties encountered weak enemy air defenses. *Oberst* von Beust clearly noted: "Losses due to weather factors, technical deficiencies, or faulty operation were greater than those attributable to direct enemy activity."[3] These same views were expressed to the writer by each of the officers interviewed.

From the information available it is not possible to obtain a clear picture of the fate of the Germans who were taken prisoner. General Volkmann noted that from 1 November 1937 to 31 October 1938 (the period he was the Legion commander), twenty-five men were taken prisoner and seven were exchanged.[4] Colonel von Beust later wrote that "no more than 30 men from the flying units managed to survive enemy captivity, i.e. who were not killed immediately after capture." He continued: "The fate of the majority of those taken prisoner by the Reds has never been clarified."[5]

In a matter of weeks after the arrival of the Legion, it was recognized the organizational structure of the headquarters, combat squadrons, maintenance groups, supply organizations, communications, and weather sections had to be reorganized. With but minor modifications their changes became the standard organizational structure of the *Luftwaffe* throughout the greater war to come.

The tremendous problems of supply for the force in Spain were painfully apparent. But corrective action was slow, cumbersome, frequently negligent, short-sighted, and in many respects seemingly impossible to overcome. Many of these problems were carried over into World War II and never corrected despite the pleas of the veterans of Spain. Lack of standardization, such as over 100 different types and models of vehicles used by the Legion, is a glaring example. Here, personal and party decisions by Hitler and Goering seem to have taken precedence over common sense. In these cases, more than one professional American officer would agree that a democracy hardly differs from a dictatorship. Without exception, the men of the Legion interviewed by this writer have noted that their urgent recommendations on these matters, based on combat experience, although recognized by some of their superiors in Berlin, too frequently would be reversed by the highest levels in Hitler's headquarters.

When the first Legionaries returned to Germany, the *Luftwaffe* was still in the early stages of its rapid growth. Most men returned to the units they had left, and some were to become instructors for the entire unit. Others were assigned to positions of influence in the expanding force at all levels of command from weather forecasting, communications, maintenance, flight-training schools, to the *Luftwaffe* High Command. Many Legionaries wrote detailed studies and reports on all phases of their experiences. General Sperrle, for example, wrote extensive reports on operations and the lessons learned. Many of Sperrle's studies still exist in the Freiburg Files. All of these had a profound impact on the *Luftwaffe*'s later operations.

Some German officers, such as General Drum, are of the view that far greater importance was attached to these reports than would have been the case if the *Luftwaffe* ". . .had already been an established entity." Furthermore, "the experiences gained in Spain were arbitrarily made into basic principles of *Luftwaffe* commitment."[6] They also point out that it was too frequently overlooked that the Legion's experiences were based on conditions unique to Spain, the nature of the Spanish war, and these experiences were gathered by a limited number of small units which were composed of officers and men of the highest quality which were the "cream of the *Luftwaffe*." Thus, their proposed methods of operation should have been weighed by the fact that in a vastly larger force, men of the same quality and experience would be spread very thin.

Officers and whole staffs from Berlin made frequent visits to Spain in order to observe operations for themselves. "These visits, which were not very popular with the Condor Legion, often failed in their purpose due to the fact that the visitors frequently accepted fleeting impressions and unique occurrences as generally valid experiences."[7] This comment was confirmed by General Plocher and every officer of the Legion contacted. There is hardly a combat officer of any land who will not agree that this is a general failing of headquarters officers and is not unique to the case of the Condor Legion.

When it became obvious that no matter how resourceful the men of the Legion were relative to the great deficiencies of their equipment, Berlin responded by shipping new and untried aircraft and concepts to Spain. Because of this it is frequently charged that the Spanish war was a testing ground for the *Luftwaffe*. Indeed it became so by chance. It would have been a dereliction of responsibility of "Special Staff W" not to have sent immediately every weapons system coming available to the men who had been committed to the battle with antiquated and inferior equipment. Some systems proved deficient, or failures, and had to be withdrawn. The He-51 immediately proved a failure as a fighter. However, its conversion to the direct ground support mission was a notable success at the time. Much of what was learned with it was to be adopted, but with much improved aircraft, into the same mission of the *Luftwaffe* during World War II.

The Bf-109 in Spain proved to be superior to enemy fighters, but its proper use was not to be realized until Captain Mölders's squadron was equipped with the Me-109 models. There is no question that the quiet and brilliant Mölders revolutionized aerial fighter tactics.

Aerial formations and tactics are designed to accomplish specific objectives at a minimal cost. To this end, World War I saw the creation of massed formations to increase firepower in large twisting dogfights. The advent of the fast low-wing monoplanes, however, emphasized the elements of maneuver to firepower in formations. With speed and maneuver came closure, and with it the need to sight the enemy first and to protect the vulnerable tail areas. Eighty percent of all aerial kills are attained with the aircraft shot down never knowing the enemy is there, and the attack usually comes from dead to the rear (or the 6 o'clock position). In the traditional formation the pilot of the new high-speed aircraft had far too much of his attention detracted by guarding against crashing into his wingman and was thereby vulnerable to enemy attack.

The formation adopted by Mölders was to have two aircraft fly as a pair (in German, a *Rotte*). Each *Rotte* was capable of acting as an independent formation in search, defense, or attack—yet it would cooperate with another *Rotte* to increase overall firepower and visual protection. The aircraft were spread 600 feet apart which permitted the pilots to concentrate on finding the enemy rather than on straining to fly in close formation. Two *Rotten* flying together (in German, the *Schwarm*) took positions resembling the extended fingers of the hand and is known as the "Finger Four" formation. The *Rotte* leader visually cleared the forward hemisphere while the wingman cleared the rear or 6 o'clock position.

In defense, if one *Rotte* was attacked, the distance between it and the other *Rotte* of the *Schwarm* permitted the other *Rotte* to turn in toward the enemy and bring its guns to bear. On the attack, each *Rotte* leader was the gunship, while his wingman maneuvered his plane in a "cone" to the rear of the lead aircraft to protect its 6 o'clock position. Thus, coordination and careful delineated responsibilities permitted Mölders to increase firepower, maneuver, and visual protection. During World War II the Royal Air Force (RAF) quickly learned it had to adopt the Mölders tactics, which were then passed on to the Americans. Even with the high-speed aircraft of the 1980s, the Mölders "Finger Four" formation is still used by the United States Air Force, except that the spread between aircraft has been increased to thousands of feet.[8]

There is no question the Legion learned well the lesson of the tactical application of air power as a close ground support weapon. This came about by accident and the nature of the Spanish war from the very beginning. The accident, as noted, was the fact that the He-51 was useless as a fighter plane, but the Legion had it, and von Richthofen decided to use it in the ground support role. The Nationalists were terribly deficient in artillery, and this weakness could be overcome by use of the Legion as airborne artillery. Thus to a large measure the Legion's concentration on the tactical use of air power and neglect of the strategic mission was due to the weakness of the Nationalist ground forces and the Spanish decision restricting its strategic application. Only on a few occasions was the Legion ever permitted to operate as a strategic force. The major exception was the brilliant performance of General Harlinghausen's Seaplane Squadron. But it, too, was switched mostly to the tactical mission when the decision was made to drive to the sea through Aragón in March 1938.[9]

Functioning as airborne artillery, the Germans learned of the dire necessity for close coordination with the ground forces. The importance of timing the ground assault with the air strikes was apparent and thus the necessity of having a Legion officer with the assault division, and he had to have immediate communications with the Legion Command Post. For such ground support operations one of the unexpected advantages of the Versailles Treaty limitations imposed on German armaments of the Weimar Republic was the denial of an air force. The result was that all future *Luftwaffe* officers, in the early period, had extensive training and experience in the infantry, artillery, or cavalry, and held a great knowledge and appreciation for the problems of the ground commanders.

The tactics developed for the Legion close support mission were the brainchild of Colonel von Richthofen, and he remained its advocate for many years through World War II. Initially there were many problems he had to overcome, partly because of conditions in Spain. It was apparent that the "dead reckoning" navigational training of the air crews was useless in this new role. They had to navigate according to landmarks, hit small and at times moving targets, while at the same time be knowledgeable of the front-line location at any given moment. Flying many missions a day, they had to be able to accept changes of targets on a moment's notice. The German bomb sight equipment was most primitive and was designed for much higher altitudes than the Legion could operate. Thus, the bomb release was dependent on practice and skill rather than technology.

It has been suggested that the success in Spain resulted in a *Luftwaffe* overconcentration on direct ground support at the expense of strategic bombing and fighter defense. It appears that this was the case. To the harassed friendly ground commander, direct air support is a welcome relief; to the enemy it can be completely demoralizing and to the flight crews most rewarding because they can instantly see the results of their efforts. General Drum summed up the matter clearly: "Of all the experience gained by the Condor Legion in Spain, it was that pertaining to the methods of tactical air employment which was most significant and most far-reaching in its effects."[10] During World War II, when the *Luft-*

waffe could maintain air superiority, the tactics developed by Richt-hofen were shockingly effective.

Not long after its commitment the Condor Legion received its few Hs-123 dive-bombers (Stukas) which were very disappointing. A year later it received the Ju-87s. Their performance left much to be desired, and their bomb delivery was far from accurate. Not until the Battle of Teruel could the Germans look upon the new Ju-87 with even a degree of con-fidence. By the end of the Spanish war, it was found to be effective against some targets unsuitable for the conventional bomber. This new weapon was under Richthofen for much of World War II and proved effective in destroying enemy fortifications. Terrifying as it was in the early period of World War II, the Stuka eventually proved to be a very vulnerable system. In Spain it had to be relieved from areas with heavy air defense because of its vulnerability when it pulled out of its steep dive. Many German airmen believe the concentration of men and resources on this system proved to be a long-range mistake.

Many veterans of the Legion are of the opinion that one of the major factors to come out of the Spanish war which had an impact on the thinking of the decision-making leadership of the *Luftwaffe*, and ulti-mately Goering and Hitler, proved to be a disaster. Simply stated, it was the concept of creating an all-purpose aircraft suited to strategic and tactical operations. This was carried to the point of Hitler insisting on a heavy multi-engined bomber being designed for both strategic and dive-bombing missions. A quick remedy for a long-range problem and a cheap price to pay for expensive results has never succeeded, but many people will always think it possible. General Drum expressed it clearly, and his opinion has been echoed by many of the old Legionaries: "In the last analysis, it would seem that there is no such thing: the result of such experiments is bound to be a hybrid, incapable of fulfilling either mission properly."[11]

Another lesson from Spain not learned by Berlin, as was also the case in Washington for a time, was to assume that high-performance and well-armed bombers in mass formation could protect themselves against en-emy fighters during daylight missions. When the *Luftwaffe* was provided with the He-111 bomber, as a replacement for the old Ju-52 converted transport, Berlin felt the fighters could be turned loose on the "free hunt." The "Special Staff W" *Daily Summaries* that still exist reveal that in 1938 the Me-109 fighters had to be used for bomber protection until the danger of enemy fighter interception was greatly reduced, then the fight-ers were turned loose on the "free hunt." From 1938 until well into the Battle of Britain this erroneous thinking was dominant in the minds of the *Luftwaffe* planners, so much so that there was practically no training between bomber and fighter pilots. When this oversight was finally re-alized, it was too late because the German fighter planes did not have the range to protect their bombers over the targets. The result was the appallingly high losses of the *Luftwaffe*-trained bomber crews. Many German flyers consider this was a loss from which the *Luftwaffe* never recovered, and from that point on it had to forego the strategic operation in the West except at night.[12] Diverting the bombers to night operation made the *Luftwaffe* once again draw on its Spanish experiences. German officers such as General Harlinghausen still view the *Luftwaffe*'s lack of consideration for the strategic application of air power as a gross mistake.[13]

In Spain, the Condor Legion was only at times concerned with the protection of its own bases other than by the German flak guns. The result was the success realized by the German flak artillery thus gave Berlin the impression that the flak cannons were the ultimate weapon for air defense, and this contributed to the neglect of a fighter defense system to protect the homeland against penetrating enemy bombers.

The Spanish war certainly proved the value of the German flak artillery. At first the guns were usually divided, with half in defensive positions and the other half as ground artillery. It was apparent that the batteries' effectiveness deteriorated if they were in positions of limited or no activity for an extended period. Because of this the guns would be moved frequently from air defense to the direct artillery support mission. Because of the need, in time the deployment against ground targets took precedence over air defense. During one 277-day period of battle, the guns were involved in 377 engagements, and only 31 of these were against air targets. Whereas they proved themselves fairly well as an air defense weapon against the aircraft flown by the enemy in Spain, they proved shattering as ground artillery against fortifications and tanks. The experiences in Spain led to the creation of a flak artillery corps which had a spectacular effect on the European campaigns of World War II.[14]

In general, the *Luftwaffe* experiences in the Spanish Civil War can be viewed as both positive and negative. Many of the Germans who survived both wars are of the opinion that in the long range the negative outweighed the positive. The lessons were there, but many were either not recognized or were ignored by the *Luftwaffe* leadership. On the other hand, there is no doubt that the individual experiences of the men involved had a tremendous impact on them, and many were to accomplish amazing records during World War II. Some of them were projected into high positions of command.

The elderly Lt. Colonel Alexander von Scheele, who led the first small group of Germans to Spain, died in the crash of the airplane he flew back to Germany. Colonel Warlimont, von Scheele's replacement as supreme commander of German forces in Spain, was to become a member of Hitler's Supreme Command (*Oberkommando der Wehrmacht—OKW*). In September 1939, he was chief of the Operations Staff but surrendered this post to General Jodl. However, he remained in *OKW* as deputy chief of staff of Operations as a lieutenant general. He was in the briefing room in East Prussia when Colonel Count von Stauffenberg placed the bomb in one of the abortive attempts to kill Hitler. Although close to the bomb blast, Warlimont, although terribly stunned, escaped injury.[15] In September 1944, after thirty-one years of service, he was placed on the reserve list. The general died in October 1976 in his home at Tegernsee after a lengthy illness. General Faupel and his wife committed suicide as the Soviets drove into Berlin.

General Sperrle became one of the few *Luftwaffe* field marshals and was placed on the reserve list in 1944. He died in 1953 in Munich. General Volkmann for a while commanded the *Luftwaffe* Flight School but with the start of the war asked to be returned to the German Army. He commanded an infantry division in France but was killed in a vehicle accident in August 1940. General von Richthofen also became a field marshal in 1943. Because of illness he was placed on the reserve list in October 1944. While a prisoner of the Americans, he died of a brain tumor on 12 July 1945. General Plocher held many important positions in the *Luftwaffe*, including commanding a paratroop division and at the end of the war was a lieutenant general. He returned to active duty with the new West German Air Force and retired from it a major general. He died on 7 December 1980 after a long illness.

Major Harlinghausen had a brilliant career in the *Luftwaffe*, which was temporarily marred by a dispute with Field Marshal Kesselring. Even more disappointing to Harlinghausen was that he had been unable to convince the High Command of the value of the aerial-delivered torpedo, which he had proven in Spain. He wanted to equip a fleet of bombers with the torpedo and attack the British Home Fleet, which was anchored, at the time, without torpedo nets in Scapa Flow. Hitler, however, had no faith in the torpedo and did not want to risk the loss of the aircraft. Harlinghausen became famous for low-level attacks against shipping, which he had developed successfully with his Condor Legion Seaplane Squadron. During World War II, he and his crew alone sank twenty-six ships. In Africa he led an eight-plane mission against a British convoy in the Suez Canal. He reached the canal but was never able to locate the convoy. Only one airplane returned to its base in Libya, and he crashed his in the desert. He and his crew were located three days later, completely exhausted in their effort to walk across the Libyan desert to the sea. His last combat mission was flown in November 1942, when his low-flying He-111 was hit over the Irish Sea. They crash-landed on the French coast and were rescued from the sea by French fishermen. Harlinghausen suffered a brain concussion, which kept him hospitalized for three months. He was then sent back to Africa for the German withdrawal and promoted to major general. On 1 December 1944, he was promoted to lieutenant general and given command of *Luftwaffe* West in a hopeless situation. In 1957, Harlinghausen joined the new West German Air Force as the commanding general of Air Force North in Munster. He retired a lieutenant general in 1961.

Captain Christ continued to serve on the General Staff and was a colonel at the end of the war. Many associates believe that he would have become a general except for his distaste for flying, which resulted from a crash-landing in which he was badly burnt. After a long illness he died a painful death in the 1950s. His assistant operations officer, the popular Lieutenant Hans Asmus, survived the Second World War and then served in the new German Air Force from which he retired a major general. Captain Werner Mölders became the highest German ace in Spain with fourteen victories. At the age of twenty-eight he was the first German pilot to have over 100 aerial victories and was made general of the *Luftwaffe* Fighter Arm. In late 1941 he was on his way back to Berlin to attend the state funeral for General Udet when his He-111 encountered bad weather and with engine failure, probably due to carburetor ice, crashed in Czechoslovakia. Killed with Mölders was his pilot Lieutenant Kolbe, who was an experienced bomber pilot from the Condor Legion. In attendance at General Udet's funeral were, at the time, three top fighter aces of the *Luftwaffe*: Colonel Lützow, Walter Oesau, and Adolf Galland, all three veterans of the Spanish war. Colonel Oesau flew with Mölders that memorable 15 July 1938, when he, Mölders, and Wolfgang Lippert scored the first victories for their "Mickey Mouse" Squadron. Galland was called back to Berlin for the honor guard for Mölders's funeral, and during the ceremony was advised by Field Marshal Goering that he was Mölders's replacement as general of the Fighter Arm. At the time Colonel Oesau commanded a Fighter Wing on the Western Front. In 1943, like so many of the German flyers, he was both physically and mentally exhausted. Over Aachen he tried to break through an American fighter screen and was shot down.

The fighter pilots of the Condor Legion learned their lessons well in the Spanish conflict. After their initial problem with inferior aircraft was resolved, they gained not only confidence in their new weapons systems, but importantly, confidence in their flying skills and developed tactics. Because of their experiences gained in Spain and then with the great number of missions flown in the Second World War (some with over 1,000) many of them are engraved high on the list of the world's aces. Some of the Condor Legion fighter pilots and their records in Spain and World War II are listed on page 262. The rank indicated is the rank held at the time they were killed or at the end of the war. There were over 5,000 German aces, and this must be considered only a partial listing.[16]

It is possible that some of the men listed might have acquired higher scores in the Second World War, but some were removed from combat flying because of other assignments. Colonel Lützow was the second German with over 100 victories in the Second World War. He became

Rank		*Victories*	
		Spain	*World War II*
Colonel	Herbert Ihlefeld	9	123
Colonel	Walter Oesau	8	115
Colonel	Werner Mölders	14	101
Major	Reinhard Seiler	9	100
Colonel	Gunther Lützow	5	103
Lt. Gen.	Adolf Galland	—	103
Major	Rudolf Resch	1	93
Major	Wolfgang Ewald	1	77
Major	Hubertus von Bonin	4	73
Lt. Col.	Gunther Radusch	1	63
Colonel	Hans Trautloft	4	53
Captain	Wilhelm Balthasar	4	40
Major	Karl-Wolfgang Redlich	2	41
Captain	Hans-Karl Mayer	8	30
Captain	Heinz Bretnuetz	2	35
Captain	Wolfgang Lippert	4	25
Captain	Herbert Schob	6	22
Captain	Walter Adolph	1	27
Major	Josef Fözö	3	24
Captain	Horst Tietzen	7	20
Major	Rolf Pingel	4	22
Lt. Col.	Wolfgang Schellmann	12	14
Captain	Harro Harder	11	11
Major	Otto Bertram	8	13
Lieutenant	Robert Menge	4	14
Lt. Col.	Eduard Neumann	2	11
Major Gen.	Walter Grabmann	6	6
Captain	Karl Ebbinghausen	6	6
Major	Joachim Schlichting	5	3

one of the *Luftwaffe*'s first jet aces and died in the crash of his jet the last few weeks of the war. Lt. Colonel Radusch's victories were at night. Colonel Hans Trautloft was one of the first He-51 pilots to go to Spain. After World War II he returned to duty with the new German Air Force from which he retired a lieutenant general. Captain Balthasar became a much respected squadron commander on the Western Front where he was shot down by the RAF. His men recovered his body and buried him alongside his father's grave (a German ace of World War I) in Flanders.

Colonel Ihlefeld, Captain Schob, and Lieutenant Menge flew as noncommissioned officers in Spain. Lt. Colonel Eduard Newmann became the commanding officer of the "Star of Africa." Lieutenant Douglas Pitcairn flew the Me-109 early in World War II and had five victories in the west but was shot down near the channel and badly injured, which put an end to his combat flying until in the twilight of the war. He returned to active duty with the West German Air Force, from which he retired a colonel.

The Legion airmen of the Bomber Group and Reconnaissance Group recognize that their experiences in Spain greatly added to their flying and combat skills. Of particular note was the added training in cross-country navigation and bomb delivery. Their many missions made them very familiar with their weapons systems, and they knew exactly what they could expect as problems for the future. Some could be corrected; others never could be.

These groups produced many outstanding airmen. One was Lt. Colonel Hermann Hogeback, who flew his first mission in Spain on 13 September 1938. His He-111 was hit and set on fire, and he had to crash-land into no-man's-land. The crew was pinned down by enemy fire through the day but was rescued that night by Moorish *Regulares*. After a stay in the hospital he returned to duty and was to fly more than 100 missions in Spain; he returned to Germany highly decorated. During the Second World War, he flew on all fronts including twenty-eight missions over London. He was shot down in the desert of Africa but managed to fly an abandoned aircraft to Crete and rejoin his squadron. Later his bomber was attacked by twelve British fighters, but two were shot down by his crewmen, permitting them to escape. In 1942, he became the commander of the same group he had started the war in as a pilot. He and his crew continued to fly repeated missions, and by the end of the war they had flown over 500. Each of his crewmen earned the Knight's Cross and was the only complete crew in the entire *Luftwaffe* to be so decorated. Colonel Hogeback added the Oak Leaves and Swords to his Knight's Cross.[17]

Another outstanding bomber flyer from Spain was Major Gerhard Kollewe who came from the Stuka wing *Immelmann*. He, too, flew against England but gained his reputation in the Mediterranean area against enemy warships. He was awarded the Knight's Cross with Oak Leaves. In October 1942, he failed to return from a mission.

A highly respected bomber pilot and commander was Colonel Baron Hans-Henning von Beust. Like many *Luftwaffe* pilots he started as an infantry officer but received his flight training through *Lufthansa*. In Spain he became the first squadron commander of the 2nd Squadron of K/88. Before he returned to Germany, he had flown over 100 missions and was awarded the Spanish Golden Cross with Swords. In Europe he flew on all fronts. In September 1941 he was decorated with the Knight's Cross and had flown 410 missions when he received the Oak Leaves. In

1943, he became very ill but returned to duty in 1944 as a General Staff officer. The last month of the war he was named general of Bomber Flyers. Following the war he joined the West German Air Force as a colonel and held many important assignments, including liaison officer to the United States Armed Forces Europe in Wiesbaden. Colonel von Beust retired in 1971.

Another was Lt. Colonel Willi Antrup, who received his flight training with German civil aviation and joined the *Luftwaffe* in 1935. In the Condor Legion, he flew the courier aircraft. During the war to follow he flew 500 missions and was awarded the Knight's Cross and Oak Leaves. He, too, returned to duty with the West German Air Force and retired a brigadier general in 1968.

Lt. Colonel Baron Siegmund-Ulrich von Gravenreuth flew with the Legion bombers 1937-1938 and was decorated with the Spanish Golden Cross with Swords. He had great success during World War II, particularly against warships and transports. He was killed in an accident on 16 October 1944. On 9 January 1945 he was posthumously promoted to lieutenant colonel and awarded the Oak Leaves to his Knight's Cross.

Colonel Herbert Wittmann flew the He-111 in Spain. He began World War II with the Bomber Wing 52 known as the Legion Condor and became its commander. He flew 467 missions during which he had to parachute more than once. He earned the Knight's Cross in 1941 and the Oak Leaves on 1 February 1945. He was a major when the war ended but returned to duty with the West German Air Force from which he retired a colonel to live in Pullach near Munich. Sergeant Engelbert Heiner flew as a bomber pilot in Spain, but during the Second World War he flew the night fighters. He had eleven victories and was awarded the Knight's Cross. Captain Rudolf Henne flew 200 missions with the bombers in Spain. In 1942 he was a captain with the Knight's Cross. His bomber was shot down returning from a strike against Marseille, but he parachuted into enemy territory and managed to work his way back to Germany. He ended the war with 540 more missions. He died on 13 April 1962.

Captain Rudolph von Moreau, who flew the first unauthorized bombing mission in Spain, later commanded the first German bomber flight. For a while he commanded the "Experimental Flight" of the Legion. When he returned to Germany, he was killed in an aircraft accident.

Captain Kurt Seyfarth flew with the long-range Reconnaissance Flight of the Legion as a lieutenant. Beginning in 1939 he flew with a Ju-52 transport group and operated on all fronts, including the attempted relief of Stalingrad. Later he rejoined the bomber force where he was awarded the Knight's Cross when he had 532 missions. After the war he became a noted sports flyer.

This is but a sampling of the accomplishments of the men of the Condor Legion. It is difficult to determine the number of the 19,000 men who served in Spain who died during World War II. Those who survived believe the number was staggeringly high. This would be but natural in that they were an elite professional force. General Harlinghausen summed up the feelings of these men:

> Putting Germany into war [World War II], our political leadership demanded great sacrifices from our forces. One could see that despite all the early successes it would end in a catastrophe. Through it all the soldiers and airmen tried, to the best of their ability, to save Germany from complete destruction.[18]

In the process, the men of the Condor Legion wrote an unusual chapter in the history of military aviation. The number who survived both wars and then returned to active duty with the new West German Air Force is indeed amazing.

Notes

1. All of these data were reduced from the "Final Report of the Condor Legion," dated 20 May 1939, prepared by the General Staff of the Condor Legion. As far as this writer can determine, this copy, made available to the writer by a member of the General Staff, is the only copy in existence.

2. General Karl Drum, "The German Luftwaffe in the Spanish Civil War (Condor Legion)," pp. 161-165.

3. Quoted in Ibid., p. 164.

4. Lieutenant General Volkmann, "Brief Report on the Employment of the Condor Legion in Spain from 1 November 1937 to 31 October 1938" (Germany: Karlsruhe Document Collection), pp. 21-22, quoted in Drum, "The German Luftwaffe," pp. 162-163. This report also lists the men and equipment lost by units and the reasons.

5. Quoted in Drum, "The German Luftwaffe," pp. 164-165.

6. Ibid., pp. 167a-168.

7. Ibid.

8. Major (USAF) Barry D. Watts, "Fire Movement and Tactics," *Top Gun Journal* 2, No. 2 (Winter 1979/80), pp. 4-24; Trevor J. Constable and Colonel Raymond F. Toliver, *Horrido!*, pp. 62-63, and discussion with Captain Pat Pentland, USAF, A-10 Weapons Officer.

9. General Harlinghausen's comment to the writer.

10. Drum, "The German Luftwaffe," p. 201.

11. Ibid., p. 187.

12. Ibid., pp. 180-181, and the writer's discussions with bomber pilots.

13. General Harlinghausen's comments to the writer.

14. Drum, "The German Luftwaffe," pp. 253-254.

15. General Warlimont's comment to the writer.

16. A partial listing of German fighter aces is in Constable and Toliver, *Horrido!*, and each of these former flyers from the Condor Legion is listed although

some figures differ from this writer's, whose were drawn from the Legion records and Captain Christ's *Diary* which shows different totals for Spain.

17. A very interesting work on the *Luftwaffe* Bomber Aces is Georg Brütting, *Das waren die deutschen Kampffleigerasse 1939-1945* (Stuttgart, 1974). Most of the information about the bomber flyers recounted here was drawn from this source.

18. General Harlinghausen's comment to the writer.

Select
Bibliography

Published Documents

United States. *Documents on German Foreign Policy 1918-1945*. Series D (1937-1945), Volume III. Washington, D.C.: U.S. Government Printing Office, 1950.

Unpublished Documents

Germany (Freiburg Collection)

RL 7/57a and RL 7/57e. *Evaluation Rügen*: Operations, Leadership, Bombardment Crews, Fighters, Reconnaissance, Flak Artillery, Communications, and Movement of Combat Forces.

RL 35-1. *War Diary of Captain L. G. Christ*, Ia of the General Staff of the Condor Legion, 1 January 1938-23 December 1938.

RL 35-2. *AS/88 Spanish Campaign July 1937-December 1937*, "Evaluations of Operation Rügen." Contains Weekly Reports of AS/88.

RL 35/3 Loz 1/24, L-12-88/3. *Report and Essays about the Spanish Civil War*.

RL 35/4, RL 35/5, and RL 35/6. *Special Staff W, Daily Situation Reports of the Condor Legion: 6 July 1938-23 September 1938*.

RL/35/4, *Enclosure to Special Staff W Report No. 538 dated 13 July 1938, Berlin*. "Report on my being taken prisoner," Tonollo.

RL 35/4, *Enclosure to Special Staff W Report No. 540 dated 18 July 1938, Berlin*. "Report as a Prisoner of War," Meyer.

RL 35/4. *Enclosure to Special Staff W Report No. 541, 19 July 1938*, "Report as Prisoner of War," Siegmund.

RL 35/4. *Harlinghausen Report to Special Staff W and Weekly Reports of AS/88,*
    20-26 June 1938; *Daily Reports 3-9 July 1938*, and *Special Staff W Report*
    No. 543, "Nationalist Fleet 1 June-11 July 1938."
RL 35/26. *War Diary of Communications Group Ln/88 5 November 1936-27*
    February 1937.
RL 35/27. *War Diary of Lt. Arend*, "Ln/88 Support for Battle of Guadalajara, 5
    March 1937-26 March 1937."
RL 2/v. 3187. *Magic Fire*, "Reports on Work of the History of the Legion."
    Part 1: "Memorandum of General Schweickhard."
    Part 2: "German Materials Delivered to Franco."
    Part 3: "Battle in the Month of August 1936."
    Part 4: "Battle in the Month of September 1936."
    Part 5: "Battle for Oviedo-October 1936."
RL 2/v. 3188. *Fight in the North: Battle March/April 1937.*
RL 2/v. 3189. *Battle in the North: April through the fall of Bilbao.*
RL 2/v. 3191. *Battle of Brunete: 5 June-26 June 1937.*
RL 2/v. 3195. *First Ebro Offensive: 9-18 March 1938.*
RL 2/v. 3196. *Second Ebro Offensive: 22 March-21 April 1938.*
RL 2/v. 3198. *Catalonia Offensive: 23 December 1938-9 February 1939.*
Service Record File. Field Marshal Wolfram Baron von Richthofen.
Service Record File. Field Marshal Hugo von Sperrle.
Service Record File. General Helmuth Volkmann.

Germany (Karlsruhe Collection)

Air War Academy Manual. Leitfaden der Luftkriegsschulen, "*Einsatz der*
    Deutschen Luftwaffe während des spanischen Bürgerkrieges."
Kohler's *Fliegerkalender*, 1940. "*Einsatz der dt. Flakartillerie in Spanien.*"
List of German Combat Aircraft.
Pitcairn, Lt. Colonel Douglas. "*Russische Flieger im Spanieneinsatz*," 1955.
Table of Performance Characteristics of German Military Aircraft, 1 December
    1938.
Volkmann, General Helmuth. "*Kurzer Erfahrungsbericht über den Einsatz der*
    Legion Condor in der Zeit vom 1.11.37-31.10.38."

Spain, Spanish Military Archives (Archivos Militar)

Condor Legion Headquarters Staff Report. Madrid: *Archivos Militar.*
Confidential Letter Sander [Sperrle] to Franco, Vitoria, 11.4.37. Madrid: *Archivo*
    de la Guerra 1936-39.
Letter from Sander [Sperrle] to General Franco, pertaining to the Campaign in
    the North, dated 2 July 1937, and the Nationalist General Staff response
    (undated). Madrid: *Archivo de la Guerra 1936-39.*
Memo from General von Thoma, on training and use of tanks, dated 29 April
    1938. Madrid: *Archivo de la Guerra 1936-39.*
Memo of Sander [Sperrle] and Franco Discussion, dated 19 December
    1936. Madrid: *Archivo de la Guerra 1936-39.*

Memo from Spanish General Staff Operation Section to Sander [Sperrle], dated 24 December 1936. Madrid: *Archivo de la Guerra 1936-39*.
Memo from Spanish General Staff to Sander [Sperrle], dated 28 December 1936. Madrid: *Archivo de la Guerra 1936-39*.
Situation Reports Condor Legion, 25-30 September 1937. Madrid: *Archivo de la Guerra 1936-39*.
Situation Reports Condor Legion, 5-19 October 1937. Madrid: *Archivo de la Guerra 1936-39*.
Spanish General Staff Memo on German antitank guns and tanks at Cáceres dated 20 December 1936. Madrid: *Archivo de la Guerra 1936-39*.
Spanish Nationalist General Staff Records of the 2nd Section. Madrid: *Archivo de la Guerra 1936-39*.

Spain, Spanish Military Archives (Segovia Collection)

Alonso Vega, Captain General Camilo. Segovia: Extract of Service Record.
Aranda Mata, Lt. General Antonio. Segovia: Extract of Service Record.
Dávila Arrondo, Captain General Fidel. Segovia: Extract of Service Record.
Kindelán y Duany, Lt. General Alfredo. Segovia: Extract of Service Record.
Millan-Astray y Terreros, Maj. General José. Segovia: Extract of Service Record.
Mola Vidal, Lt. General Emilio. Segovia: Extract of Service Record.
Monasterio Ituarte, Lt. General José. Segovia: Extract of Service Record.
Muñoz Grandes, Captain General Agustín. Segovia: Extract of Service Record.
Queipo de Llano y Serra, Lt. General Gonzalo. Segovia: Extract of Service Record.
Vigón Suerodíaz, Brigadier General Juan. Segovia: Extract of Service Record.
Yagüe Blanco, Lt. General Juan de. Segovia: Extract of Service Record.

Diaries and Memoirs

Ansaldo, Juan Antonio. *¿Para Que. . .?*. Buenos Aires: Editorial Vasca Ekin S.R.L., 1951.
Bolín Luis. *Spain: The Vital Years*. Philadelphia and New York: J. B. Lippincott, 1967.
Callega, Juan José. *Yagüe, un corazón al rojo*. Barcelona: Editorial Juventud, 1963.
Cardozo, Harold. *March of a Nation: My Year of Spain's Civil War*. London: Eyre & Spotiswoode, 1937.
Casado, Colonel Segísmundo. *The Last Days of Madrid*. London: Peter Davies, 1939.
Ciano, Count Galeazzo. *Ciano's Diary 1937-1938*. New York: Dutton, 1953.
————. *Ciano's Diary 1939-1943*. London: Heinemann Ltd., 1947.
————. *Ciano's Diplomatic Papers*. London: Odhams Press, 1948.
Forell, *Oberstleutant* Fritz von. *Mölders und seine Manner, herausgegeben*. (Werner Mölders's *Diary*). Graz, Austria: Steirische ver Lagsanstalt, 1941.
Galland, General Adolph. *The First and the Last*. London: Methuen Co., Ltd., 1955.

270   Select Bibliography

García Lacalle, Colonel Andres. *Mitos y verdades: la aviación de casa en la guerra española*. Mexico City: Ediciones Lito Offset Fersa, 1974.
García Morato, Joaquín. *Guerra en el aire*. Madrid: Editoria Nacional, 1940.
García Valiño y Marcén, General Rafael. *Guerra de Liberación española*. Madrid: Imp. Biosca, 1949.
Hidalgo de Cisneros y López de Montenegro, Ignacio. *Memorias*. 2 Vols. Paris: Société d'Éditions de la Librairie du Globe, 1964.
Hossbach, Colonel Friedrich. *Zwischen Wehrmacht und Hitler*. Hannover: Wolfenbüttel, 1949.
Hoyos, Max Graf. *Pedros y Pablos*. Munich: Bruckmann, 1940.
Iribarren, Colonel José M. *En el cuartel general de Mola*. Saragossa: Heraldo de Aragón, 1938.
Kindelán y Duany, General Alfredo. *Mis cuadernos de guerra*. Madrid: Plus Ultra, 1945.
Koehler, Klaus. *Kriegsfreiwilliger 1937: Tagebuch eines Kriegsfreiwilliger der "Legion Condor."* Leipzig: G. Heinig, 1939.
Kohl, Hermann. *Deutsche Flieger über Spanien*. Reutlingen: Ensslin & Laiblin, 1941.
Larios, José (Duke of Lerma). *Combat over Spain: Memoirs of a Nationalist Fighter Pilot: 1936-39*. New York: Macmillan, 1966.
Lent, Alfred. "The Blond Moors Are Coming." In *The Distant Drum: Reflections on the Spanish Civil War*, edited by Philip Toynbee. New York: David McKay, 1976.
———. *Wir kämpften für Spanien: Erlebnisse eines deutschen Freiwilligen im spanischen Bürgerkrieg*. Berlin: Gerhard Stalling Verlag, 1939.
Lister, Enrique. *Nuestra guerra*. Paris: Éditions de la Librairie du Globe, 1966.
Martínez de Campos, General Carlos. *Ayer 1931-1953*. Madrid: Instituto de Estudios Políticos, 1970.
———. *Dos batallas de la guerra de liberación de España*. Madrid: Edit. de Conferencias y Ensayos, 1962.
Moscardó Ituarte, General José. *Diario del Alcázar*. Madrid: Atlas, 1943.
Nelson, Steve. *The Volunteers*. New York: Masses & Mainstream, 1953.
Pitcairn, Frank. *Reporter in Spain*. London: Lawrence & Wishart, Ltd., 1936.
Regler, Gustav. *The Owl of Minerva*. London: Rupert Hart-Davis.
Rojo, General Vicente. *¡Alerta los pueblos!* Buenos Aires: Aniceto López, 1939.
———. *¡España heroica!* Mexico City: Ediciones Era, 1961.
Rolfe, Edwin. *The Lincoln Battalion*. New York: Veterans of the Abraham Lincoln Brigade, 1939.
Tinker, Frank Glasgow. *Some Still Live*. New York: Funk & Wagnalls, 1936.
Trautloft, Hans. *Als Jagdflieger in Spanien: Aus dem Tagebuch eines deutschen Legionäres*. Berlin: Nauch, 1940.
Vigón, Jorge. *General Mola, el conspirador*. Barcelona: Editorial AHR, 1957.
Wintringham, Tom. *English Captain*. London: Faber & Faber, Ltd., 1939.

Secondary Works

Abshagen, Karl Heinz. *Canaris*. London: Hutchinson, 1956.
Alcofar Nassaes, José L. *C.T.V.: Los legionarios italianos en la guerra civil española 1936-39*. Barcelona, n.p. 1972.

Amery, Julian. *Approach March.* London, n.p. 1973.

Aznar, Manuel. *Historia militar de la guerra de España 1936-1939.* 3 vols. Madrid: Editoria Nacional, 1958-1963.

Beck, Clarence D. "A Study of German Involvement in Spain 1936-1939." Unpublished doctoral dissertation, University of New Mexico, 1972.

Bekker, Cajus. *The Luftwaffe War Diaries.* New York: Ballantine, 1975.

Belforte, General Francesco. *La guerra civile in Spagna,* III. 4 vols. Milano: Intituto per gli Studi di Politica Internazionale, 1938.

Beumelburg, Werner. *Kampf um Spanien* (The Struggle for Spain). Oldenburg/Berlin: Gerhard Stalling Verlagsbuchhandlung, 1940.

Blinkhorn, Martin. *Carlism and Crisis in Spain 1931-1939.* London: Cambridge University Press, 1975.

Bolloten, Burnett. *The Grand Camouflage. The Communist Conspiracy in the Spanish Civil War.* New York: Praeger, 1961.

————. *The Spanish Revolution.* Chapel Hill, N. C.: The University of North Carolina Press, 1979.

Brissaud, Andre. *Canaris.* New York: Grosset & Dunlap, 1974.

Brome, Vincent. *The International Brigades. Spain 1936-1939.* New York: William Morrow, 1966.

Broué, Pierre, and Témime, Emile. *The Revolution and the Civil War in Spain.* Cambridge, Mass.: M.I.T. Press, 1970.

Brütting, Georg. *Das waren die deutschen Kampffleigerasse 1939-1945.* Stuttgart: Motorbuch Verlag, 1974.

Carr, Raymond. *Spain 1808-1939.* London: Oxford at the Clarendon Press, 1966.

————, ed. *The Republic and the Civil War in Spain.* London: Macmillan, 1971.

Cattell, David Tredwell. *Communism and the Spanish Civil War.* New York: Russell & Russell, 1965.

Caubín, Julián. *La batalla del Ebro.* Mexico City: n.p. 1944.

Cierva y de Hoces, Ricardo de la. *Bibliografía sobre la guerra de España 1936-1939 y sus antecedentes.* Barcelona: Ariel, 1968.

————. "The Nationalist Army in the Spanish Civil War." In *The Republic and the Civil War in Spain,* edited by Raymond Carr. London, Macmillan, 1971.

Colodny, Robert Garland. *The Struggle for Madrid: The Central Epic of the Spanish Conflict 1936-1937.* New York: Paine-Whitman Publishers, 1958.

Colvin, Ian. *Master Spy.* New York: McGraw-Hill, 1952.

Constable, Trevor J., and Toliver, Colonel Raymond F. *Horrido!* New York: Ballantine Books, 1970.

Coverdale, John. *Italian Intervention in the Spanish Civil War.* Princeton, N.J.: Princeton University Press, 1975.

Cox, Geoffrey. *The Defence of Madrid.* London: V. Gollancz, Ltd., 1937.

Crozier, Brian. *Franco.* Boston: Little, Brown, 1967.

Dahms, H. G. *Der spanische Bürgerkrieg, 1936-1939.* Tübingen: Rainer Wunderlich Verlag, 1962.

Drum, General Karl. "The German Luftwaffe in the Spanish Civil War (Condor Legion)." Unpublished manuscript, USAF, Air University, Maxwell AFB, Alabama, 1957.

Duval, General Maurice. *Les espagnols et la guerre d'Espagne*. Paris: Librairie Plon, 1939.

———. *Les Leçons de la guerre d'Espagne*. Paris: Librairie Plon, 1938.

Eby, Cecil D. *The Siege of the Alcázar*. New York: Random House, 1965.

Elstob, Peter. *Condor Legion*. New York: Ballantine Books, 1973.

Esch, Patricia A. van der. *Prelude to War*. The Hague: Nijhoff, 1951.

Foltz, Charles, Jr. *The Masquerade in Spain*. Boston: Houghton Mifflin, 1948.

Foss, William, and Gerahy, Cecil. *The Spanish Arena*. London: The Right Book Club, 1938.

Fraser, Ronald. *Blood of Spain*. New York: Pantheon Books, 1979.

García Durán, Juan. *Bibliografía de la guerra civil Española*. Montevideo: El Siglo Ilustrado, 1964.

Gibbs, Jack. *The Spanish Civil War*. London: Ernest Benn Limited, 1973.

Gómez, Oliveros, Major Benito. *General Moscardó, Sin novedad en el Alcázar*. Barcelona: Editorial AHR, 1956.

Hills, George. *The Battle for Madrid*. London: Vantage Books, 1976.

———. *Franco. The Man and His Nation*. New York: The Macmillan Co., 1967.

Höhne, Heinz. *Canaris: Hitler's Master Spy*. New York: Doubleday, 1979.

Horton, Albert G. "Germany and the Spanish Civil War, 1936-1939." Doctoral dissertation, Columbia University, 1966.

Jackson, Gabriel. *The Spanish Republic and the Civil War 1931-1939*. Princeton, N.J.: Princeton University Press, 1965.

Javier Mariñas, General Francisco. *General Varela. De soldado a general*. Barcelona: Editorial AHR, 1956.

Jellinek, Frank. *The Civil War in Spain*. New York: Howard Fertig, 1969.

Johnston, Verle B. *Legions of Babel. The International Brigades in the Spanish Civil War. 1936-1939*. State College, Pa.: Pennsylvania State University Press, 1967.

Knightley, Philip. "The First Casualty, Commitment in Spain 1936-1939," *Book Digest*, February 1976, pp. 88-111. New York: Book Digest Co., Inc. Excerpt from *The First Casualty—From Crimea to Vietnam: The War Correspondent as Hero, Propagandist, and Myth Maker*. New York: Harcourt Brace Jovanovich, 1975.

Largo García, Ramiro. "La batalla de Guadalajara," *Ejército* No. 60, January 1945, pp. 23-30.

Liddell Hart, B. H. *The German Generals Talk*. New York: Wm. Morrow, 1948.

Lloyd, Alan. *Franco*. New York: Doubleday, 1969.

Madariaga, Salvador de. *Spain*. New York: Praeger, 1958.

Maier, Klaus A. *Guernica 26.4.1937. Die deutsche Intervention in Spanien und der "Fall Guernica."* Freiburg: Rombach, 1975. Appendix 1 contains excerpts from Field Marshal Wolfram Baron von Richthofen's *Diary*.

Martinex Bande, Colonel José Manuel. A series of monographs for *Servicio Histórico Militar*. Madrid, 1969.

Mason, Herbert Molloy, Jr. *The Rise of the Luftwaffe*. New York: Ballantine Books, 1975.

Mattioli, Guido. *L'aviazione legionaria in Spagna*. Rome: L'Aviazione, 1938.

McNeill-Moss, Geoffrey. *The Siege of the Alcázar*. New York: Knopf, 1937.

Merkes, Manfred. *Die deutsche Politik gegenüber dem spanischen Bürgerkrieg, 1936-1939*. Bonn: Ludwig Röhrscheid Verlag, 1961.

Payne, Stanley G. *Falange: A History of Spanish Fascism.* Stanford, Calif.: Stanford University Press, 1961.

————. *Politics and the Military in Modern Spain.* London: Oxford University Press, 1967.

————, ed. *Politics and Society in Twentieth-Century Spain.* New York: New Viewpoints, 1976.

————. *The Spanish Revolution.* New York: Norton, 1974.

Peers, E. Allison. *Spain in Eclipse 1937-1943.* London: Methuen & Co., 1943.

————. *The Spanish Tragedy.* London: Methuen & Co., 1937.

Proctor, Raymond L. *Agony of a Neutral: Spanish-German Wartime Relations and the "Blue Division."* Moscow, Idaho: University of Idaho Research Foundation, 1974.

————. "They Flew from Pollensa Bay," *Aerospace Historian* 24, No. 4 (Winter/December 1977), pp. 196-202.

Rello, Salvador. *La aviación en la guerra de España.* Madrid: Librería y Editorial San Martín, 1969.

Richardson, R. D. "Comintern Army: The International Brigades in the Spanish Civil War." Unpublished doctoral dissertation, University of Maryland, 1969.

Robinson, Richard A.H. *The Origins of Franco's Spain.* Pittsburgh, Pa.: University of Pittsburgh Press, 1970.

Salas Larrazábal, Jesús. *La guerra de España desde el aire.* Barcelona: Ariel, 1969.

Salas Larrazábal, Ramón. *Historia del ejército popular de la República.* 4 vols. Madrid: Editoria Nacional, 1974.

Salazar, R. Hidalgo. *La ayuda alemana a España 1936-39.* Madrid: Librería Editorial San Martín, 1975.

Salter, Cedric. *Tryout in Spain.* New York: Harper, 1943.

Schliephake, Hanfried. *The Birth of the Luftwaffe.* Chicago: Henry Regnery, 1971.

Sencourt, Robert. (pseudonym George, Robert Esmonde). *Spain's Ordeal.* London: Longmans, Green & Co., 1938.

Sims, Edward H. *The Greatest Aces.* New York: Ballantine, 1967.

Southworth, Herbert Rutledge. *Guernica! Guernica!* Berkeley, Calif.: University of California Press, 1977.

Stackelberg, Karl-George von. *Legion Condor: Deutsche Freiwillige in Spanien.* Berlin: Verlag Die Heimbucherei, 1939.

Steer, George L. *The Tree of Guernica.* London: Hodder, 1938.

Talon, Vicente. *Arde Guernica.* Madrid: San Martín, 1970.

Thomas, Gordon, and Witts, Max Morgan. *Guernica.* New York: Ballantine, 1975.

Thomas, Hugh. *The Spanish Civil War,* 1st edition. New York: Harper and Brothers, Publishers, 1961.

————. *The Spanish Civil War,* 2d edition. New York: Harper & Row, 1977.

Trythall, J.W.D. *El Caudillo.* New York: McGraw-Hill, 1970.

Urrutia, Julio de. *El cerro de los héroes.* Madrid: Editorial S.E.I., 1965.

Viñas, Angel. *La Alemania nazi y el 18 de julio.* 2d edition. Madrid: Alianza Editorial, S.A., 1977.

Wood, Tony, and Gunston, Bill. *Hitler's Luftwaffe.* 3d edition. New York: Crescent Books, 1979.

Index

The personalities listed here are not identified by their political affiliations but by their nationality and the side on which they served during the Spanish Civil War. On the government side they are identified (PF) and (N) for the Nationalists. All Germans listed were with the Nationalists. The place names are all in Spain, unless otherwise noted. The following abbreviations are used:

A.:   American
A.O.:   Auslandsorganisation
             (foreign organization)
Capt.:   Captain
Col.:   Colonel
Com.:   Communications
F.:   French
Flak: Antiaircraft Artillery
F.M.:   Field Marshal
G.:   German
Gen.:   General
I.B.:   International Brigades

It.:   Italian
Lt.:   Lieutenant
Lt. Gen.:   Lieutenant General
Maj. :   Major
Maj. Gen.:   Major General
NCO: Noncommissioned Officer
N.:   Nationalist
PF: Popular Front
R.:   Russian
Recon.:   Reconnaissance
Sgt.:   Sergeant

Adolph, Capt. Walter (G. pilot), 262
Aguirre y Lecube, José Antonio
  (1904–60) (Basque president) (PF),
  135
Aircraft, German
  Dornier (Do-17) "Flying Pencil,"
  armed recon.: performance, 93-94
  Fieseler (Fi-156) "Storch," observa-
  tion: performance, 185
  Heinkel (He-45) armed recon.: per-
  formance, 92
  Heinkel (He-46) armed recon.:

shipped to Spain, 43-44

Heinkel (He-50) dive bomber: shipped to Spain, failure, 46

Heinkel (He-51) fighter: performance, 87, 89; mission change, 89

Heinkel (He-59) floatplane: in AS/88, 59-60

Heinkel (He-60) floatplane: in AS/88, 59-60

Heinkel (He-70) "Blitz" armed recon.: performance, 92-93; shipped to Spain, 33

Heinkel (He-111) bomber: performance, 94-95; arrives in Spain, 118

Henschel (Hs-123) dive bomber: shipped to Spain, 46

Junker (Ju-52) transport/bomber: performance, 85-86

Junker (Ju-87) dive bomber: arrives in Spain, 182

Messerschmitt (Bf-109 or Me-109) fighter plane: experimental models to Spain, 46; performance, 90-91; prototype in J/88, 118

Aircraft, Russian

Katiuska SB-2 ("Martin") bomber: performance, 56

Polikarpov I-15 ("Curtiss") fighter: performance, 56

Polikarpov I-16 ("Mosca" or "Rata"): introduced in Spain, 64

Air Force, Italian (*Aviazione Legionaria*): permitted combat, 37; bombs Cartagena, 55; over Madrid, 64, 66; Romero-37, 64, 69; in North operation, 118, 119, 122, 126, 136, 137, 138, 142; at Brunete, 147-52, 154; Italian Fiats, German view, 155; end in the North, 159; at Teruel, 176; Aragón offensive, 188-90; Battle of the Ebro, 223, 229; party, 238

Air Force, Nationalists, 12, 64-66; in North operation, 118, 119, 122, 136-38, 142; at Brunete, 147-52, 154; end in the North, 159; at Teruel, 176; Aragón offensive, 188-90; Battle of the Ebro, 223, 231; Catalonian offensive, 242, 243

Air Force, Republican (PF), 12, 30, 40, 45, 49, 50, 56; defends Madrid, 64-66, 81; in Guadalajara Battle, 112-14; in the North, 137; at Brunete, 145, 146, 151, 152; end in the North, 159, 161, 163, 164, 166-68; at Teruel, 173, 174, 181, 183; Aragón offensive, 190, 191, 193, 195; on the Mediterranean, 209-12, 214-17; Battle of the Ebro, 226, 227, 229-35; Catalonian offensive, 240, 243-47

Airlift from Africa: starts, 20, 22; operations, 25-28, 30-33, 252

Air Ministry (G), 19, 20, 74, 75, 94

Albacete, 12, 49, 107, 146

Albalate del Arzobispo, 188, 189

Albocácer, 208, 209

Alcalá de Henares, 50, 65, 80, 95, 101, 103, 105-7, 110

Alcañiz, 188, 189, 196-98, 202, 203, 218, 222, 224; party at, 238

Alcarraz, 196, 200

Alcázar, the (Toledo), 12, 29, 31, 45, 68, 108

Alcázar de San Juan, 45

Alcolea, 113

Alcolea del Pinar, 111, 114

Alcorcón, 65, 88

Alcorisa, 188, 189

Alfambra, 176, 178-81

Alfambra, Río, 174, 178-83, 187

Alfaro, 175, 190, 201

Alférezes Provisionales (Provisional 2nd Lts.) (N), 51

Algora, 111, 114

Alicante, 65

Almazán, 110, 111, 173, 175, 178, 180

Almería, 201, 203, 206

Alonso Vega, Col. (later Gen.) Camilo (N), 147, 161, 202, 227

Altun, 124

Amorebieta, 136-39, 140

Amposta, 196, 221-23, 241

Andalusia, 31, 85, 102, 251

Andorra (Spain), 189, 196, 197

Andújar, 67, 68

Ansaldo, Maj. Juan Antonio (N), 9

Antrup, Lt. Col. (later Gen.) Willi (G. pilot), 264

A.O. (*Auslandsorganisation*) "foreign organization" (G), 15, 17, 18, 71-72

Aragón, 49, 63, 104, 173, 174, 253, 257; Popular Front offensive, 161-62

Aragón offensive: plans for, 187-89; air order of battle, 190; first phase, 191-95; second phase, 196-203

Aramburu de Topete, Lt. (later Gen.) José (N), 181, 185, 203

Aranda Mata, Col. (later Gen.) Antonio (N), 200-202, 207, 209, 210, 213; at Oviedo, 53, 108, 163, 167; at Teruel, 176-78, 183; Aragón offensive, 188, 193, 195, 200, 201; reaches Vinaroz, 202; Levante offensive, 207, 209, 210, 213

Aranjuez, 50, 63, 82, 110, 248

Arcos de Jalón, 109-11, 113, 114

Arend, Lt. (G) (Commun. officer), 109, 110, 112-14

Arganda, 103, 105, 106

Arman, Maj. Paul ("Greisser") (R. officer), 56

Army of Africa (N), 5, 12, 13, 15, 31, 49, 80, 104, 107, 251

Army of Catalan (PF), 162

Army of the Center (PF), 147, 149, 172, 248

Army of the East (PF), 162, 163, 173

Army of the Ebro (PF), 221-35

Army of the Levante (Valencia) (PF), 172, 174, 175, 184, 239

Army of the North (N) "Dávila," 25, 31-33, 80, 103, 104, 142, 188, 193, 239

Army of the South (N) "Queipo de Llano," 25, 32, 102

Arranz y Monasterio, Capt. Francisco (N), 16, 17, 19, 20

Artesa de Segre, 201, 241-43

Ascó, 221, 222, 224, 225, 228

Asensio Cabinallas, Col. (later Gen.) José (N), 150, 151

Asmus, Lt. (G. asst. operations officer), 211, 231; in Battle of the Ara-

gón, 194; returns to Germany, 232; record, 261

Assault Guards (*Asaltos*), 6, 12

Asturias, 11, 108, 117, 133, 152, 161-63, 167

Ávila, 45, 53, 55, 64, 81, 82, 147, 177, 205, 247

Avilés, 160, 167, 168

Ayódar, 208, 216

Azaila, 188, 189, 194-96

Azuara, 189, 193, 196

Badajoz, 22, 31, 32, 205

Balaguer (G. base), 173, 196, 202, 240, 241

Balmes Alonso, Gen. Amadeo (N), 4, 6

Balthasar, Lt. (later Capt.) Wilhelm (G. pilot), 131; four victories on single mission, 181; later career and death, 262

Baños de Fitero (G. hqtrs.), 178, 180-82, 184, 190, 197, 201

Barahona (G. base), 53

Barajas, 50, 88, 95, 248

Barbastro, 196, 198, 200, 202

Barcelona, 11, 32, 40, 48, 206, 213, 214, 229, 238, 244, 245; capture of , 246-47

Barracas, 215

Barrón y Ortiz, Lt. Col. (later Gen.) Fernando (N), 150, 152, 162

Barroso y Sánchez-Guerra, Maj. (later Gen.) Antonio (N) (Chief of Operations), 107-8; advises against attack on Madrid, 63-64

Basart, Col. (PF), 146

Batea, 226, 228

Battle for Madrid, 31-32, 49-51, 53-56, 63-67

Battle in the North, 117-31, 133-43, 157-69

Battle of Aragón, 161, 162, 187-203

Battle of Brunete, 143-55

Battle of Guadalajara, 107-16

Battle of Jarama, 103-7

Battle of La Coruña Road, 80-81, 87-88

Battle of Málaga, 102-3
Battle of Sigüenza, 53-54
Battle of the Ebro, 221-36
Battle of the Mediterranean (Lev-
  ante), 206-18
Bauer, NCO (G. pilot), 216, 226
Bautista y Sánchez, Col. (later Gen.)
  Juan (N) (Commander, Navarrese
  Brigade), 147
Bebb, Capt. (English flight capt.), 5-7
Beck, Gen. Ludwig (G. Army Chief of
  Staff), 74-76
Beigbeder Atienza, Lt. Col. Juan (N),
  14
Belchite, 188, 203; first battle for,
  162; second battle for, 190-94;
  Franco visits, 196
Benasal, 208, 210
Bendler, Cmdr. (G. Navy liaison offi-
  cer), 201, 202, 227
Benicarló (G. base), 206-9, 224, 230
Benifallet, 217, 222, 228
Berlin (G. transport), 58
Bermeo, 135, 140
Bernhardt, Johannes ("Tónie") (G.
  businessman), 34; A.O. in Tetuán,
  15; Nationalist envoy to Berlin, 16,
  17; meets Hitler, 18, 19; responsible
  for economics, 48
Berti, Gen. Mario (It.), 188, 201, 214-
  16
Bertram, Lt. Otto (G. pilot), 227, 229,
  230, 233, 262
Bertram, Otto (Lufthansa represent-
  ative), 4-7
Beust, Col. Baron Hans-Henning von
  (G. pilot), 254, 263, 264
Bilbao, 32, 45, 86, 101, 117-19, 122,
  123, 125-28, 130, 131, 159, 160, 161;
  Battle of, 133-43
Biscay, Bay of (Mar Cantábrico), 13,
  62, 98, 138, 140, 160
Blankenagel, Lt. W. August (G.
  pilot), 121
Blomberg, Gen. von (G. Minister of
  War), 18, 39, 41, 57, 158; assigns
  Warlimont, 35, 36; replaces Warli-
  mont, 71-73; at Faupel meeting, 75-
  76; replaces Sperrle, 158

Boadilla del Monte, 81, 88, 148, 150
Bobera, 241, 243
Bohle, Gauleiter Ernst Wilhelm
  (Chief A.O., Berlin), 15, 17, 18, 71
Bolín, Luis Antonio (N), 5-7, 9, 12, 13
Bomber Group, Condor Legion (K/
  88), 83, 84, 101, 110; organized, 59;
  to Spain, 61; first missions, 65-67;
  problems, 85-86; receives He-111s,
  95; on the Jarama, 105, 107; in the
  North, 118-30, 135-43; at Brunete,
  146-53; end in the North, 158-60,
  163, 165-67; at Teruel, 173-84; in
  Aragón, 190-95, 201; Operation
  Neptune, 205, 206; on the Mediter-
  ranean, 207-11, 213-18; on the
  Ebro, 223-25; in Catalonia, 241-47
Bonin, Maj. Hubertus von (G. pilot),
  262
Borbón, Col. (Duke of Seville) (N),
  103
Braunshirn, Sgt. (G. pilot), 217, 232,
  235
Bretnuetz, Capt. Heinz (G. pilot), 262
Brey, Col. Franz (G. pilot), 203
Brihuega, 103, 110-14
Bronchales (G. base), 176, 179
Brucks, NCO (G. pilot), 217, 227
Bruñel (G. base), 207
Brunete, 50, 81, 88, 143, 174, 218;
  Battle of, 145-54
Bujaraloz, 191, 196, 198, 200
Burgos, 32, 57, 118, 157, 158, 160,
  239, 247
Burgos Junta (N), 49

Cabeza la Vaca (Badajoz), 205
Cáceres, 31, 32, 34, 39, 43, 44, 55, 96,
  107
Cáceres Division (N), 147, 151
Cádiz, 11, 25, 27, 33, 55, 61, 79, 80;
  Germans arrive, 21; Italians arrive,
  47
Calahorra de Boedo (Palencia) (G.
  base), 158
Calamocha, 174-76, 178, 179, 189
Calatayud, 187, 189
Calvo Sotelo, José, 5, 9
Cambrils, 199, 225

Caminreal, 179, 181, 182
Campillo, 176, 179
Canaris, Admiral Wilhelm (G. Intelligence Chief), 19, 35, 72, 201; relations with Franco, 14; visits Italy, 36-37; advises of Condor Legion, 56, 71; on replacing Sperrle, 158; visits Volkmann, 201
Candasnos, 193, 200, 222
Carabineros (Customs Guards) (N), 5, 12
Cariñena, 188, 189
Carlists (Traditionalists), 11, 12, 49, 117
Cartagena, 28, 43, 48, 201, 214: bombed, 54, 55; K/88s' first strike, 65, 66; "Operation Neptune," 203, 205, 206
Casa de Campo (Madrid), 64, 67, 80, 88, 148, 248
Casado López, Col. Segismundo (PF), view of Brunete, 153
Caspe, 188, 189, 191, 193, 194, 196-98, 203, 221, 222, 241
Castejón Espinosa, Maj. (later Gen.) Antonio (N), 226
Castellón, 198, 210-13, 218
Castellón de la Plana, 207, 208
Castile, 11, 81, 103, 147, 149, 150, 152, 157, 163
Casualties, German: A/88 (Recon.), 141, 150, 164, 165, 180, 201, 227; AS/88 (Seaplane Sqdn.), 195, 197, 199, 227, 230, 232, 243; F/88 (Flak), 130, 139, 153, 161, 165, 167, 184, 206, 212, 213, 217, 225, 230, 244, 248; Imker, 153, 161, 200, 248; J/88 (Fighter), 45, 64, 65, 87, 107, 121, 129, 139, 151, 152, 165, 174, 183, 195, 200, 201, 202, 209, 210, 211, 232, 233, 235, 247, 248; K/88 (Bomber), 29, 66, 68, 86, 101, 125, 142, 152, 165, 166, 167, 174, 178, 184, 193, 199, 201, 205, 210, 230, 233, 235, 244, 248; Ln/88 (Communications), 102, 139, 153, 161, 167, 184, 207, 234, 243, 246, 248; S/88 (Staff), 167, 199; other, 102, 130, 230, 235

Catalonia, 40, 80, 122, 187, 206, 207, 229, 238, 239, 241, 242, 247, 248
Cerro de los Ángeles, 50, 88, 103, 106
Cherta, 196, 201, 222, 226, 228, 234, 235
Christ, Capt. (later Col.) L. G. (G. operations officer), 180, 252, 261; begins *Diary*, 178; on Teruel, 180-84; Aragón offensive, 187-203; Levante offensive, 206, 209-11, 213-14; concern for Ebro attack, 217, 218, 223; Battle of the Ebro, 226-32; on Italian party, 238; sick, 239; last entry, 242; death, 261
Churruca (PF destroyer), 12, 28
Ciano, Count Galeazzo (It. foreign minister), 37, 79
Cinca, Río, 196, 200, 222
"Circo Krone," 164
Civil Guards (*Guardia Civil*), 12, 29, 67
Communications Group, Condor Legion (Ln/88), 65, 81-83, 96, 105, 153; organized, 59-61; to Spain, 62, 63; reorganized, 97; problems, 101-2; at Málaga, 103; at Guadalajara, 109-14; at Bilbao, 139; in Aragón, 190, 192, 195; on the Mediterranean, 207; in Catalonia, 243, 246
Concud, 176, 179
Condor Legion: 3, 40, 52, 53, 77, 81-86; formation of, 56-60; moves to Spain, 61-63; first casualty, 64; first bombing mission, Cartagena, 65-66; K/88 bombs Madrid, 66-67; supplies Santa María de la Cabeza, 67-68; Battle of La Coruña Road, 87-89; reequipped and reorganized, 90-98; Málaga, 102-3; Battle of Río Jarama, 104-7; Battle of Guadalajara, 109-14; Battle in the North, 117-27; Guernica bombing, 128-30; Bilbao assault, 133-42; Franco praises, 143; ordered to Brunete, 147-154; Santander operation, 157-68; new commander, 171; Alfambra and Teruel, 175-84; Aragón offensive, 187-203; Operation Neptune, 205, 206; Mediterranean offensive, 207-18; Battle

of the Ebro, 221-36; Catalonian offensive, 237-46; moves to Toledo, 247; last flight, 248; record, 253, 254

Corbera, 222, 224-26, 228, 233, 234

Corps Aragón (Moscardó) (N), 198-200, 202, 240

Corps Castile (Varela) (N), 176, 198, 207, 217

Corps Galicia (Aranda) (N), 176, 178, 183, 188, 193, 195, 198, 200-202, 207, 210

Corps Maestrazgo (Valiño) (N), 217-34, 240, 242, 243, 246

Corps *Marroqui* (Yagüe) (N), 178, 180, 183, 188, 190, 192, 195, 198-201, 221, 234, 240, 244, 245

Corps Navarre (Solchaga) (N). *See* Navarre

Corps Urgel (Muñoz Grandes) (N), 240, 242, 243, 246

Covadonga, 160, 166

C.T.V. (*Corpo Truppe Volontarie*) (It.), arrives in Spain, 80; Málaga operation, 102-4; Battle of Guadalajara, 107-15; in the North, 129, 134-35, 139, 158-59, 161, 163; Aragón offensive, 214-16; artillery on the Ebro, 232, 235; Catalonian offensive, 239-42, 244, 246

Cuatro Vientos (airfield), 30, 40, 50, 56, 83, 88

Cubells, 241, 243

Culla, 208, 210

D-AMYM (G. Ju-52 transport), 22

D-APOK "Max von Müller" (G. D-APOK airplane), 4, 7, 8, 20

Daroca, 174, 179, 180, 187, 189

Dávila Arrondo, Gen. Fidel (N), 163, 229, 239; replaces Mola, 137; decorates von Kessel, 164; at Teruel, 176; in Aragón offensive, 188

Delgado Serrano, Col. (later Gen.) Francisco (N), 227

Dieckhoff, Dr. Hans Heinrich (*Reich* Foreign Office), 17, 79

Döberitz, 20-22, 249

Dohna, Lt. Count von (G. pilot), 195

Dragon Rapide (de Havilland), 5, 6, 7

Drohne (tank battalion) (G.) (N), 43, 51, 60, 61

Drum, Gen. Karl (G. officer), 40, 58, 254, 255, 257, 258

Durango, 119, 120, 127-30, 137, 140

Durruti, Buenaventura (PF), 63

Ebbinghausen, Capt. Karl (G. pilot), 216, 226, 262

Eberhard, Lt. Kraft (G. pilot), 26, 29, 30, 47, 55, 70; died (Madrid), 64-65

Ebro, Río, 104, 161, 173, 174, 178, 182, 187-89, 195-201, 214, 215, 217, 218, 239-42, 245; Battle of, 221-36

Ecrivain, Col. (PF) (F. *Wing España*), 146

Éibar, 120, 127-29

El Burgo de Osma (airfield) (G. base), 173

El Ferrol, 47, 98

Elgueta, 120, 126, 127, 129

Elorrio, 120, 127

Ensslen, Lt. (G. pilot), 230-32

Ermúa, 120, 127

Escalona (G. base), 30, 50, 81, 150, 177, 247

Escatrón, 188, 189, 195-97, 238

Espinosa de los Monteros, Gen. Eugenio (N), 248

Estremadura, 39, 41, 226

Ewald, Lt. (Later Maj.) Wolfgang (G. pilot), 262

"Exercise Rügen," 58, 59, 61

Experimental Flight (*Versuchskommando*), Condor Legion, 47, 48, 60, 87, 90, 91, 118, 129, 264

Falange, 12, 49, 253

Faldella, Col. Emilio (It. Chief of Staff), 79, 107, 108

Fatarella, 222, 228, 233, 235

Faupel, Lt. Gen. Wilhelm von (G. ambassador, Burgos), 71-74, 79, 98; in Hitler's conference, 75-77; dispute with Sperrle, 124, 157-58; death, 260

Fayón, 218, 221-23, 226-28, 235
Fernández Heredia, Col. Enrique
 (PF), 174
Fica, 139, 140
Fighter Group, Condor Legion (*Jagd*)
 (J/88), 84, 95; organized, 59, 60, 81;
 mission changed, 87-91, 93; in the
 North, 118-27, 129, 130, 133, 136-
 41; at Brunete, 147-52; back in the
 North, 158, 159, 163-67; Teruel,
 173, 174, 176, 178-83; in Aragón,
 190-97, 199, 202; on the Mediterra-
 nean, 209-17; Ebro Battle, 221-35;
 in Catalonia, 242-47
Figueras, 241, 247
Flak, Condor Legion Antiaircraft
 Group (F/88): organized, 59, 60; in
 the North, 119-21, 123, 125, 127,
 134, 139, 141; at Brunete, 147, 152,
 153; end in the North, 163, 165; at
 Teruel, 182; in Aragón, 190-95, 198-
 200, 202; on the Levante, 206-15;
 Ebro Battle, 223, 225-30, 235; in
 Catalonia, 242, 244-47; record, 253,
 259
Fleischmann, NCO (G. pilot), 234, 235
Flix (Tarragona), 107, 196, 218, 221,
 222, 224, 225, 227, 228, 235, 241
Foreign Legion, Spanish (*banderas*)
 (N), 5, 13, 28, 49, 67, 80, 87, 104,
 105, 108, 135, 147
Fözö, Maj. Josef (G. pilot), 262
Fraga (Huesca), 196, 198, 200, 206,
 222, 240, 241
Franco y Bahamonde, Gen. Francisco
 (N), 7-11, 13, 18-21, 29, 31, 34-36,
 40, 49, 51-53, 63, 64, 66, 71-74, 75-
 77, 86, 98, 110, 115, 123, 137, 142,
 143, 150, 152, 153, 157-59, 162, 173,
 184, 197, 214, 218, 226, 227, 229,
 233, 234, 247, 248, 251; joins revolt,
 4-5; to Morocco, 6; approaches Germany, 14-16; meets Warlimont, 39;
 visits tank battalion, 41-43; learns
 of Condor Legion, 56-57; cancels
 Madrid offensive, 67; advised of
 Italian troops, 79-80; opposes Italian plans, 107-8; switches operation

North, 118; Sperrle complains to,
 124; response to Brunete, 147; responds to Teruel, 175-78; plans Aragón offensive, 187-90; visits
 Belchite, 195; rejects Berti, 202;
 congratulates Legion, 216; responds
 to Teruel offensive, 221; on Levante offensive, 207; decorates
 Volkmann, 238; plans Catalonian offensive, 239-40; last plans, 247; re-
 views Legion, 248
Franco y Bahamonde, Lt. Col. Ramón (N), 158
Franz, Lt. Col. (G. officer), 239
Freund, NCO (G. pilot), 229
Frezza, Col. (It. commander), 113
Fritsch, Col. Gen. Baron Wernher
 von (chief of the German Army),
 75-77
Fuchs, Maj. (G. officer), 65
Fuendetodos, 189, 192
Fuentes de Ebro, 162, 187-89
Fuentes de Jiloca (Franco's hqtrs.),
 197
Führer, 15, 35, 49, 249. *See also* Hit-
 ler, Adolf
Fulda (G. transport), 62

Gabriel, Lt. (G. general staff officer
 and pilot), 180, 184, 198-200, 238
Galdácano, 139, 140
Galicia Division (N), 147, 151
Galland, Capt. (later Gen.) Adolf (G.
 pilot), 131, 203, 213, 261, 262; goes
 to Spain, 98; in Battle of Brunete,
 149; termination in North, 164;
 commands "Mickey Mouse" Sqdn.,
 199, 200
Gallera, Lt. Hans Peter (G. pilot), 87
Gallur (G. base), 175, 190, 196
Gambara, Col. (later Gen.) Gastone
 (It.), 239, 240
Gamringer, Lt. (G. pilot), 233
Gandesa, 196, 198, 203, 218, 222, 241;
 first battle for, 202-3; second battle
 for, 218, 222-34
Gandia, 223, 224
García Escámez y Iniesta, Col. (later

Gen.) Francisco (N), 104
García Valiño, Col. (later Gen.) (N):
  in the North, 127-28, 161; in Med.
  offensive, 209, 214-16; with Corps
  Maestrazgo, 234, 240, 243
Garda, Gen. (It. Air C.O.), 227, 229,
  238, 248
Gestapo, 20, 41
Gijón, 12, 160, 163, 166-68
Ginestar, 222, 223, 225, 226, 228
Girgenti (G. supply ship), 34
Gockel, Lt. (G. officer), enters Bilbao,
  142
Goering, Gen. (later F.M.) Hermann
  (G. air minister), 42, 48, 128, 249,
  254, 258, 261
Gollmann, Lt. (G. pilot), 113
Goy, Lt. (G. pilot), 213, 216
Grabmann, Capt. (later Maj. Gen.)
  (G. pilot), 233, 262
Granada, 11, 32, 55, 87, 101, 103, 205,
  206
Granadella, 241, 242
Granollers, 241, 246
Gravenreuth, Lt. Col. Baron Sieg-
  mund-Ulrich (G. pilot), 264
Gredos Mountains, 104, 134
Guadalajara, 50, 104-6, 134, 174; Bat-
  tle of, 108-15
Guadalope, Río, 188, 196-98, 222
Guadarrama, Río, 148, 151
Guardia Civil. See Civil Guards
Guernica, 120, 127-31, 134, 135, 140
Guerrero, Dr. (physician, Gen.
  Balmes Alonso), 4
Guerricaiz, 120, 128-30

Hamburg (Germany), 19, 20, 33, 34,
  35, 41, 47, 97, 249
Handrick, Major (G. officer), 172
Harder, Capt. Harro (G. pilot), 81,
  149, 166, 167, 262
Harlinghausen, Maj. (later Gen.)
  Martin (G. pilot), 257, 259, 265;
  C.O. Seaplane Sqdn., 100, 172; to
  support Aragón, 191, 197-99, 201,
  203; supports Med. offensive, 212,
  213, 216; in Battle of the Ebro, 224,

226; returns to Germany, 239; re-
  cord, 260, 261
Hefele, Maj. Hans von (G. pilot), 172
Heftner, Lt. Eberhardt (G. pilot), 45,
  70
Heilmayer, Sgt. (G. pilot), 126
Hein, NCO (G. pilot), 216
Heiner, Sgt. Engelbert (G. pilot), 264
Henke, Flight Capt. Alfred (*Luft-
  hansa* pilot), 13, 22, 26; interrupted
  flight, 4, 7-11; flies to Berlin, 16, 17;
  starts airlift, 20, 252; attacks *Jaime
  I*, 28; supplies Alcázar, 29
Henne, Capt. Rudolf (G. pilot), 264
Hentschel, Capt. (G. pilot), 201
Herici, Lt. Oskar (G. pilot), 65
Hering, Capt. Hubertus (G. pilot),
  199, 200
Hermann, Capt. (G. Fighter Sqdn.
  C.O.), 201, 231
Hermann, Flight Sgt. (G. pilot), 86,
  101
Hermann, Lt. (G. Flak officer), 26
Hernández Saravia, Col. (later Gen.)
  (PF), 173, 178, 183
Herrera de Pisuerga (G. base), 158
Hess, Rudolf (G), 15, 17, 18, 71
Hidalgo de Cisneros y López de Mon-
  tenegro, Lt. Col. (later Gen.) Igna-
  cio (PF), 146, 154
Hiehn, NCO (G. pilot), 229, 230
Híjar, 189, 192, 196
Hildemann, Lt. Helmut (G. pilot), 141
*HISMA (Hispano-Marroquí de
  Transportes, S.L.)*, 20, 28, 35, 48,
  157
Hitler, Adolf, 15, 16, 17, 35, 40, 49,
  51, 182, 202, 249, 251, 254, 258; re-
  ceives Franco delegation, 18-21; im-
  portance of Ju-52, 31; assigns
  Faupel, 72; calls conference, 72-76;
  reasons for German operation in
  Spain, 77; advised of Guadalajara,
  115; relieves Faupel and Sperrle,
  157-58
Hogebach, Lt. Col. Hermann (G.
  pilot), 233, 263
Holle, Lt. Col. (first chief of staff,

Condor Legion), 58
Hossbach, Col. Friedrich (Hitler's pilot), 74, 75, 78
Houwald, Capt. (G. pilot), 26, 55, 81
Hoyos, Lt. Count (G. pilot), 28
Huerva, Río, 187, 189
Huesca, 162, 196, 202, 203; battle at, 198-200
Húmera, 67, 80, 88

Ibarrola Orueta, Col. Juan (PF), 174
Iglesuela del Cid, 208, 209
Ihlefeld, Sgt. (later Col.) Herbert (G. pilot), 209, 214, 215, 262
Imker (G. instructors), 51, 61, 153, 161, 200
Infiesta, 160, 167
International Brigades, 49, 63, 87, 105, 110, 112, 113, 145, 146, 150-52, 162, 163, 190, 193, 194, 197, 206, 221, 223
"Iron Belt," 134-39, 140, 141
Irún, 40, 49

Jaenecke, Col. Gen. (G. officer), 40, 51, 115, 254
Jaenisch, NCO (G. pilot), 223, 226
Jaime I (PF warship), 28, 206
Janisco (Mexican ship), 48
Jarama, Río, 110; Battle of, 103-7
Jerez de la Frontera, 27, 29, 30, 31, 44, 55; in airlift, 25
Joester, Capt. (G. pilot), 55
Jordana y Souza, Gen. Count Francisco (Gómez) (N), 229
Juncosa, 241, 243
Jurado Barrio, Col. (later Gen.) Enrique (PF), 153

Kamerun (G. ship), 30
Kaufmann, Lt. (G. pilot), 68
Keidel, Lt. (G. pilot), 214
Keitel, Gen. (later F.M.) Wilhelm (G), 73
Keller, Lt. (G. pilot), 211, 214, 229
Kessel, Lt. Hans Detler von (G. pilot), 164
Kesselring, F.M. Albert, 158

Kieling, NCO (G. pilot), 234
Kindelán y Duany, Col. (later Gen.) Alfredo, 13, 44, 118, 123, 124, 130, 157, 182, 197, 201, 227, 238
Klein, Lt. Gerhard (G. officer), 174
Klinkicht, Lt. (G. pilot), 201
Knüppel, Lt. (G. pilot), 30
Köhn, Willi (A.O.) (general consul), 72
Kolbe, Lt. (G. pilot), 261
Kollewe, Maj. Gerhard (G. pilot), 263
Kressmann, Lt. Col. (G. Flak officer), 201
Krock, Lt. (G. pilot), 226
Kühlenthal, Gen. (G), 14
Kuhlmann, Sgt. (G. pilot), 211, 214, 216
Kull, NCO (G. pilot), 229

La Barona, 240, 242
La Cenia (G. base), 207, 208, 210, 211, 222, 230, 231, 233, 240, 242
La Coruña, 34, 50, 102, 107; battle for road, 80, 81, 87, 88
"La Magdalena" (G. base), 176
Lanaja (airfield), 196, 201
Langenheim, Adolph (Chief A.O.) (G), 15-18
La Puebla de Hijar, 189, 191
Las Rozas, 87, 88, 148
Lehmann, Capt. (G. pilot), 81
León, 34, 45, 53, 54, 61, 81, 98, 160, 163, 172, 213, 248
Lérida, 173, 196, 198, 206, 207, 222, 229, 240, 241, 245; battle for, 200-201
Libertad (PF warship), 214
Lichtenberber, Maj. (G. officer), 194, 201
Liddell Hart, B. H., 42
Lindau, Commander (G. naval commander), 19
Lippert, Lt. (later Gen.) Wolfgang (G. pilot), 215, 217, 229, 233, 261, 262
Lister, Maj. (later Gen.) (PF), 56, 147, 152, 174, 222-24, 226, 242
Llanes, 160, 164, 165

Lohse, Lt. (G. Flak officer), 194
Lufthansa, 4, 6-8, 16, 17, 19-22, 26, 44, 85, 93, 94, 263
Luftwaffe, 19, 20, 21, 34, 36, 40, 42, 47, 57, 58, 75, 85-86, 91, 92, 94-97, 172, 238, 251, 252, 254, 255, 257-63
Lugar Nuevo, 67
Lützow, Capt. (later Col.) Gunther (G. pilot), 81, 123, 149, 261, 262

Mackensen, Hans von (G. Foreign Ministry), 157, 158
Madrid, 11, 22, 106, 248; first bombing of, 29, 30; battle for, 31, 32, 49-51, 53-56, 63-67, 79-88, 90, 101-4, 107, 109, 110, 112, 117, 145, 146, 148, 150, 151, 162, 173-75, 178, 181, 182, 184, 187, 247, 248
Madrid government, 40, 49, 54, 63, 65, 104, 152, 153
Maggalhanes (ship), 48
"Magic Fire" (code name for Spanish operation), 19, 28, 40, 46, 52, 57
Málaga (Spanish port), 27, 28, 54, 55, 61, 104, 107, 206; battle of, 102-3
Mallorca, 191, 198, 199, 209
Malraux, André (F) (PF), 51, 103
Manca, Gen. (It.), 229
Manteuffel, Gen. Hasso von (G), 69
Marovo, Col. (R) (PF), 146
Marquina, 120, 127-29
Martín, Río, 189, 196, 197
Matacán (G. base), 149
Matachana (G. base), 107
Maurer, Lt. (G. pilot), 211
Mayals, 241, 242
Mayer, Capt. Hans-Karl (G. pilot), 262
Medinaceli, 109, 111, 173
Mehnert, Maj. (G. pilot), 227, 232
Melilla, Morocco, North Africa, 6, 63, 65
Menéndez López, Col. (later Gen.) Leopoldo (PF), 174
Menge, NCO (later Lt.) Robert (G. pilot), 233, 234, 262
Mequinenza, 196, 218, 221-23, 226-28, 234, 240, 241

Merhard, Maj. (G. pilot, C.O. J/88), 81, 89
Mérida, 31, 42, 55, 101, 226
Meyer, Lt. (G. pilot), 211
Miaja Menant, Gen. José (PF), 63, 87, 150, 172
Michaelis, Lt. Manfred (G. pilot), 200
Milch, Gen. (later F.M.) (G), 19, 21, 28
Ministry of Foreign Affairs, German, 14, 15, 17 ,18, 57, 71, 72, 157, 158
Miravalles, 135-136, 139, 140, 141
Miravet, 221, 222, 224, 225, 228
Mission "Guido" (G.), 46, 52
Modesto Guilloto, Juan (PF), 147, 153, 162, 221, 227
Mola Vidal, Gen. Emilio (N), 4, 5, 13, 25, 31, 49, 103, 117-19, 121, 126, 134, 135, 138; seizes Pamplona, 11; asks Germany for supplies, 33, 34; responds to Richthofen, 122; death, 137
Mölders, Lt. (later Col.) Werner (G. pilot), 216, 229-35, 262; replaces Galland, 212-13; first victory, 214-15; tactics, 256; killed, 261
Molíns del Rey, 241, 246
Mollet, 241, 246
Monasterio Ituarte, Col. (later Gen.) José (N), 56, 63, 180, 181, 188
Monreal del Campo, 178, 179
Montalbán, 182, 188, 195, 196, 208
Monzón, 196, 240, 241
Mora de Ebro, 196, 218, 222-25, 228, 235, 241
Mora de Rubielos, 208, 215
Mora la Nueva, 217, 221-23, 228
Morata de Jiloca (Franco's hqtrs.), 187, 189
Moreau, Capt. Baron Rudolph von (G. pilot), 26, 28, 29, 44, 47, 55, 67, 91, 264
Morella, 196, 198, 208, 209, 218
Moroccan Troops, Regulares, Tabores (N), 5, 12, 13, 31, 49, 54, 67, 87, 104, 105, 108, 124, 145, 147, 263
Moscardó Ituarte, Col. (later Gen.) José (N), 29, 108, 240

Móstoles, 50, 88, 145, 148
Motril, 103, 206
Muela de Teruel (Teruel's Tooth), 175, 176
Müller, Lt. (G. pilot), 211, 214, 230
Muñoz Grandes, Col. (later Gen.) Agustín (N), 191, 193, 240, 243
Mussolini, Benito, 37, 51, 79, 107

Nathan, Maj. George (A.) (I.B.), 151
Navalcarnero, 40, 50, 54, 88, 145, 148
Navarre, 11, 117, 118, 121
Navarre Brigades, Divisions, and Corps, 136, 137, 139, 141, 147, 151, 152, 159, 161, 163-66, 178, 195, 197-201, 209, 210, 234, 240, 242-46
Nelson, Steve (A.) (I.B.), 151
Neudörffer, Capt. (G. pilot), 172
Neumann, Lt. (later Lt. Col.) Eduard (G. pilot), 164, 211, 262, 263
Neurath, Constantin von (G. foreign minister), 17, 71
Noguera Pallaresa, Río, 240, 241
Nules, 208, 214, 217
Nyassa (transport), 47

Ochandiano, 119, 120, 137; Battle for, 122-23
Oesau, Lt. (later Col.) Walter (G. pilot), 215, 216, 229, 233, 235, 261, 262
Operation Döberitz (G), 249
Operation Neptune (N), 203, 205
Orduña, 139, 160
Orgaz y Yoldi, Gen. Luís (N), 4-8, 239; appointed Field Commander, 86-87; Battle of La Coruña Road, 87; Battle of Río Jarama, 104; does not support Roatta, 110
Osorio (G. transport), 58
Oviedo, 12, 45, 53, 54, 108, 160, 163

"Pablo Flight" (Condor Legion bomber flight), 44-46, 54, 55, 64
Peñíscola, 207, 208
Pentland, Capt. Pat A. (USAF), 265
Perales, 178, 181
Perales de Alfambra, 179, 180

Pinell, 226, 227, 234, 235
Pingel, Maj. Rolf (G. pilot), 262
Pinto, Gen. (N), 118
Pitcairn, Lt. (later Col.) Douglas (G. pilot), 68, 69, 100, 171, 184, 185, 263; assigned to Legion, 58; arrives in Spain, 61; on Wohnzug, 81, 184-85; on Merhard and Sperrle, 89-90; with "Mickey Mouse" Sqdn., 118, 131; fuel procedure, 173-74
Plocher, Maj. (later Gen.) Hermann (Chief of Staff, Condor Legion), 178, 237, 239, 253, 255, 260; assigned to "Special Staff W," 57, 59-69; joins Legion, 178; at Teruel, 181-85; in Aragón, 187-88, 190-92, 197-98, 201-3; Levante offensive, 206-18; on the Ebro, 224, 229, 231, 236; Italian party, 238
Pobla de la Granadella, 241, 243
Pobla de Masaluca, 222, 226, 228
Pollard, Maj. Hugh (English), 5
Pollensa Bay, Mallorca (G. base), 158, 213, 239
Pontejos (Zamora) (G. base), 165
Post Office Box "Max Winkler" (G.), 21, 97, 114
Pozas Perea, Gen. Sebastián (PF), 162, 173
Pozuelo, 50, 67, 80, 88, 148
Prada Vaquero, Col. Adolfo (PF), 167, 248
Prieto y Tuero, Indalecio (PF), 13
Prisoners of war, German, 136, 167, 193, 197, 210, 211, 213, 227, 230, 233, 238, 246, 254

Quasinowski, NCO (G. pilot), 214, 216
Queipo de Llano y Serra, Gen. Gonzalo (N), 11, 13, 33, 39, 48, 67, 102
Quijorna, 148, 150
Quinto, 189, 196, 198, 199

Radusch, Lt. (later Lt. Col.) Gunther (G. pilot), 126, 262
Raeder, Grand Admiral Erich (G. Navy), 75
Reconnaissance Group, Condor Le-

gion (*Aufklärung*) (A/88): organized, 59, 60; in the South, 68;
problems, 83, 89, 91, 92; new air-
craft, 93, 94; Battle of Guadalajara,
113; in the North, 118, 119, 138; at
Brunete, 150, 152; end in the
North, 158, 164; at Teruel, 173,
175, 180; in Aragón, 190-91, 193; on
the Levante, 207, 214, 215, 217;
Ebro Battle, 223, 225, 227, 231,
232; in Catalonia, 240
Redlich, Maj. Karl-Wolfgang (G.
pilot), 262
Rehahn, Lt. Paul (G. pilot), 107
Reinosa, 159-61
Resch, Maj. Rudolf (G. pilot), 216,
262
Reus, 241, 244
Reuter, Lt. Ernst von (G. pilot), 152
Rey d'Harcourt, Col. Comingo (N),
176, 177
Riaño, Lt. Col. Luis (Spanish officer),
22
Ribadesella, 160, 165
Ribarroja, 222, 223, 228, 235
Richthofen, Col. (later F.M.) Baron
Wolfram von (chief of staff, Condor
Legion), 85, 97, 256-58, 260; as-
signed to Legion, 58-59, 69; urges
North Operation, 117-18; North
campaign, 119, 121-27; Guernica,
128-30; Bilbao, 134-37, 143; at Bru-
nete, 147-49; end in the North, 167;
new commander, 172; at Teruel,
176; returns to Germany, 178; as
Legion commander, 239; Catalonian
Campaign, 240, 243-48
Roatta, Col. (later Gen.) Mario (It.),
35-37, 39, 102, 103, 107-10, 112, 113
Rochel, Sgt. (G. pilot), 209, 211
Rojo Lluch, Col. (later Gen.) Vicente
(PF), 153
Rubielos de Mora, 208, 215
Rudilla, 188, 189

Sabadell, 241, 244, 246
Saénz de Buruaga y Polanco, Gen.
Eduardo (N), 162

Sagunto, 107, 188, 198, 208, 212, 214,
216
Salamanca, 26, 32, 41, 43, 53-55, 61,
63, 65, 66, 68, 71-75, 77, 81, 82, 84,
101-3, 107, 109, 110, 114, 124, 157,
171, 205, 247
Salazar, Antonio de Oliveira (minister
president of Portugal), 34
Saliquet Zumeta, Gen. Andrés (N),
147
San Blas, 176, 179
San Fernando (airfield), 101
Sanjurjo (airfield), 226, 239, 240
Sanjurjo Sacanell, Gen. José (N), 4-6;
death, 7, 13
San Martín de Valdeiglesias, 50, 149
San Mateo, 196, 207, 208, 218
San Rafael (G. base), 208, 211
Santa Magdalena de Pulpis, 207, 208
Santa María de la Cabeza (monas-
tery), 12, 67, 68
Santander, 68, 117, 119, 143, 145,
152, 162, 163, 166; battle for, 158-61
Santed (G. base) 179-82, 189
Saragossa, 54, 103, 107, 109-14, 162,
173, 175, 187, 189, 196, 200, 201,
207, 227, 234, 239, 248
Sariñena, 173, 196, 222, 241
Sarratella, 208, 210
Sástago, 189, 191
Scheele, Maj. (later Gen.) Alexander
von (G. officer), 21, 22, 26, 28, 29-
31, 35, 47, 239, 259
Schellmann, Lt. (later Lt. Col.) Wolf-
gang (G. pilot), 211, 212, 216, 217,
227, 229, 232, 262
Schlichting, Maj. Joachim (G. pilot),
262
Schmouskievich, Gen. Yacob ("Doug-
las") (R) (PF), 56, 145, 146, 150,
153
Schob, NCO (later Capt.) Herbert (G.
pilot), 233, 262
Scholz, Lt. (G. pilot), 229
Schubert, Maj. (later Lt. Col.) (G.
C.O.), 82, 109, 110, 113, 114
Schuller, Corporal Alois (G.), captured and executed, 198-99; Plocher

unveils memorial stone, 238
Schulze, NCO Helmut (G.), dies, 29;
  body returned to Germany, 34
Schumann, Lt. (G. pilot), 234, 236
Schwartz, Lt. (G. officer), 184, 238
Schwendemann, Karl (G. Embassy
  counselor), 13, 72
Seaplane Squadron, Condor Legion
  (AS/88): organized, 50, 60, 158; new
  commander, 172; in Aragón offen-
  sive, 191, 197-99, 201; Levante of-
  fensive, 212-14, 216; Battle of the
  Ebro, 223-26, 230; Catalonian offen-
  sive, 239, 243, 244, 253 257, 260,
  261
Segorbe, 208, 214, 216
Segre, Río, 196, 198, 221-23, 240, 243
Seidemann, Maj. (G. staff officer), 239
Seiler, Lt. (later Maj.) Reinhard (G.
  pilot), 262
Serós, 196, 222, 240, 241
Seseña, 50, 56, 103, 106
Seufert, Sgt. (G. pilot), 209, 211
Sevilla la Nueva, 148, 150
Seville, 13, 17, 22, 31, 32, 34, 39, 43,
  47-50, 55, 61, 62, 65, 67, 68, 72, 82,
  96, 172, 205; Nationalists' capture
  of, 11; airlift to, 20, 25-28
Seyfarth, Capt. Kurt (G. pilot), 264
Sierra de Caballs (Caballs Moun-
  tains), 223, 228, 234
Sierra de Espadán, 214-18
Sierra de Gredos, 54, 84
Sierra de Guadarrama, 30, 49, 84,
  104, 173
Sierra de Pandols, 223, 227, 228, 234,
  235
Sierra Nevada, 65, 85, 102, 205, 206
Sigüenza, 103, 107, 108, 109, 111;
  Battle for, 53-54
Singra, Battle for, 178-80
Sobradiel, 232, 233
Solchaga Zala, Col. (later Gen.) José
  (N), 159, 163, 165, 167, 212, 213,
  215, 216, 239, 246
Soria Division (Moscardó) (N), 108,
  147
"Special Staff W" (G): organized, 19;

increased support, 33, 34; and Warlimont, 37, 40-42; more support, 46-
  47, creates Condor Legion, 57;
  knows of problems, 89, 90, 97; reports, 151, 168, 216, 219, 224, 225,
  232, 258; responsibility, 255
Sperrle, Gen. (later F.M.) Hugo von
  ("Sander") (Cmdr., Condor Legion),
  80, 249, 255, 260; assigned to Legion, 58-59, 61-62; bombs Madrid,
  66; quarrel with Faupel, 77, 157-58;
  changes tactics, 82-85; faces Merhard, 89; on reconnaissance, 92; reorganization, 97; Guadalajara
  Battle, 109-10; Battle in the North,
  117-21, 124-26, 128, 133-37, 139-43;
  at Brunete, 147-50, 153; end in the
  North, 159, 167-68; returns to Germany, 171
Stege, Sgt. (G. pilot), 211
Stettin, Germany (port), 47, 58, 61,
  62, 97
Stohrer, Dr. Baron Eberhard von (G.
  ambassador to Spain), 158, 190
Szuggar, NCO (G. pilot), 229

Tablada (Seville) (airfield) (G. base),
  17, 26
Talavera, 31, 44, 147, 177
Talavera de la Reina, 81
Tamarite de Litera, 240, 241
Tarragona, 241, 244, 245
Tauste (G. base), 240
Tella Cantos, Maj. (later Gen.) Heli
  Rolando (N), 56, 63
Teruel, 32, 162, 187, 188, 196, 197,
  207, 212, 218, 258; Battle for, 174-
  84
Tetuán, Morocco, 6-8, 13-17, 19, 20,
  22, 26, 27, 39, 55, 238, 251
Thoma, Maj. (later Gen.) Wilhelm von
  (G), 42, 43, 60, 69
Tietzen, Capt. Horst (G. pilot), 216,
  226, 232, 233, 262
Toledo, 12, 32, 50, 56, 63, 68, 147,
  247, 248
Tonollo, Lt. Alfred (G. pilot), 197
Torija, 104, 110-14

Torrelavega, 160, 161
Torremocha del Campo, 109, 111
Tortosa, 195-98, 201, 222, 223, 228, 240, 241, 245
Trautloft, Lt. (later Col.) Hans, 21, 30, 55, 262
Tremp, 196, 198, 202, 241
Trijueque, 111, 112
Turia, Río, 174, 179, 182, 183, 213

Usaramo (G. freighter), 20, 21, 25, 28, 29, 33, 35, 36, 47

Valdemorillo, 148, 152
Valencia, 11, 32, 48, 80, 82, 103, 107, 108, 135, 137, 145, 146, 161, 183, 187, 188, 191, 198, 206, 208, 212, 215, 226, 244, 248
Valenzuela (G. staging base), 175
Vall de Uxó, 208, 214
Valls (Tarragona) (G. base), 241, 243, 245, 246
Varela Iglesias, Col. (later Gen.) José Enrique (N): before Madrid, 55, 63-64, 67, 80, 87; wounded, 81; on the Jarama, 104-5; at Brunete, 149-50, 152; at Teruel, 176, 184; drive to the Mediterranean, 198, 207, 209, 215
Velani, Gen. (It. Air Commander), 119, 122
Vergara, 120, 124-26
Vigo, 82, 230, 249
Vigón Suerodíaz, Col. (later Gen.) Juan (N), 118, 119, 121, 122, 124-27, 129, 134, 159, 176, 180, 181, 190, 197, 200, 227, 229, 238
Vilajuiga, 241, 247
Villafranca del Castillo, 50, 148, 150
Villafranca del Cid, 208, 209
Villalba Baja, 182, 224, 230
Villalba de los Arcos, 222, 225, 226, 228
Villa Lolita (G. hqtrs.), 209
Villanueva de la Cañada, 50, 146, 148, 150, 152
Villanueva del Pardillo, 50, 88, 148-51
Villar de Canes, 208, 210

Villarreal (Álava), 86, 120, 211
Villaverde, 148, 151
Villaviciosa, 147, 148
Vinaroz, 196, 202, 207, 208, 213, 226
Vinebre, 218, 222, 224, 225, 228
Vitoria, 45, 81, 86, 96, 117, 118, 121, 124, 125, 130, 160
Vivel del Río Martín, 187-89
Viver, 208, 216
Volkmann, Gen. Helmuth ("Veith") (commander, Condor Legion) (G): assigned to Legion, 171-72; at Teruel, 176-78, 180-84; Aragón offensive, 187, 190-92, 194, 197-98, 200-202; on the Mediterranean, 206-9; visits Berlin, 211-12; concern for Ebro, 214; Franco congratulates, 216; responds to Ebro attack, 221-24, 229; letter to Berlin, 237; decorated by Franco, 238; on prisoners, 254; death, 260
Voronov, Gen. Nikita (PF) (R. artillery officer), 56

Wandel, Lt. (G. pilot), 136, 142
Wäntig, Capt. (G. flak officer), 193
Warlimont, Col. (later Gen.) Walter ("Guido") (G), 40, 51, 68, 71, 74, 79, 80, 99, 249, 251, 259, 260; assigned as German commander, 35-37; reports to Franco, 39; asks for tanks, 41; on von Thoma and Liddell Hart, 42; letter to author, 42, 43; on Nationalist Air Force, 43, 44; concerned over demands, 45; divides responsibility, 48; view of support, 49; strikes Málaga, 54-55; surprised by Condor Legion, 56-57; meets Faupel, 72; views of Faupel, 73; meets Hitler and staff, 75; views to Hitler on Spanish War, 76; shocked at Hitler's reasoning, 77
War Ministry, German, 17, 18, 34, 35, 36, 37, 48, 71, 72, 74, 75, 168
Werner, Lt. (G. staff officer), 210, 226
Wigbert (G. freighter), 33, 34, 46
Wilberg, Gen. Helmuth (G. officer),

19, 21, 28, 34, 37, 48, 57
Wittmann, Col. Herbert (G. pilot),
  264
Wohnzug (G. living quarters), 81,
  173, 175, 178, 184, 185, 198, 199,
  201
Wötke, Lt. (G. pilot), 166

Yagüe Blanco, Col. (later Gen.) Juan
  de (N): at Brunete, 146-47; on the
  Alfambra, 178-80, 184; in Aragón

offensive, 189, 190, 195, 197-201;
  Battle of the Ebro, 221-24, 229,
  230, 234-35; Catalonian offensive,
  240, 244-46; "beasts of prey"
  speech, 253

Zaidín (G. base), 196, 207, 222, 240,
  241, 245
Zech, NCO Herbert: dies, 29; body
  returned to Germany, 34
Zuera (G. hqtrs.), 162, 196, 199

About the Author

RAYMOND L. PROCTOR is a former career officer in the United States
Army and Air Force, and currently Professor of European and Middle
Eastern History at the University of Idaho. He also wrote *Agony of a
Neutral* which has been published in both Spain and the United States,
and is one of the major contributors to *Historical Dictionary of the Span-
ish Civil War* (Greenwood Press, 1982).

Recent Titles in
Contributions in Military History

The Art of Leadership in War: The Royal Navy From the Age of Nelson
to the End of World War II
John Horsfield

A Wilderness of Miseries: War and Warriors in Early America
John E. Ferling

Iron Arm: The Mechanization of Mussolini's Army, 1920-1940
John Joseph Timothy Sweet

American Sea Power in the Old World:
The United States Navy in European and Near Eastern Waters, 1865-1917
William N. Still, Jr.

A Hollow Threat: Strategic Air Power and Containment Before Korea
Harry R. Borowski

The Quest for Victory: The History of the Principles of War
John I. Alger

Men Wanted for the U.S. Army: America's Experience with an All-Volunteer
Army Between the World Wars
Robert K. Griffith, Jr.

Bullets and Bureaucrats: The Machine Gun and the United States Army,
1861-1916
David A. Armstrong

General John M. Palmer, Citizen Soldiers, and the Army of a Democracy
I.B. Holley, Jr.

History of the Art of War: Within the Framework of Political History,
The Middle Ages
Hans Delbrück, translated by *Walter J. Renfore, Jr.*

"Dear Bart": Washington Views of World War II
Glen C. H. Perry

Fighting Power: German and U.S. Army Performance, 1939-1945
Martin van Creveld

Two If by Sea: The Development of American Coastal Defense Policy
Robert S. Browning III